KERMIT

This book was written using EMACS and EMACS-like editors on a DECSYSTEM-20, a VAX/UNIX system, and various microcomputers running Kermit (both for terminal emulation and file transfer), and the drafts were formatted using the Scribe Document Production System (Unilogic Ltd., 160 North Craig Street, Pittsburgh, PA 15213). Converted to type by Waldman Graphics, Inc. Printed and bound in the United States of America by the Murray Printing Company. Cover photos courtesy of International Business Machines Corporation and Digital Equipment Corporation.

The KERMIT File Transfer Protocol was named after the star of THE MUPPET SHOW television series. The name is used by permission of Henson Associates, Inc.

Designed by Diane Jaroch

9 8 7 6 5 4 3 2

Order number EY-6705E-DP

A list of trademarks cited in this book appears on page 372.

Library of Congress Cataloging in Publication Data
da Cruz, Frank, 1944-
    Kermit, a file transfer protocol.

    Includes index.
    1. Computer network protocols. I. Title.
TK5105.5.D27 1987   005.7'1   86-16696
ISBN 0-932376-88-6

KERMIT

A File Transfer Protocol

Frank da Cruz

Drawings by George Ulrich

digital

Digital Press

CONTENTS

PART IV–PROGRAMMER GUIDE

List of Figures

List of Tables

Foreword

It's a great pleasure to see computer programs that were written for the sheer love of it, by people who delight in improving the effectiveness of our machines. The rapid growth of Kermit as a near-universal protocol for transferring files between computers is also a convincing demonstration of the advantages of software sharing.

The authors of Kermit wisely decided not to keep their ideas proprietary, and they soon found that hundreds of people were willing and able to refine and extend the system. This book is the logical next step: It presents the concepts in tutorial fashion, and gives detailed examples of the subtle pitfalls that were discovered, so that many more people will be able to learn from the accumulated experience of the pioneer Kermit volunteers. Once this knowledge becomes widespread, we can expect further advances in both hardware and software.

People often mistakenly believe that low-level considerations of input and output are not part of "real" computer science. The truth is just the opposite. Computer scientists have a duty to understand real-world constraints and to deal with them in as "clean" a way as possible. Therefore I hope that many readers of this book will be challenged to find high-level concepts and invariant relations by which various versions of the Kermit protocol can be proved correct in a mathematical sense.

It will be very interesting to see how this system evolves in the future. Can a de facto standard continue to rely entirely on dedicated voluntary contributions and peer pressure, or will some sort of stricter rules have to be enforced? Will a steady state be reached? And how long will it be before dictionaries of the English language include the new verb "to kermit"—as in the sentence "I kermitted ten files during the Muppet Show."

Donald E. Knuth
Stanford, California

Preface

This book is for everyone who needs to move information from one computer to another. It's for the growing number of people who bring work home to personal computers so they can spend more time with their families. It's for university students with microcomputers in their dormitory rooms, and for university computer centers faced with the microcomputer explosion. It's for students, teachers, hobbyists, administrators, authors, farmers, secretaries, scientists, anyone who might want to share and communicate computer data with friends or coworkers. And it's for hospitals, space flight centers, city agencies, publishing houses, soft drink bottling plants, organizations of every kind with diverse, incompatible computers of all sizes sprouting in every room and department, who feel the same need on a grand scale. Computers are tools that should be used to improve the quality of life on earth; this book presents a tool that can improve the quality of our lives while we use computers.

Kermit is a computer file transfer protocol developed at Columbia University. The Kermit protocol has enjoyed increasing popularity in recent years, enough—I hope—to warrant publication of this book, which is intended to serve as a compendium of Kermit information, ranging from instructions for basic use to an informal description of the Kermit protocol. I won't try to put Kermit forth as the best of all possible file transfer protocols, only to describe it as it has evolved. I hope that the result is something more— and less—than a typical computer software user manual: more, because it supplies the background and motivation usually lacking in manuals; less, because it does not try to describe every command and peculiarity of each and every Kermit program; there are far too many of them, and they change too often.

I've tried to improve upon earlier Kermit publications [6, 7, 8][1] by presenting the material in a more coherent, natural sequence. Tutorial sections have been added to provide background in computing, file organization, and data communications. These are independent from the other material and may be skipped by those who don't need tutoring. Case studies illustrate ways of coping with diverse computer systems and data communications environments. The latter part of the book describes the Kermit protocol in detail, with each facet illustrated by some code from a working Kermit program. At the end are a glossary, appendixes, and an index.

The book should prove useful to three distinct groups of people: those who wish to *use* Kermit, those who wish to *support* its use within an organization, and those who wish to *create* Kermit programs. Potential Kermit users need no particular experience

---

1. Citations refer to the Bibliography at the back of this book.

with computers; any necessary background can be picked up from the tutorials. Potential supporters of Kermit programs should also be able to learn whatever they need from this book, particularly from the case studies. Those who want to create Kermit programs should have a reading knowledge of the C programming language [19] to follow the program examples given in the protocol specification.

This book may also find useful application in data communication or networking courses (Kermit is a degenerate case of networking) as an introductory text or as a case study in coping with a complicated reality. Even experienced protocol designers might pick up a few useful tidbits. After all, Kermit is able to work in environments where other protocols have not been so fortunate. And in the areas where Kermit is wanting, designers can learn from our mistakes.

Kermit is more than a file transfer protocol; it is also the *process* by which the protocol spreads and develops through the cooperation of a wide, diverse, and open international community. Most Kermit programs are written and contributed by volunteers, often working on their own time. The programs can vary markedly in both style and quality, but tend to improve with age, as improvements are added. No document can hope to pin down the Kermit universe for all time; new Kermit programs appear, old ones change, and the protocol itself evolves. Even when a program remains the same, changes in the underlying machine, operating system, or communications environment can alter its behavior. This book attempts to describe Kermit as it is today, in terms specific enough to be useful yet general enough to remain valid tomorrow, and maybe even the next day.

Acknowledgments

Because so many have contributed to the Kermit storehouse, this book has more acknowledgments than an Academy Award acceptance speech. As you flip past these pages, I hope you will come away with a feeling for the scope of the Kermit effort.

Thanks and acknowledgments must go to the Columbia University Center for Computing Activities (CUCCA, my employer), which has generously fostered our Kermit development and support efforts even when there was no apparent tangible benefit to itself; to Bill Catchings, the codesigner (with me) of the basic Kermit protocol, who worked out many of the details and wrote several Kermit programs, including the first two (for CP/M and the DECSYSTEM-20), and who suggested and coauthored the 1984 *BYTE* magazine article [8]; to Daphne Tzoar, who conquered IBM mainframe asynchronous communications and wrote the next two Kermit programs (IBM System/370 VM/CMS and IBM PC), and who tirelessly kept the BITNET Kermit distribution up to date; to Vaçe Kundakçi, who advised and helped with all IBM mainframe aspects of Kermit design and implementation; to Bruce Gilchrist, director of CUCCA, and Howard Eskin, director of academic computing at CUCCA, who encouraged our early efforts and promulgated and proselytized them beyond the walls of Columbia. Bill, Daphne, and Howard are no longer at Columbia, but Kermit will haunt them long into their new careers. Acknowledgments also to Coleen Markland, Bob Tschudi, Peter Howard, and Robert Story for running the "Kermit factory," and to Christine Gianone, who coordinates all of this while simultaneously acting as Kermit consultant and publicist.

Outside of Columbia, credit goes to Bernie Eiben of Digital Equipment Corporation, who was the first to "port" one of our Kermit programs to a new machine, and who promoted Kermit enthusiastically; to Philip Murton of the University of Toronto, who wrote the first high-level language Kermit program (in PASCAL); to Nick Bush and Bob McQueen of Stevens Institute of Technology (Hoboken, New Jersey), who suggested many improvements to the protocol and contributed several major implementations, including VAX/VMS Kermit; to Leslie Spira and her group at The Source Telecomputing Corporation for the first implementation of "eighth-bit prefixing" (for the IBM PC and Prime computers) and later for working out the sliding window extension along with Hugh Matlock, John Mulligan, Larry Jordan, and Jan van der Eijk; also to Wael Bahaa-El-Din at the University of Houston for a parallel investigation of sliding windows; to Brian Nelson of the University of Toledo for an ambitious Kermit implementation that encompasses the many DEC PDP-11 operating systems and provided the first working examples of "attribute packets" and extended-length packets; to Herm Fischer of Encino, California, for valuable contributions to the development of the MS-DOS and UNIX Kermit programs.

At this writing, there are nearly 200 different Kermit implementations. Here is a list of some of institutions from which Kermit programs have sprung, and the names of some of the contributors (located in the U.S. or Canada unless indicated otherwise): ABC-Klubben Stockholm, Sweden (Torbjörn Alm); Aberdeen University, Scotland (Brian Robertson); Advanced Computer Communications (Charles Carvalho); American Mathematical Society (Bill Hall); Atari Computer (Jack Palevich); Bankers Trust (Tad Marshall); Brigham Young University (Bryan Peterson); Brighton Polytechnic, UK (D.J. Rowland); Brown University (Peter DiCamillo); Brunel University, UK (Ralph Mitchell); Bucknell University (Cheryl Ann Poostay); Bureau of Engraving Inc. (Randy Hippe); California State University at Long Beach (Jack Bryans); Cantor Consulting (Charles J. Cantor); Carnegie-Mellon University (Dave King, Bdale Garbee); Cerritos College (Bruce Tanner); Clemson University (Larry Afrin); the Colorado School of Mines (Dan Smith, Joe Smith); Columbia University (besides those mentioned above: Jeff Damens, Bill Schilit, Howie Kaye, Chris Maio, Bob Cattani, Rich Garland, Guy Valiquette, Norman Weatherby, Peter Trei, Francis Wilson, Jon Beeson); Control Data Corporation (Duane Jergens, Ted Brown); Cornell University (Kate MacGregor, David Rossiter, Nick Gimbrone); Corporate Data Exchange (Peter Brooks); CSIRO, Australia (Andrew Hunt); Digital Equipment Corporation (Bernie Eiben, Martin Minow, Larry Campbell, Dan Schullman, Walt Lamia); Du Pont Co. (Joe Smiley); Eastman Kodak Co. (Steve Archer); General Electric Co. (Bob Wilson); Gothenburg University, Sweden (Stefan Lundberg); Grinnell College (Albert Goodman); Harvard University (Stew Rubenstein, Steve Engel); Harvard/Smithsonian Center for Astrophysics (John Chandler); Helsinki University of Technology, Finland (Kimmo Laaksonen); Hewlett-Packard Laboratories (Ken Poulton, Frank Heartney, T.W. Cook); Honeywell Information Systems (Terry Carlin, Lee Hallin, Mark Ahlstrom, David Cargo); the Hungarian Academy of Sciences (Janos Koppany); Indiana/Purdue University (Marie Schriefer, James Harvey, Jim Griffin); INFOGEM, France (Hubert de Langautier); InteCom Inc. (John Mealing); Intel Corporation (Teresa Koo); Lancaster University, UK (Alan Phillips); Leigh Instruments Ltd. (Hanh Tuan Truong); Lisp Machines Inc. (Mark David, George Carrette); Litton Data Systems (Herm Fischer); Los Alamos National Laboratory (Leah Miller, Dave Forslund); Massachusetts Institute of Technology (John Klensin); Merrell Dow Research Institute (Anthony Starks); Metro-II (Randy McLaughlin); National Aeronautics and Space Administration (Dave Tweten); Nippon Telephone and Telegraph, Japan (Ken-ichiro Murakami); the Norwegian Institute of Technology (H. Eidnes, A. Lie); Oakland University (Paul Amaranth); Oklahoma State University (Mark Vasoll, Gregg Wonderly); Philips International B.V., Netherlands (Frans van Grotel); Pima Community College (Vanya Cooper); Planning

Research Corporation (Jim Noble); Polaris, Inc. (Ed Eldridge); Prime Computer (Jeff Duncan); Queen's University (Victor Lee); Quest Research (Scott Bertilson); RCA Laboratories (John Lee, Glenn Everhart); Research Machines, Ltd., England (Chris Kennington); Rice University (Andrea Martin, Stan Barber); Rijksuniversiteit Groningen, Netherlands (Ph.P. Visser, Johan Ph. Kelders); Rutgers University (Eric Lavitsky); Rutherford-Appleton Laboratories (M.J. Loach); Salford University, UK (Tony Addyman); Soft Machines (Bob Rubendunst); Southwest Texas State University (Randall Simmons); SPSS Inc. (Gene Autrey-Hunley); Stanford University (Jim Celoni); Stevens Institute of Technology (Bob McQueen, Nick Bush, Anton Mione, Stuart Hecht, David Stevens); Stockholm University, Sweden (Per Lindberg); Technical Research Centre of Finland (Tor Lillqvist); The Source Telecomputing Corporation (Leslie Spira et al.); The Southwest Foundation for Biomedical Research (Paul Mamelka); Technische Hogeschool Eindhoven, Netherlands (J.M.H. Smeets, B.J.M. Morselt); TransEra Corp. (Robert Raymond); Tulane University (John Voigt); Universität Bern, Switzerland (Franklin Davis); Université Scientifique et Medicale Grenoble, France (Jean-Luc Archimbaud); University College, Dublin, Ireland (Barry Devlin); University of Arizona (Joellen Windsor); University of British Columbia (Bruce Jolliffe); University of California at Berkeley (Greg Small); University of Chicago (Ron Rusnak); University of Edinburgh, Scotland (Adam Albert-Recht); University of Hawaii (Ian Gibbons); University of Kansas (Wes Hubert); University of Maryland (Edgar Butt); University of Michigan (Chris Thomson, Gavin Eadie); University of Namur, Belgium (Jacques Pierson); University of New South Wales, Australia (Peter Thew); University of Oslo, Norway (Svein Johannessen, Knut Smaaland, Edward Hartmann); University of Saskatchewan (Joe Angel); University of Southern California (Bob Larson, Marco Papa); University of Tennessee at Knoxville (John Bray, James Grossen); University of Texas at Austin (Jim Knutson, Steve Padgett); University of Toledo (Brian Nelson); University of Toronto (Philip Murton); University of Trondheim, Norway (Frithjov Iversen); University of Vermont (Robert Detenbeck); University of Virginia (Olaf Pors); University of Washington (Ron Blanford, David Ragozin, John Sambrook); University of Wisconsin (pAul sTevens, David Wilson); Utah State University (Joe Doupnik); the U.S. Environmental Protection Agency (Bruce Wright); the U.S. National Institutes of Health (Chuck Bacon, Roger Fajman); Victor Technologies Canada (W. Hertha); Virginia Polytechnic Institute (R.A.L.); World Research Institute for Science & Technology (Chris Barker). I've probably omitted as many contributors as I included (not intentionally!), and the list grows constantly.

Thanks also to the Columbia University Computer Science department for playing host to Kermit network distribution during 1984; to the proprietors of the various research, educational, and volunteer computer networks for providing convenient paths for the flow of Kermit programs and information; to the Oklahoma State University Department of Computing and Information Sciences and Mark Vasoll for maintaining a complete Kermit distribution for UUCP and Kermit server dialup access; to Digital Equipment Corporation and Bernie Eiben for maintaining and providing dialup access to the Kermit files; to Lancaster University and Alan Phillips for handling much of the Kermit distribution in the United Kingdom; to the French DECUS Networks SIG and Jean Dutertre of the Institut Française du Pétrole for setting up a European Kermit "distribution tree"; to those who have set up Kermit redistribution mechanisms in Scandinavia, Australia, and elsewhere; to Richard Garland, formerly of the Columbia University Chemistry Department, Brian Nelson of the University of Toledo, Glenn Everhart of RCA, and Stephen Attaya of Wiener Enterprises Inc, for periodically submitting the Kermit collection to the various DECUS SIGs; and also to Brian for providing dialup and BITNET access to PDP-11 and other Kermit files; to DECUS, SHARE, PC-SIG, and other user groups for distributing Kermit on magnetic media; to those who have translated Kermit documents into other languages; to the various hardware and software producers who have included Kermit with their products at no extra charge; to all those who have run sessions on Kermit at industry seminars and user group conferences; and to everyone else who has helped in any way at all.

Thanks also to Richard Stallman of the Free Software Foundation, creator of the text editor EMACS [28], which was used to write many of the Kermit programs and documents (including this book), and an early champion of the idea that software can be developed by a broad, open, unorganized community without regard for personal enrichment and shared by all without secrecy or license.

And thanks to those who supplied information on various topics: to Frank Wancho, who helped with the summary of the Christensen protocol; to Bob Larson, Charlie Spitzer, Alistair Milne, (the ubiquitous) Brian Nelson, William Lawrance, Gerard Gaye, Jacob Palme, Ryan Popken, Lee Hallin, Roger Krall, and others who responded to my queries about the peculiarities of sundry computer systems.

And thanks to those who helped in the production of this book: the editors and production staff at Digital Press: John Osborn, Nancy Gustavesen, Chase Duffy, Mike Meehan, Beth French, and to Barbara Murray and Geraldine Morse for their sensitive, eagle-eyed copyediting, and to the staff of Waldman Graphics for overseeing the typesetting. Thanks also to those who read the proposal or the manuscript and provided helpful suggestions and comments: Don Knuth and Ralph Gorin of Stanford University, J. Ray Scott of Carnegie-Mellon University, Kathy Hornbach of Lear Siegler, Inc., Bernie Eiben of Digital Equipment Corporation, Bill Brindley of the DECUS Networks SIG, Bill Catchings of Foundation Computer Systems, Brian Nelson of the University of Toledo, and Vaçe Kundakçi and Christine Gianone of Columbia University. Need I say that any errors remaining after the scrutiny of this crowd are mine alone?

Thanks too to John McNamara for writing the invaluable *Technical Aspects of Data Communication* [25], and to Professor Lee Lidofsky of the Columbia University Engineering School for first getting me hooked on computers so many years ago.

Finally, thanks to all the people and organizations I may have overlooked in the foregoing, and to all those yet to come, for their contributions to Kermit Kultur.

This book is lovingly dedicated to my family: my wife, Judy, and my kids, Peter and Amy, whom I shamefully neglected during the preparation of this book, and to my mother, Vivian, and the memory of my brother Dennis.

Frank da Cruz (SY.FDC@CU20B)
New York City, March 1986

PART ONE

The Basics

1

Introduction

Computers are touching our lives in more ways every day. We see them at our schools and workplaces. Our kids have them in their classrooms, and they're asking for their own at home. Computers send us bills, keep track of our grades, our salaries, our pensions, our police records. They control our telephone system, traffic lights, aircraft, spacecraft. Bookstores are choked with new computer books, and dustbins with old ones.

As computers proliferate, the need to get information—"data"—from one computer to another becomes increasingly important. This was not a big problem in the old days, when many people shared the same large central computer. Everything was in the same place, in the same format, where it could be easily shared and moved from one application to another. But now many offices (and homes) are their own little computer centers, and no two are quite alike.

When we decentralize, we must learn to communicate. Our first sad lesson is that computer manufacturers do not make this easy for us. Whether the result of deliberate marketing decisions, or of the simple lack of pertinent standards, their products tend to be incompatible in just those areas where we need compatibility. There are many ways out of this predicament. This book presents what may be the cheapest.

History

At the height of the timesharing era at Columbia University, about 1980, our central computers began to suffer from a glut of files. Disk storage space was running out, and increasing numbers of students wanted to keep the computer files they accumulated over their academic careers. The problem could not be solved simply by buying more disks because, as somebody's law states, "Usage will expand to consume all available resources."[1]

A more decentralized approach was called for. Given the means, those who cared about saving their files from term to term would take the trouble to do it themselves. The newly popular floppy-disk-based microcomputers fit the bill nicely. The diskettes were cheap, capacious, and easily carried and stored. But how could files be transferred reliably from the university's central computers to the microcomputer floppies, and back?

---

1. This is a corollary to Parkinson's Law, which says, "Work expands so as to fill the time available for its completion."

The problem took on a new dimension with the introduction of the IBM PC in 1981, which struck a powerful blow to centralized computing. As the new generation of personal computers began to rival the large central computers in several key application areas, PCs (not only IBM) began to appear in offices all over campus, and soon spread to the homes and dormitory rooms of faculty and students. The users of these PCs needed to communicate and share their work—professors and students, researchers or authors in collaboration, administrators up and down the "chain of command." Communication was required between PCs and the central systems, between PCs and other (possibly incompatible) PCs, and between our central systems and minicomputers in the academic departments. In short, everything had to "talk" to everything else.

But how? Computer networks were not a practical alternative in 1981, and today they remain a costly one, even when you can find a network that provides the required connections. The only medium that all our computers had in common was the "communication port," the place where a terminal or a "modem" is attached. The operation of the communication port is relatively well defined and standardized, but it is not an ideal medium for bulk transfers of data (for reasons that will be covered later). On the other hand, it is usually standard equipment; with appropriate software it can do the job for little or no additional hardware expense.

Several communication software packages were on the market in 1980–81, but they were not available for all our systems. Even if they had been, the total cost would have been enormous when multiplied by the number of microcomputers, minicomputers, and mainframes we expected to arrive in the ensuing years. And even if the cost were bearable, it would not have been wise to depend upon a single commercial vendor for such an important function—the company could fail, or raise its prices suddenly, or decline to add support for some new system.

Had we been aware of public domain communication protocols and programs, particularly MODEM[2] and its derivatives, we might have been tempted to adapt them to our needs. But it turns out that MODEM would not have fulfilled one of our most basic requirements: IBM mainframe communication.

Finally, for better or worse, we took the do-it-yourself approach. We invented a new protocol and called it Kermit, after Kermit the Frog, star of *"The Muppet Show."*[3] As

---

2. MODEM is more properly referred to as the Christensen protocol; MODEM, XMODEM, and so on, are names of programs that implement this protocol. The Kermit and Christensen protocols are compared in detail on pages 303–308.

3. Why? Mostly because there was a Muppets calendar on the wall when we were trying to think of a name, and Kermit is a pleasant, unassuming sort of character. But since we weren't sure whether it was OK to name our protocol after this popular television and movie star, we pretended that KERMIT was an acronym; unfortunately, we could never find a good set of words to go with the letters, as readers of some of our early source code can attest. Later, while looking through a name book for his forthcoming baby, Bill Catchings noticed that *Kermit* was a Celtic word for *free*, which is what all Kermit programs should be, and words to this effect replaced the strained acronyms in our source code (Bill's baby turned out to be a girl, so he had to name her Becky instead). When *BYTE* Magazine was preparing our 1984 Kermit article for publication, they suggested we contact Henson Associates Inc. for permission to say that we did indeed name the protocol after Kermit the Frog. Permission was kindly granted, and now the real story can be told. I resisted the temptation, however, to call the present work "Kermit the Book."

luck would have it, the few types of systems that our protocol initially had to support—DECSYSTEM-20 and IBM 370-Series mainframes, CP/M and MS-DOS microcomputers—exhibit among them nearly every imaginable quirk and idiosyncrasy of communication style and file organization, and our protocol was designed to encompass all of them. The result has turned out to be adaptable to almost every new situation; its flexibility accounts in large measure for its popularity. It must be said, however, that had we known Kermit would eventually spread all over the globe (and beyond), we might have thought a little more carefully about the basic design before unleashing it (see "It's Too Late Now," page 307).

By 1981 we had several no-frills Kermit programs running successfully. In 1982 we began to present Kermit at computer user-group conferences like DECUS (the Digital Equipment Corporation User Society) and SHARE (the IBM user society), and we gladly gave the programs, source code, and documentation to anyone who asked. Before long, we began to receive new Kermit implementations back, and soon we had quite a collection, one that continues to grow to this day.

Sharing versus Selling

Another reason for Kermit's popularity is that it's *free*. Kermit is one example of why it's good to share software of general utility (two others are EMACS [28] and T_EX [20]). If we had elected to keep it to ourselves, or to license and sell it, or to keep the source code or protocol specification secret, it would never have reached its current level of popularity. It would never have been written for so many different computers. It would not have improved and evolved through the continuous contribution of bug fixes and new versions, complaints and suggestions. It would never have threatened to become a "de facto standard." If the spirit of the '80s is "Don't give away anything you can sell," then Kermit must be a child of the '60s.

Contrary to what you might expect from the foregoing polemic, Kermit programs are not necessarily in the public domain. Many of them bear copyright notices to protect their authors or sponsoring institutions against having their work turned into commercial products. However, these copyright notices generally grant permission to any individual or organization to use, copy, modify, or redistribute the program, source code, or documentation as long as this is not done for profit, and the copyright notice and author credits are retained. Commercial hardware and software vendors are allowed to add Kermit protocol to their products provided they do not charge their customers extra for it (at least not beyond the incremental cost of reproduction and distribution), and they agree to certain other easy terms.

Kermit distribution began at Columbia in 1981. Our original policy was: "Send us a tape and a return mailer and we'll send you the Kermit distribution." Since we were not able to make floppy disks in a wide variety of formats, we preferred to send tapes to institutional computing centers, which could take the responsibility for "bootstrapping" the desired microcomputer implementations to floppy disk and distributing them in appropriate formats to their users.

By early 1983 the demand for Kermit tapes had grown far beyond our capacity to produce them and still do our "real jobs." To get our system programmers out of the shipping room, we began to charge a distribution fee. This fee is not a software license fee. It allows us to keep up with demand by hiring production workers, and it compensates us for media, packaging, postage, computer utilization, and printing. It does not reflect the amount of software on the tape, the quality of the software, or the amount of effort that went into producing the software—only the "parts and labor" required for reproduction and shipping.

For the benefit of those who have trouble with the fee, every effort is made to funnel Kermit programs into alternative distribution channels. Kermit programs are submitted regularly to user group libraries, and they are available on many computer networks and dialup bulletin board systems. All who have received Kermit programs from Columbia or elsewhere are encouraged to share them with their friends and neighbors.

Kermit has been a comforting example of international cooperation on a personal and institutional level. Kermit runs happily in both Irelands, both Chinas, both Germanys. It can be found in the USA and the USSR, in Israel and Iraq; in New Zealand and New Caledonia, Chile and Czechoslovakia; in Malaysia and Mexico, Sweden and Switzerland, Norway and the Netherlands, and practically anywhere else you can think of. If a country has computers, many of them are probably running Kermit programs—people's basic needs are pretty much the same everywhere, and people who use computers have begun to view the ability to transmit computer data as a basic need, even a right. Kermit fosters the free exchange of information and ideas, and it works against the trend toward information as commodity (or controlled substance).

Our attitudes about sharing spring from a spirit of respect for fellow humans and other creatures. I trust and urge that Kermit be used *only for peaceful and humane purposes*. It was not created and shared to further causes of nationalism, war, oppression, or discrimination. Please use it in the spirit in which it is offered.

Kermit versus Networks

You have probably read about computer networks. Networks are based upon dedicated physical connections between computers; they are the best way to put computers into communication with each other. They're reliable, they're fast, they support a variety of functions, and they're easy to use. They overcome all the same problems that Kermit must cope with, and they do it better. So why bother with Kermit?

If you have a network, and it includes all the computers you care about, then you *don't* have to bother with Kermit. But networks are expensive, hard to install, and often designed to work only with a particular vendor's equipment. Many microcomputers have no network option available; even when there is one, the expense can be prohibitive. And when the expense is tolerable, the logistics get in the way—cables must be laid, holes drilled, satellites launched. So chances are that your microcomputer is not on a network, or if it is, that some day you will need it to communicate with some other computer that is not on your network.

Table 1-1: Major Kermit Implementations

Portable Environments

CP/M-80 (Many different systems; Assembler)
CP/M-86 (DEC Rainbow, NEC APC, several others; ASM86)
LISP (LMI, Symbolics; ZETALISP)
MS-DOS, PC-DOS (IBM PC family, DEC Rainbow, many others; MASM)
OS-9 (TRS-80 Color Computer, and various 6809 and 68000 systems; C)
Software Tools (various systems; Ratfor)
Turbo Pascal (MS-DOS, CP/M-80, Apple II DOS)
UCSD p-System (IBM PC, Terak, and other systems; Pascal)
UNIX (VAX, SUN, many others; V7, 4.x BSD, System III & V, etc; C language)

Particular Mainframes, Minicomputers Not Covered Above

Burroughs B6800, B7900 (Algol)
Cray-1, Cray-XMP (CTSS; Fortran-77)
CDC Cyber 170 (NOS, NOS/BE; Fortran-77)
Data General (RDOS; Fortran-5), (AOS; Fortran-5), (AOS/VS; Pascal)
DEC PDP-11 (RT11, RSX11M, RSX11M+, RSTS/E, P/OS, etc; Macro-11),
DEC PDP-11 (MUMPS; MUMPS-11)
DEC VAX-11 (VMS; Bliss-32, Macro-32, Pascal/Fortran, or C)
DECsystem-10 (TOPS-10; Bliss-36, Macro);
DECSYSTEM-20 (TOPS-20; Macro)
GEC 4000 (OS4000; MUM/SERC)
Gould/SEL Concept 32 (MPX-32; Fortran)
Harris 800 (VOS; Pascal)
Honeywell (MULTICS; PL/I), DPS-6,8 (GCOS; C, B), CP6 (Pascal or PL/6)
Hewlett-Packard 1000 (RTE-6/VM; Fortran) (RTE/A; Pascal)
Hewlett-Packard 3000 (MPE; SPL or Fortran)
IBM System/370 (VM/CMS, MVS/TSO, MVS/GUTS, MTS, MUSIC; Assembler)
ICL 2900 (VME; S3)
Perkin-Elmer 3200 Series (OS/32; Fortran)
PRIME (PRIMOS; PL/P)
Sperry/Univac-1100 (EXEC, OS-1100; Assembler, Ratfor, or Pascal)
Tandem Nonstop (Guardian; TAL)

Particular Microcomputers, PCs, Workstations Not Covered Above

Alpha Micro 68000 (Alpha 68K Assembler)
Acorn BBC Micro (OS1.20; ADE)
Apollo (Aegis; Pascal)
Apple II 6502 (Apple DOS; DEC-10/20 CROSS or Apple Assembler)
Apple Macintosh (SUMACC C)
Atari Home Computers (DOS; Action!)
Commodore 64 (DEC-10/20 CROSS or FORTH)
Commodore Amiga (Intuiton; C)
DEC Pro-300 Series (P/OS; Bliss-16 or Macro-11), (Pro/RT; Macro), (Venix; C)
ICL/Perq (Pascal)
Intel Development System (ISIS; PL/M), (iRMX-86; PL/M)
TRS80 Models I,III,4 (TRSDOS; ASM), Model 16 (Xenix; C), Color Computer (Asm)

Network connections must be installed by "management." They require special "interface hardware," operating system software, and so forth. Kermit programs, on the other hand, run (with very few exceptions) in the computer's "user mode," with no special privileges or changes to the system software required. Once you have a copy of Kermit on your computer, you can establish your own connection to any other computer that you can dial on the telephone or reach with a cable. Unlike proprietary networks, Kermit always comes with source code and documentation, so even if there is no Kermit program for your computer, a programmer can create one in a short time based on the Kermit programs that have already been written or the examples in this book.

Networks are becoming increasingly widespread and interconnected, but they will never encompass every computer in the world. Communication programs like Kermit will always be needed to make the connections that aren't already there: from home to work, from business trip to home base, from space to earth.

Why Is This Book So Thick?

The Kermit book is several books in one—a political tract, an introduction to computers and data communications, a reference manual, a protocol specification (not to mention 37 pages of acknowledgments). Different parts are appropriate to different audiences; very few people will need to read it front to back. Much of the material is included based on years of answering questions about Kermit, and if this book serves no other purpose than to give my phone a rest, I'll be happy.

But you might still wonder why the book *has* to be so thick. Why can't we have a one-page Kermit manual, and be done with it? Is it because Kermit programs are deficient in design, requiring people to work harder and know more than they really should have to? On a superficial level, the answer may sometimes be yes. Remember that many Kermit programs are contributed by volunteers working in their limited spare time; to get the job done at all, they may have to skimp on the frills that are the bread and butter of commercial software packages.

On a more fundamental level, it must be recognized that Kermit is a response to a very complicated problem. Most computer programs operate in self-contained, controlled environments; programmers of sufficient motivation and skill can go to great lengths to shield users of these programs from the underlying details of machine architecture and file organization. But data communication programs like Kermit cannot have this knowledge built in, because their successful operation depends upon factors *outside* the computer—a murky world filled with all kinds of pitfalls and obstructions. No matter how "artificially intelligent" a communication program may claim to be, you must sometimes lead it by the hand through the rough spots before it can begin its work. You can think of this book as a detailed guide to that uncertain, complicated world.

How to Get Kermit

The Columbia University Center for Computing Activities serves as a clearinghouse for Kermit programs and information. All who create new Kermit programs, adapt existing ones to new systems, or fix bugs in or add features to existing programs are encouraged to submit their work to Columbia for further distribution. Columbia, in turn, makes all the Kermit material, including program source, as widely available as possible.

It should be stressed again that all Kermit programs are provided "as is," with no warranty of any kind. Columbia University, the individual programmers, and the contributing institutions make no claim as to their correct operation or the accuracy of their documentation. Kermit is not a commercial venture; everyone does the best they can in the time that they have, and all Kermit users are invited to fix bugs, improve documentation, and contribute new versions, so that the collection will continue to grow and each Kermit program will continue to improve.

As of February 1986, Kermit was available for about 200 different machines and operating systems, and many additional versions were under development. Table 1-1 shows some of the major implementations, including the machine, operating system, and the programming language used. Certain of the programs can run on more than one computer. For instance, the IBM PC version runs on the IBM PC, XT, AT, and all the compatibles; the UNIX version runs on dozens of different systems. For an up-to-date list of available Kermit programs along with ordering instructions, write to:

Kermit Distribution
Columbia University Center for Computing Activites
612 West 115th Street
New York, NY 10025
USA

2

The Basics

Imagine you have written a book, and you want to submit the manuscript to your publisher, Fred, whose office is behind a high fence, marked "DEPOSIT MANUSCRIPTS HERE," with an arrow pointing to the top.[1] Your first thought is to throw the whole thing over at once, but you wisely decide against this course because the last author who submitted a large manuscript in this manner broke Fred's foot. Instead, you decide to send it a page at a time, folding each page into a paper airplane and flying it over the fence.

This method works, up to a point. Fred is able to catch each page, flatten it out, and put it into a folder before the next page arrives. But when the folder becomes full, he has to make a trip back to the filing cabinet to file the folder away and get a new empty one. Because of the fence, you don't know he's away, so you continue to send your pages across. Some fall into puddles, some are carried away by stray dogs. This happens each time Fred returns to the filing cabinet.

To make matters worse, the weather takes a bad turn. First, the wind begins to blow. Sometimes it blows a page away just before Fred can catch it. Or it seizes a page before it ever gets over the fence, so that Fred never even knows it is lost. And then it starts to rain! Whenever a raindrop strikes a page, the words run together into an illegible smear.

After the storm passes, the Banana Birds come out from hiding. Whenever these creatures see the word *banana* in print, they attack the page furiously, leaving only a hole where the word had been. They are soon joined by the Kumquat Birds, who fly off with any piece of paper bearing the word *kumquat*, which they use for building their nests. And the Mocking Birds join the fun, too; they take great pleasure in manufacturing their own airplanes, covered with meaningless scribbles, and hurling them over the fence amongst the real ones. Fortunately, the Snipper Birds (who bite off the noses of airplanes as they fly past) are away for the season, visiting some disreputable cousins.

Meanwhile, as your skill at making airplanes improves, you are able to build and throw them faster. At times, Fred can't keep up, and he loses several pages this way. He also misses pages when he is interrupted by telephone calls, or when visitors drop by.

Toward the end of the day, when only 100 pages remain to be sent, Fred is suddenly called to a meeting. Unfortunately, he doesn't have a way to let you know about this, so you continue to sail your manuscript over the fence, page by page. The pages that

---

1. This is the first of many silly analogies you will find in this book. It does not reflect the actual method used to submit the present manuscript.

A Banana Bird

A Kumquat Bird

A Mocking Bird

are lucky enough to survive the birds fall prey to the puddles and dogs. And to top it off, Fred forgot to close the file cabinet drawer before he left, so all the pages he had already filed blow away in a sudden gust of wind.

This story illustrates, without going into any technical detail, the kinds of hazards that await us when we set out to transfer computer files. The manuscript is a file, the fence is the separation between the two computers; the wind, the rain, and the birds represent just a few unexpected properties of the communication medium. The dogs and puddles correspond to the infamous "bit bucket" into which arriving data is[2] consigned when the computer is not ready to process it. The file cabinet is the computer's disk, and the folders are the system's disk buffers. You and Fred are the computers themselves, with their differing capabilities, speeds, and jobs to do.

If you had first tried submitting your manuscript on a sunny, calm, dry day (with the birds wintering in the south), all might have worked perfectly. Yet the hazards are real, and if you perform this operation often enough, they will take their toll: a normally "clean" telephone connection will be attacked by a sudden burst of noise; a seemingly attentive computer will turn its back on you at a critical moment; some rare arrangement of characters in your data will plunge a piece of communication equipment into catatonia. A set of rules and procedures, a *protocol*, is needed to ensure that when problems like this arise, they can be detected and corrective action taken.

What Is a Protocol?

A protocol is a kind of etiquette, much like the conventions people follow regarding introductions, greetings, conversation, and parting. Computers must observe similar conventions if they are to exchange information with one another. They must agree to speak the same language, at the same speed. They should know how to say hello and goodbye to each other. They may have to agree that only one of them can talk at a time (unless they're New Yorkers!). It doesn't matter very much what the rules are, as long as the two parties can agree upon and follow them. Such a set of rules is called a protocol.

Kermit is a *file transfer* protocol. Its rules are designed to ensure that computer files[3] can be transferred from one computer to another correctly and completely, despite the many pitfalls that lie in the way. As a crude example, here is a protocol for submitting manuscripts to Fred's Press:

---

2. Yes, I know *data* is the plural of Latin *datum*, and I should say *data are*, or perhaps *data sunt*. But alas, the word has entered English usage as a collective (singular) noun, despite the best efforts of the *Académie Anglaise*.

3. Because you're reading this book, you probably have some idea of what files are. For now, let's just say a file is a collection of information stored in approximately permanent form under a given name, usually on a magnetic medium like a disk; files are described in detail in the Primer section of this book (starting on page 48).

- In order to avoid injury to Fred, don't throw the whole manuscript at once. Fold each page into a paper airplane, and fly the pages over the wall one by one. Number them sequentially, so Fred can detect when a page is missing.

- Start your manuscript with a title page, so Fred can tell who it's from and where to file it. Launch the title page first.

- Send the pages in order. After sending a page to Fred, wait for a receipt before sending the next page, to be sure he's ready for it.

- To foil the Banana and Kumquat birds, substitute special code words on your airplanes for *banana* and *kumquat*. If Snipper Birds are in the vicinity, fold the airplanes so that the nose contains no writing.

- If you wait too long for a reply from Fred, send another copy of the same page. If you send, say, five copies with no reply, you can assume Fred has gone to a meeting, in which case you give up and try again later.

- After you have sent the last page, you should send a special message telling Fred that the transmission is complete. This message requires a receipt, so the previous rule applies to it.

Of course, Fred must observe his end of the protocol:

- Begin by waiting for a title page. Ignore any papers that are not title pages. When the title page arrives, open the appropriate file drawer, get an empty folder, and then send back a receipt for the title page.

- When an expected page arrives successfully, decode any code words and then put it in the folder. If the folder becomes full, go file it and get another empty folder. Then send back a numbered receipt for the page, and wait for the next page.

- When a page arrives that has scribbles, smears, the wrong page number, or the same page number as last time, send back a request for another copy of the desired page. This takes care of the wind, rain, Mocking Birds, and lost receipts.

- When a special message arrives indicating that the manuscript has been completely sent, file away the last folder, close the file drawer, and send a final receipt.

Now you have a fairly general and robust protocol for throwing a manuscript over a fence. A real file transfer protocol must address the same concerns, which might be stated somewhat more formally as follows:

- *Identification:* The name of each file should be transmitted with, but distinct from, its contents, so that it can be automatically stored under its correct name on the target computer system.

- *Delimitation:* The beginning and end of each file should be marked clearly, so that the target system can be certain that it has received it completely, with no extraneous material at the beginning or end.

- *Transparency:* Information must be encoded during transmission to exclude patterns that could trigger interference by intervening communications or computing equipment.

- *Synchronization:* Information must not be transmitted to the target system faster than it can be processed.

- *Sequencing:* The target system must be able to ensure that no data has been lost or erroneously duplicated.

- *Error Correction:* The target system must be able to detect when information has been corrupted during transmission, and recover the damaged information.

- *Timeout:* At least one of the systems must be able to detect when expected data does not arrive in a reasonable amount of time, and request retransmission.

- *Format Conversion:* If the information is to be used on the target system (rather than simply stored there), it must be converted to a form that is useful on the target system.[4]

We'll return to all these topics throughout the book.

How the Kermit Protocol Works

A file is transferred from one computer to another by a *pair* of Kermit programs, one running on each computer, as shown in Figure 2-1. The Kermit programs carry out the Kermit protocol by sending messages to each other through their communication ports. This section describes the protocol briefly, just enough to give you an idea of how it works. All the material presented here is covered more thoroughly in subsequent sections.

The Kermit protocol is *character-oriented*; data is transmitted in the form of discrete characters, like A, B, C, rather than in some other form. The communication medium itself is character-oriented, because it was designed for use by character devices like data terminals. Most computers agree about how characters are represented, and they agree that there are 128 of them altogether, of which 95 are printable (like A, B, C, 1, 2, 3), and the other 33 are reserved for control or formatting purposes. These characters compose the ASCII character set [5] (listed in Appendix D on page 340). The control characters sometimes cause computers and communication devices to react unpredict-

---

4. Format conversion didn't come up in our story, because Fred is not picky about the manuscript format. But another publisher might want your margins rearranged, your spacing changed, or your English translated to Sanskrit.

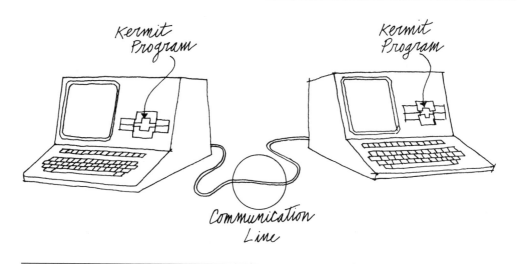

Figure 2-1. Two Computers, Two Kermit Programs

ably, just as the names of certain fruits provoke the neighborhood birds to intercept our paper airplanes. To promote transparency, Kermit encodes control characters as printable character sequences during transmission, just as we disguised the hazardous fruit names in our manuscript.

Kermit transfers data by breaking it up into pieces and encapsulating the pieces within *packets*, much as we broke our manuscript into separate pages for transmission. In data communication, a packet is a sequence of characters arranged so that the beginning and end, and the location of various control and data fields, can be unambiguously identified. The control fields are used for synchronization, sequencing, and error detection, and the data field usually contains a piece of the file being transferred. A Kermit packet is shown in Figure 2-2.

| MARK | LEN | SEQ | TYPE | DATA | CHECK |

Figure 2-2. Kermit Packet Layout

The MARK identifies the beginning of the packet. The length field (LEN) specifies how long the rest of the packet is. The sequence number (SEQ) is used to detect lost or duplicated packets. The TYPE field indicates the purpose or contents of the packet: file name, file data, end of file, etc. The CHECK field contains a quantity formed by combining all the other characters in the packet in some way (like adding them up). The sender of the packet computes this value and includes it at the end of the packet. The receiver of the packet does the same computation and checks the result against the value recorded in the packet. If the two values agree, the packet is accepted; if they disagree, the packet has been corrupted and retransmission is requested.

Figure 2-3 shows how a typical file transfer proceeds. The transfer is synchronized, because the file sender waits for a response to each packet before sending the next one. The receiver has time to file away the data, free from concern that the next packet will arrive prematurely. The file sender begins the transfer by transmitting a Send-Initiation packet to the receiver (packet zero in the figure). The "Send-Init" and its response are greeting messages, in which the two programs settle upon etiquette: the longest packet that will be tolerated, how long to wait for a packet before timing out, and so forth. Then the sender transmits a File-Header packet (packet 1 in Figure 2-3) to tell the receiver the name of the file that is about to arrive. Then come as many File-Data packets (packets 2 and following) as are required to transmit the entire contents of the file, which is encoded in printable characters to promote transparency. The sender follows the data packets by an End-of-File packet (27). The File-Header, File-Data, End-of-File sequence is repeated for each file to be sent, and the transaction is closed by an End-of-Transaction packet (packet 54 in the figure).

The file receiver sends an ACK (positive acknowledgment) packet back to the sender for each packet that has been received correctly. Then both Kermit programs advance their current packet sequence numbers and move on to the next packet. If a packet is corrupted in transit by noise or loss of characters (packet 4 in the figure), the check will be wrong and the file receiver will NAK (negatively acknowledge) it, causing the sender to retransmit the same packet.

If the file sender does not receive an ACK within the prescribed timeout interval (packet 30), it retransmits the same packet. If the file receiver does not receive an expected packet within the timeout interval, it sends a NAK for the expected packet. The receiver uses the packet number to detect when the same packet arrives more than once (like packet 30) to avoid writing redundant data into the file. Because the file sender must receive a valid ACK for each packet before transmitting the next one, there is never a gap in the data. Finally, if the same packet is retransmitted too many times, the protocol will declare that the transfer has failed.

Conventions Used in This Book

Before we proceed to the basic Kermit commands and examples, let's endow some commonly used words with specialized meanings:

- *Computer:* For the purposes of this book, a computer is a device that can communicate over a "serial communication port," store and manage files, and run programs (like Kermit). A computer may also be called a *computer system*, a *system*, or a *machine*.

- *Micro:* This term is used synonymously with *microcomputer*, *personal computer* (PC), and *workstation*. It denotes a self-contained, primarily single-user computer system. These can range in power from a hobbyist's inexpensive home computer to an engineer's

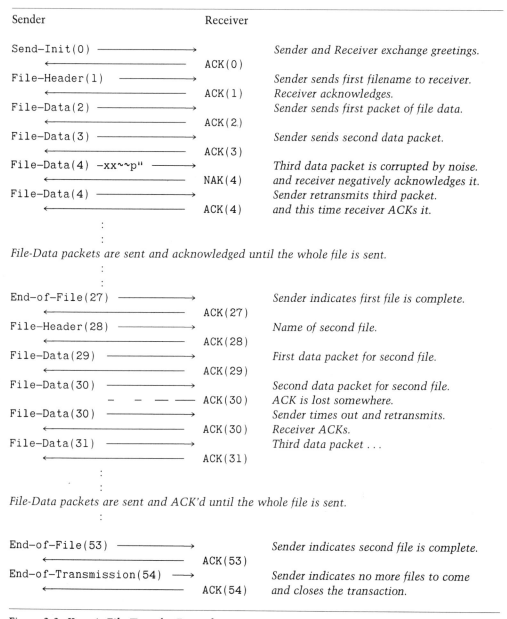

Sender		Receiver	
Send-Init(0) ────────→			*Sender and Receiver exchange greetings.*
←────────	ACK(0)		
File-Header(1) ────→			*Sender sends first filename to receiver.*
←────────	ACK(1)		*Receiver acknowledges.*
File-Data(2) ────→			*Sender sends first packet of file data.*
←────────	ACK(2)		
File-Data(3) ────→			*Sender sends second data packet.*
←────────	ACK(3)		
File-Data(4) -xx~~p" ────→			*Third data packet is corrupted by noise.*
←────────	NAK(4)		*and receiver negatively acknowledges it.*
File-Data(4) ────→			*Sender retransmits third packet.*
←────────	ACK(4)		*and this time receiver ACKs it.*

File-Data packets are sent and acknowledged until the whole file is sent.

End-of-File(27) ────→			*Sender indicates first file is complete.*
←────────	ACK(27)		
File-Header(28) ────→			*Name of second file.*
←────────	ACK(28)		
File-Data(29) ────→			*First data packet for second file.*
←────────	ACK(29)		
File-Data(30) ────→			*Second data packet for second file.*
− − − − ACK(30)			*ACK is lost somewhere.*
File-Data(30) ────→			*Sender times out and retransmits.*
←────────	ACK(30)		*Receiver ACKs.*
File-Data(31) ────→			*Third data packet ...*
←────────	ACK(31)		

File-Data packets are sent and ACK'd until the whole file is sent.

End-of-File(53) ────→			*Sender indicates second file is complete.*
←────────	ACK(53)		
End-of-Transmission(54) ──→			*Sender indicates no more files to come*
←────────	ACK(54)		*and closes the transaction.*

Figure 2-3. Kermit File Transfer Example

NOTE. The monospace typeface used in this figure and elsewhere in the book for computer output and programming code does not distinguish between the lower-case letter "l" and the numeral "1." I hope this constraint will not cause confusion in the program examples.

$100,000 automated design workstation. The distinguishing characteristic of these systems, from Kermit's point of view, is that the user's primary access is through a special *console* (keyboard and screen) that is distinct from the primary communication medium (the serial port).

- *Mainframe:* This term is used synonymously with *minicomputer* or *timesharing system*. From Kermit's viewpoint, all of these have in common that they are shared simultaneously by more than one user. Users communicate via terminals, over communication lines that serve simultaneously as their primary access to the system *and* the primary communication medium.

- *Local:* This means the same in Kermit jargon as it does in everyday speech: "nearby." The local system is the closer of two systems, the one you interact with more directly. A *local Kermit program* can interact with you via the keyboard and screen while it is transferring files on a separate communication line. A micro is usually, but not always, local.

- *Remote:* By the same token, *remote* means "far away." When two computers are connected via Kermit, the more distant one is remote—if you have to go through computer A to reach computer B, then A is local and B is remote. A *remote Kermit program* uses the same communication line to transfer files that it uses to interact with you, which means it cannot interact and transfer files at the same time. A mainframe is usually, but not always, remote.

- *Host:* In computer jargon, a host is a computer system that can accommodate multiple simultaneous users (guests) and offer them a variety of services. This book uses the word *host* to refer to a remote mainframe or timesharing system.

Over the years there have been many different styles of "user interface" (computer jargon for how a computer communicates with a human) ranging from plugboards and switches to cards and "job control language"; from terminals and commands to mice and windows. The most common form of human-machine interaction today is still the terminal and command model, and this is the one we use in this book, even though some Kermit programs use others.

Within the terminal and command model, there are several variations. Our focus is on the interactive prompting, or conversational, style. The computer issues a *prompt* and you respond by typing a *command*; the computer displays the results of your command, and then prompts you for your next command. And so on. This form of interaction is called a *dialog*. The prompt is the computer's way of telling you that it is ready for your next command. Kermit programs tend to have prompts like "Kermit>" and simple commands composed of words, usually in the form of short imperative sentences. In the following example, the program's prompt "Kermit>" is followed by the command "send foo.bar":

```
Kermit>send foo.bar
```

The computer types `Kermit>` and you type `send foo.bar`.

A command is composed of one or more *fields*. A field is like a word in a sentence; it is surrounded by spaces, or else appears at the beginning or the end. The fields of Kermit commands are either specific *keywords*, like SEND, SET, EXIT, HELP, FILE, ON, OFF, or else *operands*, like numbers or filenames. In the description of a command, a keyword is shown literally, whereas an operand is shown as a *parameter*, a symbol for which you are to substitute a real value. For instance, if the parameter is *number*, then you might substitute 13.

Here is the notation that is used to describe Kermit commands, as well as in sample dialogs with the computer. A few additional conventions appear on page 119.

1. Parameters are shown in *italics*. For example, a command to delete a file might be shown like this:

`delete` *filename*

which means that you would type the word `delete` and the following space literally, and then you would type the name of an actual file. The most common parameters are:

filename   The name of a single file

filespec   A file specification, possibly referring to more than one file

number   A number, usually in decimal notation

The method for specifying a group of files depends on the particular computer system. Usually it is done by including a "wildcard" character in the filename. For instance "`*.TXT`" might denote all files whose names end with "`.TXT`".

2. In sample dialogs between a person and a computer, the part typed by the person is in green ink, and the part typed by the computer is in plain black ink. In command descriptions, colored ink is not used.

3. In command descriptions there is an implied carriage return at the end of the line. In other words, when you see the end of a line, you should type a carriage return unless otherwise indicated.

4. `<CR>` means "type carriage return." This is used in contexts where the implied end of line might not be obvious.

5. `<NOCR>` means that although the end of the line would normally imply a carriage return, you shouldn't type one here.

6. `CTRL-A` represents the Control-A character, one of the control characters from the ASCII alphabet. Similarly, `CTRL-B` represents Control-B, and so on. To enter a control character from the keyboard, hold down the Control (CTRL) key and press the indicated letter.

7. `^A` is an alternative notation for Control-A, sometimes called "uparrow" notation. Computers often display control characters in this form.

The following sample dialog shows how to "log in" to a (hypothetical) host computer and start a file transfer with Kermit. The lines are numbered to help us talk about them afterward:

```
(1) @ login username
(2) Password: password
(3) User username logged in at 6:45pm Monday, 7 October 1985
(4) @ kermit
(5) Kermit-XX>send filespec
(6)   ^]c <NOCR>
(7) Kermit-MS>receive
```

In line (1) the system has issued a prompt consisting of an atsign (@) and a space. You type login, a space, and then your own username, and you enter the command with a carriage return.

In line (2) the system responds by prompting for your password, which you type. In line (3) the system issues a message; the sample shows that you would really see your own username in the message, rather than the word *username*.

In line (4) you get the system's atsign prompt again, and you type kermit, which tells your computer to run the Kermit program. When the program starts, it issues its own prompt, Kermit-XX>. Note that the system and the program have different prompts, so that you know which one you are talking to; the system command language interpreter recognizes one set of commands and Kermit another.

In line (5) you tell the Kermit program to send a file.

In line (6) you type a control character, Control-Rightbracket, followed by the letter "c," with no carriage return. This cryptic sequence invokes another program's prompt, another *different* Kermit program on a *different* computer. To this program, you type receive. And then . . .

But before we get ahead of ourselves, let's see what it takes to establish communication between two computers.

Getting Connected

This section explains how to connect one computer to another. If you already know how to make the connection you want, feel free to skip ahead to page 27 (Terminal Emulation).

Before two computers can communicate, there must be a physical connection between them. In some cases, the connection is already there: a hardwired (dedicated, permanent) line, or a terminal network. But you may have to make the connection yourself by dialing a phone number or installing a cable. Once you have the physical connection, you need software (like Kermit) that knows how to use it, and you need to know how to use the software.

The following discussion assumes you are connecting a micro to a mainframe, but it would also apply to connections between micros, or between mainframes, with minor and obvious changes in wording.

Cables, Connectors, Modems, and Ports

Before you can establish a physical connection, you need an asynchronous serial communication port, sometimes called an asynchronous adapter, an RS-232 port, an EIA connector, or some other combination of these words. We'll just call it the serial port. All terminals come with a serial port, and many, but not all, microcomputers carry them as standard equipment. All mainframes have them too (with a few exceptions we'll discuss later). The serial port generally appears on the back of your micro as a connector with two rows of pins (or holes), either 25 or 9 of them, as shown in Figure 2–4. But if you don't see such a connector, read the next few paragraphs before rushing out to buy a serial port.

The connector is there for you to plug a cable into. If you have a cable that will reach the other computer, you need no more, provided the cable is wired correctly and the plugs fit (Figure 2–5). If the other computer is too far away, you can call it up on the telephone, using a *modem* (MOdulator-DEModulator). Modems come in two basic forms, internal and external. An external modem (Figure 2-6) is separate from your microcomputer. It connects to the micro's serial port with one cable and to the telephone with another cable. Older external modems, called acoustic couplers, connect to the phone's handset with rubber cups. An internal modem (Figure 2-7), on the other hand, is inside your micro. It is connected internally to (or incorporates) your micro's serial port, so that all you see from the outside may be a modular phone jack. In this case, you can still communicate, but only by telephone.

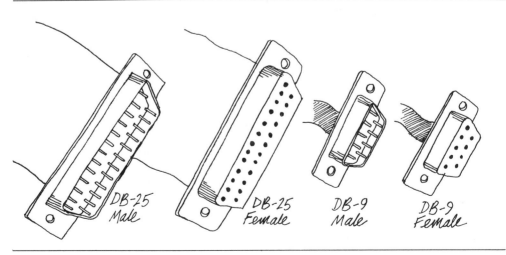

Figure 2-4. Common Connector Configurations

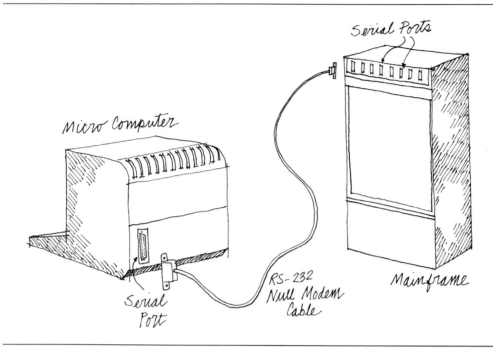

Figure 2-5. Direct Hookup

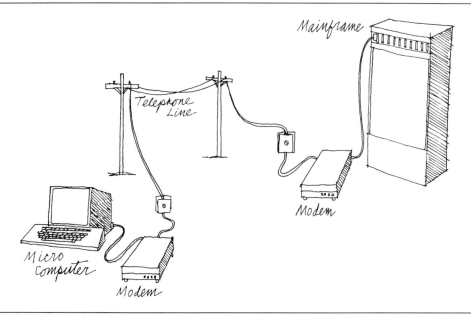

Figure 2-6. Direct-Connect External Modem Hookup

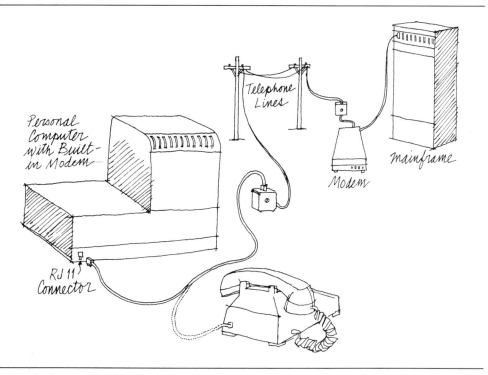

Figure 2-7. Internal Modem Hookup

If you have an internal modem, you can skip ahead to "Dialups," page 25. But you should be aware that Kermit does not necessarily work with any particular internal modem, even if it works with an external modem on the same system. The only way to be certain is to try. If you're in the market for a modem to use with Kermit, don't buy an internal modem unless you already know it will work with Kermit on your system.

The kind of data communication cables we use are called EIA cables or RS-232-C cables. A cable consists of an outer sleeve containing from 4 to 25 insulated wires, which terminate at pins (or holes) within D-connectors at each end (Figure 2-4). These connectors come in different shapes, different "genders," with different numbers of wires, and with different pin assignments. You will need a cable with just the right combination of all these.

- *Gender:* A connector is called "male" if pins protrude from it, and "female" if it has holes. Only connectors of opposite gender can "mate." For better or worse, this kind of terminology is firmly rooted in data communications and also among electricians.[5] Although there is a standard [9] that says computers and terminals should have male connectors, you are just as likely to find them with female ones. Male connectors are sometimes called plugs, and females receptacles.

- *Shape:* D-connectors come in two major shapes, DB-25 (currently the most common) and DB-9[6] (gaining popularity), described by international standards [15,16] respectively, and shown in Figure 2-4. The DB-25 connector has two rows of pins (or holes), 13 on top and 12 on the bottom. The DB-9 has 5 on top and 4 on the bottom. Both are shaped like horizontally elongated trapezoids with rounded corners. The shell of the male connector fits around the female connector, and the pins go into the holes. Properly speaking, only the 25-pin version is an RS-232 connector.

- *Wires:* All data cables must have at least four wires—one for transmit, one for receive, and two for ground. When modems are involved (or when the serial port is intended for use with a modem), additional wires carry signals used to monitor and control the phone connection. When the transmit lead of one connecter goes to the receive lead of the other, and vice versa, the cable is called a null modem cable, or a modem eliminator. A null modem is used to connect one computer directly to another.

Manufacturers exhibit little consistency in the importance they attach to the various pins. For this reason, computer supply houses often sell cables in several varieties—for instance, with 4, 8, 10, 15, or 25 wires, and options as to which sets of pins are con-

---

5. As far as I can tell, no particular merit is ascribed to either gender.

---

6. Although "DB-9" is in common usage, it is probably a misnomer. Supply catalogs indicate that the letter following the D denotes the connector's shell size, and that the shell size for 9-pin connectors is E, not B.

nected. However, it is not always true that more wires are better; in null modem cables, especially, certain modem signals need to be ignored, or cross-connected. There have been cases where wiring, say, pins 9 or 10 (used for test voltages) has caused damage. The only way to know which cable is right is to consult your dealer or the technical documentation for your equipment.

The following sections discuss direct and dialup connections as they most commonly occur. If this information is not enough to get you connected, consult the primers and case studies in later sections of this book.

Direct Connections

A direct connection between two computers can be established by running a communication cable between their serial ports. But finding the right cable can be a major hurdle. Most computer-to-computer connections require a null modem cable, because the data that one system transmits is to be received by the other. So first, get a null-modem cable that has a connector of the right shape and gender on each end and try it out. If it doesn't work, then (1) the cable is defective, (2) it has too few or too many wires, or (3) you really needed a straight-through cable after all.

If you find yourself stuck with an uncooperative cable, you may have to do the kind of fiddling described in the data communications primer (see "Cables and Connectors Revisited," page 102). Don't be timid. This book should include enough information to make you an expert interfacer.

The RS-232-C standard [9] says that 50 feet (about 15 meters) is the maximum distance for a direct connection. In practice, direct-connect cables are often several hundred feet long. The maximum length depends upon the environment, the cable, and the devices involved. If you need a direct connection over a longer distance (like several thousand feet), you can use "line drivers" or specially shielded or low-capacitance cables available from computer supply houses.

Direct connections can also be made over even longer distances, but not without considerable investment of time and money in synchronous modems, leased dedicated phone lines, microwave towers, satellite dishes, construction permits, FCC licenses, and so on. Kermit may be used over long-distance direct connections, but it is beyond the scope of this book to tell you how to establish those connections in the first place (see McNamara [25]).

Dialups

When direct cabling is not feasible, computers may be connected through the telephone system using modems. In the typical case, a mainframe has a "dialup line" available, consisting of a serial port connected to an "auto-answer" modem, which in turn is connected to a telephone. You initiate a connection by dialing the appropriate phone number, waiting for the computer to answer, and then activating your modem. The mechanics of this process vary, depending on your modem. Consult your modem manual for any details that you don't find here.

You should be aware that there are several different, incompatible, types of modems. Two modems work together only if they observe the same conventions as to the coding and transmission of data on the phone line, and operate at the same speed. The speed is called the "baud rate," which is roughly equivalent to ten times the number of characters the hardware can transmit per second; 1200 baud is equivalent to 120 characters per second. The most common transmission standards in North America are called Bell-103 (110–300 baud), Bell-212A (1200 baud), and Racal-Vadic VA3400 (also 1200 baud, but incompatible with Bell-212A).[7] Many modems automatically recognize two or three different standards. These are called double (or triple) modems. You should ensure that the modems you propose to use are compatible.

The local modem is called an "originate" modem, because it initiates the call (if it has an Originate/Answer switch, it should be set on Originate). The modem is situated between your micro and the telephone. The modem connects to the telephone, using either a modular phone jack (RJ-type, usually RJ11) supplied with the modem,[8] or acoustic cups. In some cases, the modem is installed between the modular outlet on your wall and the telephone itself, using a telephone wire with RJ11 jacks at each end. Consult your modem manual for installation instructions.

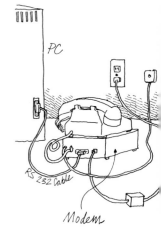

Unlike computers and terminals, external modems are fairly predictable in their use of connectors. Every modem should have a female DB-25 connector, so the modem end of your cable should have a male DB-25 connector, and the cable should always be straight-through, with 10 wires for the transmit, receive, ground, and modem signals. Your problem is reduced to finding such a cable with a connector of the appropriate shape and gender on the other end; these should be stock items in computer stores.

Before attempting to establish a dialup connection, you must use Kermit or some other software to set the baud rate of your PC's serial port. This is normally done with a command like SET SPEED or SET BAUD. Your PC's baud rate must be the same as the baud rate of the serial port on the remote computer; if they do not match, no meaningful communication can take place. Furthermore, your baud rate must be one supported by the modems involved in the connection.

If your modem has a built-in dialer, see the following paragraphs for how to use it with Kermit. Otherwise, you must make the connection manually. The usual procedure is as follows:

1. Dial the computer's phone number. If the line is busy or doesn't answer, try again later. If a person answers, you probably dialed a wrong number—apologize and try again.

---

7. In Europe, Bell-103 is generally not used; 200–300 baud techniques (mostly variations on CCITT Recommendation V.21) tend to differ from country to country. For 1200 baud, most European countries recognize CCITT V.22, Bell-212A, or both. At 2400 baud, several different, competing, proposed standards are emerging in the U.S. and Europe (AT&T 2224, V.22*bis*, V.26*ter*). See Table 4-3 on page 91.

---

8. This type of modem is called a "direct connect" modem. If you have a such a modem, but your phone lacks modular jacks, you can convert the phone and the wall outlet using parts available in any hardware store.

2. When the computer answers the call (after one or two rings), you will hear an audible tone, usually high in pitch.

3. If you have a direct-connect modem, switch it from voice to data (unless it does this itself automatically). If you have an acoustic coupler, insert your handset into it with the phone cord on the correct end.

4. If your modem has a "carrier" light, it should now come on. This means that the two modems are engaged and communicating according to the same standard.

Terminal Emulation

By now, you should have a physical connection. Your PC must be instructed to transmit and receive data over this connection. These instructions are carried out by a software program, like Kermit.

In addition to its file transfer function, Kermit provides "terminal emulation" for microcomputers. This means that the Kermit program can be told to make the micro behave as if it were a terminal: to send the characters you type on the keyboard out the serial port, and to display all the characters that arrive at the serial port on your screen. No error detection or correction is done, any more than a real terminal would do. Terminal emulation is not part of the Kermit protocol, only a convenient tool to aid in its initiation. The particular terminal being emulated may range from a "dumb" terminal with no special features to some particular "smart" terminal, depending on the needs, whim, ambition, and skill of the contributing programmer.

The Kermit command that activates terminal emulation is CONNECT. After you issue the CONNECT command, you are communicating with whatever device is connected to your serial port. If you have a direct line to another computer, or if you have already dialed up a computer, then you are connected to that computer. However, if you have the type of modem that dials the phone for you, then you will be communicating with the modem itself. Autodial modems contain their own little computers with which you may have a dialog. You tell them to dial a number, they tell you whether they succeeded or failed. For instance, if you have a Hayes-like modem [14], you could type

```
ATD7654321<CR>
```

to have it dial the telephone number 765-4321. It might respond (depending on the setting of certain switches on the modem) with "CONNECT" upon successful connection with a modem on the other end, or "NO CARRIER," meaning that the phone didn't answer, or there was no modem connected to it. If the call was placed successfully, the modem will automatically become transparent so you can communicate directly with the dialed system. Consult your modem manual for details.

By this time, you should have reached the remote computer. Now you need to do something to get its attention. Typing a carriage return or two is usually enough to provoke a response. If you see a meaningful message on your screen, you're connected.

Otherwise, the problem might be that your cable is not wired correctly, the modem is set up wrong, the baud rate is incorrect, etc. Consult Chapter 6, "Common Problems and How to Fix Them," page 172.

One final element of terminal emulation must now be mentioned: the "escape sequence." You might have wondered how you ever get back to your local computer after you've CONNECTed to the remote one. During terminal emulation, the Kermit program looks at every character you type, and if it is *not* a certain predesignated "escape character," it is transmitted. If it *is* the escape character, then the program waits for you to type another character, which is taken to be a command, such as "C" for "Close Connection." The escape character most often chosen is one that would rarely, if ever, need to be typed at the remote system. A typical choice is Control-Rightbracket: the mystery of the cryptic "^]C" from page 20 is now revealed. The basic functions of terminal emulation are illustrated in Figure 2-8.

To summarize, terminal emulation is a mechanism that makes your PC behave like a terminal; it enables you to communicate with two different computers using the same keyboard and screen. CONNECT sends you to the remote system, and the escape sequence brings you back to the local one. If this discussion has left you confused, then follow the examples to get a feel for how it works.

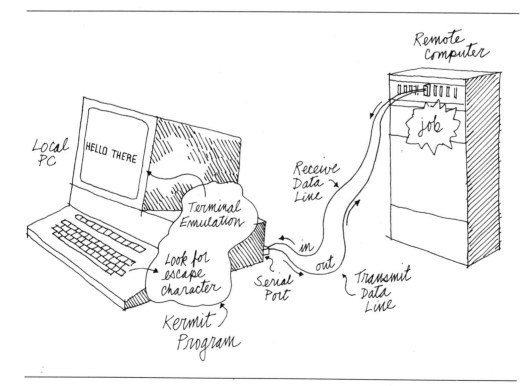

Figure 2-8. Terminal Emulation

How to Transfer Files with Kermit

The Kermit protocol, and most Kermit programs, allow you to send a file reliably from a microcomputer (PC) to a host, from the host to the PC, from host to host, or from PC to PC, usually without any special regard for the nature of the particular machines involved. The scenarios are similar, differing mainly in the details of how to establish the connection.

The most common use of Kermit is between a PC and a mainframe, and this discussion assumes you are sitting at a PC which:

• Is turned on and working

• Is connected directly or via dialup to the mainframe

• Has a Kermit program available on its disk or other local storage

• Has sufficient free disk space to store new files

It is also assumed that you have the ability to log in to the mainframe, store or read files there, and that a Kermit program is available on the mainframe. When one of the systems lacks a Kermit program, you can't use the Kermit protocol to transfer files (see page 9 for how to get Kermit).

From system command level on your PC, run your local Kermit program and issue the CONNECT command. Now you're "talking" to the remote host. At this point you must get its attention, log in, and then run the remote Kermit program.

Once you have a Kermit program on each end of the connection, the next step is to tell *each* Kermit what to do. Suppose you want to transfer a file from the remote computer to your PC. You would first tell the remote Kermit to SEND the file, then "escape back" to the PC Kermit and tell it to RECEIVE the file. The transfer begins—you can sit back and watch, or go make yourself a sandwich. While the packets go back and forth (as shown in Figure 2-3), the PC Kermit will produce a running display on your screen (see Figure 2-9), and it will notify you when the transfer is complete.

The desired file should now be on your PC disk. The Kermit protocol has ensured that the file arrived correctly and completely. Now you must clean up after yourself: CONNECT back to the remote host, exit from Kermit on the host, log out from the host if you're done, escape back to PC Kermit and exit from it. Now you can do whatever you had planned for your file—edit it, print it on your PC printer, etc. Transferring a file in the other direction works the same way, but with the SEND and RECEIVE commands interchanged.

If you have to exchange several files in both directions, you will soon tire of escaping back and forth and typing SEND and RECEIVE commands on each end. Most (but not all) mainframe Kermit programs can be put into a "server mode" of operation, which simplifies the process considerably, and most (not all) PC Kermit programs provide the special commands required for communicating with Kermit servers. A Kermit server (on the mainframe) takes all its commands in packet form from the local Kermit program (on the PC). For example, if you tell the local Kermit to SEND a file, the remote Kermit server need not be told to RECEIVE it—it will do so automatically.

Basic Commands

The fundamental Kermit commands are described here very briefly. Details of syntax may vary among systems, and additional options may be available. A detailed presentation of Kermit commands is given in Chapter 5, and that may have to be supplemented by documentation for your particular Kermit program. Note that when initiating a file transfer, you must issue your command (SEND, RECEIVE, or SERVER) to the remote Kermit first, then escape back to the local Kermit and issue the corresponding command (RECEIVE, SEND, or GET).

- ?

Typed almost anywhere within a Kermit command: List the commands, options, or operands that are possible at this point.

- HELP

Display a summary of Kermit commands and what they do.

- CONNECT

Act as a terminal to the remote system until the escape sequence is given.

- SET BAUD *number*

Set the serial port's speed to the given baud rate. Sometimes available as SET SPEED. When not available in either form, use a system utility to set the baud rate. The SET command also has many other options.

- SEND *filespec*

Send the file or file group specified by *filespec* to the other Kermit, which must be given a RECEIVE command, or else must be in server mode.

- RECEIVE

Passively wait for a file or file group to arrive from the other Kermit, which must be given a SEND command.

- GET *filespec*

Actively request a Kermit server to send the specified file or files.

- REMOTE *command*

Some Kermit servers may be asked to perform functions beyond sending and receiving files. These are invoked by the REMOTE command. For instance, REMOTE DIRECTORY will ask the remote Kermit server to send a file directory listing of the specified remote files to your screen, and REMOTE DELETE will request the server to delete the specified remote file.

- BYE

Ask the server to terminate and log out your job from the remote system, so that you need not CONNECT back and clean up.

- FINISH

Ask the server to terminate, but leave your remote job active so that you can CONNECT to it again.

- EXIT

Exit from the Kermit program.

File Types

Before we proceed to real examples, there's one more thing you should know. Kermit is normally set up to work with *text* files. If you want to use Kermit to transfer *binary* files, you may have to take some special measures.

A text file is one that has been created by a human agent, or that is intended for reading by a human. It contains only printable characters and formatting control characters, like carriage return, linefeed, formfeed, and tab. It might be a document, or electronic mail, or program source. Most likely, it was entered into the computer by typing it into a text editor, but it might also be the output from a computer program.

A binary file is not intended to be directly understood by humans; it may be composed of any arbitrary patterns or sequences. Binary files are usually used to control a given device, or as input to a computer program. Examples include executable program files (like KERMIT.EXE on the MS-DOS diskette), some word-processor documents (but not others), numerical data in internal binary format, raster graphics for display, control codes for a laser printer, and so forth.

For purposes of file transfer, the key question is whether the file is to be received in a form that is useful on the target system. For text files to be usable after file transfer between unlike systems, it is often necessary to convert the format. For instance, IBM hosts store text files using a different alphabet than most other computers use. Different systems may represent boundaries between lines of text in different ways.

Binary files, on the other hand, generally cannot and should not be converted to another system's format, because their contents are meaningful only on their home systems. Machine instructions for one system cannot be executed correctly on another kind of system; internal representation of numbers will vary from system to system.

When most Kermit programs are told to send a file, they will perform format conversions appropriate to text files unless instructed to the contrary. Computers cannot be relied upon to tell the difference between text and binary files automatically, and I don't think you'd want them to try—you are the one who knows what the file is, and how it is to be used on the target system. If you really want files to be transferred without conversion, you will usually have to take special measures. The method differs from system to system, but in general the technique is to issue the following command (or one like it) to *each* Kermit program:

```
SET FILE TYPE BINARY
```

File formats and methods for coping with them will be recurring topics of this book.

Examples

The examples that follow cover the most common uses of Kermit—PC to host, PC to server, PC to IBM mainframe, PC to PC, and host to host. If your particular situation is not covered adequately by these examples, first check the handouts or built-in help text for the Kermit programs you are using. If these don't help, then pester the people who run your computer systems to explain their communications setup to you. If they can't—or "they" are *you*—well, that's what the rest of the book is for.

PC to Host   In this example, you are sitting at a PC, which is connected through its serial port to a DECSYSTEM-20 host computer, a typical timesharing system. The details of its operation are not important; it could be a VAX/VMS system, a UNIX system, or many other non-IBM hosts. The PC is local, the DEC-20 is remote. This example also applies almost literally to any other microcomputer implementation of Kermit. You have started up your PC and have the Kermit program on your disk. Begin by running Kermit on the PC. Use Kermit's CONNECT command to turn your PC into a terminal. Log in on the DEC-20 and run Kermit there. Here is an example of this procedure with the commands that you type printed in green. The material lined up on the right-hand side is our commentary, not what you see on the screen.

```
A>kermit                                      Run Kermit on the PC.
Kermit-MS V2.29
Type ? for Help

Kermit-MS>                                     This is the Kermit prompt for the PC.
Kermit-MS>connect                              Connect to the DEC-20.
(Connecting to host, type Control-]C to return to the PC)
                                               You are now connected to the DEC-20.
CU20B                                          The system prints its herald.
@login user password                           Log in.
```

(*Various greeting or notice messages are displayed.*)

```
@kermit                                        Run Kermit on the DEC-20.
TOPS-20 Kermit Version 4.2(257)

Kermit-20>                                     This is DEC-20 Kermit's prompt.
```

You are now ready to transfer files between the two machines.

The following example illustrates how to send files from the DEC-20 to the PC.

```
Kermit-20>send *.for                Send all my FORTRAN files.
^]c                                 Now escape back to the PC.
(Back at PC)                        The PC tells you you're back.
Kermit-MS>receive                   Tell the PC that files are coming.
```

If you take more than about 5 seconds to get back to Kermit-MS and issue the RECEIVE command, the first packets from the remote Kermit may arrive prematurely and appear on your screen, but no harm will be done, because the packet will be re-transmitted automatically until the PC acknowledges it.

Once the connection is established, the PC will show you what is happening. First it clears the screen and waits for incoming packets; as packets arrive, the current file name and packet number will be continuously displayed on the screen (Figure 2-9). When the PC's Kermit-MS> prompt returns to your screen (with an accompanying beep to catch your attention) the transfer is done. Notice the screen display. The status should be indicated as Complete. If not, an error has occurred and an appropriate message should be displayed to tell you why.

After you're finished transferring files, CONNECT back to the host, EXIT from the remote Kermit program, log out, and escape back to the PC as you did previously:

```
Kermit-MS>connect                   Get back to the host.
(Connecting to host type CTRL-]C to return to PC.)
Kermit-20>                          Here we are.
Kermit-20>exit                      Get out of Kermit-20.
@logout                             Log out from the DEC-20

Logged out Job 55, User username, Accout account, TTY 146,
  at 7-Oct-85 15:18:56, Used 0:00:17 in 0:21:55

^]c                                 Escape back to the PC.
(Back at PC)
Kermit-MS>exit                      Exit from the PC's Kermit.
```

The files you transferred should now be on your PC disk. To send files from the PC to the DEC-20, follow the same procedure but interchange the SEND and RECEIVE commands.

The procedure outlined above demonstrates the minimum service you should expect from any micro-mainframe Kermit connection, namely the ability to send files in either direction by explicitly issuing complementary SEND and RECEIVE commands for each transfer.

```
          File Name:    FOO.BAR
 KBytes Transferred:    17
Percent Transferred:    58%
            Sending:    In Progress

  Number of Packets:    193
  Number of Retries:    2
         Last Error:    None
       Last Warning:    None
```

Figure 2-9. Sample File Transfer Display Screen

PC to Kermit Server Kermit server operation is a bit more advanced in the sense that you will not necessarily find it available in a particular pair of Kermit programs. The remote Kermit must have a SERVER command, and the local Kermit must have a GET command and either FINISH or BYE (or both). If these conditions are not met, then you'll have to stick with basic operation.

To use a Kermit server, you must connect to the remote host, log in, and run the remote Kermit program, just as in the first example, but then issue the SERVER command. After putting the remote Kermit in server mode, you no longer have to tell one side to SEND and the other to RECEIVE. Nor do you have to connect back to the remote side to clean up and log out when you're done. Using the server, you can send as many files back and forth as you like without ever having to connect back to the remote host. Some servers perform additional functions, too, including directory listing, file deletion, or disk usage reporting, invoked by the REMOTE command from the local Kermit. (However, note that not all server-compatible PC Kermit programs provide REMOTE commands, and not all Kermit servers can respond to them.)

The following example demonstrates the use of a Kermit server. The user is sitting at a PC and the remote host is a DEC VAX running UNIX. Again, the particular machines and operating systems don't matter very much.

```
A>kermit                                   Run Kermit on the PC.
Kermit-MS V2.29

Kermit-MS>                                 The PC Kermit's prompt.
Kermit-MS>connect                          Connect to the UNIX system.
(Connecting to host, type Control-]C to return to the PC)

4.2 BSD UNIX                               The UNIX system prints its herald.
login: username
Password: password
Last login: Mon Oct 7 18:42:16 on ttyi6
```

(The UNIX system prints various login messages here.)

```
% kermit                                    Run UNIX Kermit.
C-Kermit, 4C(057) 31 Jul 85, 4.2 BSD
Type ? for help
C-Kermit>server                             Tell it to be a server.
```

```
C-Kermit server starting. Return to your local machine by typing its
escape sequence for closing the connection, and issue further commands
from there. To shut down the C-Kermit server, issue the FINISH or BYE
command.
```

```
^]c                                         Now escape back to the PC.
(Back at PC.)
Kermit-MS>send foo.*                        Send all the "foo" files from my micro.
```

(The screen displays the progress of the transfer.)

```
Kermit-MS>remote dir *.c                     See what C programs are on the UNIX
                                             system.

 ls -l *.c
-rw-rw-r--  1 fdc 20368 Jun 14 16:18 ckudia.c
-rw-rw-r--  1 fdc  8514 Jun 14 16:18 ckuscr.c
-rw-rw-r--  1 fdc 17836 Jun  3 16:53 cutape.c
-rw-rw-r--  1 fdc  2457 Oct  7 14:55 foo.c
Kermit-MS>remote delete foo.c                Get rid of an unwanted UNIX file.
 rm -f foo.c [OK]                            Kermit shows the UNIX translation.
Kermit-MS>get *.c                            Download the remaining C programs to
                                             the PC.
```

(The screen displays the progress.)

```
Kermit-MS>exit                              Exit from Kermit back to DOS.
A>
```

(Here you can do some work on the PC, edit files, whatever you like.)

```
A>kermit                                    Run Kermit-MS some more.
Kermit-MS>send new.c                        Send another file.
Kermit-MS>bye                               Done; shut down and log out the Kermit
                                            server.

A>
```

This is much simpler. Once you've started the Kermit server on the remote end, you can run Kermit as often as you like on the micro without having to go back and forth. Make sure to shut the server down when you're done by typing the BYE or FINISH command. If you use BYE, you don't have to connect back; if you use FINISH, you may connect back and do other work on the host before logging out.

Note the use of the REMOTE command. The REMOTE DIRECTORY (shortened to REMOTE DIR in the example) caused the UNIX Kermit server to display a listing of the specified files on the PC's screen, and the REMOTE DELETE command caused the file foo.c to be deleted from the UNIX system. If only a basic Kermit program had been available on the remote system, the user in this example would have had to CONNECT and escape back five times, rather than just once, to do the same work.

PC to IBM Mainframe   IBM System/370 series mainframes have a style of data communication different from most other computers. Because of this, the following example must use some terms that haven't been presented yet.[9]

The preferred means of communication between an IBM mainframe and a user is IBM's 3270-Series full-screen block-mode terminal. Most PCs do not bear any resemblance to a 3270; the communication medium, hardware interface, and even the character alphabet are different. Under what conditions, then, can a PC be connected to an IBM mainframe?

Most IBM mainframes have a "communications front end," called a 3705 (there are also equivalent or more advanced models from IBM as well as other companies). The 3705 may be configured to allow ordinary asynchronous ASCII terminals, or PCs that emulate them, to operate in "line mode," as opposed to 3270-style full-screen block mode. Line-mode operation is sometimes called "TTY mode," or even "TWX mode." If your system has a 3705 or equivalent front end with asynchronous ASCII line-mode ports, then you may use Kermit with it through those ports, as long as your PC has the requisite SET commands, described below.

Systems that do not provide line-mode ports may provide "protocol converters" for communicating with ASCII terminals and PCs. A protocol converter is a device or software package, residing anywhere along the communication path, that translates between the IBM character set and the PC's ASCII character set, from 3270 screen formatting commands to appropriate commands for the PC's screen, and from the PC's function keys to 3270 function keys. Kermit can transfer files through a protocol converter only if the protocol converter can be commanded to turn off its data format conversion function. However, most Kermit programs can be used for terminal emulation through protocol converters, even ones that can't be made transparent.

As of this writing, the only protocol converters that have the required capability— and which IBM host Kermit programs understand how to control—are the IBM Series/1

---

9. These terms will be covered in the data communications primer, which begins on page 70. IBM mainframe communications is covered in detail in "The IBM World," page 108.)

and equivalents (4994, 7171) supporting the Yale ASCII Communications System. We refer to this combination generically as the Series/1. If you don't know whether your IBM host has the prerequisites for Kermit file transfer, check with your system manager. It might help to bring this book with you. If the Kermit program on your IBM host gives you an error message like "An ASCII terminal must be used," then you are probably accessing the system via a protocol converter that cannot operate transparently, or that the host Kermit program does not know how to control. Again, consult your system manager—there may be a better way into the system.

Once you've determined that you can make a connection to the IBM mainframe, you must be prepared to cope with the idiosyncrasies of the IBM style of communication by entering some special SET commands to your local PC Kermit. Don't worry yet about what they mean; just work through the following example.[10] Note that some SET commands apply to line-mode connections, others to Series/1 connections; see Table 2-1. Our connection is between a PC and an IBM mainframe running the VM/CMS operating system:

```
E>kermit                                    Run Kermit on the PC.
Kermit-MS>
```

(These are the special commands for IBM host communication:)

```
Kermit-MS>set local-echo on              (Line mode only)
Kermit-MS>set flow none                  (Line mode only)
Kermit-MS>set handshake xon              (Line mode only)
Kermit-MS>set timer on                   (Line mode and Series/1)
Kermit-MS>set parity mark                (Line mode and Series/1)
```

(Connect to the IBM host, log in, and start Kermit there.)

```
Kermit-MS>connect
(Connecting to host, type Control-]C to return to PC)
<CR>
WELCOME TO CUVMA                         Greeting is displayed.


VM/370 ONLINE                            The system's herald.
<CR>                                     Type a carriage return.
!
```

---

10. A brief explanation of these special commands is given after the example, and they are described thoroughly in Chapter 5, "Kermit Command Reference."

```
.login username                              Log in.
ENTER PASSWORD:
password                                      Enter your password.
LOGON AT 16:17:28 EDT MONDAY 10/07/85
CUVMA CMS 3.1 8409 01/25/85
.<CR>                                         Type another CR.
```

(Various messages are displayed.)

```
R;
.<CR>                                         And another.
CMS
.kermit                                       Run the Kermit program.
Kermit CMS Version 2.01
Enter ? for a list of valid commands

KERMIT-CMS>.server                            Put it in server mode.
Entering server mode. . .
^]c <NOCR>                                    Escape back to the PC.
(Back at PC.)
Kermit-MS>
```

(Files may be transferred in the usual manner.)

```
Kermit-MS>bye                                 Shut down the server.
```

The five special SET commands shown above are often available bundled together into a single command, like DO IBM, or SET IBM ON. Most PC Kermit programs have such an IBM "macro" command, or provide the separate commands that compose it, although the syntax may vary. The special SET commands are as follows:

• SET LOCAL-ECHO ON
Sometimes available as SET DUPLEX HALF or SET ECHO LOCAL. You need this command for line-mode terminal emulation; without it, the characters that you type will not echo on your screen.

• SET PARITY MARK
PC Kermit programs usually do not use parity. But you need a SET PARITY command in order to communicate with IBM hosts. The actual parity could be something other than "mark." If MARK doesn't work, try EVEN, ODD, or SPACE (in that order).

• SET FLOW NONE
Use this command only for line-mode connections, if your PC Kermit supplies it. If your PC Kermit does not supply this command, then the feature that it turns off probably was not present anyway.

Table 2-1. Typical Settings for IBM Mainframe Communication

	Line Mode (3705)	Protocol Emulator (Series/1)
Terminal Emulation	Parity Mark Flow None Local Echo	Parity Even Flow XON/XOFF Remote Echo
File Transfer	Parity Mark Handshake XON Flow None Timer On	Parity Even Handshake None Flow XON/XOFF Timer On

• SET HANDSHAKE XON

Your PC should provide a command like this in order for you to transfer files with an IBM mainframe over a line-mode connection. If your PC lacks this command, try SET RECEIVE END 17 or SET RECEIVE END 21; if these commands are present, they might accomplish the same effect.

• SET TIMER ON

PCs usually have their timers turned off, on the assumption that the mainframe Kermit will provide the timeouts. But IBM mainframes cannot time out. If your PC doesn't have this command, you will have to watch the file transfer display and type a carriage return on the PC's keyboard if the transfer appears to be stuck.

Table 2-1 summarizes the settings required for terminal emulation and file transfer for communicating with an IBM mainframe, in line mode and through a Series/1-type protocol converter. The particular value of the parity setting may vary from site to site, and possibly among different devices within the same site. The flow setting should be XON/XOFF only if your PC supports this style of flow control. See the data communications primer (starting on page 70) for an explanation of parity and flow control, and see "Common Problems and How to Fix Them" (page 172) for some additional hints.

PC to PC It is possible to use Kermit to transfer files between two microcomputers, both in local mode.[11] You must start by connecting the two PCs. If they are nearby,

---

11. Some microcomputers can be commanded to behave like mainframes (according to our definition) by assigning their consoles to their communication ports (the MS-DOS CTTY command is an example). This effectively puts them in remote mode, and it's equivalent to the PC-to-host case we have already covered, except that you might have to issue a command like SET DISPLAY OFF to the remote PC to suppress its file transfer display.

you can use a null modem cable, in which case, you can skip ahead to step 4 in the following list. Otherwise, you'll have to establish a dialup connection. For this you will need two compatible modems, one in originate mode (the normal mode for a PC's modem), the other in answer mode. Not all modems have an answer mode, so before you proceed make sure that one of the two modems has this option. The procedure is as follows:

1. User B puts her modem in answer mode, runs Kermit, sets the serial port speed to (say) 1200, and gives the CONNECT command.

2. User A makes sure his modem is in originate mode, runs Kermit, sets the port speed to match user B's, and dials user B's number, and gives the CONNECT command (if the modem has a dialer, then CONNECT comes before dialing).

3. User B's modem should answer the phone automatically, and both carrier lights should come on. If not, check the modems, cables, switches, and so on.

4. At this point, the two PCs should be connected. To test the connection, user A and user B can send messages to each other—whatever user A types should appear on user B's screen and vice versa. Users A and B can use this property of the connection to coordinate their activities.[12]

5. When the connection is tested successfully, both users should escape back to their respective Kermit command levels.

6. The user who wants to receive a file should type RECEIVE.

7. The user who wants to send a file should type SEND *filespec*.

Repeat as needed. Since not all PC Kermits are capable of timing out, it is important that the RECEIVE command be issued before the SEND, to avoid a deadlock. Alternatively, one or both of the PCs may be given the SET TIMER ON command to activate an otherwise dormant timeout mechanism, if that command is available.

If one of the PC Kermit programs supports server operation, the remote operator need not be present. For instance, if you have an MS-DOS machine at your office, you can put your office modem in answer mode when you go home, and leave Kermit running on the PC in server mode. When you get home, you can dial up your office PC and you will be connected to a Kermit server, with which you can transfer files repeatedly, as long as its disk space holds out.

---

12. User A will see only the characters that User B types, and vice versa, unless the SET LOCAL-ECHO ON, SET DUPLEX HALF, or equivalent command is given. Even then, the display may appear somewhat odd, because—depending on the actual Kermit versions involved—the linefeed that host computers usually supply after you type carriage return may be missing. If that happens, you can type a linefeed (or Control-J) after each carriage return.

Host to Host   Some mainframe Kermits are capable of initiating a connection. This will be true if the host Kermit has SET LINE and CONNECT commands, and if the host system has a dialout modem or a dedicated connection to another system.

Host-to-host connections work just like PC-to-host connections except that before you give the CONNECT command, you must give the SET LINE command so that the local host Kermit program knows it must use the indicated device rather than the job's console terminal. By doing this, you put the host Kermit program, which normally runs in remote mode, into local mode. This arrangement is illustrated in Figure 2-10; notice how your commands and the Kermit program's responses go over the console terminal line, while the Kermit packets are transmitted on a separate terminal line specified by the SET LINE command.

In the following example, UNIX Kermit uses an autodialer to call up a DECsystem-10. Note the SET LINE, SET MODEM, and SET BAUD commands that are necessary (in this case, at least) when telling the Kermit program to use a line other than the one

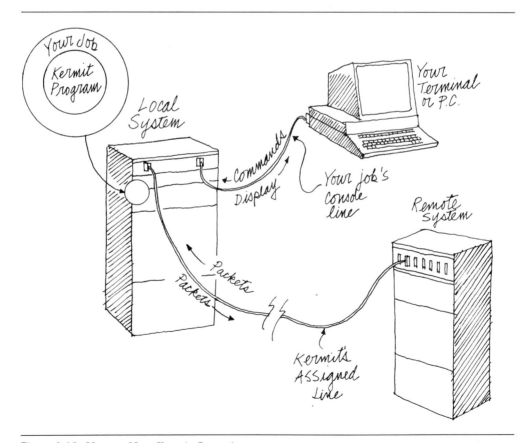

Figure 2-10. Host-to-Host Kermit Operation

it normally expects to use. The SET LINE command specifies the terminal device to be used for connecting to the remote system, and the SET MODEM and SET BAUD commands provide information about how to use the specified device. These commands are described in detail in "Kermit Command Reference," Chapter 5, starting on page 116.

```
%                                          This is the UNIX prompt.
% kermit                                   Run UNIX Kermit.
C-Kermit Version 4C(057)
Type ? for help
C-Kermit>set modem hayes                   Specify type of modem.
C-Kermit>set line /dev/ttyi8               Specify communication line.
C-Kermit>set baud 1200                     Specify baud rate.
C-Kermit>dial 765-4321                     Tell the modem to place a call.
(Call completed)                           When the call is complete,
C-Kermit>connect                           connect to the remote system.
(Connecting to host, type ^\C to return)
<CR>
Stevens T/S 7.01A(10) 20:20:04 TTY41 system 1282
Connected to Node DN87S1(101) Line # 57

Please LOGIN or ATTACH

.log 10,35                                 Log in to the remote system.
JOB 51 Stevens T/S 7.01A(10) TTY41
Password: password
20:20   26-May-84        Sat

.r kermit                                  Run Kermit.
TOPS-10 Kermit version 2(106)

Kermit-10>server                           Enter server mode.

Kermit server running on the DEC-10 host. Please type your escape sequence
to return to your local machine. Shut down the server by typing the Kermit
BYE command on your local machine.

^\C                                        Escape back to UNIX Kermit.

(Connection closed, back at C-Kermit)

C-Kermit>get switch.ini                    Request file from server.
```

```
^A for status report, ^F to cancel file,
^B to cancel batch.
SWITCH.INI......%..%%.......[OK]

C-Kermit>bye                                    Shut down the server.
C-Kermit>exit                                   Exit from the local Kermit.
%
```

Note the display that occurs during the file transfer. When mainframe Kermit programs are used in local mode, the display is typically serial (one character after another) rather than full-screen. In this case, dots appear when packets are successfully transmitted, and percent signs appear when an error-correcting retransmission occurs.

If you are seated at a PC during this operation, using Kermit for terminal emulation, you are actually controlling three Kermit programs at once. This can lead to some confusion. For instance, after CONNECTing from the local host to the remote host, you might accidentally type the "wrong" escape sequence, and find yourself back at the PC instead of the local host (and if you're not paying attention, you might even find yourself transferring files between the remote host and the PC, *through* the local host). If the local host and the PC Kermit programs both have the same escape sequence (you can use SET ESCAPE to change this), then you will have to type the escape character twice before typing the C, in order to escape back to the local host. Typing it once before the C gets you back to the PC.

Use of Kermit over Public Networks Kermit may be used over public networks like Telenet, Tymnet, UNINET, and Datapac. A public network is a commercial service that provides its subscribers access to distant computers with a local phone call, in areas where the service is available. To use the public network, you dial a special-purpose computer called a PAD (Packet Assembler/Disassembler) in your area, just as you would dial any other computer. In a brief dialog with the PAD, you identify yourself for billing purposes, establish any required communication settings, and then request to be connected to the desired host computer. The result is equivalent to dialing the host computer directly, except that you pay for a local, rather than long-distance, phone call; you are billed for your use of the network; and you have to cope with certain features of the network.

The PAD provides an error-free connection between itself and the selected host, no matter how far away, but your telephone connection to the PAD is not normally protected from noise or interference, so you will need a file transfer program like Kermit to provide the necessary error detection and correction. But using Kermit over a public network may require some special measures:

1. The PAD has an escape sequence which you can type if you need to return to the PAD from your connection to the remote host, just as Kermit provides an escape sequence to get you back to the local Kermit program from terminal emulation. If the

PAD's escape sequence is composed of printable characters, then you must do whatever you can to disable it, or change it to a nonprintable character sequence. Any sequence of printable characters can occur in a Kermit packet, and if the PAD's escape sequence happens to appear, the connection will be broken.

2. Use SET commands to adapt both Kermit programs to the network's communication environment. Many networks require you to SET PARITY MARK (or ODD or EVEN). Others may require you to reduce Kermit's packet size using SET SEND (or RECEIVE) PACKET-LENGTH 60 (the normal length is 80 or 90). You might also have to increase the timeout interval using SET SEND (or RECEIVE) TIMEOUT 20 (or some other number bigger than the usual 5 or 10) in order to account for the delays of the network.

There are also numerous settings that can be established at the Kermit or PAD level to improve performance and cut down on network fees. These will be discussed in later sections, after we have filled in some technical background.

The End of the Easy Part

I hope the material presented so far is enough to get you started with Kermit, at least when used in conjunction with the documentation that accompanies your particular Kermit program. Most of the common arrangements have been covered in cookbook fashion. If you can follow the examples and achieve useful results, then you need read no further. Otherwise (you're still reading?), you will need to do a little detective work. For this, you need some background in computers, file organization, and data communication. If you don't feel you have sufficient background, read the primers immediately following. They should provide all you need. After the primers comes a complete Kermit command reference, which includes descriptions of the many commands that control Kermit's behavior in the areas covered by the primers. Then comes a chapter called "Common Problems and How to Fix Them," in which your knowledge of computers, file organization, data communication, and Kermit commands can be combined to overcome the many obstacles that can confront you when you attempt to connect two possibly unlike systems over a possibly hostile medium.

The second half of the book attempts to answer the question, "How can I get a Kermit program running on my computer?" There are two possibilities. In the first case, a Kermit program has already been written for your computer. Your problem is reduced to getting a copy of it that you can run. This can be as simple as copying a friend's disk, or as difficult as writing a "bootstrap" program (a sample bootstrap program is provided). In the second case, no Kermit program exists for your computer. For the stout of heart, directions are given for writing a new Kermit program, beginning with suggestions for program organization and "user interface," and winding up with the detailed protocol specification, complete with programming examples.

The remainder of the book is taken up by a comparison of Kermit with other protocols, a glossary, appendixes (including a compact Kermit command summary), a bibliography, and an index. The appendixes, the table of contents, the glossary, and the index are there to help you find what you need. Please use them.

PART TWO

Primers

3

Computers and Files

This part of the book presents some basic concepts of computing, files, and data communication. These sections are self-contained, and you can skip them if you already have the necessary background; they contain no particular reference to Kermit. Some sweeping statements are made that may not be completely true in all cases; in the interest of brevity a great many but-if's and except-for-when's are omitted.

Hardware and Software

Computers are made out of hardware—metal, silicon, rubber, paint, etc. An important part of the hardware is called the memory , or more precisely, the internal memory (to distinguish it from external memories like magnetic disk or tape). The internal memory is also referred to variously as short-term memory, volatile memory, and core[1] memory. The computer must bring information into its internal memory before it can manipulate it.

Another part of the hardware is the instruction decoder. Every computer has a fixed repertoire of instructions it can execute. A computer instruction is usually a very simple operation like "copy the contents of location 123 to location 234" or "add the contents of location 345 to the contents of location 1" or "if location 456 contains a zero, then go to location 567 and execute the instruction stored there."

A program is a sequence of machine instructions which, when loaded into the computer's internal memory, can be executed by the computer. Software is another word for program (or programs). The thing that makes computers so useful is that the same piece of hardware can execute a potentially unlimited amount and variety of software. Unlike, say, a chain saw, a computing machine can totally change its demeanor, its very essence and purpose, in a fraction of a second, simply by executing another program.

A program is written in a programming language. There are two kinds of programming languages: assembly languages and high-level languages. In an assembly language each statement corresponds to one machine instruction. Assembly language programs are translated into machine instructions by relatively simple programs called assemblers. Unlike an assembly language, a high-level language can express complex operations in a single statement. High-level languages are translated into machine instructions by very complicated programs called compilers.

---

1. A holdover from the days when memories were made out of little magnetic rings called cores.

Here's an example of a single statement in the C language [19] (a high-level language):

```
for (i = j = 0; i < 10; i++) j += i;
```

This means "set the variables i and j to zero, and then for every value of i less than 10, add the value of i to j." In other words, add up all the integers (whole numbers) from 0 to 9. The C compiler translates this statement into machine instructions, like those represented by the following assembly language statements (for a hypothetical assembler):

Instruction	Commentary
CLR I	*Clear location I, i.e., set its contents to zero.*
CLR J	*Clear location J.*
A: MOV T, I	*Copy I into T (note the label A).*
SUB T, 10	*Subtract 10 from T.*
BZ T, B	*If the result is zero, go to location B.*
ADD J, I	*Add the contents of I to the contents of J.*
INC I	*Increment I (i.e., add 1 to the contents of I).*
JMP A	*Go back to A.*
B: ...	*At location B, J contains the desired sum.*

This should suggest the level at which most computers operate. Assembly languages like this one use alphabetic symbols to represent machine instructions and locations. Normally, the C compiler would directly produce the numbers that these symbols represent. Note that control passes from one instruction to the next unless an instruction explicitly transfers control elsewhere, either conditionally (like BZ) or unconditionally (like JMP).

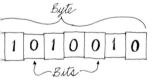

How Computers Represent Data

Computer data is composed of binary (base 2) numbers, sequences of 0's and 1's. One binary digit is called a bit (abbreviated b). Computers use the binary system because bits can be made out of little switches that are either off (0) or on (1). If you've ever seen the wheels and gears inside an old mechanical decimal calculator, you can appreciate the simplicity of the binary system[2].

A computer's memory is broken up into discrete chunks of various sizes. The big chunks may be called pages or segments. A smaller chunk (usually 16 or 32 bits) is called a word (abbreviated W). A smaller chunk still (usually 8 bits) is called a byte (abbreviated B). Computers refer to memory locations by their addresses, which are just numbers ranging from zero up to some maximum number. The number of addresses a

---

2. Appendix E, "Binary, Octal, and Hexadecimal Numbers," explains the binary system in some detail, plus some alternative notations for expressing binary numbers.

computer can have is called its address space. An address specifies the location of either a byte or a word, depending on the design ("architecture") of the computer. Computers have built-in instructions to operate on either bytes or words, or both.

All data is represented in the computer as words or bytes filled with 0's and 1's. A particular sequence of bits has no intrinsic meaning or value. The same bit string could be a legitimate machine instruction, an address, a whole number, a "floating-point number," a string of characters, or some other kind of code. The interpretation depends upon the hardware or software that is using it—for instance, the bit string 0100000101000010 might represent the ASCII characters AB to a text editor, or the decimal number 16706 to a program that is performing calculations, or a machine instruction to the computer's instruction decoder.

In most computers a word is used to hold instructions, numbers, or addresses. The word size in bits is usually a power of two (see Appendix E if you don't know what this means). The most common word sizes are 16 and 32 bits, but other sizes, including 4, 8, 12, 18, 24, 36, 48, 64, 72, and 128 (or larger), may be encountered. The word size determines the precision with which numeric calculations may be performed, the magnitude of numbers that may be represented, and the address space of the machine. Bytes, on the other hand, are used to hold characters. The most common byte size is 8, but sizes of 5, 6, 7, 9, and 12 (or more) may also be found. Most machines have a fixed byte size, but some have instructions for manipulating variable-length bytes.

Machines may address either bytes or words. Byte-addressed machines are concerned that numbers and addresses begin on "word boundaries"—usually addresses that are multiples of 2 or 4. Word-addressed machines, on the other hand, must provide special instructions for manipulation of individual bytes that are packed within a word.

Operating Systems

One program that every computer has is an operating system. The operating system (OS) is there even when your application program is running. The OS provides such services as managing files and getting data from and sending data to external devices (the computer jargon is input/output, or I/O); it saves you from having to know about the details of the machinery or the format of the disk. On timesharing systems, where many people use the same computer simultaneously, the operating system also provides each person with the illusion of a dedicated, exclusive machine.

The operating system runs your programs for you. When you type run foo, the operating system finds the program called foo, loads it into memory, and starts the program by pointing the instruction decoder at the program's first instruction. After that, the operating system stands back and watches your program execute, and provides assistance whenever your program calls upon it.

On some systems, particularly microcomputers, your program shares the operating system's address space—your program can read information directly from the operating system and in some cases even alter it. On other systems, the operating system has its own address space, and your program can communicate with it only through special "system calls."

By definition, a program is restricted to its own address space. An address space in execution is called a process. A timesharing system can have many processes active at once; the operating system protects them from each other and schedules their access to resources they must share. Each user has a job (or session) which may consist of one or more processes, depending on the OS. A job is created when the user logs in and persists (under normal conditions) until the user logs out.

There is an important distinction between the operating system and a user program. The operating system is able to service the input/output devices for which it is responsible in "real time," as the data arrives. Your program cannot do this because it might not even be running when its requested input comes in; the operating system may have scheduled some other program to run. Therefore the operating system keeps the data that you have requested in a "buffer" until your program is ready to read it.

The Console Terminal

Whether you are a user of a timesharing system or of a single-user microcomputer, you have some primary means of communicating with the system. This is called your "console."[3] It consists of a primary input device, usually a keyboard, and a primary output device, usually a screen.

On a microcomputer, the console is definitely special. It's an integral part of the machine, its "face." It does not (with few exceptions) attach to the micro as if it were a terminal, over a communication line. It is always available for use, even when other communication devices are active. Auxiliary input devices such as mice, trackballs, light pens, joy sticks, and touch screens may be associated with a micro's console.

A timesharing system does not have a single console, but rather one for each user. Your timesharing console is your only communication channel to your job, and it usually is connected to the computer over a communication line, as a terminal. It's where you log in, issue commands, read the results of your commands, and log out.

The operating system treats the console differently from other devices, because the device that it must communicate with in this case is controlled by a person, and people have more complicated needs than most input/output devices. The system allows the console user to type certain characters to interrupt an operation in progress. It might pause after each screenful of output until the user types a go-ahead signal for the next. It might transmit messages to the console screen. It might echo keyboard input on the screen, and it might use certain input characters to allow users to correct typing mistakes in their commands. Certain characters might be translated to others upon input

---

3. The terminal with which the system operator controls a timesharing system may also be called its console. We are not using the word in that sense.

or output. Long lines might be split so as not to run off the edge of the screen. Most operating systems also take into account the type of terminal that is being used, and issue terminal-specific formatting commands to facilitate command line editing: line erase, character erase, screen clear, and so on. Some combination of these services is provided by all timesharing systems for the job console terminal, and usually none of them will be found on a bare terminal device, through which data can normally pass transparently in both directions.

Most timesharing operating systems assume that a job's console is a terminal, not a PC. This is a very important distinction. A terminal transmits characters only as fast as a person can type them (ten characters per second at most), but a computer can display vast amounts of data at the console in response to a very short request. For this reason, the operating system may be designed for a 10-to-1 or 100-to-1 ratio of console output to input. When the console is actually another computer, this design assumption can easily be violated, resulting in poor performance, loss of data, or worse.

The timesharing console is designed for interaction with a human, and not for direct communication with another computer. When machine-to-machine communication (such as file transfer) must take place through a console device, the console's normal services and characteristics must be disabled. When the operating system does not allow the console to be turned into a "raw" device, then the two machines must find a way to circumvent its special services.

Disks, Diskettes, Formats

We have discussed how data is represented in the computer's short-term internal memory. When data must be stored for longer periods, it is kept on a magnetic medium called a disk. Information stays on a disk after the computer is turned off, whereas the internal memory is erased. A disk is a rotating platter (or stack of platters) on which bits are stored and retrieved magnetically, by a read-write head (one for each recording surface) similar to the arm of a record player, except that the disk head can jump back and forth across the surface randomly, whereas the tone arm of a record player is stuck in a single continuous groove. For this reason, a disk is called a random-access device, and may be contrasted to a reel of magnetic tape, which is a serial storage medium.

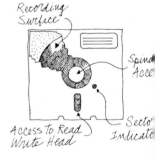

Disks are of two major types: floppy and hard. On a microcomputer, a hard disk is a permanent part of the system, capable of storing 5, 10, or more megabytes. A floppy disk (or diskette) is a removable, single-platter, inexpensive, compact medium capable of storing between 100 kilobytes and 1 megabyte (or thereabouts—the numbers keep increasing). Mainframe disks have capacities of 100MB or more, often in free-standing cabinets occupying their own floor space.

Each platter of the disk is divided up into slices, like the slices of a pie, called sectors. The sector boundaries are intersected by concentric circular tracks. A typical diskette has 40–100 tracks and 10–32 sectors on one or both sides, and mainframe disks have

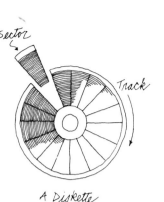

A Diskette

many more tracks on each of multiple recording surfaces. The part of a track that lies between two sector boundaries is called a block. A disk block contains a fixed number of bytes, usually a power of two, between 128 and 8192.

Just as a computer's memory locations are identified by addresses, so are locations on the disk. A disk address is formed from an encoding that specifies the platter, sector, and track of the desired block. A block is the minimum amount of data that can be read from or written to a disk in a single operation. Disk addresses are "coarser" than memory addresses because they need to address more data in the same number of bits.

The speed with which data can be transferred between disk and internal memory is called the disk's transfer rate, or bandwidth. Floppy disk transfer rates are usually in the range of 5K–25K bytes per second. Hard disk bandwidth is typically in the 250K–5000K range. For any particular read or write operation, the disk head must first move to the correct track and sector, and this "seek time" is often the bottleneck in disk data transfer.

The exact technique used to record information on disk varies with the manufacturer and type of disk. In fact, it is safe to state as a general rule that no system will be able to read a disk written on a different manufacturer's system. More often than not, the same will be true even for different models produced by the same manufacturer. There are no commonly accepted standards (except for 8-inch floppy disks, which are now falling into relative disuse).

Directories, Files

The millions of bits that the computer stores on a disk must be organized in some way so that desired information can be recalled when needed or discarded to make room for new data. For this reason, every computer that has a disk also has a file system. A file system consists of zero or more files and a directory where file names can be looked up and the corresponding locations determined. The directory is a special file whose starting location is known, so the computer can always find it. Figure 3-1 shows a simplified disk layout. Address 0 contains the "home block," which in turn contains the starting addresses of the storage allocation table and the directory. Each directory entry occupies one disk block, and consists (in this example) of a filename, the starting disk address of the file, and the file's length. The zero stored at disk address 102 indicates the end of the directory. The example is simplified because the directory and the files are contiguous. In practice, a file's disk blocks are usually scattered all over the place and linked together with "pointers," or located through a "file index block."

Some file systems permit the existence of more than one directory. In this case, the disk's top-level directory will contain a list of directories, rather than files, and these directories in turn will list the files. This mechanism allows more than one person to share a disk without sacrificing privacy or security. It can be repeated to potentially any level, depending upon the system, with files and directories mixed together in each

Disk Address	Contents	
0	10 100	*(Home block)*
⋮		
10	1000000001111...	*(Storage allocation table)*
⋮		
100	F00.BAR 743 15860	*(Directory entries)*
101	F00.BAZ 1072 7255	
102	0	
⋮		
⋮		
743	This is some data from the file F00.BAR,	
744	which goes on and on...	
⋮		
⋮		
1071	...till the end.	
1072	This is the first line of the file F00.BAZ,	
1073	which goes also goes on and on...	

Figure 3-1. Simple Disk Organization

directory. A system with only a top-level directory is called a flat file system (Figure 3-2) and a system with more than one level is a hierarchical file system (Figure 3-3). These figures are schematic illustrations; in reality, the information is organized more along the lines of Figure 3-1.

A system with multiple single-level directories is a special, but common, case. The major purpose of this arrangment is to allow files to be grouped together according to owner or purpose. When multiple directories exist, files of the same name may reside in one or more directories simultaneously, and directories can have the same names as files in other directories. This is illustrated in Figure 3-3.

A computer may have more than one disk active simultaneously. Each disk can have its own file system. To identify a file uniquely, it may therefore be necessary to specify the disk unit, one or more levels of directory, and finally the filename.

A new disk starts out blank. Before it can be used, it must be formatted, either by the manufacturer or by the user, with a program that comes with the system. Part of the formatting process is the creation of a storage allocation table—a list of disk addresses that are free for use.[4] Certain disk addresses are preassigned by the operating system for the beginning of the (top-level) directory. When you create a file on the disk, the operating system looks in the storage allocation table for free addresses, creates a

---

4. In practice, the storage allocation table is more likely to be a "bit vector," in which bit number *n* is 0 if disk address *n* is free, and 1 if it is in use.

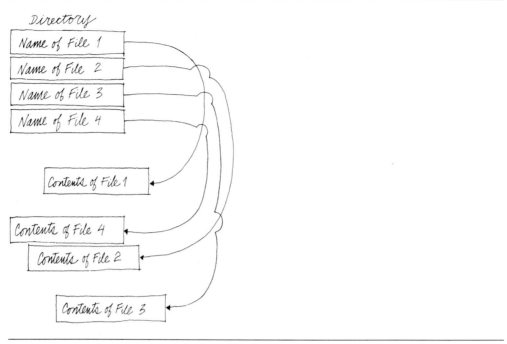

Figure 3-2. A Flat File System

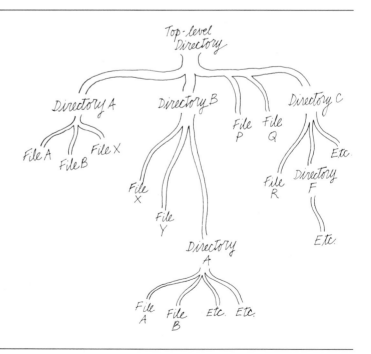

Figure 3-3. A Hierarchical File System

directory entry for the file, and then stores the contents of the file (and the directory entry itself) on the disk in those free locations, afterward marking each address involved in the process as "used" in the storage allocation table. When you delete a file, the directory and data locations are removed and marked as "free" in the storage allocation table. The format of the directory entries, the data entries, and the storage allocation table are all managed by the operating system, so you don't need to be concerned with the details. You merely issue the appropriate file management commands.

Although disk formats need not concern the user of a particular computer, the fact that formats are different and incompatible among different computer systems does become a concern as soon as there is a requirement to move a file from one system to another: you cannot simply take a diskette from, say, an IBM PC and plug it into the disk drive of, say, an Apple II, and expect to be able to access the files.

Naming Conventions for Files

It is very common for files to have two-part names, in which the first part is made up arbitrarily by the file's creator, and the second part specifies the type of file it is, according to some convention (which need not be observed). The two parts are separated by a delimiter, usually a period. There is usually a length restriction on each part, often six or eight characters for the first part, and three for the second. The second part is called the file type. On a particular system, a file type of FOR might mean the file is a FORTRAN program, C might designate a C program, TXT might be some kind of text, EXE an executable program image.

Many systems require that filenames be composed only of letters and numbers. Some systems allow letters only, or if numbers are allowed, then the first character of the name must be a letter. Most systems, but not all (UNIX is a well-known exception), observe no distinction between upper- and lowercase letters in filenames.

A file is (usually) fully specified by the device it's on, the directory it's in, and its name. Most systems, however, support the notions of "current disk" and "current directory." When you omit these fields from a file specification, they "default" to the current device and directory.

The syntax for file specifications varies considerably among systems, but there are several widespread conventions. A device name terminates in a colon, a directory name is enclosed in brackets, a dot separates the file name from the file type. For instance, the VAX/VMS file specification

```
DSKA:[KERMIT]FOO.BAR
```

would mean the file named FOO.BAR in the directory KERMIT on the device DSKA.

Another common notation separates the fields with slashes, as in these UNIX file specifications:

```
/dev/dska/kermit/foo.bar
/dev/dska/kermit/new/foo.bar
```

Note that there is no distinction between device and directory in UNIX file specifications, and that the "path" through a directory tree is denoted by simply stringing the directory names together, separated by slashes.

Some systems mix the previous styles, and may also use different kinds of brackets or slashes:

```
A:\KERMIT\NEW\FOO.BAR        (MS-DOS)
DSKA:<KERMIT.NEW>FOO.BAR     (DECSYSTEM-20)
```

Notice the different methods used to specify the subdirectory NEW of the KERMIT directory.

There are systems whose file specifications differ radically from this general model (see Table 3-4). The exact format of the file specification, the restrictions on the length and contents of each field, and the conventions used for delimiting the fields become a matter of great concern when files must be transferred between unlike systems. The difficulties are greatest when files are moved from a system with very flexible naming conventions to a system with very restrictive ones.

File Organization

The most common arrangement of data within a file is sequential, with one byte following another and no apparent gaps. A random access file, on the other hand, may (or may not) have gaps of any size. Two common types of random access file are the relative file, in which records may be accessed by record number, and the indexed or "hashed" file, in which records are accessed via key or some other classification method. Sequential files may also have internal keys or record numbers. The important criterion is whether the file can be reproduced by copying only its contents; only sequential files have this property. Random access files are meaningful only in combination with additional information external to the data, such as a list of addresses or keys. Sometimes this information actually *is* in the file, but in a device- or system-dependent form.

Sequential files themselves vary in format. Text files typically consist of one or more lines, or "records." Different systems represent record boundaries in different ways. One common way is to include control characters at the end of each line, typically carriage return (CR), linefeed (LF), or both (CRLF). This is called stream format. There is also a fixed format, in which all records must be the same length (like 80 bytes); any shorter record is padded out with a sequence of blanks or other innocuous characters, and any longer record is truncated or "wrapped." And there is a variable format, in which each record is preceded by a length field. Another style has "carriage control"—the first byte of each record tells the printing format of the record: whether it starts a new page, a new line, overstrikes the previous line, skips a line, etc. This format is mainly for use with printers, but is also found in files created by FORTRAN programs.

In general, only sequential files can be transferred between unlike systems, because nonsequential files usually have system or device dependencies built into their representations. For text files to be useful after transfer to an unlike system, it is often necessary to convert them to the prevailing format for the target system—stream, fixed, variable, etc.

File Management

Most operating systems provide you with a set of commands for managing files. Although the syntax will vary, and some commands may be lacking on some systems, the following list should give you an idea of the common operations:

- CREATE

  Create the specified file. If this command exists, it probably invokes a text editor. If it doesn't, you probably have to invoke an editor explicitly to create the file.

- DELETE

  Remove the file from the directory. Operating systems differ in their approach to file deletion. The most common method is to remove the file's directory entry, and mark the file's blocks as free in the storage allocation table. A variation on this method also scrubs the blocks clean, lest the data fall into the wrong hands—a desirable precaution on shared file systems. A less common method retains the file, but sets the "deleted" attribute, allowing the file to be "undeleted" at a later time. Common synonyms for DELETE include REMOVE and ERASE, and various abbreviations of these words.[5]

- DIRECTORY

  List the names of the specified files, or all files in the current device or directory, possibly along with some of their attributes. This lets you find out what files are in a directory, or on a disk. Some systems provide many options to aid in file management—pattern matching on the file names, selection by date, size, or other criteria. A common synonym is LIST.

- TYPE

  Display the contents of the specified file on the screen. This command is useful for reading text files; binary files generally spew forth as squiggly characters and blotches, with the cursor jumping all over the screen and the beep sounding insistently.

---

5. For instance, UNIX uses "rm" for REMOVE. While this may seem cryptic, it is an improvement over what the command was called in early UNIX versions: "dsw," an abbreviation of the Russian word for *goodbye*.

- COPY

Make a second copy of the specified file, under the specified new name, or to the specified device. The original file is undisturbed. This command can be used to create a new file by copying from the console terminal to that file, providing the system gives you a way to signal an "end of file" at the console.

- APPEND

Add one file to the end of another file. This operation is called concatenation, or simply catenation.[6]

- RENAME

Change the name of the specified file to the new name specified. This is generally done by changing the directory entry, leaving the contents of the file undisturbed. On some systems, this technique can be used to "move" a file to another directory.

- CWD

Change Working Directory, i.e., change the default directory and/or device for file specifications to that specified. This command provides the illusion of moving about the file system, hopping from one directory to another. Synonyms include CD, CHDIR, CONNECT, and sometimes simply a disk name.

In hierarchical file systems, there are also commands for creating and deleting subdirectories. And in shared file systems, there are commands to control how others may access your files; typically you may grant or refuse any combination of read, write, append, directory listing, and execute access separately to yourself, your group, and the general public. Write permission usually implies delete permission.

Encoding of Text

Text, like any other kind of data, is stored in the computer's memory and on disk as binary numbers, sequences of 0's and 1's. The computer screen or printer displays the character equivalent of a binary number according to some convention. The most widely accepted convention is ASCII, the American Standard Code for Information Interchange [5], listed in detail in Appendix D.

The ASCII alphabet is a 7-bit code consisting of $2^7 = 128$ characters, numbered 0 through 127. The first 32 (numbered 0 through 31) plus the last one (number 127) are the control characters. Among the control characters are the format effectors carriage return (CR, or Control-M), linefeed (LF, Control-J), horizontal tab (HT, Control-I), and

---

6. The UNIX command is "cat." UNIX has no TYPE command, so cat is used instead, with the desired file catenated to the terminal.

formfeed (FF, Control-L), which are commonly found in text files. The remaining control characters are used for device control or other purposes, and are not usually found in text files.

The 95 characters in the range 32 through 126 comprise the graphic, or printable, set. These are the characters that actually cause ink to appear on paper: the upper- and lowercase alphabet, the decimal digits, punctuation marks, and other symbols. The space character is also considered a graphic character. Table 3-1 shows the ASCII alphabet as it is employed in the U.S. and Canada (Appendix D provides much more

Table 3-1. The ASCII Alphabet

0	^@	NUL	32	SP		64	@		96	'
1	^A	SOH	33	!		65	A		97	a
2	^B	STX	34	"		66	B		98	b
3	^C	ETX	35	#		67	C		99	c
4	^D	EOT	36	$		68	D		100	d
5	^E	ENQ	37	%		69	E		101	e
6	^F	ACK	38	&		70	F		102	f
7	^G	BEL	39	'		71	G		103	g
8	^H	BS	40	(		72	H		104	h
9	^I	HT	41	)		73	I		105	i
10	^J	LF	42	*		74	J		106	j
11	^K	VT	43	+		75	K		107	k
12	^L	FF	44	,		76	L		108	l
13	^M	CR	45	-		77	M		109	m
14	^N	SO	46	.		78	N		110	n
15	^O	SI	47	/		79	O		111	o
16	^P	DLE	48	0		80	P		112	p
17	^Q	DC1	49	1		81	Q		113	q
18	^R	DC2	50	2		82	R		114	r
19	^S	DC3	51	3		83	S		115	s
20	^T	DC4	52	4		84	T		116	t
21	^U	NAK	53	5		85	U		117	u
22	^V	SYN	54	6		86	V		118	v
23	^W	ETB	55	7		87	W		119	w
24	^X	CAN	56	8		88	X		120	x
25	^Y	EM	57	9		89	Y		121	y
26	^Z	SUB	58	:		90	Z		122	z
27	^[	ESC	59	;		91	[		123	{
28	^\	FS	60	<		92	\		124		
29	^]	GS	61	=		93	]		125	}
30	^^	RS	62	>		94	^		126	~
31	^_	US	63	?		95	_		127	RUB

detail). Other countries make certain substitutions: in England, the # symbol is replaced by the £. In Scandinavia, some of the more esoteric graphics, like "}", are replaced by special alphabetic symbols, like "ø".

Note the distinction between the characters that represent the decimal digits and the numeric values of the decimal digits themselves. The character 0 (zero) is stored within a computer byte as the number 48 (binary 0110000), whereas the number zero is stored as binary zero (0000000), which corresponds to the ASCII character NUL. The numeric coding of each character turns out to be quite important, since it determines the "collating sequence"—the "alphabetic" ordering you get when the computer sorts ASCII text. As you might expect, the letters are numbered consecutively, but since the uppercase letters precede the lowercase, "B" comes before "a" in the ASCII collating sequence.

Also observe the patterns in the table. The uppercase letters line up with the lowercase ones (they are offset by $32 = 2^5$); the control characters line up with their printable equivalents (the offset is $64 = 2^6$). These patterns allow certain common conversions to be made arithmetically. ASCII characters are generated by ASCII terminals, which have typewriterlike keyboards. Control characters are produced by holding down a special key marked Control and pressing the corresponding letter, A for Control-A, B for Control-B, and so on. This method of generating control characters has resulted in a strong association between ASCII character number 1 and Control-A, character number 2 and Control-B, and so on. However, these characters are more properly designated by their formal names, SOH (Start of Header), STX (Start of Text), etc., which are given in Appendix D.

Although manufacturers of most popular computers use ASCII encoding for text both internally and when communicating with external devices, there is a major exception (and it *is* major)—IBM. IBM favors its own EBCDIC (Extended Binary Coded Decimal Interchange Code) encoding, an 8-bit 256-character code, on its mainframes and minicomputers, but it has adopted ASCII on its PC family. Several other mainframe manufacturers also employ the EBCDIC code, selected portions[7] of which are shown in Table 3-2, taken from the IBM System/370 Reference Summary [29].

Note the differences from ASCII. The nonprintables are not listed as control characters because EBCDIC terminals do not have Control keys. Most EBCDIC characters have different numeric values from their ASCII equivalents, although a few coincide (SOH, ETX). There are "holes" in the alphabet, most noticeably between the letters I and J, and R and S, in both the lower- and uppercase sets. The EBCDIC lowercase letters precede the uppercase letters, which is the reverse of the ASCII arrangement. The collating sequences of EBCDIC and ASCII are very different.

The fact that there are two principal competing codes might lead you to expect a widely adopted standard for translating between them. But that would be too easy. Many

---

7. Why don't I just show the whole thing? OK, I confess . . . I'm writing this book using ASCII computers, with no way to enter those EBCDIC printable characters that ASCII doesn't have, like cent-sign, not-sign, corner brackets, etc. This is just the kind of problem that this section is meant to illustrate.

Table 3-2. Selected Portions of the EBCDIC Alphabet

0	NUL	75	.	110	>	145	j	200	H	240	0
1	SOH	76	<	111	?	146	k	201	I	241	1
2	STX	77	(	:	:	147	l	202		242	2
3	ETX	78	+	:	:	:	:	:		:	:
:	:	79	:	123	#	152	q	209	J	249	9
:	:	80	&	124	@	153	r	210	K		
26	UBS	:		125	'	:	:	:	:		
27	CU1	:		126	=	162	s	217	R		
28	IFS	90	!	127	"	163	t	:	:		
29	IGS	91	$	128		164	u	:	:		
30	IRS	92	*	129	a	:	:	226	S		
:	:	93	)	130	b	169	z	227	T		
:	:	94	;	131	c	:	:	:	:		
37	LF	:		:	:	:	:	233	Z		
38	ETB	:		136	h	193	A	:	:		
39	ESC	107	,	137	i	194	B	:	:		
:	:	108	%	138		195	C	:	:		
:	:	109	_	:		:	:	:	:		

computer people no doubt owe their livelihoods to the fact that there is not, and they spend a good deal of their time devising their own custom translations. In fairness, it must be said that much of the confusion dates from the days when both alphabets were in a state of development [23], and that many of today's dubious translations were "correct" at the time they were originally made. But the problem runs deeper still.

Translation from one character set to another is done through a translation table—"translate table" for short—which is simply a list of numbers. The number at position n in the table is the translation of character number n in one set into the other set. For instance, the number at position 71 in the ASCII-to-EBCDIC table is 199—71 is the ASCII value for the letter G and 199 is the EBCDIC value for that letter (Table 3-3). When an ASCII value of 71 arrives at an EBCDIC system (say, from an ASCII terminal), the translation is done immediately by replacing it with the seventy-first element from this list.

Each translate table should have an inverse; if an EBCDIC-based system is receiving characters from an ASCII device, it probably will also want to send characters back to that device. Thus it will also need an EBCDIC-to-ASCII table. This should simply be the inverse of the ASCII-to-EBCDIC table.

But what about the fact that there are twice as many EBCDIC characters as 7-bit ASCII? The maker of the EBCDIC-to-ASCII table has some hard choices: some ASCII characters will have multiple EBCDIC equivalents. What happens when an EBCDIC file that has been translated to ASCII needs to be translated back to EBCDIC? Will it be the same as the original? Probably not, because any distinction between those EBCDIC

Table 3-3. Parts of an ASCII-to-EBCDIC Translate Table

ASCII	EBCDIC	ASCII	EBCDIC	ASCII	EBCDIC	ASCII	EBCDIC
0	0	32	64	70	198	91	173
1	1	33	90	71	199	92	224
2	2	34	127	72	200	93	189
3	3	35	123	73	201	94	95
4	55	36	91	74	209	95	109
5	45	37	108	75	210	96	121
6	46	38	80	76	211	97	129
7	47	39	125	77	212	98	130

characters that had to be mapped to a single ASCII character will have been lost. Since EBCDIC has more characters than ASCII, it is not possible to have an invertible translation from EBCDIC to ASCII.

But if you only care about ASCII files, your problem is reduced to picking out 128 unique values from the EBCDIC set to correspond to the 128 ASCII values. Translations from ASCII to EBCDIC and back can be invertible given a properly designed table. Such a table is furnished in the IBM System/370 Reference Card, and in Appendix D, and this is about as close as we can come to a standard in this area.

Before leaving the topic of character sets, I should also mention that there is a recent trend to create 8-bit sets based on ASCII. The lower half of the set is standard ASCII, and the upper half contains special characters. There is very little agreement as to what these special characters should be, although several standards have been proposed. The intention is usually to provide a selection of characters with diacritic marks (umlauts, accents, etc.) for use in Europe, or alternative alphabets like Greek, Hebrew, or Cyrillic. Users of IBM or DEC microcomputers will be familiar with these special characters, as they often appear on the screen by accident.

Versions of Files

In most file systems, there can be only one copy of a file with a particular name in a particular disk or directory. If you create another file with the same name in the same place— for instance, by editing the original file and then saving it—the original file is obliterated. Some file systems, however, allow multiple copies (called versions or generations) of the same file to coexist. The first and original copy is version 1, the next copy is version 2, and so forth. Such systems generally remove the oldest version automatically when you create a new one, or else provide you with the ability to remove old versions explicitly.

When file versions may coexist, file transfer becomes a less hazardous affair. File name conflicts do not arise, and treasured files are not accidentally blotted out. When the file system does not provide this feature, file transfer programs must take pains to handle name collisions by inventing unique names for new files to prevent the undesired destruction of old ones.

End of File

A particularly important attribute of a file is its length. Unfortunately, not all file systems record a file's length in the file's directory entry. Among those that do, some may do so precisely, indicating the exact number of characters or bytes in the file, while others record only the number of blocks.

Systems that record the length imprecisely usually have no way to determine the exact end of a file; the best they can do is guess that it is somewhere in the last disk block, or define it to be at the end of the last disk block.[8]

Programs that run on such systems may adopt a convention for marking the end of the data by including a special character (such as ASCII Control-Z) at the appropriate place within the file. Of course, such a convention precludes use of the special character itself as a data character, and it depends on all application software to observe it when creating or reading files.

Other File Attributes

Now we know about a file's specification (device, directory, name), organization (sequential, random), type (text, binary), encoding (ASCII, EBCDIC), version, and length. These are a file's most important attributes. But a file can have other attributes, too, depending upon the particular file system. These are typically recorded in the file's directory entry.

Some of the nicer attributes are externally recorded tidbits having no bearing on how the contents of the file are interpreted: date and time of creation, name or account of creator, protection code, etc. The more insidious attributes specify the "access method" for the file— how to interpret it: fixed versus stream, keyed versus relative, and possibly even that the file is really a directory or a program to be executed. If a file whose interpretation depends upon such externally recorded attributes is transferred to an unlike system and then brought back, it may have been rendered useless through loss of these attributes, even though the data itself remains intact.

---

8. If this sentence were a file on such a system, it might look like this when you type it at your terminal:xs~%_nna<xxlxknamx/''''

Characteristics of Selected Systems

Table 3-4 lists a selection of micros and mainframes according to some of the characteristics we've been discussing. It's only a small table, and it can't be considered very accurate because many of the listed parameters change from one release of the operating system to the next, or from one model of the machine to another. The word and byte sizes are given in bits.

The column "Filespec Format" shows the notation used to fully specify a file in the normal case (network node names and other esoterica excluded); DEV means a device name, DIR means a directory name (in a hierarchical file system, DIR . . . means an arbitrary path through the directory tree). If the directory field is specifed by a numeric project and programmer number, that is shown as "p,pn." Digits refer to the maximum length of the file name and type fields, respectively, and ".v" or ";v" on the end of the filespec shows the format for specifying file version or generation numbers when these are allowed. An entry like DEV: [DIR.DIR. .]9.3;v would indicate a file specification that begins with a device name that terminates in a colon, followed by a directory name

Table 3-4. Characteristics of Selected File Systems

System/OS	Word Size	Text Byte Size	Filespec Format	Text Code	Text EOR	EOF
CP/M-80	8	8	DEV:8.3	ASCII7	CRLF	block
Intel MDS/ISIS	8	8	DEV:6.3	ASCII7	CRLF	byte
MS-DOS	16	8	DEV:\DIR\DIR...\8.3	ASCII8	CRLF	byte
UCSD p-System	16	8	DEV:15	ASCII7	CR	byte
Apple Macintosh	32	8	(free)	ASCII8	CR	byte
OS-9	—	8	dev/dir/dir.../29	ASCII7	CR	byte
UNIX	—	8	dev/dir/dir.../14	ASCII7	LF	byte
Hewlett-Packard 1000	16	8	6::DEV	ASCII7	CRLF	word
Prime/Primos	16	8	<DEV>DIR>DIR>...>32	ASCII7 –	LF	word
DEC PDP-11/RT-11	16	8	DEV:6.3	ASCII7	CRLF	block
DEC PDP-11/RSTS/E	16	8	DEV:[p,pn]6.3	ASCII7	CRLF	byte
DEC PDP-11/RSX-11	16	8	DEV:[p,pn]9.3;v	ASCII7	RCW	byte
DEC VAX/VMS	32	8	DEV:[DIR.DIR...]39.39;v	ASCII7	RCW	byte
DECsystem-10	36	7	DEV:6.3[p,pn]	ASCII7	CRLF	byte
DECSYSTEM-20	36	7	DEV:<DIR.DIR...>39.39.v	ASCII7	CRLF	byte
IBM VM/CMS	32	8	8 8 DISK	EBCDIC	F,V	RCW
IBM MVS/TSO	32	8	44	EBCDIC	F,V	RCW
Sperry 1100/OS 1100	36	9	DIR*12.12/v	ASCII7,8	RCW	RCW
Honeywell DPS8/MULTICS	36	9	dir>dir>...>32	ASCII8	LF	bit
Honeywell DPS8/GCOS	36	9	user/dir/dir.../12	ASCII8	RCW	RCW
CDC Cyber 170/NOS	64	6, 12	7	SIXBIT	RCW	RCW

in square brackets, in which multiple directory levels are separated by periods, followed by the filename, with a maximum of nine characters in the name and three in the type, and a dot separating the name and type, followed by a version number.

In the Text Code column, ASCII7 means 7-bit ASCII, ASCII8 means "extended ASCII," and SIXBIT is a 6-bit code including only half of 7-bit ASCII. ASCII7 − is "negative" ASCII, in which the high-order bit of each 8-bit byte is set to 1. In most other cases, where an n-bit ASCII character is stored in an m-bit byte (and m is greater than n), the high-order bits are set to zero.

"Text EOR" and "EOF" show the convention for marking the end of a record (line) in a text file and the end of the text file itself, respectively; CR means Carriage Return, LF means Linefeed, RCW means that a Record Control Word describes each record. F,V means there's a selection of fixed and variable records in which the variable records are described by RCWs. In the EOF column, byte means an accurate byte count is kept in the directory, block means the length of the file is known only in blocks, word means the length is known only to the nearest word, RCW means a special record control word indicates the end of the file.

- CP/M-80 files are stream format, stored in 128-byte blocks, and the length is recorded as the number of blocks. The end of a text file occurs, by convention, at the first Control-Z character in the file. A binary file's length is a whole number of blocks, as recorded in the directory. Lines of text are separated by carriage-return–linefeed sequences (CRLFs).

- The MS-DOS file system started out as a copy of the CP/M file system, but with the file creation date and file length to the exact byte recorded in the directory entry. Version 2 of MS-DOS added a fully hierarchical directory structure, like that of UNIX, but with backslashes rather than slashes as separators. MS-DOS files are simple streams of bytes. Lines of text are separated by CRLFs. Many CP/M applications were carried forward to MS-DOS, and brought the Control-Z convention along with them.

- The UCSD p-System is a Pascal-oriented operating system that runs on a variety of microcomputers. It has a 2-level file system, consisting of volumes and subvolumes. File names may or may not include a file type; if they do, certain types are treated specially by the operating system, such as those ending in .TEXT. Lines of text are separated by bare carriage returns. Files are stored in contiguous blocks, and must therefore have space preallocated for them at creation. Text files may be stored with space compression, using ASCII 16 (DLE) as the compression lead-in character. Every text file has an empty leading "page" (2 blocks) for storing environment information. The special treatment of files based on a 4-letter type (when many common systems restrict the file type to 3 letters), and the foreknowledge of a file's size required before the file can be created, pose special problems for file transfer.

- The word size of the Apple Macintosh is either 16 or 32 bits, depending on whether you think the Motorola 68000 is a 16- or a 32-bit microprocessor. The original Apple Macintosh had a flat file system over which "folders" could be superimposed to lend an illusion of structure. The second release of the Macintosh file system is truly hierarchical. Macintosh file names can be arbitrary text strings, like "This is the name of my file." Macintosh files each have two pieces, a data fork and a resource fork, which makes file transfer a tricky affair. Text is recorded in extended (8-bit) ASCII to allow addition of special characters to the basic ASCII set; lines of text are separated by bare CRs.

• The UNIX operating system runs on many different machines of varying word size. Unlike most other systems, UNIX distinguishes between upper- and lowercase letters in filenames. There is no formal notion of file type, and any number of dots may appear at any position in the filename (nevertheless, certain conventions are observed). Berkeley UNIX allows files to have very long names. The file system is fully hierarchical, with subdirectories stored as ordinary files within their superior directories. Files are simple streams of bytes, with the length known exactly. Text lines are terminated by a "newline" character, which is almost always LF.

• OS-9 is a derivative of UNIX that runs on a variety of microcomputers. Its text files are just like UNIX's, except the line terminator is CR instead of LF.

• The Hewlett-Packard 1000 minicomputer comes with a flat file system having no directory structure (a limited hierarchical file system is available as an option; it works by building a file system inside a regular HP-1000 file). The HP-1000 has 16-bit words, with ASCII characters stored 2 per word. A file's length is known to the nearest word.

• The Prime 50 series computers have a fully hierarchical file system modelled after that of Honeywell MULTICS. Text is recorded in "negative ASCII," with lines separated by LF, or LF NUL (the NUL is added when the line has an odd number of characters); the file's length is always an even number of bytes. Text files are stored with blank compression (and with trailing blanks removed), and they may contain special codes for print formatting. These codes, and the compression lead-in, are distinguished from textual data by having their high-order bit set to 0 rather than 1.

• DEC's RSX and VMS operating systems provide a vast array of file types, organizations, and attributes via FILES-11 and RMS. File type and record delimitation depend upon the file's recorded attributes. The usual style on FILES-11 and RMS is variable records (with length fields), padded to an even length, with carriage control implied via directory attributes. RT-11 does not use FILES-11; it has simple stream files with CRLF separating lines of text, but records the file length only to the nearest block; the final block of a file is padded to the end with NUL characters (when a file has real zero bytes as data at the end, the end of the data cannot be distinguished from the padding). RT-11 files are contiguous, requiring that disk space be preallocated for new files.

• The DECSYSTEM-20, and its close relative the DECsystem-10, have an unusual word length: 36, not a power of 2. These machines have special instructions to manipulate bytes of any size from 1 to 36. Text files are normally packed as five 7-bit bytes into a single 36-bit word, with 1 bit left over. Some text files have line sequence numbers, which occupy a full word; such files have each line padded out with nulls to a word boundary. Native binary files occupy the full 36-bit word, whereas foreign binary files are usually stored in the four leftmost 8-bit bytes, with 4 bits left over. On the DEC-20, a file's byte size is recorded in the directory entry; on the DEC-10 it is not. The DEC-10 has [p,pn] style directories, whereas the DEC-20 allows named subdirectories to any level, so long as the total number of characters in the directory specification, including the dots that separate each level, does not exceed 39.

• The Honeywell DPS series with GCOS has a fully hierarchical file system similar to that of UNIX, but the files are record-oriented rather than simple streams, with a record control word preceding each record to indicate its length, and a special RCW to mark the end of file. These machines have a 36-bit word, but unlike the DEC-10 and DEC-20, divide them up into four 9-bit bytes for the purposes of storing characters.

• An IBM VM/CMS disk has a flat file system, but a user is allowed to create many "virtual disks," each with its own file system. The file specification consists of the file name, the file type, and the disk name (called the "file mode"), separated by spaces. It is rare to find a file system that allows spaces within a file specification, as these can cause no end of ambiguity within commands, especially when these file specifications must be typed on foreign systems. CMS knows the number of blocks in the file, but leaves it up to the access method appropriate to the file's format to determine the actual end. Text files are encoded in EBCDIC rather than ASCII. The MVS operating system has a similar file structure, but file specifications contain no disk name, and may be up to 44 characters long, but a period is required at least every 8 characters. Like the HP-1000, MVS supports environments in which file systems are created inside single files. In the MVS case, these are called "partitioned datasets."

• The CDC Cyber with NOS has a flat file system; file names are seven characters long, period—no file type, no device specification, no version number. Text is stored in many different ways, including at least three different 6-bit character sets (no lowercase letters), and some variations on 7-bit ASCII, with text packed within words in various different ways. To add to the confusion, some sites have also devised their own custom character sets. A line of text is normally terminated by a machine word that has at least 12 zero bits right justified. End of file is indicated by a machine word filled with zeros.

The diversity exhibited by these few systems is only the tip of the iceberg. During the 1960s and '70s, the trend was for every computer to have a unique operating system. In the 1980s, manufacturers have swung in the other direction, adopting one of the popular "portable" operating systems like UNIX or MS-DOS, but many of the "proprietary" operating systems will continue to thrive alongside them. Each file system poses its own set of problems when its data needs to be shared with an unlike system. In the foregoing list, there are consistent incompatibilities in the following areas:

• Character set

• Delimitation of text lines

• End of file detection

• Compression or formatting codes within files

• Filename format and length

• Difference between text and binary files

• Difference between native and foreign binary files

• Requirement to preallocate

Every combination of two unlike systems can pose a unique set of problems. But it is impractical to expect that every system should have specific knowledge of the peculiarities of every other system with which it expects to exchange data. This is the paradox that a file transfer protocol must confront.

4

Data Communication

Our discussion so far has presented a simplified model of a computer and its file system, as shown in Figure 4-1. We now complicate this model by adding a window, or "port," to the outside world, as in Figure 4-2. Reality is still a bit more complex, since the console itself may be a port. But wherever the port is, let's see how it works.

Data communication takes place when signals are transmitted over some medium. The medium most commonly used is ordinary copper wire, but others may be used too: coaxial cable, optical fiber, and even empty space. As long as these media can mimic the behavior of copper wire well enough that the communicating devices can't tell the difference, the "traditional" practices discussed here still apply.

Several binary codes have been used over the years for transmitting characters over communication lines, including variable-length Morse code, 5-bit Baudot code [25] (variants of which are still used to transmit telegrams and telexes), 7-bit ASCII code [5], and 8-bit EBCDIC code [23]. With the usual prominent exception, almost all contemporary computer and terminal manufacturers use 7-bit ASCII encoding for character transmission regardless of the preferred internal encoding.

Besides the medium and the character encoding, there are several other parameters that may characterize the common data communication arrangements. Oddly enough, some of the most important parameters don't have widely accepted names, even though their values do. These include the serial-or-parallel parameter, the synchronous-or-asynchronous parameter, and the full-or-half-duplex parameter. The values of these parameters can occur in any combination, although some combinations make more sense than others.

Serial Transmission

There are two ways to transmit the bits that make up a character: all at once (in parallel) or not all at once (in series). Parallel transmission assigns each bit of a character to its own wire (Figure 4-3). Because of timing problems and the extra expense for additional wires, both of which increase with distance, parallel transmission is generally used only for very short distances, like that between a microcomputer and its printer.

Serial transmission sends each bit of a character over a single wire, one after the other, in a series (Figure 4-4). Serial bits are distributed over *time*, whereas parallel bits are distributed by *position*. A character transmitted in parallel is like a picture, which you can see all at once; in series, it's more like speech, in which words arrive one after the other. Although serial transmission is slower than parallel, it is the predominant mode of communication between computers today.

Instruction
Decoder
Memory
Disk
Console

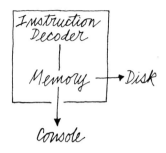

Figure 4-1. A Computer

Instruction
Decoder
?
Port
Memory
Disk
Console

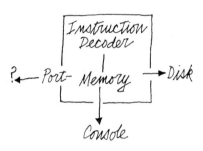

Figure 4-2. A Computer That Can Communicate

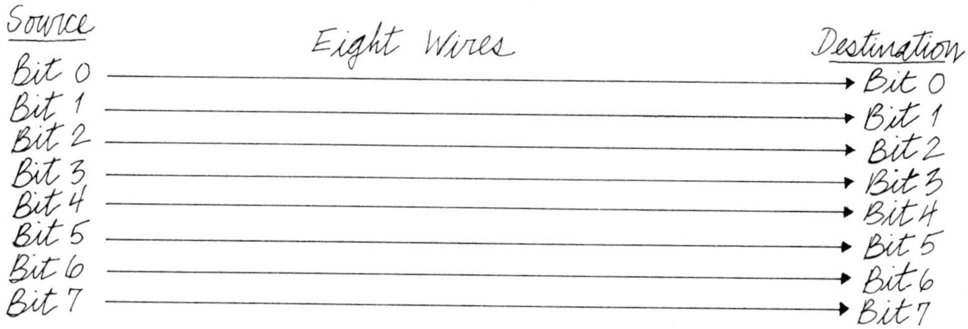

Source
Eight Wires
Destination
Bit 0
Bit 1
Bit 2
Bit 3
Bit 4
Bit 5
Bit 6
Bit 7
Bit 0
Bit 1
Bit 2
Bit 3
Bit 4
Bit 5
Bit 6
Bit 7

Figure 4-3. Parallel Transmission

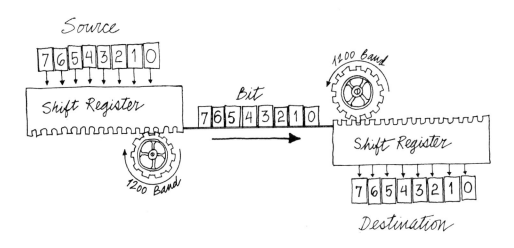

Figure 4-4. Serial Transmission

Asynchronous Transmission

When the bits in a character arrive all at once, in parallel, there is little confusion about where one character ends and the next begins. But when they arrive in series, we need an unambiguous way to delimit them. Two methods are used: clocking, associated with synchronous transmission, and framing, associated with asynchronous transmission. Clocked synchronous transmission is the faster of the two, but it is also more expensive; it requires special equipment to provide the timing signals that keep receiver and transmitter synchronized.

Asynchronous transmission is much more common. It is designed for use between humans and machines, rather than between machines and machines. The distinction is that a person can cause a character to be transmitted from a terminal at any (unpredictable) time by pressing a key, whereas two computers communicating synchronously will know exactly when to expect characters because they share a common clock pulse.

You can visualize the difference between synchronous and asynchronous serial communication like this: suppose you want to get a drink of water from a hose, but the person controlling the spigot is out of sight and likes to turn it on and off a lot. In the synchronous case, your friend calls to you when the water is about to go on and off, but in the asynchronous case you have figure it out for yourself. Synchronous communication requires a separate, "out-of-band" communication channel for control information. If the hose is very long, you won't be able to hear your friend and you'll have to find some (asynchronous) way of getting a drink without being squirted in the face (like buffering the hose in a pail, but let's not get ahead of ourselves).

Data transmission, whether serial or parallel, synchronous or asynchronous, is accomplished by applying agreed-upon voltages to the communication line for agreed-

upon intervals. In RS-232, the standard for asynchronous data transmission [9], a "high" voltage (+3 volts or higher) represents a binary zero, and a "low" voltage (−3 volts or lower)[1] represents a binary 1. In data communication jargon, a zero is a "space" and a one is a "mark." The application of positive and negative voltages—called bipolar signalling because the two values have opposite polarity—allows legitimate signalling elements to be distinguished from line power interruptions, unlike the unipolar technique (signal versus no signal) originally used in telegraphy.

The restriction of legitimate signals on a transmission medium to a small number of discrete voltage ranges (in this case two of them) is called digital communication. This is in contrast to common voice or video transmission, in which signals may vary continuously over a wide spectrum. Digital transmission reduces the probability that illegitimate signals will be taken as legitimate ones.

Baud Rate

Digital transmission can occur over a wide range of speeds, depending upon the characteristics of the devices and the communication medium involved. A short wire between two computers can convey data reliably at relatively high speeds, whereas a noisy cross-country telephone connection can do so only at much lower speeds. Data communication speed is measured by the number of significant voltage transitions that can occur per second. This is called the signalling rate, or "baud rate," and in the case of binary digital transmission it is equivalent to the number of bits per second, because there are only two significant voltage states.

To allow devices to exchange data at the highest rate appropriate to the prevailing conditions, a selection of speeds must be provided. In an attempt to ward off chaos, various standards organizations have made lists of acceptable baud rates [2, 30, 11]. The standards all say that baud rates should be multiples, halves, or quarters of 600, plus a few others (on which the standards tend to disagree). The common baud rates are 110, 150, 300, 600, 1200, 2400, 4800, and 9600. 110 and 150 baud are for Teletypes; 300 and 1200 are in common use over telephone lines; 2400 and above are used mainly with direct connections (2400-baud telephone connections are also becoming practical). Higher speeds like 19200 and 38400 are also beginning to appear for direct connections; slower speeds like 50 and 75 baud are used for international cable traffic. I once read that power utility companies even use their power transmission lines to carry power-grid switching information at very low speeds, like 12.5 baud.

The baud rate can generally be characterized as ten times the number of characters per second (cps), for instance, 1200 baud is 120 cps. Table 4-1 shows how long it takes to transmit selected amounts of data from 1K (1024) bytes to 1024K (a megabyte) at various baud rates, assuming the data flows continuously (which hardly ever happens).

---

1. RS-232 specifies an upper limit of 25V on the magnitude of these signals. In practice, they rarely exceed 15V.

Table 4-1. Transmission Times for Selected Baud Rates

KBytes	Baud: 110	300	1200	2400	4800	9600	19200
1	1.7m	34.1s	8.5s	4.3s	2.1s	1.1s	0.5s
2	3.4m	1.1m	17.1s	8.5s	4.3s	2.1s	1.1s
4	6.8m	2.3m	34.1s	17.1s	8.5s	4.3s	2.1s
8	13.7m	4.6m	1.1m	34.1s	17.1s	8.5s	4.3s
16	27.3m	9.1m	2.3m	1.1m	34.1s	17.1s	8.5s
32	54.6m	18.2m	4.6m	2.3m	1.1m	34.1s	17.1s
64	1.8h	36.4m	9.1m	4.6m	2.3m	1.1m	34.1s
128	3.6h	1.2h	18.2m	9.1m	4.6m	2.3m	1.1m
256	7.3h	2.4h	36.4m	18.2m	9.1m	4.6m	2.3m
512	14.6h	4.9h	1.2h	36.4m	18.2m	9.1m	4.6m
1024	29.1h	9.7h	2.4h	1.2h	36.4m	18.2m	9.1m

(s = second, m = minute, h = hour)

You are sometimes asked to specify input and output baud rates separately. Some years ago, "split-speed" communications enjoyed a brief vogue, predicated on the (no longer valid) assumption that traffic from the terminal to the computer would be light compared to that in the other direction (because computers can spew out data faster than people can type). A typical split-speed arrangement was 75 baud input and 1200 baud output, from the point of view of the dialup user. While some environments may still require or encourage split-speed communications, the general rule today is equal rights for input and output.

The UART

In the early days, it was rarely possible to connect computing equipment from two different manufacturers. There was little regard for standards (when they existed at all), and wide variations of interpretation even when attempts were made to follow the early standards. By 1969, the RS-232 standard had matured to its present level (RS-232-C), and it wasn't long before manufacturers began to mass-produce a device to implement this standard. Today, thanks to this device, called a Universal Asynchronous Receiver/Transmitter (UART, pronounced "you-art"), we can take RS-232 connections for granted. Computer makers who once recoiled at the thought of allowing a competitor's equipment to communicate with their own have now come to accept the idea, and they routinely equip their products with standardized UARTs.

The UART allows a wide variety of terminals to communicate uniformly with a wide variety of computers, and computers themselves to exchange data over asynchronous serial connections. The UART is represented schematically in Figure 4-4 as the contraption at either end of the wire. Recall that characters are stored in the computer within bytes, and a byte is a row of 7 or 8 bits which the computer treats as a single

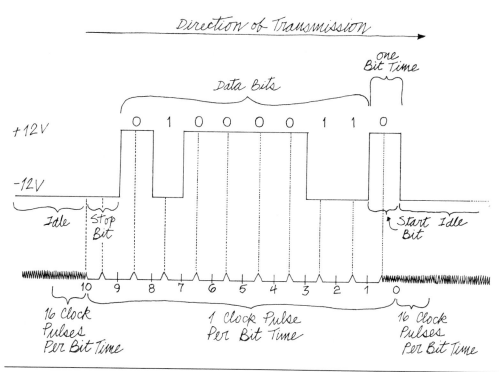

Figure 4-5. Asynchronous Serial Transmission of the Letter C

unit (in parallel). The UART's task is to convert a byte in the computer's memory to a series of voltages on the communication line, and vice versa. Conceptually, this is a simple task. To transmit a byte, the UART simply feeds the bits (in voltage form) to the line, one at a time, in the prescribed order (exactly *which* order was once the subject of some debate [3]).

But how does the UART on the receiving end know where one character ends and the next begins? The transmitting UART observes a "framing" convention, which works like this: whenever no data is flowing, the UART applies a steady negative voltage (a mark condition) to the line. The mark looks just like a binary 1. To signal the beginning of a character, the UART raises the voltage to the space condition for one bit time. As soon as the receiving UART sees this 1-to-0 transition, it samples the line voltage eight more times to assemble a byte, which it makes available to the computer for copying. When the transmitter has finished sending the character, it goes back to its idle state by applying the mark condition to the line for at least one bit time.

Figure 4-5 shows how the ASCII letter C (67 decimal, 01000011 binary) would be transmitted by the UART. Note that the least significant (low-order) bits go first.[2] The

2. Pictures like this one are intrinsically confusing. In the example shown, time is backward. But if the mirror image were shown, then the data would look backward.

space at the beginning of the character is called the start bit and the mark at the end is called the stop bit. Ten bit times are required to transmit 8 bits of data. This constitutes a 20 percent overhead, and it is part of the price we pay for the convenience and economy of asynchronous transmission. The times given in Table 4-1 include this overhead.

At this point, it's worth mentioning that communications equipment or programs often require you to specify the number of stop bits. This question is an artifact of earlier times when clunky mechanical printing contraptions (like ASR33 Teletypes) needed some time to settle down after printing a character. Today's equipment should be able to make do with one stop bit at any baud rate, although it is still customary to use two stop bits at 110 baud.[3]

Now let's look at the UART's operation in a little more detail. Before any communication can take place, the two UARTs must be set to the same baud rate, which is the inverse of the bit time (for instance, 1200 baud means a bit time of $1/1200 = 0.000833$ second). When the UART's input line is in the idle state, the receiver samples the input line at a rate many times faster than the bit rate, typically 16 times faster, or once per 0.000052 second at 1200 baud. This furious activity is necessary because the UART *does not know* when the character will start to arrive. This is why the transmission is said to be asynchronous; the process is somewhat akin to staring constantly into a hose to see when the water will arrive.

As soon as the UART receiver detects the 1-to-0 transition (at bit time 0 in Figure 4-5), it continues "furious sampling" for half a bit time (until bit time 0.5) and then slows its clock down to tick exactly once per bit time, so that the line is sampled as closely as possible to the "middle" of each data bit. At the same time, a counter is set to the number of data bits expected (usually 8). Then for each clock tick, the line is sampled, the sampled voltage is converted into a bit and inserted into a shift register (in which the earlier bits are moved over one position to make room), and the counter is decremented (decreased by 1). The process continues until the counter reaches zero. At that point (bit time 9.5 in the figure) the UART checks to make sure the line is in mark state. If not, it informs the computer that a framing error has occurred. Otherwise it copies the character from the shift register to a holding register (to make room for new arrivals), and indicates to the computer that a character has been received successfully. At this point the computer may copy the character from the UART's holding register into its own memory. If the character has not been removed by the time the UART is ready to copy the next character into the holding register, the UART signals an overrun condition to indicate that data was lost.

The UART has two channels for communicating with the computer: one for data and one for control information. The control channel, consisting of status and error bits

3. Of course, at such a low baud rate, the *last* thing you want to do is add extra transmission overhead. If you have to communicate at 110 baud for some reason, try it first with 1 stop bit, and switch to 2 only if necessary.

Table 4-2. Typical UART Parameters

1	+5V Power	21	Reset All
2	−12V Power	22	Transmitter Buffer Empty
3	Ground	23	Data Strobe
4	Received Data Enable	24	End of Character
5–12	Received Data 1–8	25	Serial Data Output
13	Receive Parity Error	26–33	Parallel Data Input 1–8
14	Framing Error	34	Control Strobe
15	Overrun	35	No Parity
16	Status Word Enable	36	Two Stop Bits
17	Receiver Clock	37–38	Bits Per Character (5, 6, 7, 8)
18	Resets 19	39	Even Parity Select
19	Received Data Available	40	Transmitter Clock
20	Serial Data Input		

("flags"), provides an out-of-band method for communicating information about the data. Table 4-2 shows the parameters associated with each of the 40 UART signals.

Now you can see why the asynchronous serial communication medium is said to be *character-oriented*. The computer itself is shielded from the serial nature of the transmission by the UART. It sees the UART, and therefore the communication line, strictly as a character-at-a-time input/output device. This is a paradoxical situation, because the wire itself is a purely serial path, subject to perturbations that take no account of the character orientation of the devices on either end.

Noise and the Telephone System

Serial data communication is often called "telecommunication" because so much of it occurs over telephone lines. Telephone lines have some special characteristics that will be discussed later, but one worth mentioning now is that they can be very noisy.

Your own experience with ordinary telephone calls should give you an idea of what can go wrong with a phone connection. The signal may be weak. There may be hissing sounds or pops. Someone else's conversation may be superimposed on yours. The signal might disappear altogether for short intervals. There may be annoying delays in voice transmission. Your words might echo back to you some seconds after you speak them.

These problems have many causes, not least among them that some parts of the telephone network are nearly a century old. A vast array of potentially noisy junctions and switching equipment establishes and maintains telephone circuits. And telephone lines, like all communication lines, are subject to interference from other nearby electrical energy sources— power cables, motors, alarms, even other transmission cables— as well as loose connections, frayed insulation, and so on.

The noise that occurs during a phone conversation usually does not prevent the desired information from being exchanged—people can talk louder, talk slower, or repeat themselves. Digital data does not fare as well in these circumstances. The meaning of human speech distorted by static can often be inferred from context, but digital data, once corrupted, is hard to reconstruct. Techniques have been developed to detect transmission errors in digital data, but most of them presuppose that errors involve only individual bits. Unfortunately, the kinds of noise that affect a communication line tend to occur in bursts that wipe out many bits in a row.

The telephone system has elaborate noise reduction mechanisms built into it, but they cannot be depended upon entirely. If more demands are placed on the phone system than it can handle, if furious switching or dialing activity mangles data beyond recognition, if devices malfunction or electrical interference occurs, there's little the system itself can do to correct the signals.

The BREAK Signal

If the serial asynchronous communication line were capable only of transmitting properly framed characters, certain desirable operations would not be possible. Here are two examples:

- Automatic baud rate adjustment—If your device is running at one baud rate, and the device on the other end of the connection at another rate, neither device will be able to decode the other's transmissions. It is sometimes necessary to "wake up" the remote device to this fact and have it adjust its baud rate.

- Escape from transparency—If some intermediate device connects your system to a remote computer, you would probably want it to pass all characters through transparently, just as if your system were connected directly. But then how would you get the device's attention when you need to communicate directly with it, for instance, to ask it to connect you to a different system?

One technique that can be used in both situations is the intentional generation of a framing error. This can be done by putting the communication line into the space condition for more than a whole character time. Such a condition is called a BREAK signal.[4] Since the baud rate at the receiving end may not be known, a BREAK must last longer than the longest possible character time. The lowest baud rate in common use is 50 baud (for international telecommunication), which gives a bit time of 0.02 seconds (20 milliseconds) and a character time of 0.2 seconds (200 milliseconds) at 10 bits per character. It is therefore commonly agreed that a BREAK signal should last slightly longer than one 50-baud character time, or 275–300 milliseconds, so it can never be confused with valid character data at any baud rate.

An interesting property of the BREAK signal is that if the receiving computer elects to ignore the UART's error indication, the data is received as an ASCII NUL. The BREAK

---

4. BREAK is customarily spelled in all uppercase; don't ask me why.

key has become a common shortcut for entering a NUL from the terminal—easier than, say, typing Control-Atsign. What's even more interesting is that the data comes through as a NUL at any baud rate.

Generation of a framing error is a cheap way to achieve an out-of-band signal. When a device that is expecting valid data gets·an error instead, it can trigger special action. A computer that is initially connecting to a device whose baud rate is unknown can switch, under program control, to another baud rate if framing errors occur. A communication device whose normal mission is to pass along all character data transparently can "wake up" when it detects a framing error and find out what the user wants.

Such handy uses of the BREAK signal have prompted most asynchronous terminal manufacturers to include a BREAK key on the keyboard. The prevalence of the BREAK key has in turn prompted software designers to take advantage of it by including the BREAK signal among valid inputs expected from the user. For instance, a text editor might require a BREAK signal to switch from text collection to command mode. This sort of thing could be expected to work in the days when a terminal was a terminal, and was connected directly to a computer. But today's terminals are more likely to be microcomputers that might not be programmed to generate BREAK signals, and the connection is just as likely to be through some intermediate device that may not pass BREAK through transparently. Since so many applications and devices expect to have access to the BREAK signal, it is important to understand this problem, even when it can't readily be solved.

Connectors and Pin Assignments

Let's recapitulate our discussion of cables and connectors. A data communication cable has a D-connector on each end; D-connectors, like ordinary power plugs and sockets, come in two genders—male and female. As a general rule, computers and terminals have male connectors and modems have female ones. The most common connector used for asynchronous serial communication is called the DB-25 connector, shown in Figure 4-6. Each pin is associated with a particular signal by the Electronic Industries Association (EIA) Standard RS-232-C [9].

The RS-232-C standard describes how Data Terminal Equipment (DTE) and Data Communications Equipment (DCE) may be connected. A DTE is a terminal or a computer. A DCE is a modem, multiplexer, or similar piece of communication equipment (explained later). Most descriptions of signals assume that a DTE is connected to a DCE, but in practice it is just as common to have two DTEs connected directly to each other. Technical literature generally specifies that a signal is "from DCE" or "to DCE" (or, conversely, to DTE or from DTE). We've shown this directionality in the figures simply as (IN) and (OUT), respectively.

Of the twenty-five RS-232 signals, ten are commonly used in asynchronous data communication:

• *Protective Ground, or Frame Ground (FG, Pin 1)*
This circuit is to protect the human operator from electrical shock. It is bonded to the equipment frame or to the ground pin of the power connector.

• *Transmitted Data (TD, Pin 2)*
This is the circuit for sending out data from the DTE. It is interesting to note that by definition a DCE *receives* data on its TD circuit. The DTE's transmitter keeps this circuit in the mark state when no data is being transmitted.

• *Received Data (RD, Pin 3)*
This is the circuit used by the DTE for receiving data from the DCE. Thus the DCE *transmits* on its RD circuit. This circuit is also in the mark state when no data is being transmitted.

• *Request to Send (RTS, Pin 4)*
When On (set to 1), this circuit announces the intention of the DTE to transmit data over its TD circuit.

• *Clear to Send (CTS, Pin 5)*
When On, announces the DCE's readiness to receive data from the DTE on the TD circuit. When Off, indicates that the DTE should not transmit.

• *Data Set Ready (DSR, Pin 6)*
Indication from the local DCE (e.g., a modem) that it is connected to the DTE in data transmission mode, and not in voice or test mode.

• *Signal Ground (SG, Pin 7)*
This circuit provides the common electrical reference against which the voltages of the other signals are measured. Also called Common Return. The DTE and the DCE should have the same ground connection at the power plug. Common ground reference is required for bipolar signalling.

• *Carrier Detect (CD, Pin 8)*
Indication to the DTE from the local DCE that it is receiving a carrier signal from the remote DCE (the local modem tells the terminal that it has a data connection to the remote modem). Also called Received Line Signal Detector (RLSD) or Data Carrier Detect (DCD). Transition from Off to On indicates establishment of connection (call answered by modem); transition from On to Off indicates loss of connection (hangup).

• *Data Terminal Ready (DTR, Pin 20)*
Indication from the terminal or computer (DTE) that it is operational and ready to communicate with the DCE. Used in conjunction with DSR and RI to control dialing or other communications equipment.

• *Ring Indicator (RI, Pin 22)*

Indication from the DCE (presumably an autoanswer modem) that a ringing (calling) signal is being received from the telephone.

The remaining RS-232 circuits are used for synchronous communications, testing, or other purposes. Figure 4-6 shows the pin assignments for a male DB-25 connector as it appears from the outside, from the point of view of the DTE (computer or terminal). OUT means the signal goes out from the DTE to the DCE; IN means the reverse. The female connector's pin assignments form the mirror image of those shown in the figure.

Although RS-232-C specifies the pin assignments for the 25-pin connector, the physical configuration of the connector has been left to the manufacturers. The DB-25 configuration shown in Figure 4-6 has achieved the widest acceptance. The shape, size, and distance between the pins, the exact shape and size of the shell, the location and size of the mounting holes, have all achieved an amazing degree of uniformity in the absence of a formal standard. Nevertheless, you will encounter the occasional pair of DB-25 connectors that will not mate, usually because of differences in the hood, or the placement of the screws.

The 9-pin connector is gaining in popularity because of its adoption by IBM on its PC/AT and by Apple on the Macintosh as a means for saving precious mounting space.

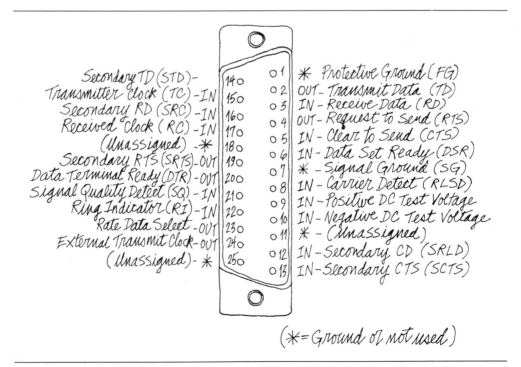

Figure 4-6. DB-25 Pin Assignments

Its configuration is specified in RS-449 [12]. The two manufacturers use the nine pins in entirely different ways, but in both cases the choice reflects a tacit recognition that 25-signal RS-232 in all its glory is not required for ordinary asynchronous data communication. IBM assigns selected RS-232 circuits to the nine pins on the PC/AT's port, as shown in Figure 4-7. Apple, however, uses its 9-pin connector to implement the newer EIA RS-422 standard [10], which specifies a way for data to go faster over greater distances than RS-232-C by employing balanced pairs of receive and transmit signals. The Macintosh serial port (female, shown in Figure 4-8) may also be used for RS-232-C communication with appropriate wiring, as shown in Figure 4-17 on page 107.

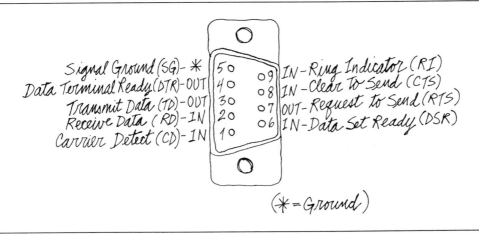

Figure 4-7. IBM PC/AT 9-Pin RS-232-C Serial Port Pin Assignments

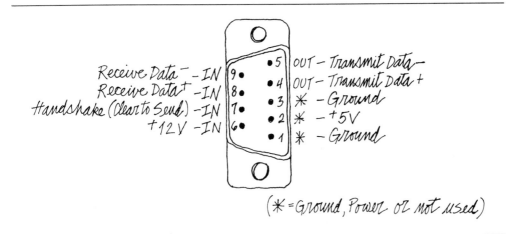

Figure 4-8. Macintosh 9-Pin RS-422 Serial Port Pin Assignments

Duplex and Echo

Our discussion of UARTs failed to mention one of their best features: they can receive and transmit at the same time. But this is not to say that all computers that employ UARTs can take full advantage of this capability. When two connected systems do so, the connection is said to be full-duplex. Full-duplex transmission requires two wires for data—one to receive, one to send.

For a variety of reasons, it is sometimes necessary for two DTEs to agree that only one can transmit at a time. This kind of communication is called half-duplex, meaning that traffic can go two ways (duplex), but only one way at a time (half). Another mode, called simplex, means traffic can only go one way, period.

When a terminal and a computer are connected in full-duplex, it is customary for the computer to "echo" the characters it receives from the terminal. This means that every character that arrives at the computer's receiver is processed and then copied (perhaps with alterations) to its transmitter. The terminal, meanwhile, copies every character that is typed on the keyboard to its own transmitter, and copies every character that arrives at its receiver to the screen. This arrangement is illustrated in Figure 4-9, and it differs from half-duplex operation in which the terminal, rather than the host, echoes what is typed on the keyboard.

You might wonder why communication would ever need to be half-duplex if (as is usually the case) there are wires for both receiving and transmitting. One reason is simply that certain manufacturers feel it promotes more efficient use of their computers, since the terminal relieves the host of the burden of echoing, and it simplifies the console device driver software. Another reason is conservation of signalling bandwidth, which we'll get into when we discuss modems on page 90.

Full-duplex operation has two prominent advantages: it allows the user to monitor the quality of the connection, and it allows the host to control what appears on the user's screen. To give a concrete example, suppose you're trying to log in to a full-duplex system, and you type your username as ABC; if it appears on your screen as AXW then you can infer that the line is noisy. Assuming, however, that the line is clean, the host can ask you to type your secret access password, and then refrain from echoing it so that the inquisitive person looking over your shoulder cannot discover it.

These characteristics of full-duplex communication also allow another desirable feature: typeahead. This lets you send characters to the computer before it has asked you for them. For instance, you can type three commands in a row, even though the computer might not have finished executing the first command by the time you have finished typing the third. And since the computer can control the echoing of characters, it can arrange the output so that your commands and their responses all come out in the correct sequence on your screen. While any full-duplex system has the potential to provide this service, not all of them do.

On both full- and half-duplex systems, it often happens that you wish to interrupt some long display of output from the computer. Since full-duplex systems allow you to transmit to them at the same time they are transmitting to you, they normally provide

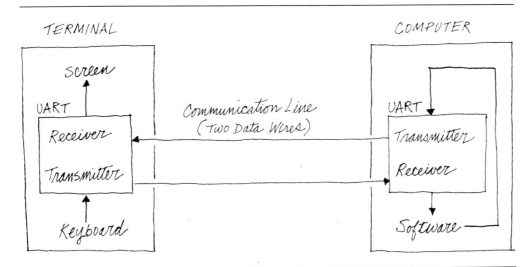

Figure 4-9. Full-Duplex Communication

```
RD←WHEN CAN I TRANSMIT?<XON>—TD
TD—<XON>WON TIMSNART NAC UOY→RD
```

Figure 4-10. Half-Duplex Communication with In-Band Handshaking

special interruption characters for this purpose. Half-duplex systems, on the other hand, are not prepared to receive input while they are performing output. The typical method for interruption in this situation is the BREAK signal; detection of the resulting framing error is interpreted by the computer as an interruption command.

Handshake

Full-duplex transmission also has a more subtle advantage. No coordination is necessary between the two devices as to which currently has permission to transmit. A half-duplex connection, on the other hand, has to manage this problem. The method employed is called handshaking, and it is indeed a matter of etiquette. Only one device talks at a time, and when it is finished, it grants permission to the other side to talk.

There are two ways to do handshaking, in the data itself or with out-of-band RS-232 signals. The out-of-band method requires extra wires for circuits like Request to Send (RTS) and Clear to Send (CTS). In this protocol, transmission may occur only when the receiver's CTS signal is On.

Handshake

The in-band handshaking method is less foolproof than RTS/CTS, but it's cheaper because fewer wires are required. In this case, the transmitter of a message concludes it with a specially designated character, such as ASCII DC1 (usually called XON), as shown in Figure 4-10. The receiver is not supposed to transmit unless the last character it has received is an XON.

In-band handshaking is more sensitive to noise than is the RTS/CTS method. Since RTS and CTS are steady signals with their own wires, they have a certain robust quality. A serial in-band handshake character stricken by noise, however, will leave the intended recipient waiting forever for its turn to transmit. The apparent advantage in simplicity of the in-band method is offset by measures that must be taken to recover from deadlocks. And it should be noted that the handshake character itself is no longer available for transmission as an ordinary data character. A connection that uses in-band control information is not wholly transparent. It is said to be opaque to those characters that are used for control purposes.

Flow Control

Half-duplex handshaking is a method of flow control. That is, it's a way to control the flow of data in one direction or another. However, it is a very rudimentary form. When one side gets the go-ahead to transmit, it sends data with absolutely no assurance that the receiver will have a place to put it. And in data communication, Having A Place To Put It is among the paramount virtues. But how can one computer really know that another is truly prepared to receive an abundance of data?

The "brute-force" approach to this problem (and the one used in the half-duplex environment) is for the receiver to allocate very big places to put arriving data. These places are called buffers. Buffers are like soft cushions that keep mutually antagonistic things from bumping against each other; in this case, the buffer isolates the stringent "real-time" requirements of the UART from the casual attitude of the user program, just as a bucket would allow our thirsty friend from page 72 to get a drink without risking a squirt in the face.[5]

Remember that the UART must be relieved of each character before the next one comes in, or else its holding register will overrun. Since user programs are usually not in a position to service the UART's demands promptly, every operating system provides, at a very low level transparent to the user and even to the programmer, a "device driver" for the UART, which takes care of all this. The driver copies data from the UART, in real time, into a buffer from which the user program removes characters at its leisure, making room for more characters to enter. This arrangement is called a FIFO—First In First Out—list, or a *queue*.

---

5. But don't think that the bucket solves all our friend's problems. There's still the question of how to prevent the bucket from overflowing, and what to do with the water coming out the hose when drinking from the bucket.

To help you appreciate what device drivers do for you, here's a short program fragment in C that implements a kind of do-it-yourself half-duplex handshaking:

```
(1) tty = fopen("/dev/tty02","rw");            /* Open the device */
(2) while (1) {                                /* Forever, do...  */
(3)   while ((c = getc(tty)) != XON) putc(c,stdout); /* Read characters */
(4)   while ((c = getc(stdin)) != XON) putc(c,tty);  /* Send characters */
(5)   putc(c,stdout);                          /* Send handshake  */
(6) }
```

Statement (1) opens a communication line, tty02, for reading and writing; a file pointer, tty, is associated with the communication line. This means that any input or output to the line will go through the appropriate device driver. Statements (2) and (6) indicate that statements (3) through (5) are to be repeated endlessly. Statement (3) is a loop that gets characters (getc) from the communication line (tty) and copies them (putc) to the screen (stdout) until an XON character is encountered; the XON is not copied to the screen. Invoking getc with the tty file pointer automatically brings the communication-line device driver into play, which handles the details of UART control—timing, status bits, error indications—and manages an internal buffer that your program never sees. Your program has only to "get the next character," which it can expect with some confidence to be there. Statement (4) allows you to type a reply at the console (stdin); each character you type is sent out the communication line until you type an XON (Control-Q). Again, the communication-line device driver takes care of the timing, buffering, and UART control. Statement (5) sends the XON that grants the other system permission to take its turn.

We've said that the half-duplex solution to the buffering problem is simply to dedicate large portions of the computer's memory to buffers. This is done in hope that more than a buffer's worth of data will never be sent all at once. If this should happen, the computer would lose the extra data. But if the receiver had some way of telling the sender to stop, *while* the transmission was in progress, then the loss could be avoided. The ability to do this is called full-duplex flow control.

Did you ever take the top off your toilet tank and watch what happens when you flush? Your toilet provides an excellent example of full-duplex flow control. The tank is like a queue: water exits from the bottom when you flush, and enters from the top to refill the tank. The flow into the tank is controlled by a float that monitors the water level. When the water gets high enough, the float shuts a valve to turn off the water. When the toilet flushes, the float goes down and opens the valve to let in more water.

Just as half-duplex handshaking comes in two forms, so does full-duplex flow control. One form employs the out-of-band RTS/CTS signals, with the same advantages and drawbacks of the half-duplex case: more transparent and foolproof, but less cheap and less widely available. The more common method uses special characters imbedded in the data stream; one example is called "XON/XOFF." It works like this: when the communication-line device driver notices that its input buffer has reached some measure of fullness (that is, before it is completely full), it transmits an XOFF character, like

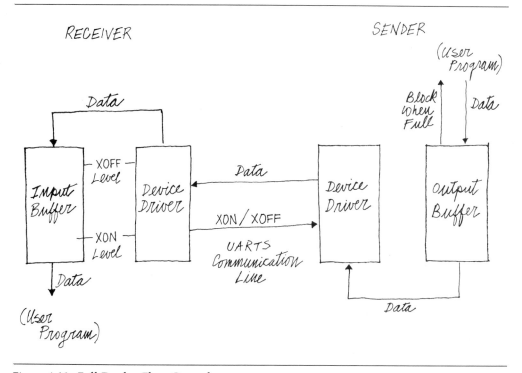

Figure 4-11. Full-Duplex Flow Control

when the float shuts the valve. When the other system sees the XOFF, it stops trans-mitting.[6] Eventually, the application on the receiving side removes enough characters from the buffer to bring it beneath a certain threshold; this is like flushing the toilet. The device driver notices that there is room in the buffer again and sends an XON character to resume the transmission, like when the tank float drops and opens the valve. The XON and XOFF functions are generally assigned to the ASCII characters DC1 (Control-Q) and DC3 (Control-S), respectively.

The effect of an XOFF can ripple back through multiple layers of hardware and software. Even in the case where only two computers are involved, the XOFF causes the device driver on the sending side to stop transmitting. However, the user application may still be writing characters to its output buffer. If the XOFF condition is not cleared before the sender's output buffer fills up, the sender application will be blocked (pre-vented from executing) until the receiver starts to accept data again. Figure 4-11 shows the software aspects of full-duplex flow control schematically, for data flowing in only

6. A toilet is a self-contained mechanism, whereas the two computers are independent. The toilet valve's response to the float is immediate, but a computer must plan for some delay before its message gets across and the other computer responds.

one direction. Of course, data can flow in both directions in a full-duplex channel, so in reality both sides have input and output buffers and may be doing XON/XOFF to each other simultaneously.

The receiver's XOFF and XON thresholds must be carefully chosen. The XOFF point should occur early enough to allow the XOFF to reach the other end and be processed before the receiver's buffer fills, but late enough so as not to waste buffer space. The XON should be sent late enough to ensure that adequate buffer space has been freed, but not so late as to degrade transmission performance by making the transmitter wait unnecessarily. And the XOFF and XON thresholds must not be so close together that inordinate amounts of time will be spent transmitting and processing these flow control signals themselves.

The drawbacks of XON/XOFF are similar to those of half-duplex XON handshaking, but compounded. If an XOFF is corrupted or lost, the transmitter will continue to send even though the receiver is running out of buffer space. But note the difference: the receiver will just send another XOFF when the next character arrives, so no harm will be done as long as the XOFF threshold is set appropriately. But if an XON is lost, a deadlock could ensue. Deadlocks are also possible in the rare situation in which both sides XOFF each other simultaneously, and when an XOFF is spontaneously generated on the communication line by noise. Overruns can occur if an XON is generated by noise, but only during an XOFF condition. The advantages of XON/XOFF however, are apparent. Large amounts of system storage need not be dedicated to buffers, applications can be character-oriented rather than line-oriented, transmissions can be smooth rather than jerky, and typeahead is possible.

Before we leave the topic of flow control, two more in-band schemes should be mentioned. One is called ENQ/ACK. In this protocol, which can work on either full- or half-duplex channels, the transmitter requests permission to transmit by sending an ENQ character (ASCII Control-E). The receiver responds with an ACK (Control-F) character if it believes it has (or after it has allocated) adequate buffer space. This method suffers the same drawback as half-duplex handshake: there is no assurance that the buffer is big enough to accommodate the data to be transmitted. The other is called ETX/ACK, and is typically used when data traffic is one-way, as between computers and printers. Transmitted data is terminated by an ETX character; the receiver replies with an ACK character as soon as the ETX character has been removed from its input buffer, indicating its readiness to receive the next transmission.

The primary proponent of half-duplex communication and XON handshake is IBM (in its System/370-series mainframes); XON/XOFF is championed by DEC and many other manufacturers; ENQ/ACK is favored by Hewlett-Packard; ETX/ACK survives on Diablo printers. There are also computers that provide no flow control at the system level, and leave it to user-level software to manage the problem. Flow control will only work if both computers involved have been told to do it, and to do it the same way. If one computer is doing XON/XOFF and the other ENQ/ACK, then each will see the other's flow control signals as ordinary data characters. On the other hand, when in-band flow control is occurring successfully, the XON and XOFF (or ENQ and ACK) characters will not be available for use as data.

Parity

Parity is used for detecting errors in binary information. The creator of a binary quantity determines whether the number of 1-bits in it is even or odd, and appends an additional 0-bit or 1-bit to achieve the desired parity. Any entity reading the data may perform the same calculation to see if the recorded parity bit agrees with the one calculated. When there is disagreement, it is certain that the data (or the parity bit) has been corrupted. In data communication, parity is applied to characters; our concern is with how it is applied to 7-bit ASCII characters.

Recall that ASCII characters have 7 bits, numbered from 0 to 6, with 0 being the least significant bit (LSB) and 6 the most (MSB). Recall too that most bytes are 8 bits long, and most asynchronous serial transmission includes 8 bits between the start and stop bits. The "eighth" bit (really bit number 7) is the one that is used for parity.

A Snipper Bird

There are five kinds of parity: even, odd, mark, space, and none. Of these, only even and odd are true parity; the others reflect the remaining possible conditions or uses of the eighth bit. But in common usage, when you are asked to select the desired parity, you will usually be given five choices rather than two.

Even parity means that there is to be an even number of 1-bits in the character, *including* the parity bit. Thus the even parity bit is 1 if there is an odd number of 1-bits in the 7-bit ASCII value, and 0 otherwise. Odd parity is just the opposite; it ensures that the overall number of 1-bits in the character is odd (Figure 4-12). Mark parity always sets the parity bit to 1, and space parity always sets it to zero. No parity means that the eighth bit is left alone.

Parity generation and checking are not required features of a communication link. In fact, they are the exception rather than the rule. When parity is not being "done," the link is said to have no parity. Note the difference between no parity and space parity; when parity is "none," the high-order bit may be used to transmit actual computer data as it is stored in 8-bit bytes within the computer. Space parity sets the high bit to zero, wiping out the data bit from that position.

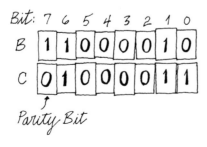

Figure 4-12. The ASCII Letters B and C with Odd Parity

Is parity useful? In theory, it allows the receiver of transmitted characters to determine whether the characters are good or bad. But even in theory, odd and even parity
can only catch errors that affect an odd number of bits in a character, which means
they will *not* catch double-bit, 4-bit, or even 6-bit errors. For instance, if the binary
sequence 11010101 (ASCII letter U with odd parity) were received as 11101010 (ASCII
letter j), the sequence would appear entirely valid to the receiver, even though 6 of the
8 bits had been flipped by noise. And of course, space or mark parity can't catch *any*
errors in the 7 data bits; these can be used only to detect when the parity bit itself has
been toggled. (Flip and toggle mean to change the value of a bit from 0 to 1 or vice
versa.)

Parity was really designed for use in computer memories, where failures are likely
to be discrete, affecting only one bit per word or byte. In this setting, a single-bit error
is far more likely than a double-bit error, and errors of 3 or more bits are hardly worth
worrying about (by the time the memory degenerates this far, the computer is useless
anyway). What makes parity particularly useful in memories is the fact that "advanced"
forms of it, involving extra parity bits, can be used not only to detect errors but also to
correct them "on the fly" [13]. But character parity is entirely inappropriate to serial
data communication, where lengthy error bursts are the rule, and single-bit errors are
curiosities.

Parity serves little useful purpose in data communications. Some terminals check
parity: if an incoming character has a parity error, the terminal displays a special kind
of blotch on the screen to let the human operator know there is noise on the line. But
what can the person, or the terminal, do about it? Nothing. Even though parity generation and checking are built into UARTs (Table 4-2), there is no provision for error
correction. And since telecommunication noise tends to span character boundaries,
corruption is just as likely to be caught by framing anyway.

Despite all the factors weighing against it, many manufacturers of computers and
communication equipment as well as providers of data communication services are
great believers in parity, and insist that you use it if you want to communicate with,
or through, their products. Ironically, one of the most commonly required parities is
mark, which provides next to nothing in the way of error detection. The use of parity
prevents us from transmitting 8-bit data conveniently and efficiently. It constricts the
medium an additional 10 percent (remember, the start and stop bits already took away
20 percent). The price is paid on every single character, with little tangible return.

Modems

Just as you use your telephone to call another person, you can also use it to call a
computer if you have a modem—a Modulator/Demodulator. The modem works by
translating the digital output of your computer's UART into the same kind of analog
waveforms that you would generate by speaking, which can be carried over the phone

wires as "audible" tones in the normal voice frequency range. Modems are necessary because serial digital data cannot survive the filtering and amplifying functions that are applied along an analog telephone circuit.

Phone calls are full-duplex in nature. Both parties can speak and listen at the same time because each phone has a separate transmit and receive circuit. Therefore, it is easy to see how modems can be used to establish a full-duplex data connection. In fact, if digital/analog conversion were all that modems did, we wouldn't need to discuss them, because they would just be invisible boxes on the communication line. But there is a lot more to telephones than voice transmission. They also dial, ring, hang up, and emit dial tones and busy signals. And there's also a lot more to modems than turning bits into sounds.

The modem that is local to your terminal or PC is called an originate modem, and the one on the computer is called an answer modem. For two modems to communicate, the caller must be in originate mode, and the callee must be in answer mode. This is because each modem transmits on one frequency and receives on another in order to share the same wire.

In addition, both modems must observe the same modulation/demodulation technique (frequency shift keying, etc.) and the particular frequencies or amplitudes used. Table 4-3 lists the popular methods. The Bell (now AT&T) standards predominate in North America, and the CCITT recommendations predominate in Europe. As you can see from the table, some modems are able to load one baud with more than one bit's worth of information. This is because their signals assume more than two values, unlike digital bipolar signals, and this is why "baud" is not always a synonym for "bits per

Table 4-3. Popular Dialup Modem Protocols

Modem Type	Data Rate	Modulation	Baud Rate	Duplex
Bell 103	110,300	FSK	300	Full/FDM
Bell 201	2400	DPSK	1200	Half
Bell 202	1200	FSK	300	Half
Bell 212	1200	DPSK	600	Full/FDM
Bell 2224	2400	QAM	600	Full/FDM
CCITT V.21	200–300	FSK	200	Full/FDM
CCITT V.22bis	2400	QAM	600	Full/FDM
CCITT V.26ter	2400	DPSK	1200	Full/ECT
VA 3400	1200	DPSK	600	Full/FDM

DPM = Differential phase modulation   FDM = Frequency division multiplexing
DPSK = Differential phase shift keying FSK = Frequency shift keying
ECT = Echo cancellation technique   QAM = Quadrature amplitude modulation

second." The half-duplex modems are able to achieve their speeds by transmitting in one direction at a time, using the entire bandwidth of the connection (except for a tiny reverse channel used for line-turnaround handshaking).

You needn't be concerned with the particulars of modulation technique or frequency assignment, but you should be aware that the two modems must match in these respects (the VA 3400 and Bell 212 entries look the same in the table, but are still incompatible). Most modems of recent vintage attempt to support two, three, or more of the protocols listed in the table, often by automatically recognizing the behavior of the modem on the other end of the connection. These techniques are fraught with pitfalls, especially when the connection crosses an international boundary.

Figure 4-13 shows a modem connection between a terminal (or a PC) and a computer. Your terminal and modem tell each other they are "on line" via the DTR and DSR signals, respectively. Your modem will not operate unless it sees the DTR signal, and your terminal might not be willing to communicate with the modem unless it receives the DSR signal. When the call is placed, the remote modem will notice that the phone is ringing, and it will send the RI (Ring Indicate) signal to the computer. If the computer is up, it will respond by bringing up DTR on its end, and then the remote modem will answer the phone and produce a carrier tone on the phone line.

When your local modem detects the carrier tone, it turns on its CD (Carrier Detect) signal, which tells your terminal that the data connection is made, and sends its own carrier signal back to the remote modem. At this point, you can log in and conduct a session with the computer. When the remote computer wishes to terminate the session (e.g., because you logged out), it can turn off DTR, which tells its modem to stop transmitting the carrier tone, which tells your local modem to turn off CD, which tells your PC that the connection is broken.

If you turn off your terminal, your local modem will notice that DTR has gone Off and will stop transmitting carrier; the remote modem will turn off CD so that the remote computer can dispose of your job and condition the modem for receiving another call. If your terminal is really a PC, your communication software can use this trick to "hang up" the phone.

Just as a connection between two DTEs can be full- or half-duplex, so can the DTE/DCE connection. While most modems allow full-duplex operation through a technique like frequency division multiplexing, some, like Bell 201 modems, require the entire bandwidth of the phone circuit in order to communicate at their rated speed. Even those modems that are capable of full-duplex operation may have a switch to put them in half-duplex mode. When a modem is half-duplex, it requires the exchange of additional signals with the DTE. When the DTE wants to transmit, it must raise RTS (turn it On). If the modem senses that the communication line is not in use, then it raises CTS and puts itself into transmit mode. The DTE is then free to transmit. When transmission is done, the DTE lowers RTS, and the modem puts itself in receive mode. Sometimes a similar sort of ritual is done on full-duplex connections. It all depends on the particular modems, computers, and software.

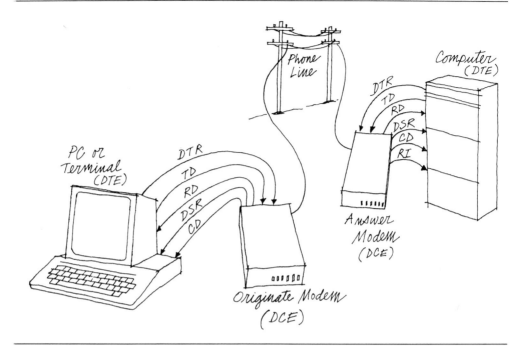

Figure 4-13. A Data Connection with Modems

Internal and External Modems

Now that we have an idea of how modems work, let's talk about some considerations in selecting and using them.

An internal modem is one that plugs directly into a "slot" in the "backplane" or "motherboard" of your microcomputer. Internal modems come as standard or optional equipment from the manufacturers of certain microcomputers, or they can be purchased for certain popular microcomputers (like the Apple II or the IBM PC) from independent sources. An internal modem connects directly to your telephone line via an RJ-type modular phone jack.

An external modem is one that is connected to your computer's serial port with an RS-232 connector. It may connect to the phone line with a jack, or it may have an acoustic coupler—a pair of rubber cups for your phone receiver's earpiece and mouth-piece.

Each type has its advantages and drawbacks. The primary advantage of an internal modem is price. It's cheaper than an external modem because it does not require the packaging or power supply, or a separate RS-232 port. Also, it doesn't take up any desk space, but then neither do external modems that fit under the phone. Its drawbacks, however, are worth considering:

1. It takes up a valuable slot in the PC.

2. It can be used only on the type of PC it's designed for.

3. It is not easily moved from one computer to another.

4. It probably requires special software to control it.

The last point is particularly important, and we'll be returning to it later.

Feature for feature, an external modem is more expensive than an internal modem, and it may (or may not) occupy valuable space on your desk. But it has the following advantages:

1. It does not take up a slot in your PC.

2. It can be used with any PC that has a serial port.

3. It is easily portable.

4. It is transparent to most software.

5. When the software and the modem do not agree about RS-232 modem signals, the cable can be rewired to compensate.

The point about transparency applies at the basic input/output level. If it's a "smart" modem, it may still need special software to exercise its "intelligence." But this is true of internal modems too. A final point worth noting about external modems is that some of them come equipped with an array of status lights and perhaps a speaker. These allow you to monitor the progress of your connection conveniently. Typically, there will be at least a carrier light. Many also have receive and transmit data lights, and other lights that show answer/originate mode, high/low speed, even DTR and DSR. The speaker allows you to hear the dial tone, ring, busy signal, carrier, and the modulated data.

Smart versus Dumb Modems

Until recently, all modems were "dumb"; they did only modulation and demodulation, and took care of the modem signals. And really, this is all a modem needs to do. The data is transmitted, and the modem signals provide the out-of-band control information that allows computers and phones to cooperate with a minimum of manual intervention. The one place where a person had to step in was in the initial establishment of the connection—the dialing, and the switching of the modem to data mode.

Many modern modems are designed to automate these chores. They include not only the required communication circuitry, but also a little computer that is capable of carrying on a dialog with its user through the terminal or PC. The most common method used is the one developed by Hayes for its Smartmodem series [14]. The Hayes modem has a command language built into it, which allows you to dial a number, redial the number, set various parameters, and so on, simply by sending it commands in the form of ASCII characters. It responds to dialing commands with result codes that tell you whether the operation was completed successfully. For instance, to dial the number 765-4321, you would issue the command "ATD7654321" (followed by a carriage return). The modem places the call, and then returns a code like 1 (connected), 3 (no carrier), 6 (no dial tone), 7 (busy), or 8 (no answer). It may also return the words themselves, depending on some switch or mode settings. Most manufacturers of smart modems use the Hayes command language, but some do not. The language is actually quite complex; the manual is more than 40 pages long. Therefore, there is usually a program that mediates between the user and the modem, presenting the user with command menus and interpreting the result codes. If you have a PC, you can use such a program (or write one yourself). If you have a terminal, you must deal with the modem's command language and result codes yourself.

The problem with smart modems is that data destined for the remote computer must pass through the same channel that is used for commands to the modem. What happens when the data stream contains a sequence of characters that happens to correspond with a valid modem command? The answer to this question varies from modem to modem, but in general it depends upon what "mode" the modem is in, command or connect. Some modems are always listening for commands, no matter what. Others have ways (manual or automatic) to be put into transparent mode. The Hayes, for instance, enters transparent mode automatically when remote carrier is detected, but then it provides an "escape" mechanism to get back into command mode—three plus signs in a row (+++), with at least a full second of "silence" before and after.

None of this would concern us if we only intended to be interactive terminal users of the remote computer. If we happened to put the modem into command mode by mistake, we'd notice right away. But when a file is being transferred through the modem under program control, watch out! My favorite story about this concerns a professor who had enjoyed great success with a certain file transfer program (Kermit, in fact) until he tried to use it on a certain longish file. Every time he tried to send the file, the transfer would fail in the same place. Eventually, he gave up and found some other way to transfer it. Some weeks later, he was astonished to find that his phone bill included charges for several calls to Tasmania. It turned out, of course, that he was using an autodial modem that did not have a transparent mode—or at least, not a very good one—and his file contained just the right sequence of characters to instruct the modem to place the call. He has since changed modems.

WELCOME
TO
TASMANIA

A
Kumquat
Bird

Digital Phone Service

AT&T and other carriers are gradually converting the telephone system from analog to digital signalling. At some time in the future, it may be possible to make dialup data connections without modems, perhaps at speeds up to 56 kilobaud. This is possible even now within organizations that have their own digital phone systems. But note that most current terminals, PCs, and mainframes cannot handle speeds beyond 9600 or 19200 baud—their UARTs simply don't go that fast. Most likely, a new generation of chips based on RS-422 will begin to take over. Let's hope these will be "upward compatible" from the current equipment, so that most software will continue to work. It will be interesting to see how software performs that was designed under the assumption that input/output speed was the limiting factor.

Other Communication Equipment

Besides modems, there are myriad devices that can situate themselves between your terminal or PC and a remote computer. Some of them are completely transparent and need not concern you at all, for instance, microwave or fiber optic equipment that might be used to extend the local terminal network.

Other communication devices—multiplexers, port contention units, network terminal servers, front ends—might not be wholly transparent. They can pose the same kind of problems that smart modems do, and they might also cause trouble of a more subtle nature.

The most common problem is *opacity*, in which some piece of equipment, somewhere along the communication path, has two modes of operation—transparent and conversational. It flips from transparent to conversational mode when it sees a certain "sacred character." In some cases, it will allow one copy of the sacred character to pass through if it gets two in a row. This means that any software that wishes to transmit that character must know to double it. Since there may be many such devices, with many different sacred characters, a general solution to the problem is not easily found.

Speaking of sacred characters, it is interesting to note that if you have two boxes in the path, each having the same sacred character, then you must transmit four in order to get one through to the remote host. Why? The first box swallows one of each pair, passing on the remaining two to the second box, which swallows one and passes the last survivor on to the host. What if there are three boxes? Then you must transmit six, right? Wrong—eight (figure it out). In fact, to transmit one copy of a sacred character through n such boxes, you have to send 2^n copies of the character—that's 1024 copies for only ten boxes!

But opacity can get even worse; we should be grateful to those boxes that allow us to get sacred characters through them at all, no matter how many times they make us type them. We should say that these boxes are semi-opaque, because there are also *fully* opaque boxes that do not let certain characters or sequences through them at all. These special sequences might be understood by the box as commands, for instance, to turn echoing off and on, to switch to another system. The only way to send data through such boxes is to make sure the data does not contain any of these sequences.

Boxes of varying degrees of opacity sometimes allow themselves to be put into "transparent mode" by means of a command in the data stream. This is the preferred way to transmit arbitrary data through them. But once in transparent mode, a box will no longer be able to respond to commands in the data stream, and there will often be no way to restore its previous level of opacity.

And there may be a few more surprises:

A Banana Bird

- Communication boxes often want to do their own flow control. XON/XOFF seemed simple (?) when only two directly connected computers were involved. Imagine what can happen when an intermediate box also wants to do flow control. Or when your computer doesn't want to, but the box does—for instance, when your computer wants to send the XOFF character as data to the remote computer, through the box.

- Some communication boxes (particularly those called statistical multiplexers) try to squeeze extra "thoughput" out of the communication line by allocating a bigger chunk of bandwidth in one direction than the other, assuming a low ratio of terminal typein to computer typeout. This is fine until someone connects a PC and tries to transfer a file *to* the computer.

- Boxes, like multiplexers, terminal servers, line drivers, and so forth, might also find it amusing to play with modem signals—particularly RTS, CTS, DTR, and DSR—and your terminal or PC may not be set up to handle them in the required way. Fortunately, you can often outsmart such boxes by fiddling with the wires in your end of the cable (see page 102).

- Another common problem with communication boxes is *parity*. Communication front ends, multiplexers, and public network access nodes may impose parity on the communication line. In some cases, they demand that the communicating devices only transmit characters with the desired parity; in others they surreptitiously apply the parity themselves and deliver the data to the intended recipient in its new form.

Public Data Networks

Public data networks (PDNs) like Telenet and Tymnet are subscription services that allow you to establish dialup data connections to distant computers with only a local phone call to the nearest access point, called a node or PAD (Packet Assembler/Disassembler). PDNs have their own "backbone" communications subnetwork, a finite resource consisting of trunk lines and satellite links, which all their subscribers share. Some subscribers (hosts) are providers of services and others are users. The network can have a very complicated topology (layout), with each PAD typically connected to at least two other PADs, making for many different paths through the network from one PAD to another.

The PAD breaks your data up into packets, much like Kermit packets, sending each one in the general direction of the PAD that serves the host you have selected. Intermediate PADs forward your packets along whatever route seems best at the moment. Each packet may travel a different route, and packets may arrive at their destination out of order. The destination PAD checks incoming packets for errors, requests retransmission if necessary, shuffles the good packets back into the right order, decodes them, and feeds a reliable stream of data to the host computer. Messages from the host to your PAD receive the same treatment.

The responsiveness of a packet-switched network depends on the distance a packet must travel, the number of routing switches it must make, and the load on each of the devices through which your packets must travel. It is possible for long delays to occur. When timing is critical, these delays must be accounted for.

The two PADs work together very much like two Kermit programs, but with added complications from the need to route packets through a complex network, while handling multiple simultaneous sessions, and serving as intermediate routing nodes for other PADs. The set of interconnected PADs, and the hosts they connect, is called a packet switched network (PSN). The detailed operation of most public PSNs conforms to CCITT Recommendation X.25 [32]. Such networks include Telenet, Tymnet, Uninet, Datapac, Transpac, and Cisipac.

Your local PAD is a kind of timesharing computer. You dial it up as you would any ordinary timesharing system, and the connection between your PC and the PAD can have the same problems as any dialup connection—noise, gaps in transmission, buffer overflows, etc.[7] After identifying yourself (if required), you request the PAD to connect you to the desired host. The connection is more or less transparent except for an escape character or sequence that allows you to get back to the PAD. The escape sequence for Telenet is <CR>@<CR>; for Tymnet, a single Control-P.

---

7. Some networks have attempted to remedy the situation by moving a good chunk of the X.25 protocol to the PC itself. Most notable among these efforts is Tymnet's X.PC effort, whose intention is to provide multiple reliable data streams between the PC and one or more hosts on the network. At this writing, these efforts are still in their early stages.

Because PCs and terminals can have different styles of communication, the PAD allows you to change selected parameters to suit your needs. These parameters are defined in CCITT Recommendation X.3 [31], and a command language for setting and querying them is given in CCITT Recommendation X.28 [33].

When you establish your connection to the host, the host's PAD automatically sets certain parameters in your local PAD. For instance, if the host is half-duplex, it might request that your PAD echo the characters you type in. You may use local PAD commands to inspect and override these settings and defaults. The normal syntax is

PAR? *p,p,p, . . .*

to inspect settings, and

SET? *p:v,p:v,p:v, . . .*

to change them, where *p* is a parameter number and *v* is a parameter value.

Twelve parameters are covered by X.3. They are shown in Table 4-4. Six additional parameters are not covered by X.3, but are widely accepted. Parameter 13 controls linefeed insertion after carriage return (0 = no linefeed insertion, 1–7 specify various insertion options). Parameter 14 selects the amount of padding to be inserted after a linefeed (0–7 pad characters). Parameter 15 controls whether the PAD is to provide local line editing (0 means no, 1 means yes), and 16–18 specify the ASCII values of the characters to be used for editing, when selected: the character delete character, the buffer delete character, and the line redisplay character, respectively.

In addition to the standard parameters, most PDNs provide a selection of private parameters. In a SET? or PAR? command, a list of private parameters is introduced by a parameter with a special number, like 0. For instance, in the command

SET? 5:1,12:1,0:33,39:0

39 is a Telenet private parameter. You will have to consult your PAD manual for a list of private parameters, since these are different for each network.

Parameters 1–15 give you some of the tools you need to configure a PAD for file transfer; Table 4-5 shows the preferred settings for these parameters. Parameter 1 is set to disable the PAD's recognition of its escape sequence in case it occurs as data within a packet. If you know that it cannot occur as data within a packet (for instance, <CR>@<CR> will never occur within a Kermit packet), then you should not change Parameter 1, because once you disable the escape mechanism, the only way to get the PAD's attention again is to hang up and redial. Parameter 3 is set to make a file transfer packet coincide with a network packet. This maximizes throughput, and it minimizes expense on networks where billing is per packet. You will probably want to change this parameter back to its original value if you return to use the host interactively.

Table 4-4. X.3 PAD Parameters

Parameter Reference Number	Parameter Function	Valid Parameter Values	What It Does
1	Escape from data transfer state	0	Escape not possible
		1	Escape possible
2	Echo control	0	PAD will not echo
		1	PAD will echo
3	Data forwarding characters	0	None
		1	A–Z, a–z, 0–9
		2	CR (others omitted)
4	Data forwarding timeout	0	None
		1–255	n/20 seconds
5	Flow control by PAD	0	None
		1	XON/XOFF
6	Suppression of PAD service signals	0	Suppression on
		1	Suppression off
7	Action on BREAK	0	No action
		1	Send interrupt packet (others omitted)
8	Suppression of data delivery to terminal	0	Data delivered
		1	Data discarded
9	Padding after CR	0	No padding except on PAD generated FEs
		1–7	1–7 character times
10	Line folding	0	No line folding
		1–255	Line folding after 1–255 characters
11	Terminal speed (read-only)	0–18	Code for baud rate (list omitted)
12	Flow control by terminal	0	Flow control off
		1	Flow control on

Table 4-5. Preferred X.3 Parameters for File Transfer

Parameter Reference Number	Parameter Function	Preferred Value	Reason
1	Escape sequence	0 = Disabled	The escape sequence might occur in the data.
2	Echo	0 = Off	Packets shouldn't echo.
3	Data forwarding characters	2 = CR	CR is a typical packet terminator.
4	Data forwarding timeout	0 = None	Let the file transfer programs do this.
5	Flow control by PAD	0 or 1	Depends on your PC.
6	Suppress PAD service signals	0 = Suppress	Messages would interfere with packets.
7	Action on BREAK	(n/a)	Applies to interactive terminal mode only.
8	Suppress data	0 = Don't	(Used with 7.)
9	Pad after CR	0 = Don't	Let file transfer programs control this.
10	Line folding	0 = Don't	Interferes with packets.
11	Terminal speed	(n/a)	
12	Flow control by terminal	0 or 1	Depends on PC.
13	Linefeed insertion	0 = Don't	Only slows things down.
14	Linefeed padding	0 = None	Only slows things down.
15	Line editing	0 = Disabled	To prevent alteration of packets.

While the settings in Table 4-5 may be necessary for file transfer to occur, they are probably not sufficient. The file transfer programs themselves will have to cope with several problems not covered by the X.3 parameters:

• **Buffer Overruns:** The PAD may have a small input buffer, perhaps smaller than the length of a file transfer packet. If this is the case, you will experience problems with file transfers from the PC to the remote host. If your PC is capable of XON/XOFF flow control, then this should be used, and selected at the PAD via parameters 5 and 12, provided the flow control characters XON (Control-Q) and XOFF (Control-S) do not occur as characters within the packets (they are not used in Kermit packets). If XON/XOFF can't be used, the file transfer program will have to send shorter packets.

- **Delays:** Network delays may strain the file transfer program's assumptions about how long it should wait for a packet. The timeout interval may have to be increased. In any case, the use of a stop-and-wait file transfer protocol over a network with built-in delays will result in very poor performance. Performance can be improved by using longer packets, or by using a sliding window technique.

- **Parity:** There is no X.3 parameter that lets you control parity. This is a serious problem because many PDNs (Telenet, for example) use parity by default, and provide no way— not even a private parameter—for the user to disable it. Some networks, however, allow the host to disable parity. The host-to-PAD interface is defined by CCITT recommendation X.29 [34], and it is entirely different from the X.28 user-to-PAD command language. When the host has not disabled parity for you, communication of 8-bit data becomes problematical. In particular, a file transfer protocol (like Kermit) must do something special to get 8-bit data through the 7-bit channel that is provided.

Kermit has commands and features for coping with these problems. These are presented in Chapter 5, "Kermit Command Reference."

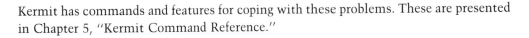

Cables and Connectors Revisited

In data communication, the most severe problems sometimes have the easiest solutions. And what data communication problem could be more severe than total failure to communicate? The solution is often as simple as reinserting a plug that wiggled loose, or changing a baud rate. When these quick remedies fail, the trouble is often in the cable and connector wiring. This section covers diagnosis and treatment of wiring problems.

Remember that a straight-through, no-nonsense cable is used to connect a DTE (computer or terminal) to a DCE (modem or multiplexer). If you are using such a straight-through cable to connect a computer to a modem, but you're getting no results, then your cable probably does not have enough wires. Cables for asynchronous DTE-DCE communication should have 10 wires, connecting each of the following pins from one connector to the other: 1, 2, 3, 4, 5, 6, 7, 8, 20, and 22. You can test the continuity of each of these wires in your cable, using a little tester made from a flashlight bulb, a battery, and a couple of pieces of wire, stuck together with tape or gum (or solder, if you're a technical type). If your cable is correct, then you probably have a hardware problem with your PC or modem, or a software problem (see "Common Problems and How To Fix Them," page 172).

If you try to use a straight-through modem cable to connect a DTE to another DTE, or a DCE to a DCE, you'll find right away that no data gets through. This is because each side is transmitting to the other's transmitter, and the receivers aren't receiving anything. The solution, you may recall, is a null modem cable. But there's more to making a null modem cable than just swapping the transmit and receive leads. Other signals must be accounted for too, in ways that vary depending on the particular systems involved: there is no standard null modem cable. Building your own from an existing cable is sometimes necessary.

Before you start taking connectors apart, you should try to lay your hands on a "breakout box." This handy device lets you experiment with connector signals quite painlessly by moving little jumper cables around between pins that correspond to the various RS-232 signals. They also have lights to show when current is flowing on each of the 25 circuits, and switches to break or complete each circuit. You can buy a breakout box from a computer supply house for about $100. Supply houses also carry other useful items:

- "Gender menders" are two-faced connectors that allow you to change the gender of a connector. A male-male model changes a female connector to a male, and vice versa.

- Modem eliminators are two-faced connectors that let you to convert a straight-through cable to a null modem cable (or vice versa). They come in any combination of genders, and can also be used in conjunction with gender menders.

- Loopback connectors allow you to use Kermit or other communication software to test whether data is actually getting out the serial port, by echoing it right back to you. They can be inserted at any place along the communication path where you would put an RS-232 connector.

- Line monitors allow you to actually watch two-way traffic on the communication line in character form on a display screen. These tend to be quite expensive, but their cost is easily justified in any organization where data communication is important.

If you don't want to tinker with breakout boxes or the insides of connectors, you can go to your local computer store and explain your problem. But don't buy anything unless they agree to let you return it.

Here is your bag of tricks for making a null modem cable. Only trial and error will determine the right combination. Consult Figure 4-14 for terminology and orientation. Begin by removing the hood from your connector (Figure 4-15). Observe which signals are connected. Some connectors have tiny pin numbers embossed near each hole, or at the corners. If yours lacks these labels, then orient your connector according to the figure. The connector pictured is a male. A female has its holes in the opposite order.

Pin 1 (Protective Ground) is connected straight through in all cases, and so is pin 7 (Signal Ground). The two devices on either end of the data cable should always have a common electrical ground. All pin numbers refer to the RS-232-C 25-pin connector assignments (explained on page 80), but a couple of examples are given afterward for 9-pin connectors. No more than ten wires should ever be necessary. It is assumed that you already have two connectors of the right shape and gender.

1. Exchange Receive and Transmit. It will always be necessary to swap TD (pin 2) and RD (pin 3) in *one* connector (not both).

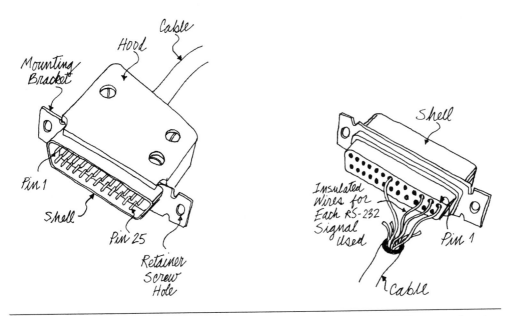

Figure 4-14. DB-25 Connector Exterior   Figure 4-15. DB-25 Connector Interior

2. Exchange CTS and RTS. If the two computers raise RTS (pin 4) when they wish to transmit data, and wait for CTS (pin 5) from the modem before actually transmitting it (this scheme allows half-duplex modems to turn the line around), you can cross-connect their RTS and CTS signals to enable full-duplex transmission as in Model A (the "official" null modem) in Figure 4-16.

3. Jumper RTS to CTS. If the local system uses RTS/CTS and the remote system doesn't, you can have the local automatically grant itself permission to send by simply feeding its own RTS output signal into its CTS input. This is done with a "jumper" within the local connector—a short wire connecting the two pins directly (a section of paper clip sometimes suffices).[8] This technique is commonly called a fakeout, and it may be used in the local connector whenever you're sure the remote system doesn't care about RTS/CTS handshaking.

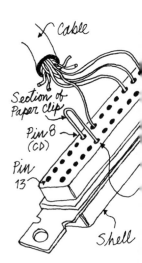

4. Connect Jumpered Local DSR,CD to Remote DTR. If the local communication software believes it's talking to a modem, it might require the modem to be on line (DSR, pin 6) and detecting carrier (CD, pin 8). If you trust the remote system to keep its DTR (pin 20) signal up as long as the system itself is up, you should feed the remote system's

---

8. Use of the paper clip is illustrated in the margin. The paper clip is about the same thickness as an RS-232 connector pin, and generally provides sufficient conductivity. But watch out —it's not insulated, and care must be taken not to cause undesired shorts. Don't close your connector with a paper clip inside; make a proper connection with insulated wire.

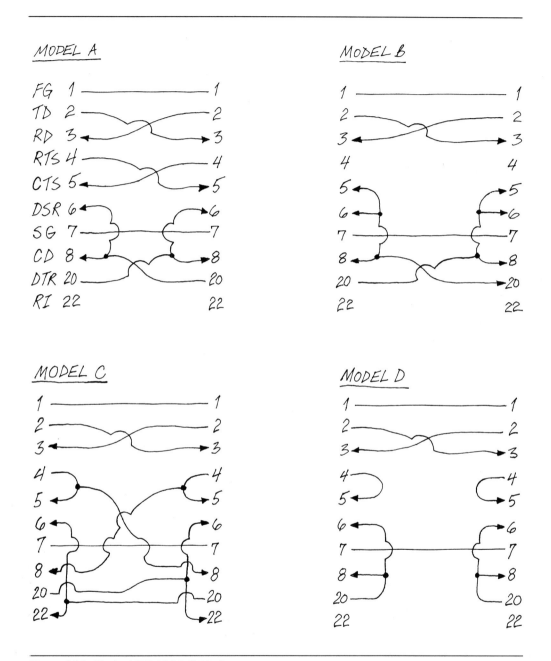

Figure 4-16. Typical DB-25 Null Modems

DTR signal into both DSR and CD on the local connector. This provides the required modem simulation and also allows the local computer to detect when the remote one is turned off or crashes. The same technique applies at the other end (just switch "local" and "remote" in the preceding sentences).

5. Connect Jumpered Local DSR,CD,CTS to Remote DTR. If Trick 4 doesn't work, then maybe you also need Clear to Send (pin 5) to be on.

6. Jumper Local DSR, CD, and DTR. Similar to Trick 4, and perhaps more popular. Keeps the connection open even if remote DTR drops. Use this trick if you don't trust the other system's DTR, or if you don't have enough wires in your cable. This technique is used in Model D in the figure—the quintessential fakeout cable.

7. Connect Local DTR to Remote RI. This will be necessary if the remote system wants to be called up before it will talk to you. It might also prove necessary to jumper the remote's Ring Indicator (pin 22) to its Data Set Ready (pin 6), if you don't already have that turned on some other way.

Figure 4-16 shows several sample null modem configurations, types that are commonly carried by computer supply houses. Model A is a "real" null modem, for use between two systems that fully honor DTE/DCE signalling conventions. Models B and C are variations on Model A, in which each computer still signals the other in some way, using DTR or RTS (or both). Model D is the other extreme, in which all modem signals are faked by jumpers within the local connector, and only real data is transmitted between the two computers. These examples are all symmetrical, but that need not always be the case. The system on one end may require certain signals which the other system can do without.

By the way, you can take one of the connectors from Model D and turn it into a loopback connector by jumpering pin 2 to pin 3, and pin 1 to pin 7.

Figure 4-17 shows a sample null modem cable for the Macintosh, with a 9-pin connector on the Mac side and a DB-25 on the other, possibly suitable for connecting to a PC's serial port (no guarantees!).

Figure 4-18 shows a sample modem (not null modem) cable for the PC/AT, which uses a 9-pin D-connector on its RS-232 port. This example illustrates not only the pin assignments but also how simple things are when you connect a DTE to a DCE the way you're "supposed to." Conversion to a null modem is left as an exercise for the reader.

One final word of caution: don't assume you can connect lots of cables together and come up with a working connection, even though each cable may work independently. This situation commonly arises when an ad hoc connection between two PCs is suddenly required. A cable of the required length with the appropriate connectors on each end can rarely be found. The typical approach is to round up a pile of shorter cables, most of them unmarked as to their internal connections, and form a long "data extension cord." This never works the first time, usually because an even number (possibly

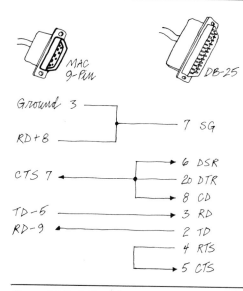

Figure 4-17. A Sample Macintosh Null Modem

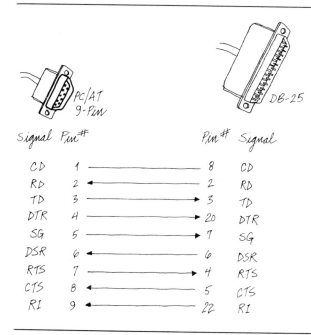

Figure 4-18. A Sample PC/AT Modem Cable

0) of null modem cables has been included, each cancelling the effect of the other. Adding or removing one null modem cable might be all that's required to get the data flowing. If not, then the cable is probably not carrying the required modem signals (DTR, DSR, etc.) through from one end to the other, perhaps because some of the cables have fewer wires than others. In that case, the appropriate fakeouts are required in the connectors at each end.

The IBM World

The International Business Machines Corporation deserves its own special section in our data communication primer because IBM is the leading manufacturer of mainframes *and* of PCs, because IBM "sets its own standards," and because IBM mainframe communication causes more problems and raises more questions among Kermit users than any other area touched by Kermit.

While most computer systems are full-duplex, IBM mainframes are half-duplex; most computers use ASCII, IBM prefers EBCDIC; most user-host interaction is character-at-time, IBM terminals are block mode; most terminal-host cabling is RS-232, IBM prefers coaxial cable. The list goes on. For many years, IBM equipment was designed to be used solely with other IBM equipment.

IBM has a variety of product lines, from large System/370 and XA mainframes, through several lines of minicomputers, office systems, and word processors, to the IBM PC family. IBM also manufactures a wide range of communication equipment, from modems to front ends to networks. The IBM PC family represents a radical departure from IBM's traditional philosophy. These are "open" systems whose architecture encourages interconnection with other manufacturers' equipment. Communication is asynchronous, serial, full-duplex, and ASCII. There is nothing special about these machines, at least from the standpoint of data communication, so we need dwell on them no further.

The other IBM product lines are a different story. Each has its quirks; this section discusses the big 370-series mainframes. Other IBM products—the System/34, /36, /38, Displaywriter, etc.—present completely different communication environments that are just as complicated but, of course, totally different from the one described here, and probably also from each other.

The IBM 370 series of computers is the direct descendant of its 1960s-vintage 360 series. The 370s once had "names" like 370/148, 370/168, but some years ago the 370/*model* naming scheme was abandoned in favor of four-digit numbers for the newer models, like 3031, 3033, 4341, 4361, 3081, 8083. These models are still 370s inside, with the same instruction set and basic architecture. In general, any program that runs on any 370-series machine will run on any other (with the exception that programs using "extended addressing" will not run on machines that don't support it).

Over the years, a number of operating systems have appeared for the 370. First, there is the successor to OS/360—MVS (Multiple Virtual Storage). Like OS/360, it is a "batch" system, not a timesharing system. However, it allows a selection of conversational subsystems to be run as batch jobs. These have names like TSO (Time Sharing Option) and CICS (Customer Information Control System). Another 370 operating system is called DOS/VSE, but it has fallen into relative disuse as a primary operating system. Several universities have developed their own operating systems for 370s, including MUSIC (McGill University System for Interactive Computing), MTS (Michigan Time-sharing System), and GUTS (Gothenburg University Timesharing System, actually an MVS subsystem).

The other major 370 operating system is called VM/370 (Virtual Machine/370). Unlike MVS, VM is a timesharing system; the user's normal access is through an interactive program such as CMS (Conversational Monitor System). VM provides each user with the image of a dedicated machine, with an operator console, dedicated disk and tape drives, and so on. The image is so complete that the user can even run other operating systems, such as MVS, DOS/VSE, or OS/VS1, as "guests" under VM.

IBM prefers to configure its mainframes with its own EBCDIC 3270-series block-mode full-screen terminals, which transfer entire screens of data at a time rather than single characters, with provisions for transmitting only selected fields from the screen, e.g., those that changed since the last transmission. Up to 32 of these block-mode terminals are connected by coaxial cable to model 3274 "cluster controllers," which in turn connect to the mainframe either directly or through a communications front end. This arrangement is shown in Figure 4-19. Many IBM mainframe applications are inherently full-screen and will only work in conjunction with 3270-series terminals.

Despite IBM's preference for 3270-style communication, users of IBM mainframes have a legitimate need to access the mainframes with their existing ASCII asynchronous equipment—terminals and computers (some of them of IBM manufacture). Two major approaches have evolved: front ends and protocol converters.

The 3705 Front End

The IBM communication front end that provides asynchronous communication is the 3705 (a newer model is called the 3725, and 3705 equivalents are available from other manufacturers). It is really intended less as a front end for asynchronous ASCII terminals than as a connection point for remote 3274 cluster controllers, remote job entry (RJE) stations, unit record equipment (card readers and line printers), and so forth. The 3705 provides half-duplex line-at-a-time ASCII service, but does not permit the use of full-screen applications. Thus IBM mainframe application programs must include explicit support for either line-mode 3705 communication, full-screen 3270 operation, or both. Line-mode 3705 communication is sometimes called TTY mode, or TWX mode, because it was originally intended for use with Teletype machines (TTY is an abbreviation of Teletype, and TWX stands for Teletypewriter Exchange).

The IBM mainframe operating system includes a device driver (or, in IBM parlance, an access method) for 3705-attached asynchronous ASCII devices. Its functions include device control, buffer management, and ASCII/EBCDIC translation. We've already dis-

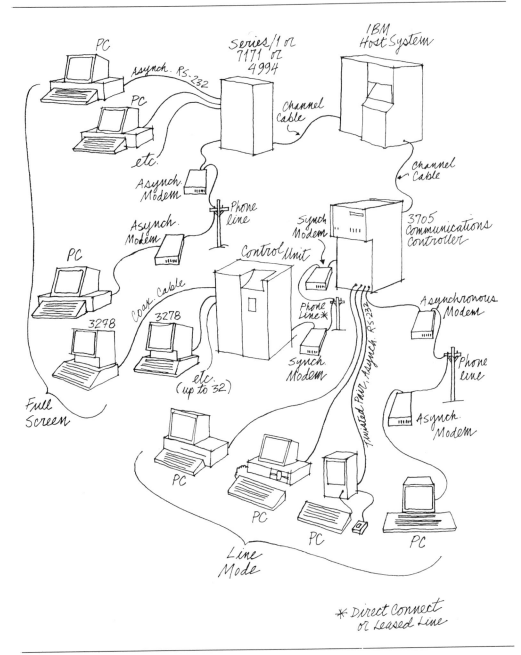

Figure 4-19. IBM Mainframe Communication Environment

cussed the problems of ASCII/EBCDIC translation, but let's review them briefly. There is no formal standard ASCII/EBCDIC translation. The closest we have is the table given in the System/370 Reference Summary [29]. For purposes of file transfer, any translation between the two must be "invertible," but because there are twice as many characters in EBCDIC as in ASCII there can be no invertible translation from EBCDIC to ASCII and back. The IBM table, however, *is* invertible from the ASCII standpoint. Unfortunately, many (perhaps most) IBM mainframe sites alter their system's "standard" translate table, which at least destroys any assumptions that file transfer software might make about it, and at worst results in an ambiguous (noninvertible) table.

In MVS, the access methods for TTYs are TCAM (Telecommunications Access Method) and VTAM (Virtual Telecommunications Access Method, which also handles SNA—IBM Systems Network Architecture—"network virtual terminals"). VM handles the console specially with an internal console driver that is similar in function to TCAM, but it allows external TTY devices to be controlled directly by user-selected software (e.g., by VTAM running in MVS under VM). The VM TTY console driver has a peculiar quirk: it provides no facility to time out a read request already in progress. This makes it difficult to write programs that provide unattended file transfer.

We've said that the 3705's asynchronous terminal service is record-oriented. This means that it provides the mainframe with input from the terminal only when one of a predetermined set of terminator characters is encountered in the input stream. The common terminators are Control-M (carriage return, CR), Control-D (EOT), Control-E (ENQ), Control-F (ACK), Control-Q (DC1 or XON), and Control-S (DC3 or XOFF). The table of terminators is kept within the 3705 in 8-bit format, where it cannot be (easily) altered. Perversely, the 8-bit terminator values include a parity bit, typically mark, odd, or even. This means that if the terminating carriage return of an incoming line does not have the right parity, the front end won't recognize the terminator, and it won't pass the line on to the mainframe. In this case, parity is not being used to detect errors; it is purely an obstruction.

We've also said that IBM line-mode TTY service is half-duplex. This is because an IBM mainframe can have only one command (read or write) active on a device at a given time. Before a user application issues a read request to TCAM or VM, it allocates a buffer that it believes will be big enough to hold the largest possible input, then it transmits the handshake character to indicate it is ready to read, and then it issues a read request to the 3705, indicating the location of the buffer. This request completes only when a terminator is recognized by the 3705. Upon completion, the mainframe may issue a write request or another read request. If the TTY device transmits while a write operation is in progress, or at any time when a read request is not active, the data will be discarded by the 3705. (The only exception occurs when the TTY sends a BREAK signal to interrupt the write.)

As a consequence of all this the system cannot echo characters as it receives them. Thus it becomes the responsibility of the local device to provide any desired echoing. Typeahead cannot be accommodated, nor can any other kind of bidirectional data transfer. Now you should understand why the following communication parameters must be used when communicating through IBM mainframes through 3705 and equivalent front ends:

• Parity (usually mark, odd, or even)

• Half-duplex with XON (or equivalent) handshake

• Local echo

• No full-duplex flow control

• Timeouts, when necessary, must be done by the TTY device

Protocol Converters

The other way to connect asynchronous ASCII devices to IBM mainframes is to disguise them as 3270s. This approach has many advantages, not least among them that it allows ASCII terminals access to the full-screen applications that would otherwise be denied. The deception is accomplished by means of a "protocol converter," situated somewhere between the ASCII device and the user application on the IBM mainframe.

In its most common form (a box external to both systems) the protocol converter takes the IBM channel cable in one side and an RS-232 connector in the other. It translates between ASCII and EBCDIC, and it translates the mainframe's 3270 screen-formatting directives into ASCII screen control sequences appropriate to the ASCII terminal or PC, and it translates the ASCII terminal's function key codes into 3270 PF-key codes. There is no particular reason why the link between the protocol converter and the ASCII device need be half-duplex, and in many cases it is indeed full-duplex, complete with XON/XOFF flow control and typeahead.

Some protocol converters attempt to optimize throughput by transmitting to the ASCII device only those characters or fields that have changed since last time. For example, suppose the screen has the word KERMIT in the upper left corner, and the IBM system wishes to overwrite it with the word GARMENT. The protocol converter might "home the cursor," write the letters GA, then issue a command to position the cursor two spaces forward, and then write the letters ENT. The computer believes it has transmitted the word GARMENT but the device receives GA<xxx>ENT, where <xxx> is the cursor command. The result on your screen will be correct, but if you were trying to capture the transmitted information into a file, you'd have a rude surprise in store.

If all protocol converters behaved the same way, it would be possible to write (very complicated) communication programs that accounted for this behavior. But, of course, each manufacturer's product is different, and probably each version of a single manufacturer's product behaves differently from the other versions. In any case, there is not necessarily a way for a program on either the mainframe or an ASCII PC to determine what, if any, protocol converter is being used and what its characteristics are.

The protocol converter is an extreme example of an opaque box. You can hope to transfer files through it only if you have the ability to turn off all of its format conversion functions. Some protocol converters allow you to do this, and some don't. Those that do no doubt do so in different ways. The prospects for file transfer are therefore bleak, but not hopeless.

The most widely understood protocol converter (at least by Kermit programmers) is the IBM Series/1 minicomputer running the Yale ASCII Communications System. Equivalent IBM products have names like 7171 and 4994. These systems provide a relatively straightforward way for a program to take them into and out of transparent mode so that files may be transferred through them with little difficulty, except for the usual complications with buffering, flow control, parity, format conversion, etc., which are not insurmountable.

Data Communication Parameters of Selected Systems

Table 4-6 lists some data communication aspects of selected systems. Communication is based on RS-232-C and DB-25 connectors, with speeds ranging from 50 to 9600 baud, unless otherwise indicated. The information in the table is gathered from sundry sources, and should not be considered definitive, especially since some of these characteristics can change as new models, front ends, or operating system releases appear, and also because local changes are often made. The primary intention of the table is to convey a feeling for the variety that must be accounted for when we want data communication to occur. An asterisk (*) in the Flow Control column means that flow control is not necessarily supplied by the system but may be provided by communication software.

Table 4-6. Communication Characteristics of Selected Systems

System	Duplex	Flow Control	Required Parity	Remarks
Apple Macintosh	Full	*	None	9-pin RS-422, speeds to 56Kb
DEC-20/TOPS-20	Full	XON/XOFF	None	Small input buffer
DEC VAX, PDP-11	Full	XON/XOFF	None	
Honeywell DPS8/GCOS	Half	XON	None	"@" sacred
HP-1000 RTE-6/VM	Full	ENQ/ACK	None	
HP-3000 MPE	Half	XON	None	
IBM PC/AT	Full	*	None	9-pin RS-232, speeds to 38Kb
IBM 370 VM/CMS/3705	Half	XON	Mark	EBCDIC, big input buffer
IBM 370 VM/CMS/7171	Full	XON/XOFF	Even	ASCII, small input buffer
Prime/Primos	Full	XON/XOFF	Mark	"?" sacred
Sperry 1100/OS 1100	Full	XON/XOFF	Odd	Prefers block-mode polled i/o

*Depends on communication program

PART THREE

User Guide

5

Kermit Command Reference

From this point on, it is assumed that the computing and data communication terms covered previously can be used without elaboration. If you run across words you don't understand, consult the Index to find references to more detailed discussions.

The Kermit commands are grouped and described according to function—terminal emulation, file transfer, parameter setting, and so on—in the approximate order in which you need to know about them. An alphabetical command summary can be found in Appendix B.

Please remember that Kermit programs are written by volunteers who did not necessarily include every command listed here, and that some systems have special features or requirements resulting in additional system-dependent commands. The command descriptions given in this chapter are as general and complete as possible, but you should consult the documentation for your particular version of Kermit to find out if there are differences.

"This is an optional feature of the Kermit protocol, not supported in all Kermit programs." That's a phrase you will see repeated throughout this chapter. Why are so many features optional? Why aren't all Kermit programs the same? It's mainly because a program that includes all the features of the protocol is more than most volunteers have the inclination or time to tackle. Only the very basic sending and receiving operations are mandatory,[1] and the rest is optional. The protocol is designed to let any two Kermit programs tell each other what features they have, so that the most rudimentary implementation can still communicate with the most advanced, and the oldest with the latest. And then there are the myriad settings, options, and frills that are outside of the protocol, but which make a Kermit program more pleasant to use, or more adaptable to unusual settings. These are included or omitted at the discretion of the programmer.

Terminology and Syntax Review

Before proceeding, let's briefly review our terminology and notation. In most connections between two Kermit programs, one program is remote and the other is local. The remote Kermit is usually running on a mainframe, which you have connected to through a PC or other computer, which is local. When a Kermit program is remote, all file

---

1. And there may be exceptions even in these fundamental areas. One person, who wrote a Kermit program for an exceptionally cantankerous machine, elected to omit the SEND command because "the [name omitted] is so user-hostile, no one has developed software on it worth sending."

transfer is done over the job's controlling terminal line, its console, the same line on which you logged in, and to which you type interactive commands. What the remote system believes to be your terminal is really another computer, usually your local microcomputer, running its own copy of Kermit. During file transfer, the remote system is cut off from your keyboard and screen.

When a Kermit program is local, file transfer is done over an external device, other than the console, such as a microcomputer's serial communication port or an assigned terminal line on a mainframe. The local Kermit is connected in some way (like a dialout mechanism) to another computer. A local Kermit is in control of the screen; a remote Kermit has no direct access to it. Since the local Kermit can control the screen, the keyboard, and the port separately, it can update the screen during file transfer with status information, watch for interrupt signals from the keyboard, and transfer packets on the communications port, all at the same time. If the remote Kermit tried to do this, the status information would get mixed up with the packets, slowing down the file transfer and possibly interfering with it.

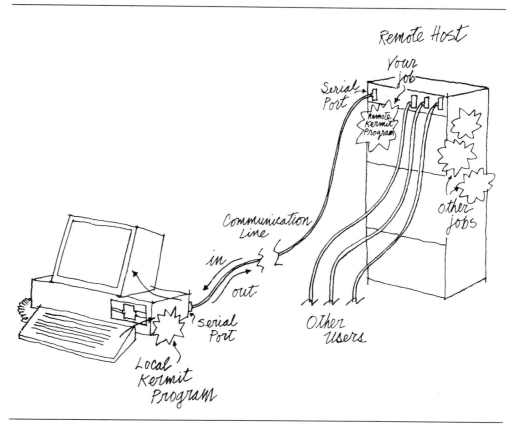

Figure 5-1. Local and Remote Kermit Programs

Microcomputer Kermit programs run in local mode unless instructed otherwise. Mainframe Kermits run in remote mode unless some special command places them in local mode. Some commands make sense only for remote Kermits, others only for local, but most can be used with either. Local and remote operation of Kermit is shown schematically in Figure 5-1.

The Command Dialog

Most Kermit programs communicate with you through interactive keyword-style command dialog. The program issues a prompt to indicate that it is waiting for you to type a command. The prompt is usually of the form

```
Kermit-xx>
```

where xx indicates the version of Kermit: Kermit-MS> for MS-DOS Kermit, Kermit-11> for PDP-11 Kermit, and so on.

In response to the program's prompt you may type a keyword, like SEND or RECEIVE, possibly followed by additional keywords or operands, each of which is called a field. Ideally, and usually also in practice, you should be able to abbreviate keywords to any length that makes them distinguishable from any other keyword valid for that field, and you should be able to type a question mark at any time to get information about what's expected or valid for the current or next field. This style of interaction is called menu on demand. An additional feature, sometimes included, is called completion or recognition, and is usually invoked by typing the Escape key (written here as <ESC>). If the portion of the current keyword or file name typed so far is enough to identify it uniquely, the rest is filled in automatically; otherwise a beep is sounded to let you know that more characters are required. The combination of abbreviation, menu on demand, and completion allows both novice and experienced people to use the program without penalizing one group to favor the other.

The following example illustrates how ? and <ESC> work. You type set and then a question mark to find out what the SET options are. Then you continue the command at the point where the question mark was typed, adding a d and another question mark to see what SET options start with d. Then you add a u to select duplex (the only SET option that starts with du) followed by <ESC> to complete the current field, then another question mark to see what the possibilities are for the next field, and so forth. The command is terminated and entered by a carriage return. Before carriage return is typed, however, the command can be edited or erased using Backspace or other command editing keys provided by your system. Finally, the same command is entered again with a minimum of keystrokes, each field abbreviated to its shortest unique length. In the example, the parts you type are printed in green; all the rest is system typeout:

```
Kermit-xx>set ? one of the following:
 debugging        delay            duplex          escape
 file             handshake        IBM             line
 parity           receive          send
Kermit-xx>set d? one of the following:
 debugging   delay      duplex
Kermit-xx>set du<ESC>plex ? one of the following:
 full   half
Kermit-xx>set duplex h<ESC>alf
Kermit-xx>set du h
```

Liberal use of the ? feature will let you rapidly learn any differences between your Kermit program's command set and the one described here.

In practice, many Kermit programs conform fully to this model (which happens to be based on the DECSYSTEM-20 command interpreter), but there are also many that do not. Of those, some are entirely menu-driven, others respond only to UNIX-style command line arguments, and still others are partial implementations of the DEC-20 style—for instance, abbreviations of keywords might not be allowed, or help is not given when ? is typed.

Commands generally do not take effect until you "enter" them by typing carriage return. Most Kermit programs allow you to edit your commands before you type the terminating carriage return, in order to correct typing mistakes. The method varies from system to system. The most common editing functions are character deletion (usually accomplished by typing the Backspace or Delete key) and line deletion (often by typing Control-U).

Consult your particular Kermit program's documentation for details about help menus, keyword abbreviation, completion, and editing. Now let's review and expand our syntax notation.

anything   A parameter. The symbol shown this way is replaced by an operand of the specified type (number, filename, etc.).

[*anything*]   A field enclosed in square brackets is optional. If omitted, the field defaults to an appropriate value. You don't type the brackets.

{x,y,z}   A list of alternatives is enclosed in curly braces; you type one of the alternatives.

number   A number entered in prevailing notation, usually decimal. Some Kermit programs expect you to type numbers in octal or hexadecimal. These alternative notations are explained in Appendix E.

character   A single character. Some Kermit programs allow the character to be typed literally; others require you to type its numeric ASCII value in decimal, octal, or hexadecimal. These values are included in the ASCII table in Appendix D.

filespec	A file specification, i.e., the name of a file, possibly including a search path, device or directory name, or other qualifying information, and possibly containing "wildcard" or pattern-matching characters to denote a group of files.
^X	Control characters are written using uparrow notation, except for those that already have more common names, like CR (^M) and LF (^J). Control characters are produced by holding down the key marked CTRL (or Control) and typing the appropriate character, e.g., x.
<CR>	Carriage Return. Included when the carriage return that is normally implied by the end of a line is not clear.
<NOCR>	Don't type a carriage return, even though the end of the line implies that you should.
<ESC>	Type the Escape key.

Commands are shown in uppercase, but most Kermit programs let you enter them in any combination of upper- and lowercase. Here are some examples of command syntax descriptions.

• EXIT
Type `exit`, followed by a carriage return.

• SEND *filename*
Type `send`, followed by a space, followed by the name of an actual file, followed by a carriage return.

• DIRECTORY [*filespec*]
Type `directory`, a space, and then either a carriage return or a file specification followed by a carriage return.

• DEFINE *name* [*value* [, *value* [, . . .]]]
Type `define`, a space, and then a name that you make up, then a list of zero or more values separated by commas, followed by a carriage return.

• SET FILE {DISPLAY, WARNING} [{ON, OFF}]
Type `set file`, then a space, then either `display` or `warning`, and then either a carriage return or `on` or `off` followed by a carriage return.

Invoking Kermit Programs

Every system has its own way of letting users run programs and every Kermit program has its own peculiarities, so it would be silly to try to give general directions for running Kermit programs. But I'll try anyway.

First, let's ignore the workstation-based menu-driven Kermit versions, like those on the Apple Macintosh or DEC Pro-350. Menus are supposed to explain themselves. The remaining Kermit implementations tend to fall into two categories: interactive and command line. When an interactive program is invoked, it issues a prompt and you give it a command. The process repeats until you issue a command, like EXIT, that tells it to stop executing. This is the model used throughout this book. The command line model is much more rigid; all the operands (commands, options, arguments, data) for the program are included on the same command line that invokes the program. You have to know what they are in advance and type them all correctly. The set of programs that makes up the UNIX environment provides the best-known example of this style of program invocation. For instance, UNIX Kermit can be invoked with a command like:

```
kermit -1 /dev/ttyi4 -b 1200 -cntp m -r -a foo
```

which means something like "Using line `ttyi4` at 1200 baud, half-duplex with hand-shake and mark parity, connect to the remote system, then receive a file, storing it under the name `foo`, and then connect back when done."

UNIX Kermit allows both command line and interactive operation, but it uses different syntax for each. Many other Kermit programs allow only one style or the other, but some allow both, usually with consistent syntax. The normal convention for command line invocation is for the program to terminate and disappear after processing of the given operands is complete. When the program is invoked without operands on the command line, it will either begin interactive dialog or else it might print a help message to the effect that command line operands are required, perhaps indicating what they might be.

Those Kermit programs which allow both interactive and command line operation usually extend the convention slightly. When command line operands do not specify any action, like CONNECT or SEND, the program enters dialog mode anyway. If you typed

```
kermit set line 27
```

you probably did not intend for the program to disappear before you could use it to communicate with the system at the other end of line 27.

Many Kermit programs are set up to process an initialization file upon startup. The "init file" may contain any valid Kermit commands. If you find that you always use certain options, then you can save yourself a lot of repetitive typing by collecting them together into the init file. For instance, if you have a PC on your desk at the office with a direct line-mode connection to an IBM mainframe, your init file might look like this:

```
set speed 9600
set parity mark
set duplex half
set flow none
set handshake xon
set timer on
connect
```

The init file must have a certain name, and be in a certain place, so that your Kermit program can find it. Usually the name is something like KERMIT.INI and the place is in your home directory or the current disk and/or directory. Consult the documentation of your particular Kermit program for details about invocation and initialization files.

Terminal Emulation Commands

Before you can transfer files with Kermit, you must be able to communicate with the remote system at least enough to get the remote Kermit program running, which means that you must establish a terminal session there. Kermit provides the CONNECT command for this purpose, plus several related commands.

The CONNECT Command

Syntax: CONNECT [*line*]

For use in local mode only. Establishes a terminal connection to the system at the other end of the specified or currently selected communication line. On a microcomputer this is normally the serial port. On a mainframe you will have to specify a terminal line number or other identifier, either in the CONNECT command itself, or in a prior SET LINE command. A SET PORT command will be necessary on a microcomputer to select an alternative serial port, like COM2 instead of COM1.

The terminal connection established by the CONNECT command is exactly what you would get with an ordinary terminal. It is "unguarded." No error-correcting protocol takes place. All microcomputer versions of Kermit should have a CONNECT command, and in most cases a particular type of terminal, such as a DEC VT52 or VT100, or a Heath/Zenith 19, will be emulated. Mainframe Kermits may or may not have a CONNECT command. If you want to connect two mainframes with Kermit, the one that is to initiate the connection must have a CONNECT command. Mainframe Kermits that have CONNECT commands generally do not emulate any particular kind of terminal. They assume that you are already using a real terminal or a terminal emulator as your console to the system.

Before issuing the CONNECT command, you may have to use the SET command (page 148) to make any necessary adjustments to the default or current communication settings, including SPEED (or BAUD), DUPLEX (or ECHO), PARITY, FLOW-CONTROL, and HANDSHAKE. Most Kermit programs use full-duplex, no-parity communications by default, but check the documentation of your particular program for details.

When you issue the CONNECT command, the Kermit program will print a brief message telling you how to get back. Be sure you remember it!

```
Kermit-xx>connect
(Connecting to remote host, type ^]C to get back)
```

(Terminal session with host conducted here.)

```
^]C<NOCR>
(Back at local Kermit.)
Kermit-xx>
```

During terminal emulation, every character you type (except one) is sent immediately out the communication port (with any selected parity tacked on to it), and every character that arrives at the port is displayed on your screen (usually with the parity bit stripped). In half-duplex connections, keyboard characters are also echoed immediately to the screen. When a particular terminal is being emulated, selected control sequences among the incoming characters are interpreted to produce the indicated effects, like clearing the screen, positioning the cursor, or making characters blink.

Some Kermit programs have a LOG command to allow the terminal session (everything that appears on your screen) to be recorded in a disk file called the session log. This provides "raw" (unguarded) capture of information (like interactive dialogs) that cannot ordinarily be transferred with Kermit, or of files from remote systems that do not have Kermit programs. Some postprocessing with a text editor is usually necessary. See "Raw Download and Upload," page 169.

The one keyboard character that is not sent immediately out the port is called the escape character. Its purpose is to get the attention of the Kermit program again. The escape character—not to be confused with ASCII ESC—is usually a control character that you would not otherwise have reason to type, typically ^] (Control-Rightbracket), ^\ (Control-Backslash), or ^^ (Control-Uparrow or -Circumflex). Most Kermit programs allow you to change it using the SET ESCAPE command.

When you type the escape character, Kermit treats the next character you type as a command. The combination of the escape character and the subsequent single-character command is called the escape sequence. Your Kermit program may furnish any or all of the following escape commands:

C   Close the connection and return to the local Kermit.

S   Show the status of the connection.

B   Send a BREAK signal.

0   (Zero) Send a NUL (0) character.

D   (Or H) Drop the line, hang up the modem.

P   "Push" to the local system command processor without breaking the connection.

Q   Quit logging session transcript.

R   Resume logging session transcript.

F   Record the current screen in a file.

?   List the available escape commands.

Note that

• The "C" command will always be available.

• Letters may be typed in either upper- or lowercase.

• To transmit the escape character itself, type it twice in a row.

It is possible to use Kermit to connect to a remote system, on which you invoke Kermit to connect to an even *more* remote system. The process can be repeated indefinitely, but escaping back through the same path without skipping any intermediate systems could present problems. The recommended method is to make sure each system's Kermit uses a different escape character. If the escape characters are the same, remember that you can transmit one copy of your local escape character by typing it twice, so you can escape back from the doubly remote host to the remote host by typing ^]^]C if your escape character is ^].

Here's an example showing use of the CONNECT command:

```
Kermit-xx>set baud 9600            Specify the speed.
Kermit-xx>set parity odd           Specify parity, if any.
Kermit-xx>set duplex half          And other nonstandard parameters.
Kermit-xx>connect                  Connect to the remote system.
(Connecting to host, type ^\C to return)
```

(Carry on your dialog here.)

```
^\C<NOCR>                          Type the escape sequence when done.
(Back at PC)
Kermit-xx>
```

The DIAL Command

Syntax: DIAL *number*

If your connection to the remote system is to be made with an autodial modem, you may use Kermit's DIAL command to place the call, *if* your Kermit program has a DIAL command, *and* if it is designed to control the type of modem that you have. As of this writing, DIAL commands are pretty scarce among Kermit programs. For each type of modem they intend to support, they need detailed knowledge of the modem's command and control structure. And when that involves RS-232 signals like DTR, DSR, RTS, CTS, RI, and CD, then detailed knowledge of the system's serial driver (or serial interface itself) is also required, and the interaction between the modem's behavior and the system's behavior becomes a major source of complication. Even if the programmer figures it out for a particular machine/modem combination, it might all change with some new release of system software, or be totally different on some otherwise compatible system.

Anyway, if your Kermit program has a DIAL command that works with the kind of modem that you have, you may use it subject to any restrictions or peculiarities listed in the documentation for your Kermit program or for your modem. Beyond that, there are still a few things to watch out for:

• The communication settings for communicating with your modem might not be the same as those for communicating with the system it is to dial.

• If your Kermit program supports more than one kind of modem, then you will have to give a SET MODEM command before dialing, to let the program know which kind of modem it's dealing with.

• If you are using a mainframe, or if your modem is connected to other than the normal port on your micro, you must give the appropriate SET LINE or SET PORT command first.

Once you issue the DIAL command, you may have to wait as long as a minute to allow dialing to take place. If you have lights or a speaker on your modem, you can use them to monitor the progress of the call.

If the connection cannot be completed, Kermit will print a message to that effect, usually indicating the reason—line busy, no answer, etc. If the connection is completed, you can issue a CONNECT command to use it. The Kermit program will attempt to monitor the connection and will notify you if carrier should drop, provided the modem and its connection to the computer are set up to allow this.

Some Kermit programs provide SET DIAL and SET PHONE commands to let you adapt the DIAL command to a previously unknown type of modem, to select pulse or tone dialing, and possibly to enter phone numbers into a directory.

Here's an example of the DIAL command:

```
Kermit-xx>set modem hayes          Specify modem type.
Kermit-xx>set port 2               Specify which port to use.
Kermit-xx>set baud 1200            Specify the speed.
Kermit-xx>set parity odd           Specify other parameters.
Kermit-xx>dial 7654321             Dial the number, wait for response.
(Call completed.)
Kermit-xx>connect                  Connect to the remote system.
(Connecting to host, type ^\C to return)
```

The HANGUP Command

This command, when available, explicitly hangs up the telephone connection initiated by the most recent DIAL command, usually by dropping DTR on the port, or sending a "long BREAK." In most cases, such connections are broken automatically when you log out from a remote system. Use the HANGUP command on those occasions when the automatic mechanism doesn't work, for instance, when the remote system crashes but the front end or port selector you have dialed does not drop DTR. If your Kermit program lacks a hangup command, you can escape back to the modem's command level (+++ on the Hayes, with a second's pause before and after) and then type the modem-specific hangup command (on the Hayes it's ATH0).

How to Dial without a DIAL Command

If you have a modem with a built-in dialer, but your Kermit program lacks a DIAL command, you can control your modem directly by issuing the CONNECT command and then typing modem-specific commands to your modem.

Each autodial modem works in its own way. We'll discuss the Hayes Smartmodem, because it's the most common, and in general is typical of most other modems even if they differ in detail. If you do not have a Hayes or Hayes-compatible modem, consult your modem manual for the details of its command language.

Let's assume the Hayes modem is displaying result codes as words and is echoing your typein when it's in command state (these are the factory settings). Let's also assume the modem is set up correctly to work with your phone and your PC. Consult the Hayes manual for details about the settings.

To place a call with the modem, first issue any appropriate SET commands (SET LINE, SET SPEED, SET PARITY, etc.), and then issue a CONNECT command. At this point you will be communicating directly with the modem's command interpreter. If you type AT (uppercase) followed by carriage return, you should see the response OK. This indicates the modem is ready to accept commands. To dial the number, just type "ATD" followed immediately by the phone number (just as you would dial it), followed by carriage return. Here's an example:

```
Kermit-xx>set baud 1200              Specify the speed.
Kermit-xx>set parity even            Specify any nonstandard parameters.
Kermit-xx>connect                    Connect to the remote system.
(Connecting to host, type ^\C to return)
AT
OK
ATD7654321
CONNECT
```

(At this point, you can communicate with the remote system.)

If the call is completed successfully—the party answers with a carrier tone —then the word CONNECT will appear on your screen, as shown. Otherwise, you will see NO CAR-RIER, NO ANSWER, BUSY, or some similar message.

If the connection is successful, the Hayes modem will automatically leave command state, raise the RS-232 CD (Carrier Detect) signal, and enter communication mode, in which it will remain until either carrier drops, or you type the modem's escape sequence (+++ with a pause before and after). In either case, the modem will return to AT command state.

If carrier drops, the Kermit program probably won't notice. If it doesn't have a DIAL command, it probably also lacks any other intelligence about modems and their signals. In particular, the program might not raise the PC's DTR signal or keep it up consistently. Since most originate modems will not operate in the absence of a DTR signal, you may have to set a DTR-override switch on the modem (on the Hayes, it's switch number 1), or feed some other signal that is known to be on into the modem's DTR input (for instance, by installing a jumper between DSR and DTR in the RS-232 connector that plugs into the modem).

Commands for Transferring Files

The basic commands for transferring files are SEND, RECEIVE, and GET. These commands will be described in detail starting on page 135, but first let's discuss, in somewhat more detail than before, how these commands work.

The mechanics of file transfer depend upon whether the remote Kermit is in server mode. If it is, you may issue repeated SEND and GET commands to it from your local Kermit program. Otherwise, you must issue a SEND or RECEIVE command to the remote Kermit and then escape back to the local Kermit and issue the complementary RECEIVE or SEND command for each file or file group to be transferred.

Transferring a file from a (local) microcomputer to a (remote) mainframe is called uploading. File transfer in the opposite direction is called downloading. This terminology is in common use and is not particular to Kermit. When the remote Kermit is in server mode, downloading is initiated from the local Kermit with a GET command and uploading with a SEND command. When server operation is not being used, downloading is done like this:

1. CONNECT to the remote system and run Kermit.

2. Give the SEND command to the remote Kermit.

3. Escape back to the local Kermit.

4. Give the RECEIVE command.

Uploading goes like this:

1. CONNECT to the remote system and run Kermit.

2. Give the RECEIVE command to the remote Kermit.

3. Escape back to the local Kermit.

4. Give the SEND command.

When a file transfer starts, your local Kermit program will display the progress on the screen, usually indicating the name of the current file, the number of packets sent so far, the number of retransmissions, and so forth. When the transfer is complete, the program will sound a beep, and the status of the operation will be indicated by a message like OK, Complete, Interrupted, or Failed. At that point you should find yourself at either system or Kermit command level, depending upon how you invoked the local Kermit program.

Text Files versus Binary Files

We've touched on this topic before, but it bears repetition. Most Kermit programs are initially set up to transfer text files, and they take pains to do any conversion necessary to make these files useful on the target system. If you want to transfer binary files, you have to give explicit commands to the sending and receiving programs to skip this conversion. A binary file is usually of no use on a system different from the one it was created on. The most common reason for transferring binary files between unlike systems is for archiving or sharing. For instance, a university might keep a library of public-domain microcomputer software archived on a central timesharing system.

When downloading binary, executable programs, be sure you have put both Kermit programs in the correct mode for transferring binary files (described under the SET FILE command, page 151). But even if you have done this, there is always the possibility that a program was uploaded incorrectly in the first place, or that there is something else wrong with it.

WARNING: Before running a downloaded program for the first time, take *every possible precaution* to protect your system and other files from damage.

Download these files to disks that don't contain any other important files, and remove all other disks. Turn off or disconnect printers and other peripheral equipment.

If the program has been stored or transferred incorrectly, then your computer could find itself executing totally random instructions, resulting in a crash of your machine or erasure of your disks, or worse. Some systems protect themselves against this sort of hazard by verifying that a file is in correct executable program format before attempting to run it, but many other systems (usually microcomputers) do not.

Filenames

Every file sent by Kermit is preceded by a packet containing the file's name. This is called a file header, and it allows the receiving Kermit program to store incoming files under their correct names automatically. The filename is stripped of device, directory, path, generation, or attribute fields before transmission. In other words, just the name and type are included, usually separated by a period, with letters all uppercase. This is Kermit's "canonic form" for filenames. The sending system converts the name to this form if necessary, and the receiving system does any necessary translation to local format, for instance, by truncating excessive characters from the name or type fields, translating illegal characters to X's, converting alphabetic case, or changing the punctuation that separates file name and type. If the name corresponds to the name of an existing file, the receiving Kermit will normally overwrite the old file.

There are ways to alter the normal behavior—supplying an alternative name to send the file with, supplying an alternative name to store it under upon arrival, using a SET FILE NAMES command to enable or disable conversion of the filename to canonic form, or using a SET FILE WARNING command to enable or disable the automatic renaming of arriving files to unique names in order to prevent destruction of previously existing files of the same name. These techniques are given in the descriptions of the SEND, RECEIVE, and GET commands (starting on page 135) and of the SET FILE command (page 151) later in this chapter.

Packet Encoding

During transmission, text files are converted to ASCII stream format, with a carriage return and a linefeed (this character pair is commonly called a CRLF) at the end of each line. This is Kermit's canonic form for text files. The receiving Kermit expects arriving text files to be represented this way, and it converts the arriving text stream into normal text format for its system. If the way the system stores text files is the same as Kermit's canonic form, then there need be no distinction between text and binary files on that system (this is true, for instance, of MS-DOS). Binary files are sent exactly as they are stored, byte for byte.

All file data, text and binary, is encoded for transmission to prevent interference from communications equipment and console drivers. Each control character within the data is translated to a two-character printable sequence consisting of a control prefix, normally the # character, followed by the printable ASCII character mnemonically closest to the control character—Control-A becomes #A, Control-B becomes #B, etc. The

CRLF line terminator comes out looking like #M#J. The control prefix is applied regardless of parity or the setting of the high-order (eighth) bit. If the eighth bit is used for data (i.e., parity is NONE, see SET PARITY) then its value is preserved in the prefixed character.

If communication line parity is being used (i.e., not NONE), the protocol allows a special encoding for binary files, called "eighth-bit prefixing," that permits 8-bit data to pass through a 7-bit communication channel. This is an optional Kermit feature, and not all Kermit programs have it. If either Kermit does not agree to use this feature, 8-bit binary files *cannot* be sent correctly through a 7-bit channel—the high-order bit of each byte will be lost (in which case preprocessing is recommended; see below). The eighth-bit prefix is usually &; the 8-bit byte 11000001 (ASCII letter A with its high-order bit set to 1) would be transmitted as &A. If the low order 7 bits are in the control range, the control prefix is also applied: 10000001 comes out as &#A.

The sending Kermit will also ask the other Kermit whether it can handle a special prefix encoding for repeated characters. If it can, then files with long strings of repeated characters will be transmitted very efficiently. Columnar data, highly indented text, and binary files are the chief beneficiaries of this trick. The normal repeat-count prefix is ~ (tilde), and it is followed immediately by a character whose ASCII value is 32 greater than the repeat count. For instance, 29 A's in a row would be represented as ~=A. Repeat counts can be applied to characters that already have other prefixes. For instance ~^&#A represents 62 Control-A characters in a row, each with its high-order bit set to 1.

Finally, the control prefix is used to quote itself and any other prefix character that appears in the data: ##, #&, #~. The eighth-bit and repeat-count prefix characters are not quoted if these options have not been successfully negotiated or if they happen to appear as a repeat count.

Here is an example of encoded 7-bit ASCII data:

```
First line#M#JL~?ong Line ##2#M#JLast Line#M#J
```

which translates to:

```
First line
Loooooooooooooooooooooooooooooooong Line #2
Last Line
```

Preprocessing

Sometimes it is not sufficient to transfer only the contents of a file. On some systems certain kinds of files are not useful unless additional information accompanies them. In those situations, it may be necessary to preprocess the file for transmission and postprocess it after. In other situations, pre- and postprocessing may be used to simplify an otherwise tedious process or to speed up transmission. Here are some examples:

• For some reason, 8-bit binary files can't be transferred over the available communication path. The easiest workaround is to "hexify" the binary file before sending it, and "de-hexify" it upon receipt. This can be done outside of Kermit, using a pair of simple programs that convert between 8-bit binary bytes and pairs of hexadecimal digits ($00000000_2 = 00_{16}, \ldots, 11111111_2 = FF_{16}$; see Appendix E).[2] Fancier methods can be used to encode more efficiently, but to ensure the widest possible transportability the encoding should be restricted to the ASCII printable characters, perhaps just the digits and uppercase letters.

• Some popular application (like a spreadsheet or database) is available on two computers, but the data file format differs. Such applications will almost always have an "export" or conversion utility to put the file into transportable format.

• A very long file must be transferred, and a very effective compression program is available outside of Kermit. It may be considerably faster to compress, transfer, and decompress than to transfer the original file. Of course, symmetrical compression and decompression programs must be available on either end.

• A file of complex record structure or with externally recorded attributes must be transferred between two systems of the same type, but Kermit does not have any way to preserve the structure or attributes during transmission. Examples include Macintosh applications and VAX/VMS RMS files. Many systems provide a utility to convert such difficult files, together with their directory entries and other external information, into ordinary sequential streams of bytes that may be transmitted by Kermit, for reconstruction by a complementary program upon receipt. Macintosh BinHex is one such utility.

• A complex hierarchical structure of directories and files is to be transferred between two like systems, and the files themselves may be of mixed type (text and binary) and of arbitrary complexity (record structure, attributes, etc.). Most systems have a utility for backing up disk directories onto "savesets" on magnetic tape, and some may allow this utility to write the saveset to a disk file rather than to a tape drive. In this case, you can use Kermit to transfer the saveset (a single file) and then use the backup utility on the target system to restore the files from the saveset. Examples include the UNIX "tar" program and the VAX/VMS BACKUP program.

Settings

Kermit programs allow you great flexibility in changing file and communication parameters by using the SET command, which is described in detail starting on page 148. Before attempting to transfer any files, be sure that you have issued all necessary SET commands first. In particular, before attempting to transfer binary files be sure to issue

---

2. This simple hex file format should not be confused with Intel hex format, which includes checksums and additional information.

the SET FILE TYPE BINARY (or equivalent) command to *both* Kermit programs.[3] Similarly, before attempting to transfer files over a communication channel that requires parity, you must issue the appropriate SET PARITY commands. Before attempting to communicate with an IBM mainframe, you will probably have to use SET commands to adjust parity, duplex, echo, timeout, flow control, and handshake. XON/XOFF or similar flow control may be used during file transfer, if available.

The Kermit protocol allows the sender to transmit information about a file in a special Attributes packet, including whether the file is text or binary. Unfortunately (as of this writing), very few Kermit programs support this optional packet type. As a general rule, therefore, it is not possible to mix text and binary files in the same file group without preprocessing.

Interruption of File Transfer

Once a file transfer is in progress, you should be able to interrupt it by typing one of the following control characters on your keyboard:

^X   Cancel the current file, discarding any portion of it transferred so far, and proceed to the next one, if any.

^Z   Cancel the current file and all subsequent files, and return to command level.

^E   Cause an intentional fatal protocol error. Equivalent to ^Z, but will work in situations where ^Z will not. Transmits an Error packet to the remote Kermit.

^C   Emergency Exit. Equivalent to ^E, but makes no attempt to notify the remote Kermit, which may be left in an indeterminate state (most likely timing out repeatedly, retransmitting its last packet every few seconds until its retry limit is exhausted). Use this only as a last resort, or if you have reason to believe there is no Kermit program at the other end (e.g., because you forgot to start it).

CR   Retransmit the last packet. Useful on connections that don't time out automatically (see page 133).

^A   Print a status report on the transfer in progress, without actually interrupting it; useful with Kermit programs whose file transfer display is not continuously updated.

Not all local Kermits provide all of these interruption commands, and those that do might assign them to different characters (or mouse buttons, etc.). Consult your system-dependent Kermit documentation for details.

---

3. The rare exception occurs when a system stores text files in exactly the format to which Kermit would convert them for transmission, in which case no conversion is done, and there is no need for a SET FILE TYPE BINARY command. One such system is MS-DOS.

The first two interruption commands (^X and ^Z) call upon an optional feature of the Kermit protocol not necessarily supported by the remote Kermit program, even when it is by the local one. This poses little problem when sending files, since the local Kermit is in control. When receiving files, the worst that can happen is that these interruption commands will be ignored by the remote Kermit. In that case, ^E or ^C can be used instead if they're available.

The local Kermit program should inform you of the interruption options that are available each time you start a file transfer. For instance, UNIX Kermit might give a message like

```
CTRL-F to cancel file, CTRL-R to resend current packet
CTRL-B to cancel batch, CTRL-A for status report
```

It uses different interruption commands because the normal ones are already assigned by the system to other uses.

Timeouts

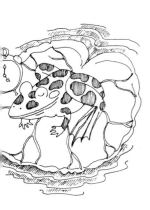

When two Kermit programs are sending packets to each other, there is always the possibility that a packet will be lost in transit or damaged badly enough to prevent its recognition as a packet. After Kermit A has transmitted a packet, it waits for a reply from Kermit B. If Kermit A's packet is lost, then both Kermit A and Kermit B will be waiting for a packet. This situation is called a deadlock, and a mechanism is required to break it. The mechanism is called a timeout. The Kermit program sets a timer (like the alarm on a clock) before issuing an input request to the serial port. If the input request is not satisfied within the timeout interval, the alarm goes off and the program takes some action to break the deadlock, usually retransmission of its last packet.

Sometimes the alarm goes off prematurely because the timeout interval is shorter than the amount of time required for a packet to arrive. Timers are usually set for operation on point-to-point, uncongested connections. However, when the connection is over a packet network, delays caused by congestion, routing, or satellite transmission may exceed the normal timeout interval. Similarly, when one or both of the systems involved is a timesharing system, it is always possible that the demands placed upon it will make it so slow that it can't transmit its packets within the allotted time. Most Kermit programs include SET commands that allow you to increase the timeout interval, but this can have the side effect of increasing the time to detect packets that really have been lost.

Ideally, the timeout interval should be set to

$$\frac{Packet\text{-}length \times 10}{Baud\text{-}rate} + process + delay + slop$$

where *Packet-length* is the number of characters in the packet, including any padding and terminator characters, *process* is the number of seconds required to process a packet, *delay* is the transmission delay in seconds, and *slop* is the number of seconds you're willing to wait for the packet after it's due. The *process* time can vary with system load and other factors (the amount of compression/decompression being done, whether or not disk buffers are being dumped), and *delay* can vary with the load on the network and other factors (e.g., the route taken by each packet). Most Kermit programs don't take these factors into account automatically, but you should consider them when adjusting timers.

Most Kermit programs are capable of timing out, and it is sufficient for only one partner of a pair to have a timer in order for a file transfer operation to proceed unattended—without human intervention. Nevertheless, it is sometimes necessary to transfer files between two Kermits, neither of which has a timer. This is what the "CR interruption" is for: it causes the program to do what it would have done had it timed out, namely retransmit its most recent packet. As usual, consult the program-specific documentation for any Kermit you intend to use to determine whether it can time out, and what manner of manual intervention is provided for.

Performance

The basic, "classic" Kermit protocol is of the stop-and-wait variety. Each packet requires a reply, and the next packet won't be sent until the reply arrives, or the sender times out waiting for it. Furthermore, a regular Kermit packet is relatively short—96 characters long at most. These characteristics of the Kermit protocol have allowed it to thrive in hostile environments, but the price is unnecessarily high when the environment is friendlier. Under the best conditions, basic Kermit transfers files at 50–80 percent of the baud rate. On connections with built-in delays, such as public networks or satellite links, throughput decreases dramatically.

Two extensions to the Kermit protocol allow improved performance, provided the two Kermit programs support them. The first extension increases the maximum packet length. It should be used only when the connection is relatively noise-free, since retransmission incurs a very high overhead when packets are long. Long packets are also the only way to boost performance in half-duplex connections. In practice, it doesn't make sense to have packets much longer than about 1000 characters—the benefits from packets longer than that are offset by the cost of retransmission.

The second extension, for use only on full-duplex connections, is the sliding window extension. This technique allows continuous transmission of packets, providing the receiver can reply within a certain interval called the window size (which is the maximum number of packets that may be unacknowledged at a given time). Retransmission, when necessary, is not costly, so this method is appropriate to noisy connections.

The file transfer commands SEND, RECEIVE, and GET are now described.

The SEND Command

Syntax: SEND *filespec1* [*filespec2*]

The SEND command causes the file or group of files specified by *filespec1* to be sent to the other system. The command can be issued from either a remote or a local Kermit program. There are two forms of the SEND command, depending on whether *filespec1* specifies a single file or a file group. The most common method for specifying a group of files is by including "wildcard" characters in the file specification. For instance, if FOO.FOR is a single file, a FORTRAN program named FOO, then *.FOR might be a group of FORTRAN programs. Most systems allow some kind of wildcard notation, usually one symbol, like *, to match any string of characters, and another, like ? or %, to match any single character. Some also provide notation for matching any of a group of characters or strings, or any letter within a given range. The important point is that a single file specification is used to select multiple files.

Sending a File Group If *filespec1* contains wildcard characters, then all matching files will be sent, in directory-listing order, each under its own name. If a file can't be opened for read access, it will be skipped. Some Kermit programs allow the initial file in a wildcard group to be specified with the optional *filespec2*. This allows a previously interrupted wildcard transfer to continue from where it left off, or it can be used to skip some files that would be transmitted first. Examples:

```
send *.txt              Send all files of type .TXT.
send *.txt file3.txt    Same, but starting with FILE3.TXT.
```

Check the specific documentation for your Kermit program to see if the second form is allowed and if it behaves as described here. If it is not provided, you might be able to achieve the same effect using SET FILE SUPERSEDE.

Sending a Single File If *filespec1* does not contain any wildcard characters, then the single file it specifies will be sent under its own name. Optionally, *filespec2* may be used to specify a different name under which to send it; *filespec2* is not parsed or validated locally in any way.

```
send foo.txt            Send the file FOO.TXT.
send foo.txt fred.txt   Send FOO.TXT as FRED.TXT.
```

Optional Syntax: An alternative to the second form might be provided on some systems, particularly those that allow spaces in filenames, to remove any ambiguity between *filespec1* and *filespec2*. If you are sending a single file, you may type the SEND command without a filespec. In that case, Kermit programs that support this option will prompt you for the local filespec on the subsequent line, and the name to send it under on the line after that:

```
Kermit-xx>send<CR>
 Local Source File: profile exec
 Remote Destination File: profile.xec
```

If the program does not support the optional syntax, it will give you an error message like "Not confirmed," which means that it did not see a carriage return where it expected one, namely after a file specification.

SEND Remote Operation When you SEND from the remote system, you are downloading a file, typically from a mainframe to your microcomputer, with the remote Kermit *not* in server mode.

After issuing the SEND command to the remote Kermit program, you have to escape back to the local Kermit program and issue a RECEIVE command. After a few seconds, the file transfer should start. You will see the progress displayed on your screen.

A remote Kermit program will wait a length of time, usually from 5 to 30 seconds (see SET DELAY), after you have given it the SEND command until it actually starts to transmit packets. When the delay period expires, the first packet will be transmitted. It might look something like this:

```
^A, Sp+ @-#Y1~
```

If the packet is not answered within the remote Kermit's timeout interval (normally about 5 seconds), it will retransmit the same packet. If you have not escaped back to your local Kermit quickly enough, you will see this packet on your screen. Don't worry: as long as you escape back and give the RECEIVE command within about a minute or two, the protocol will work. If you take more than

$$Delay \ + \ (\ retry\text{-}limit \ \times \ timeout\text{-}interval \ )$$

seconds to escape back and give the RECEIVE command, then the remote Kermit will give up and return to command level. In that case, you should just issue the SEND command again.

SEND Local Operation In this case, you are uploading a file from your local system (usually a PC) to a remote system (usually a mainframe). You should already have started the Kermit program on the remote system, issued either a RECEIVE or a SERVER command, and then escaped back to the local Kermit. As soon as you issue the SEND command, the transfer should start with no delay.

If you notice a file being sent that you do not really want to send, you may cancel the operation by typing either Control-X or Control-Z. If your local Kermit supports these options, they will work even if the remote Kermit does not support them, except that a remnant of the current file might be left behind on the remote system.

The RECEIVE Command

Syntax: RECEIVE [*filespec*]

The RECEIVE command tells a Kermit program to wait for the arrival of a file or file group sent by a SEND command from the other system. You may include the optional *filespec* field as the name under which to store the incoming file; otherwise, the name is taken from the incoming file header. If multiple files are received when the optional *filespec* is given, only the first one will be renamed; the others will be stored under the names they were sent with.

If an incoming file does not arrive in its entirety, the receiving Kermit program will normally discard it, and it will not appear in your directory. You may change this behavior by using the command SET INCOMPLETE KEEP, which will cause as much of the file as has arrived to be saved in your directory.

RECEIVE Remote Operation   When the remote Kermit program is given the RECEIVE command, you are uploading files to it. After you have given the RECEIVE command, you should escape back to your local Kermit and give the SEND command. The same cautions about timing apply as for the remote SEND command, except that in this case you may see a NAK packet on your screen:

^A# N3

Just escape back and give the SEND command within a minute or two so that the retry limit is not exceeded. If it is, you can still CONNECT back to the remote system and reissue the RECEIVE command.

RECEIVE Local Operation   When you give a RECEIVE command to your local Kermit, you are downloading files to it. You must already have issued a SEND command to the remote Kermit and escaped back to the local Kermit. See the foregoing description of the remote SEND command.

PLEASE NOTE: You cannot use the RECEIVE command to request files from a Kermit server. You must use the GET command for that. RECEIVE is passive, GET is active.[4]

---

4. Some very early Kermit programs may still survive in which RECEIVE was passive and RECEIVE *filespec* did what GET does.

As files arrive, their names will be shown on your screen, along with a continuous display of the packet traffic. If your local Kermit program supports file interruption commands like ^X and ^Z, you may issue them, but with no guarantee that the remote sender will honor them. If it doesn't, the files will continue to arrive. You can either let them come and then delete them afterward, or else you can try interruping the entire transfer by typing ^E or ^C (in that order). Again, recall that methods for entering these interruption commands may vary; consult your particular program documentation.

The GET Command

Syntax: GET [*remote-filespec*]

The GET command requests a remote Kermit server to send the file or file group specified by *remote-filespec*. Note the distinction between the RECEIVE and GET commands: RECEIVE instructs the program to wait passively for files to arrive, whereas GET actively sends a request to a server.

The GET command can be used only when Kermit is local, with a Kermit server active on the other end of the line. This means that you must have CONNECTed to the other system, logged in, run Kermit there, issued the SERVER command, and escaped back to the local Kermit. GET is equivalent to a SEND/escape-back/RECEIVE sequence, except that afterward the remote Kermit remains in server mode rather than returning to command level.

The remote filespec is any string that can be a legal file specification for the remote system. It is not parsed or validated locally. It may denote a single file or a file group in the remote system's own file naming syntax.

As files arrive, their names will be displayed on your screen, together with a continuous indication of the packet traffic. As with the RECEIVE command, you may type Control-X to request that the current incoming file be canceled, or Control-Z to request that the entire incoming batch be canceled, with no guarantee that these requests will be honored. If you type Control-E, you will terminate the file transfer, but the server will remain in server mode.

Optional Syntax: If you are requesting a single file, you may type the GET command without a filespec. In that case, Kermit programs that support this optional multiline syntax will prompt you for the remote filespec on the subsequent line, and the name to store it under when it arrives on the line after that:

```
Kermit-xx>get<CR>
 Remote Source File: aux text
 Local Destination File: al auxfile bl
```

If the program does not support the optional syntax, it will give you an error message like "Not confirmed." The reason for the multiline syntax is that the remote filespec might contain characters that could confuse the local Kermit's command interpreter, like the spaces in the example above. If the syntax were

```
get aux text al auxfile bl
```

how would the local Kermit program know which goes with what?

Commands for Server Operation

To alleviate the tedium of repetitive escaping and connecting back and forth, the Kermit protocol provides a way for the local Kermit to relay commands in packets to a remote Kermit specially set up for this purpose as a "Kermit server." Server operation is an optional feature of the Kermit protocol. Not all remote Kermit programs are capable of acting as servers, and not all local Kermits are capable of sending the command packets required to control Kermit servers.

The SERVER Command

The SERVER command instructs Kermit to cease taking commands from the keyboard and to receive all further instructions in the form of Kermit packets from other Kermit programs. Your local Kermit program must have commands for communicating with remote servers, including at least GET and SEND, plus either FINISH or BYE. If your local Kermit does not have a BYE or FINISH command, then it does not have the full ability to communicate with a Kermit server and you should not put the remote Kermit program into server mode. If you do, you might not be able to get it out again—most Kermit servers ignore whatever you type at them, and won't even echo it. If you find yourself stuck in this situation, try typing a FINISH packet:

```
^A$ GF4
```

That's a Control-A, followed by a dollar sign, one space, then GF4, and a carriage return.

Any nonstandard parameters should be selected with SET commands before putting Kermit in server mode. For instance, if you plan to transfer binary files, you will have to SET FILE TYPE BINARY. If you later decide to transfer text files, you'll have to FINISH server operation, connect back, and SET FILE TYPE TEXT before starting any transfers, unless both the local Kermit and the remote server support either Attribute packets or the REMOTE KERMIT or REMOTE SET command.

After issuing the SERVER command, escape back to your local Kermit program and issue SEND, GET, REMOTE, BYE, or FINISH commands from there. If you don't escape back fast enough, you may see a NAK packet on your screen:

```
^A# N3
```

Don't worry; the server is in no hurry to receive commands; it will not time out. In fact, you may leave the server running on the remote end for hours at a time without communicating with it. The periodic NAKs are issued by the server for the benefit of local Kermits that don't time out, to cover the case when a command packet is transmitted, but lost. Many Kermit server programs provide an option (SET SERVER TIMEOUT) for turning off these NAKs in case they cause trouble.

During a session with a server, you may use the interruption commands ^X, ^Z, and ^E as described, but they return the server to server command wait rather than to Kermit or system command level, so that you can issue further commands to the server from your local Kermit program.

When you have finished with the remote server, you should issue a BYE or FINISH command from the local Kermit to shut it down. This will cause the server to complete any pending actions, to close any open logs, and generally to clean up after itself.

The BYE Command

The BYE command is issued from the local Kermit program in order to shut down a remote Kermit server and request that it log out its job. If the BYE command succeeds, there is no need to CONNECT back to the remote system and clean up. The job will be gone, and any dialup connection should have been dropped. If the server responds with a message like "Unknown Kermit server command" or "Error—Can't log out," you'll have to use the FINISH command instead, CONNECT back, clean up, and log out yourself.

The FINISH Command

The FINISH command is issued from the local Kermit program to shut down a remote Kermit server without having it log itself out. This allows you to CONNECT back to your remote job, where you may find yourself either at Kermit or system command level, depending on the program.

The REMOTE Command

A local Kermit program may provide a REMOTE command for requesting special functions of a remote Kermit server. If the server does not understand the command or offer the requested service (all of these commands and services are optional features of the Kermit server), it will reply with a message like "Unknown Kermit server command." If it does understand, it will send the results (if any) back to be displayed on your screen. The REMOTE commands follow.

• REMOTE CLOSE *function*
Deactivate remote logging of the specified function and close the associated log file (see REMOTE LOG).

- REMOTE COPY *filespec1 filespec2*

Request that the file specified by *filespec1* be copied to *filespec2* on the remote system. The optional multiline syntax may also be allowed.

- REMOTE CWD *[directory]*

Change working directory. Set or change the default device and/or directory specification for remote file references. If no directory name is provided, the server will change to the job's default directory. Otherwise, you will be prompted for a password, and the server will attempt to change to the specified directory. If access is not granted, the server will provide a message to that effect. Details of operation vary. Some systems (like UNIX) allow directory changing without a password; others require one. On some systems (like the DEC-20) the CWD operation grants owner access to the accessed directory; on others (like UNIX) it doesn't.

- REMOTE DELETE *filespec*

Delete the specified file or files. The names of the files that are deleted may or may not be displayed on your screen. Again, details vary. On some systems, file deletion is irrevocable; on others deleted files may be resurrected.

- REMOTE DIRECTORY *[filespec]*

The names of the files that match the given file specification will be displayed on your screen, possibly along with additional information about file sizes, dates, or other attributes in the remote system's syntax. If no file specification is given, all files from the current directory will be listed.

- REMOTE HELP

A list of available server functions is displayed.

- REMOTE HOST *[command]*

The given command is passed to the server's host command processor, and the resulting output is displayed on your screen. This command, when available, serves as an "escape clause" allowing remote execution of other commands not explicitly provided for.

- REMOTE KERMIT *[command]*

The given command, which is expressed in the server Kermit's own command syntax, is passed to the server for execution. This is useful for changing settings, logging, and other functions for which explicit REMOTE commands are not available.

- REMOTE LOG *function [filespec]*

Activates remote logging of the specified function, such as DEBUGGING, TRANS-ACTIONS, or PACKETS, to the specified remote file. If the filespec is omitted, use the remote Kermit program's default name for the specified log. See the LOG command, page 146, for details.

- REMOTE PRINT *filespec [options]*

Prints the specified remote file on the remote system's printer, using the specified options, which are expressed in the syntax of the remote system's printing commands.

- REMOTE PROGRAM [*command*]
  The command is sent to the program started by most recent REMOTE RUN program, and the program's response is displayed on the screen. If no command is given, a newline character is sent.

- REMOTE RENAME *filespec1 filespec2*
  Changes the name of, or moves, the remote file *filespec1* to *filespec2*.

- REMOTE RUN *program-name* [*command-line*]
  The remote Kermit is asked to run the indicated program with the indicated command line. The program's terminal output is sent back to your screen. Not all systems provide the mechanisms required to support this command.

- REMOTE SET *options*
  A remote version of the SET command.

- REMOTE SHOW [*options*]
  Requests the remote server to display the selected SET parameters, or all of them if none are specified.

- REMOTE SPACE [*directory*]
  Requests information about disk usage in the current or specified remote directory—quota, current storage, or amount of remaining free space—to be displayed on your screen.

- REMOTE SUBMIT *filespec* [*options*]
  Submits the specified remote file for batch or background processing on the remote system, with options specified in the remote system's syntax.

- REMOTE TYPE *filespec*
  Displays the contents of the specified file(s) on your screen.

- REMOTE WHO [*name*]
  Asks the remote system to send you a list of who is logged in, or requests information about the named user.

Again, remember that any particular Kermit server program is not guaranteed to have all, or any, of these commands. It's also possible that some commands might be available that aren't listed here. The REMOTE commands that occur most commonly are CWD, DELETE, DIRECTORY, HELP, and TYPE. Any REMOTE command that results in the display of a lot of information on your screen can be canceled with the ^X, ^Z, or ^E commands, if available.

Commands for Local File Management

Even though your system provides its own commands for file management, it may be inconvenient for you to exit from the Kermit program, issue file management commands, and continue or restart the Kermit program. For this reason, many Kermit programs provide built-in commands for local file management. The LOCAL commands are mostly the same as the equivalent REMOTE commands, except that they lack the REMOTE prefix (in some implementations, a LOCAL prefix may be allowed or required). Check the documentation for your particular program to find out what local file commands are available and whether their syntax differs from that given here.

- COPY *filespec1 filespec2*
Local *filespec1* is copied to local *filespec2*.

- CWD [*directory*]
Changes your working directory to the specified device and/or directory.

- DELETE *filespec*
Deletes the specified file or files.

- DIRECTORY [*filespec*]
Provides a directory listing of the specified files.

- HOST *command*
Requests the local host operating system to execute the given command. Often available in some other syntax customary for the particular system, like ! for UNIX.

- PRINT *filespec* [*options*]
Prints the specified local file(s) on a local printer with the specified options expressed in the local print facility's own syntax.

- PROGRAM [*command*]
Gives the command to the program selected in the most recent RUN command. This allows an "inferior" program or process to be kept around and invoked from time to time without incurring the overhead of loading and starting it each time. Available only, but not necessarily, if there is also a RUN command.

- RENAME *filespec1 filespec2*
Changes the name of *filespec1* to *filespec2*.

- RUN [*filespec* [*command*]]
Runs the indicated program with the supplied command. The RUN command can be available only on systems that allow one program to run another, and its behavior can vary from system to system. For instance, the program might disappear after completion, or it might remain available for further use via the PROGRAM command. When a command is not specified, the program may be started interactively, depending on the nature of the program and the host operating system. If no filespec is given, the program will be restarted or continued, if that is possible.

- SPACE
Displays local disk quota, usage, and/or free space.

- SUBMIT *filespec* [*options*]
Submits the specified file for batch (background) execution, with the specified options.

- TYPE *filespec*
Displays the specified file(s) on the screen.

- WHO [*name*]
Lists the users logged into the local system, or the named user.

There may also be an additional local command that allows you to get at functions not otherwise provided:

- PUSH
Invokes the local system command interpreter in such a way that it can return to Kermit, with all Kermit's previous environment and settings intact. Kermit should tell you what command gets you back to Kermit, like EXIT or POP.

Some Kermit programs may provide commands for these or other functions in the syntax of their own system, when this would cause no confusion. For instance, CP/M Kermit may use ERA in place of (LOCAL) DELETE, UNIX Kermit might use ! instead of PUSH or (LOCAL) HOST.

Bureaucratic Commands

Like most other programs, Kermit needs commands to terminate its execution, provide help, keep records, and so forth.

The HELP Command

Syntax: HELP [*topic*]

Typing HELP alone prints a brief summary of the available commands and possibly instructions for obtaining more detailed help on particular topics. Most Kermit implementations also allow the use of ? within a command to produce a short help message. For instance, `help ?` might list the topics for which help is available.

The EXIT Command

The EXIT command tells the Kermit program to do any necessary cleaning up (like closing log files) and then to terminate. Some systems allow the same program image to be restarted or continued; others do not. Consult your Kermit program documentation.

The TAKE Command

Syntax: TAKE *filespec*

This command instructs Kermit to take further commands from the specified file and to execute them until the end of the file is reached. The file may contain any valid Kermit commands, including other TAKE commands, and it should contain *only* Kermit commands or other notation that is legal at Kermit command level (for instance, some Kermit programs allow comment lines to be preceded by a special symbol, like semicolon). You may include the CONNECT command in a TAKE command file, but you cannot include text after the CONNECT command to be transmitted to the remote system, nor the escape sequence to get back. A separate mechanism, called a login script, must be used if you want to carry on a "canned" dialog with the remote system from a command file (see page 164).

Command files provide a way to group related commands together so that they can be executed conveniently (the DEFINE command provides another way). For instance, if you put the following commands into a file called IBM,

```
set parity mark
set flow none
set handshake xon
set duplex half
set timer on
connect
```

then you could execute them all at once simply by typing take ibm. Some aspects of command file execution can be controlled using the SET TAKE command.

The ECHO Command

Syntax: ECHO *string*

The specified string is printed on the screen. Useful for monitoring TAKE command file execution. Special characters may be included in the string by prefixing their numeric ASCII values with a backslash (\).

The COMMENT Command

Syntax: COMMENT [*string*]

Has no effect at all. Used for putting comments in TAKE files. Some Kermit programs may substitute the system's customary comment character, like semicolon (;) or exclamation mark (!), for the keyword COMMENT.

The RUN Command

Syntax: RUN [*program* [*arguments*]]

The RUN command provides another "escape clause" from Kermit. It runs the specified program with the arguments (operands, commands) provided. The RUN command allows you to write programs to supplement Kermit's functions. For instance, if your Kermit lacks a DIAL command, you can write your own program to do the dialing. Then from within Kermit you can issue a command like

```
run dial 7654321
```

The RUN command is an optional Kermit feature; its presence depends not only on whether the programmer felt like including it, but also on the capabilities of the underlying system. Some systems provide no mechanism for one program to invoke another. Others may allow it, but provide no way of passing arguments.

The QUIT Command

Syntax: QUIT

QUIT is a synonym for EXIT.

The STATISTICS Command

Gives statistics about the most recent file transfer. For instance, here's what was reported by UNIX Kermit after receiving a 5K binary file at 9600 baud from a PC, using repeat-count compression:

```
Total File Characters   : 5792
Communication Line In   : 1813
Communication Line Out  :  173
Elapsed Time            :    6 sec
Effective Baud Rate     : 9653
Efficiency              :  101%
```

Admittedly, the performance shown here is somewhat better than typical.

The LOG Command

Syntax: LOG (DEBUG, PACKETS, SESSION, TRANSACTIONS) [*filespec*]

Record the specified information in the specified log file.

• LOG TRANSACTIONS

Directs Kermit to log transactions, such as files successfully sent or received or files that could not be successfully sent or received. A transaction log can be used to record the progress of a long, unattended multifile transfer. Here's a typical transaction log:

```
Transaction Begins Saturday, 8 Feb 1986 12:18:14
   Sending FIND.EXE as FIND.EXE at 12:18:19
     File type binary
     End of file OK
        File characters       : 5796
        Communication line in  : 134
        Communication line out : 1777
   Sending GAME.EXE as GAME.EXE at 12:18:20
     *** ^X Interrupt, Discarded ***
   Skipping GAMES.DIR at 12:18:22
     Reason: Can't send directory file
   Sending KERMIT.EXE as KERMIT.EXE at 12:18:24
     File type binary
     End of file OK
        File characters       : 43754
        Communication line in  : 2956
        Communication line out : 44725
Transaction Ends 12:19:54
Files: 2
Total file characters       : 49550
Communication line in       : 3090
Communication line out      : 46502
Elapsed time (seconds)      : 94
Effective baud rate         : 5314
```

• LOG SESSION

Creates a transcript of a CONNECT session on the specified device (e.g., printer) or disk file. The log is closed when connection is closed. In some implementations, logging can be "toggled" by typing the CONNECT escape character followed by Q (Quit logging) or R (Resume logging) or similar single-character commands. Session logging is useful for recording dialog with an interactive system and for "capturing" from systems that don't have Kermit. No guarantee can be made that the file will contain a correct and complete transcript, since no error checking takes place. See "Raw Download and Upload," page 169.

• LOG DEBUGGING

Records internal state and variable information in the specified file. When reporting Kermit program or protocol bugs, you should accompany the report with a debugging log for the failing transfer.

• LOG PACKETS

Record all the communication line packet traffic in the specified file. Also handy for tracking down protocol problems, and helpful when submitted along with problem reports.

Logging of any kind will slow down file transfers to some degree. Log files can be closed with the CLOSE command, as in CLOSE DEBUG, CLOSE SESSION, etc.

The SET Command

Syntax: SET *parameter* [*parameter*] [*value*]

The SET command establishes or modifies communication, file, or other parameters. When a file transfer operation begins, the two Kermits automatically exchange special initialization messages, in which each program provides the other with certain information about itself. This information includes the maximum packet size it wants to receive, the timeout interval it wants the other Kermit to use, the number and type of padding characters it needs, the control character it needs to terminate each packet (if any), the block check type, and the desired control, eighth-bit, and compression prefixes. Each Kermit program has its own preset default values for these parameters, and normally you need not concern yourself with them. You can examine their values with the SHOW command. The SET command is provided to allow you to change them in order to adapt to unusual conditions. Some SET options are also provided for areas not directly involved in protocol negotiations. The commonly used SET commands are now described in alphabetical order.

SET BAUD

Syntax: SET BAUD *number* **or** SET SPEED *number*

Set or change the baud rate on the currently selected communications device. The way of specifying the baud rate varies from system to system. In most cases, the actual decimal number (such as 1200 or 9600) is typed. Systems that do not provide this command generally expect that the speed of the line has already been set appropriately outside of Kermit. Common values are 300, 1200, 2400, 4800, 9600. If the SET BAUD or SET SPEED command is not available, then you will have to use a system command or utility to accomplish this function before running Kermit.

SET BLOCK-CHECK

Syntax: SET BLOCK-CHECK {1, 2, 3}

Kermit normally uses a one-character block check, or "checksum," on each packet. The sender of the packet computes the block check based on the other characters in the packet, and the receiver recomputes it the same way. If these quantities agree, the packet is accepted and transmission proceeds. If they disagree, the packet is rejected and retransmission is requested.

However, the block check is not a foolproof method of error detection. The normal single-character Kermit block check is only a 6-bit quantity (the low-order 8 bits of the arithmetic sum folded upon itself). With only 6 bits of accuracy, the chances are one in 2^6—that is, 1/64—that an error can occur which will not be detected in the checksum, assuming that all errors are equally likely. The likelihood of errors slipping through is even greater with binary files, since all carries out of the eighth bit are discarded.

You can decrease the probability that an error can slip through, at the expense of transmission efficiency, by using the SET BLOCK-CHECK command to select more rigorous block check methods. Note that all three methods will detect any single-bit error, or any error in an odd number of bits. The options are:

1. The normal single-character 6-bit checksum.

2. A two-character, 12-bit checksum. Reduces the probability of an error going undetected to 1/4096, but adds an extra character to each packet.

3. A three-character, 16-bit cyclic redundancy check (CRC), CCITT format. In addition to errors in any odd number of bits, this method detects double-bit errors, all error bursts of length 16 or less, and more than 99.99 percent of all possible longer bursts. Adds two extra characters to each packet [24].

The single-character checksum has proved quite adequate in practice, much more effective than straightforward analysis would indicate, since all errors are *not* equally likely, and a simple checksum is well suited to catching the kinds of errors that are typical of telecommunication lines. The other methods should be requested when the connection is very noisy or when sending binary files.

The two- and three-character block checks are not available in all versions of Kermit; if the other Kermit is not capable of performing the higher-precision block checks, the transfer will automatically use the standard single-character method.

SET DEBUGGING

Syntax: SET DEBUGGING {ON, OFF}

Selects or disables recording of debugging information, either on your terminal or in a file. Some Kermit programs may use other commands to control debugging, like LOG DEBUG, or simply DEBUG, or they may have other options for SET DEBUGGING to specify what is being recorded—packets, state transitions, internal program information, and so on.

SET DEFAULT

Syntax: SET DEFAULT *device*

Some microcomputer Kermit programs use this command to switch disks, in the same way disks are switched from system command level by typing their names (as in CP/M or MS-DOS).

SET DELAY

Syntax: SET DELAY *number*

Specifies how many seconds to wait before sending the first packet after a SEND command. Use when remote and sending files back to your local Kermit. The delay gives you time to escape back and issue a RECEIVE command before the packets start to arrive. The normal delay is 5 seconds. Use this command to change the normal delay, for instance to give yourself time to move the communication cable from one PC to another before the packets start to arrive. In local mode or server mode, Kermit does not delay before sending the first packet.

SET DESTINATION

Syntax: SET DESTINATION *device*

Specifies an alternative device for arriving files, e.g., a different disk than the current one, a printer, a tape, the screen.

SET DISPLAY

Syntax: SET DISPLAY {ON, OFF, ...}

This command controls the file transfer display that normally occurs only in local mode. Use OFF to allow a file transfer to proceed in the background while doing other work in the foreground, on those systems that allow such a thing. SET DISPLAY OFF might also be used to prevent the display from interfering with packet characters when using a microcomputer's normally local-mode Kermit with the console redirected to the serial port (e.g., by the MS-DOS CTTY command). There may also be other display options like GRAPHIC or TEXT, RANDOM or SERIAL, VERBOSE or TERSE, to select the style of display.

SET DUPLEX

Syntax: SET DUPLEX {FULL, HALF}

Specifies whether the connection to the other system is full- or half-duplex. Half-duplex usually implies local echo and handshake; full-duplex usually implies remote echo and

XON/XOFF flow control. You might find some or all of these parameters tied together in a particular Kermit program. The SET DUPLEX command may be available as SET ECHO or SET LOCAL-ECHO. Most Kermit programs are initially configured for full-duplex operation. Half-duplex is necessary when connecting to IBM mainframes.

SET ECHO

Syntax: SET ECHO {LOCAL, REMOTE}

Specifies who does the echoing during CONNECT, the local or the remote system. See SET DUPLEX.

SET EOF

Syntax: SET EOF *option*

EOF is the common abbreviation for end-of-file. The SET EOF command specifies the method to be used for detecting the end of an outbound file or for marking the end of an inbound file. For instance, some MS-DOS applications require text files to have a Control-Z at the end, while others will ignore one if it's there, and still others will treat the Control-Z as a data character. Binary files, which contain arbitrary bit patterns, may contain Control-Zs at any point. On such a system, the SET EOF command would enable and disable the Control-Z convention. Consult your particular Kermit program's documentation for applicability and syntax. This function might also be lumped with the SET FILE options.

SET ESCAPE

Syntax: SET ESCAPE *character*

Specifies or changes the character to use in order to get the attention of the local Kermit program during terminal emulation. This would normally be a character you don't expect to be using on the remote system, a control character like ^\, ^], ^^, or ^_. Most versions of Kermit use one of these by default. See the description of CONNECT, page 122, for an explanation of the escape character.

SET FILE

Syntax: SET FILE *parameter value*

Establishes file-related parameters. Depending on the characteristics of the system, it may be necessary to tell Kermit how to fetch an outbound file from the disk, or how to store an incoming file. The actual parameters you can specify in this command will vary from system to system, and you should consult the documentation for your particular version of Kermit. Here are some typical ones:

• SET FILE BYTE *number*
Specifies the byte size for file I/O on systems with bytes of different lengths. Also useful on systems with fixed byte size when only a certain number of bits is to be extracted from or stored in each byte; for example, it might be desirable to send the output of certain word processors in 7-bit bytes because they use the eighth bit to indicate some special effect like italics or boldface that can't be used on the target system.

• SET FILE FORMAT *value* [*value*]
For use on systems with a variety of file formats (stream, record, etc.) for specifying parameters like fixed versus variable, block size, record length, carriage control, etc. The syntax will tend to reflect the terminology of the host system.

• SET FILE NAMES {CONVERTED, LITERAL}
Normally CONVERTED, which means that outbound filenames have device, directory, generation, attribute, and other information stripped, with only the file name and type remaining, with lowercase letters raised to upper, "strange" characters changed to X's or deleted, a period separating the file name and type, and additional periods deleted. LITERAL means that none of these conversions are done, and is intended for use between like systems. For inbound files, LITERAL means to attempt to store the file exactly as indicated by the name (this requires that any device or directory path must exist and be write-accessible) and CONVERTED means to do whatever conversions upon the name are needed to put it into legal and conventional format for storing in the current area. CONVERTED option may be called NORMAL in some Kermit versions, and NAMES might be called NAMING.

• SET FILE SUPERSEDE {ON, OFF}
Rejects any incoming file that has the same name as an existing file. Useful for restarting wildcard groups after a failure. Normally OFF.

• SET FILE TYPE {BINARY, TEXT}
Normally TEXT, meaning that the file is to be converted to or from canonical form, that is, ASCII stream with carriage-return/linefeed sequences (CRLFs) at the end of each line. BINARY means no conversions are done upon the file data.

• SET FILE WARNING {ON, OFF}
Normally OFF, which means that incoming files will silently overwrite existing files of the same name. When ON, Kermit will check if an arriving file would overwrite an existing file. If so, it will construct a new unique name for the arriving file and warn you that it did so to allow you to find the file once it has arrived.

CAUTION: If the arrival of a file is cancelled, and a file of the same name previously existed, *and* the file warning feature is not enabled, then the previous copy of the file may be destroyed.

Some systems may lack one or more of these file settings, name them differently, or supply additional ones like record length, block size (record-oriented systems), or allocation method.

SET FLOW-CONTROL

Syntax: `SET FLOW—CONTROL {NONE, ENQ/ACK, ETX/ACK, XON/XOFF, ...}`

Specifies the system-level flow-control method for both terminal emulation and packet protocol. System-level flow control is not necessary to the Kermit protocol, but it can be beneficial when the same method is available on both systems. The most common type of flow control on full-duplex systems is XON/XOFF. The options for the Kermit SET FLOW command are usually restricted to the system's normal method (e.g., XON/XOFF, ENQ/ACK), and NONE (which is used to disable this feature). NONE should be selected if the Kermit program on the other end does not support the same kind of flow control.

When a system does in-band flow control, it is usually opaque to the characters used for this. They are swallowed by the system or the front end and are not passed to the application program as data. SET FLOW NONE allows these characters to pass through transparently, at the risk of buffer overflows. Use SET FLOW NONE on half-duplex connections, where you should SET HANDSHAKE instead.

SET HANDSHAKE

Syntax: `SET HANDSHAKE` *option*

For file transfer with half-duplex systems. This lets you inform the Kermit program of the line turnaround character transmitted by a half-duplex host to indicate it has ended its transmission and is granting you permission to transmit. When a handshake is set, Kermit will not send a packet until the half-duplex host has sent the specified character (or a timeout has occurred). Usually has no effect on terminal emulation. The options may include XOFF, CR, LF, ESC, and NONE. Some Kermit programs may require the option to be specified by typing the character literally or entering its numeric ASCII value. If you use this command to enable handshaking, you should also SET FLOW NONE.

SET IBM

Syntax: `{SET, DO} IBM [ {ON, OFF} ]`

Many Kermit programs provide this command as a quick way to set all the parameters required for communication with an IBM mainframe in line mode, typically PARITY

MARK, HANDSHAKE XON, FLOW NONE, DUPLEX HALF, TIMER ON. If your Kermit program has this command, but it sets one of the parameters wrong for your IBM system, you can issue the correcting command after the SET IBM command, e.g.,

```
set ibm on
set parity even
```

"IBM" may be either a "hardwired" command in your Kermit program, or a (perhaps predefined) macro.

SET INCOMPLETE

Syntax: SET INCOMPLETE {KEEP, DISCARD}

Specifies what to do when a file transfer fails before it is completed. The options are DISCARD (the default) and KEEP. If you choose KEEP, then if a transfer fails to complete successfully, you will be able to keep the incomplete part that was received. Make sure, when using this command, that you don't mistake an incomplete file for a complete one.

SET INPUT

Syntax: SET INPUT {CASE, DEFAULT-TIMEOUT, TIMEOUT-ACTION} *value*

Controls the behavior of the INPUT command (see the sections on Login Scripts and Raw Download and Upload, beginning on page 169). SET INPUT CASE {IGNORE, OBSERVE} tells what to do about alphabetic case in search strings. DEFAULT-TIMEOUT tells how long to wait for some specified string to appear in the input before timing out, if the INPUT command itself does not include a specific interval. TIMEOUT-ACTION tells whether to PROCEED with the script or to QUIT from it when a timeout occurs. See the section on Login Scripts for details.

SET KEY

Syntax: SET KEY {SCAN *number*, F*n*} *value*

This command allows key remapping or keystroke macros to be defined on microcomputers. For instance, if your micro's keyboard has the Escape key in the "wrong place," you can use this command to "move" it. Or you can assign a commonly typed sequence of characters to a single rarely used key. The exact syntax varies from system to system, but in general you can select function keys (like F1, F2), or any key at all by scan code (which you can obtain from your micro's technical manual or by using the SHOW KEY command). The value associated with a key can be any character string, including a single character. To include a character in the value string that could otherwise not be typed at Kermit command level, you can substitute its ASCII value (usually in octal notation), preceded by a backslash (\). Here's an example:

```
Kermit-xx>show key
Press a key: '
  Scan Code:  96
  Definition:
Kermit-xx>set key scan 96
Definition string: \33
Kermit-xx>show key
Press a key: '
  Scan Code:  96
  Definition: \33
Kermit-xx>
```

See your particular Kermit documentation for details.

SET LINE

Syntax: SET LINE [*terminal-designator*]

Specifies the terminal line to use for file transfer or CONNECT, to which all subsequent communication-related SET commands will apply (e.g., SET BAUD, PARITY, DUPLEX). The SET LINE command is found on mainframe Kermits, which normally run in remote mode using their own controlling terminal for file transfer. Specifying a separate line puts the program in local mode. If the terminal designator is omitted, the program reverts to remote mode.

SET MODEM

Syntax: SET MODEM *modem-type*

Specifies the type of modem to be used for the DIAL command, when more than one type might be supported by the Kermit program, so that it will know how to control the dialer. Example: SET MODEM HAYES. To specify that no modem is in use (normally the default condition) use SET MODEM NONE (or possibly SET MODEM DIRECT).

SET PARITY

Syntax: SET PARITY {EVEN, ODD, MARK, SPACE, NONE}

Allows a Kermit program to accommodate to a system or transmission medium that uses or requires parity. If you fail to use this command under these conditions, then file transfer cannot take place, because the packets might not get through at all, or if they do, the block check will be wrong.

Kermit programs that run on mainframes that require parity (like IBM or Prime) are already set up for parity operation and need not be given a SET PARITY command. Kermit programs that intend to communicate with such mainframes, however, must be told about parity.

Two Kermit programs that are running on systems that don't normally use or require parity, but which are connected over a channel that does (for example, a public network like Telenet) will *both* need to be given SET PARITY commands.

Both Kermit programs should be set to the same parity. The specified parity is used both for terminal connection and file transfer. During terminal emulation, incoming characters will have their parity bits stripped before display. The choices for SET PARITY are:

NONE (The default) Eight data bits and no parity bit.

MARK Seven data bits with the parity bit set to one.

SPACE Seven data bits with the parity bit set to zero.

EVEN   Seven data bits with the parity bit set to make the overall parity even.

ODD   Seven data bits with the parity bit set to make the overall parity odd.

NONE means no parity processing is done, and the eighth bit of each character is available for data when transmitting binary files. When set to other than NONE, 8-bit binary files can be transferred only if both Kermit programs agree to use the optional eighth-bit prefixing technique. Those Kermit programs which support this technique will automatically bid to use it when parity is set to other than NONE.

SET PORT

Syntax: SET PORT *port-designator*

Specifies the communication port for file transfer or CONNECT. This command is found on microcomputer Kermits that run in local mode. SET PORT does not change the remote/local status but simply selects a different port for local operation on systems that have more than one communication port. Some microcomputer Kermit programs that have this command allow settings like parity and duplex to be assigned on a per-port basis, so that you can switch among multiple connections conveniently.

SET PROMPT

Syntax: SET PROMPT *string*

This command allows you to change the program's prompt. This is particularly useful if you are using Kermit to transfer files between two systems of the same kind, in which case you can change the prompts of the Kermit programs involved to include appropriate distinguishing information.

SET RECEIVE

Syntax: SET RECEIVE *parameter value*

Establishes parameters to request or expect for incoming packets, as follows:

- SET RECEIVE END-OF-PACKET *character*
(or EOL or END-OF-LINE). Asks the other Kermit to terminate its packets with the specified character, carriage return (ASCII 13) by default.

- SET RECEIVE PACKET-LENGTH *number*
Maximum length packet for the other Kermit to send, between 10 and 94 (decimal) in standard, classic Kermit. The maximum length may be as high as 9024 if the long packet extension is available and 857,374 with "extra long" packets.

- SET RECEIVE PAD-CHARACTER *character*
Requests the specified padding character be appended to incoming packets (see SET SEND PAD-CHARACTER, below).

- SET RECEIVE PADDING *number*
The desired number of copies of the requested padding character.

- SET RECEIVE PAUSE *number*
How many seconds to pause before acknowledging a packet. Setting this to a nonzero value will slow down the rate at which data packets arrive, which may be necessary for systems that have sensitive front ends and cannot accept input at a high rate.

- SET RECEIVE START-OF-PACKET *control-character*
Instructs Kermit to look for the specified control character to mark the beginning of incoming packets. Normally SOH (Control-A, ASCII 1) (see SET SEND START-OF-PACKET, below).

- SET RECEIVE TIMEOUT *number*
Sets the value of the timeout field to be sent to the other Kermit, which tells it how many seconds to wait for a packet before sending a NAK or retransmitting. A value of zero tells it not to time out, to wait forever for each packet.

SET RETRY

Syntax: SET RETRY [{INITIAL, PACKETS}] *number*

Set the maximum number of retries allowed for:

• INITIAL

How many times to try establishing the initial protocol connection before giving up, normally something like 15.

• PACKETS

How many times to try sending a particular packet before giving up, normally 5. If a line is very noisy, you might want to increase this number.

SET SEND

Syntax: SET SEND *parameter value*

Specifies parameters to use when sending packets. These may be in effect only for the initial packet sent, since the other Kermit may override them during the protocol parameter exchange (unless noted below).

• SET SEND END-OF-PACKET *character*

(or EOL, or END-OF-LINE). Specifies the ASCII character to be used as a line terminator for outbound packets, if one is required by the other system, carriage return by default. You will have to use this command in order to get the first packet through to the rare system that requires a line terminator other than carriage return.

• SET SEND PACKET-LENGTH *number*

Specifies the maximum packet length to send, between 10 and 94 in unextended Kermit programs, or up to 9024 or 857,374 when the long-packet extensions are available. Shorter packet lengths can be useful on noisy lines, or with systems or front ends or networks that have small buffers. The shorter the packet, the higher the per-packet overhead, but the lower the chance of a packet being corrupted by noise, and the less time to retransmit corrupted packets. Lengthening the packets increases the throughput on clean lines. This command overrides the value requested by the other Kermit during protocol initiation, so don't use it to make packets longer than the other Kermit can accommodate. If you request a number larger than 94, but the other Kermit can't do long packets, then a smaller number will be used automatically. Kermit programs always use unextended packets unless explicitly directed to the contrary.

• SET SEND PAD-CHARACTER *character*

Designates a character to send before each packet. Normally, none is sent. Outbound padding is sometimes necessary for communicating with slow half-duplex systems that provide no other means of line turnaround control. It can also be used to send special characters to communication equipment that needs to be put in transparent or no-echo mode, when this can be accomplished by feeding it a certain control character.

• SET SEND PADDING *n*

Tells how many copies of the pad character to send, normally 0 (zero). It is rarely necessary to issue SET SEND PAD-CHARACTER and PADDING commands, since the other Kermit will request any required padding in its Send-Init packet.

• SET SEND PAUSE *number*

How many seconds to pause before sending each data packet. Setting this to a nonzero value may allow a slow or heavily loaded system enough time to consolidate itself before the next packet arrives. Normally, no per-packet pausing is done. Some Kermit programs allow the number to include a fractional part, as in SET SEND PAUSE 0.5. The PAUSE parameter is not part of the Send-Init parameter exchange.

• SET SEND START-OF-PACKET *character*

The start-of-packet character is the only control character used "bare" in a Kermit packet. It is Control-A by default. If a bare Control-A causes problems for your communication hardware or software, you can use this command to select a different control character to mark the start of a packet. You must also issue the corresponding command (SET RECEIVE START-OF-PACKET) to the Kermit on the other system (providing it has such a command). This technique also allows the protocol to survive communication front ends that echo all the characters they receive, when the Kermit program itself is not smart enough to discard the echoed packet (some are, some aren't). The start-of-packet character is not a Send-Init parameter (how could it be?).

• SET SEND TIMEOUT *number*

How many seconds to wait for a packet from the other Kermit before sending a NAK or retransmitting. A value of zero means "don't time out; wait forever." This overrides any Send-Init timeout parameter provided by the other Kermit. It is often necessary to increase the timeout interval when using communication media (like public networks) with built-in delays. The benefit is in fewer timeouts; the cost is in longer time to recover from lost packets.

SET SERVER

Syntax: SET SERVER *parameter* [*value*]

Sets server-related parameters in preparation for putting the program into server mode:

• SET SERVER TIMEOUT [*number*]

Set the server command loop NAK interval to the given number of seconds. Normally, a Kermit server will send a NAK every 30 seconds or so while waiting for commands in order to break the deadlock that would occur if the local Kermit's command packet were lost and the local Kermit is not doing timeouts. These NAKs are triggered by a timer that is separate from its normal packet timer (which you can set from your local Kermit via SET RECEIVE TIMEOUT), and they are not part of protocol negotiation. If you do not interact with the Kermit server for a very long period of time, your system might become clogged by all these NAKs, possibly XOFFing the server. If this happens, you can tell the server to send the NAKs less frequently or not at all. Use SET SERVER TIMEOUT 0 to disable the NAKs altogether.

SET SPEED

Syntax: SET SPEED *number*

Sets the speed (baud rate) of the currently selected port or line. Sometimes available as SET BAUD.

SET TAKE

Syntax: SET TAKE {ECHO, ERROR}

This command controls the behavior of the TAKE command. SET TAKE ECHO {ON, OFF} tells whether the contents of a command file should be displayed on the screen during execution. SET TAKE ERROR {PROCEED, QUIT} tells whether the Kermit program should continue to execute a command file after an error has occurred.

SET TERMINAL

Syntax: SET TERMINAL {*type, parameter value*}

For microcomputer Kermit programs that include built-in emulation for more than one type of terminal, use this command to select which emulator to use, e.g., H19, VT52, VT100, VT102, NONE. Also used to select terminal specific features like autowrap, color, etc.

SET TIMER

Syntax: SET TIMER {ON, OFF}

Turns the timer ON or OFF in the Kermit program to which this command is issued. If ON, SET SEND/RECEIVE TIMEOUT commands are processed as described above, and the timing parameters from the Send-Init negotiation are honored. If OFF, timeouts will not be done, no matter what commands you have issued, or what the other Kermit requests. Microcomputers usually have their timers OFF on the assumption that most file transfer is done with mainframes that are capable of providing more intelligent timeouts. It is sufficient for only one Kermit program to have a timer active. If both have timers going, there could be unnecessary collisions.

SET TRANSLATION

Syntax: SET TRANSLATION *"string1"* *"string2"*

This command provides a mechanism for coping with opaque communication equipment. It has nothing to do with the Kermit protocol, in the sense that no coordination between the two Kermit programs is involved. SET TRANSLATION simply specifies that after a packet is already fully formed, the specified transformation is to be done upon it before it is transmitted. The objective is for the packet to arrive at its destination exactly as it was formed before the transformation was applied. Therefore, only those transformations are useful which accomplish this objective. Example:

```
SET TRANSLATION "@" "@@"
```

would allow @ to get through a box that uses @ as an escape character, but passes one copy of it through if it receives two in a row.

The string arguments may contain any characters, but each should be enclosed in double quotes so that the two strings can be distinguished. Unusual characters, or double quotes themselves, may be quoted by preceding their numeric ASCII values with backslash. Translation occurs only during packet operations, not during terminal connection (you can use SET KEY for that).

SET WINDOW

Syntax: SET WINDOW *[number]*

Enables Kermit's full-duplex sliding window protocol extension for increased throughput, especially when communicating over a full-duplex channel with built-in delays, like a public network. This feature allows continuous sending and receiving of packets, so that the sender need not wait for the receiver's ACK before sending the next packet. The window size specifies how many ACKs may remain outstanding at a time, between 0 (zero, the normal value) and 31. Experiment to determine the best value for a given connection and Kermit program. Usually a number somewhere between 4 and 16 is sufficient to achieve continuous transmission. If the other Kermit does not "do windows" (most as yet do not), then a window size of 0 will be used automatically.

Performance may also be improved by increasing the packet size, provided both Kermits support the long-packet protocol extension and the connection is relatively clean. Long packets and sliding windows may be used together, but there's no reason why they should be. When using sliding windows, the packet length should kept be relatively short (80–90 characters) to reduce retransmission overhead.

The DEFINE Command

Syntax: DEFINE *macroname* [*phrase*, [*phrase*, [. . .]]]

The DEFINE command lets you set up a "macro" to allow convenient association of one or more commands or SET parameters with a single keyword of your choice. The phrases in the syntax specification are either Kermit commands, as you would type them at command level, or SET options, separated by commas. Some Kermit programs allow any Kermit command to be included in a macro definition, while others allow only SET options (anything you would type after SET).

If you use Kermit to communicate with several different kinds of systems, you may set up a macro for each, for instance:[5]

```
COMMENT Settings for IBM mainframe with 3705 front end:
DEFINE IBM3705 SET PARITY MARK, SET DUPLEX HALF, SET HANDSHAKE XON, -
  SET FLOW NONE, SET TIMER ON

COMMENT Settings for IBM mainframe with 7171 protocol emulator:
DEFINE IBM7171 SET PARITY EVEN, SET DUPLEX FULL, SET HANDSHAKE NONE, -
  SET FLOW XON/XOFF, SET TIMER ON, SET SEND PACKET-LENGTH 60

COMMENT Settings for VAX with UNIX or VMS:
DEFINE VAX SET PARITY NONE, SET DUPLEX FULL, SET HANDSHAKE NONE, -
  SET FLOW XON/XOFF, SET TIMER OFF

COMMENT Settings for GTE Telenet
DEFINE TELENET SET PARITY MARK, SET TIMER ON, SET RECEIVE TIMEOUT 20, -
  SET WINDOW 16
```

(When the Kermit program allows only SET options in macro definitions, the commands would be DEFINE IBM PARITY MARK, DUPLEX HALF, HANDSHAKE XON, etc.). You may then type SET (or DO, depending on the syntax your program provides) IBM, SET VAX, and so forth, to set all the desired parameters with a single command.

Another handy use for macros is to allow rapid adaptation to different conditions of line noise:

```
DEFINE CLEAN BLOCK 1, REC PACKET 94, RETRY PACKET 5
DEFINE NOISY BLOCK 2, REC PACKET 60, RETRY PACKET 10
DEFINE AWFUL BLOCK 3, REC PACKET 40, RETRY PACKET 20
```

(or DEFINE CLEAN SET BLOCK 1, etc.).

---

5. These definitions are examples only. Most Kermit programs do not allow command continuation as shown; these long commands had to be split between lines so they would fit on the page. Also, particular settings may vary from site to site.

As noted, those Kermit implementations which provide a macro facility may differ in the ways they expect the macro to be invoked:

1. By name—just use its name as a command, e.g., AWFUL.

2. The DO command, e.g., DO AWFUL

3. As an option in a SET command, e.g., SET AWFUL

As usual, consult the documentation for your particular program for details.

In general, Kermit programs do not provide a way to "undo" the effect of a macro, but you can always define another macro to restore things the way they were before, like the CLEAN macro shown in the previous example. You may also redefine an existing macro in the same manner as you defined it (just issue another DEFINE command using the same name), and you can undefine an existing macro by typing an empty DEFINE command for it, for instance:

```
DEFINE AWFUL
```

Macro definitions take up space in memory, so you cannot have an unlimited number of them. You can list all your macros and their definitions with the SHOW MACROS command, which should also show you how much space remains for additional definitions. Macros are most conveniently defined in a TAKE command file (such as your Kermit initialization file, which is TAKEn automatically each time you run the program), so that you need type their definitions only once.

The SHOW Command

Syntax: SHOW [option]

The SHOW command displays the values of the SET parameters. If a particular option is not requested, a complete display will be provided. Here is the output of UNIX Kermit's SHOW command:

```
Communications Parameters:
 Line: /dev/acu, speed: 1200, mode: local, modem-dialer: hayes
 Parity: none, duplex: full, flow: xon/xoff, handshake: none

Protocol Parameters:      Send      Receive
 Timeout:                   10          7
 Padding:                    0          0
 Pad Character:              0          0
 Packet Start:              1          1
 Packet End:               13         13
 Packet Length:            90         90
```

```
Block Check Type: 1, Delay: 5

File parameters:
  File Names:   converted      Debugging Log:    none
  File Type:    text           Packet Log:       none
  File Warning: off            Session Log:      none
  File Display: on             Transaction Log:  none

Incomplete File Disposition: discard, Init file: .kermrc
```

Some Kermit programs provide a SHOW command for every SET command, e.g., SHOW SEND TIMEOUT. Others group related parameters together for convenient display, e.g., SHOW PACKET, SHOW COMMUNICATION. SHOW VERSION displays information about the Kermit program version.

SHOW KEY is for use in conjunction with SET KEY on microcomputer Kermit programs that provide key redefinition. In response to SHOW KEY, the program asks you to press a key. When you press it, the program tells you the scan code (for use in conjunction with SET KEY SCAN) as well as any redefinitions currently in effect.

SHOW MACROS is used to display currently defined command macros, along with any relevant information about their consumption of memory. See DEFINE.

Login Scripts

A handy feature to have in any communication program is a "login script" interpreter. Login scripts are used to automate frequently performed interactions with remote computers. They can relieve you of the tedium of repetitive or complicated tasks, and they can allow routine interactions with remote computers to occur unattended, perhaps late at night when phone rates are low and timesharing systems are fast.

The special INPUT, OUTPUT, CLEAR, and PAUSE commands may be combined with other Kermit commands in a TAKE command file to provide the ability to initially connect and log in to a remote system, initiate file transfers in either direction, log out, and disconnect.

Each of the special commands honors all the current communication settings—speed, parity, duplex, flow control, etc.—and is usually coordinated with session and transaction logging to allow transcripts to record the progress of unattended operations.

The CLEAR Command

Syntax: CLEAR

Clears the input and output buffers of the currently selected line and attempts to break any flow control (XOFF) deadlock.

The PAUSE Command

Syntax: PAUSE [*number*]

Pauses the specified number of seconds before executing the next command. The default interval is 1 second.

The INPUT Command

Syntax: INPUT [*interval*] [*string*]

Looks for the given string for the specified number of seconds on the currently selected communication line. If no interval is specified, then the default interval is used, which may be specified by SET INPUT DEFAULT-TIMEOUT, and which is normally 5 seconds. Specifying an interval of 0 means "no timeout; wait forever for the specified string."

Characters coming in from the line will be scanned for the search string, and when a match is found, the command will terminate successfully. If the string is not found within the given interval, the command will terminate unsuccessfully. While the INPUT command is active, all incoming characters will appear on your screen.

The search string may contain any printable characters. Control or other special characters that you could not normally type as part of a command may be included by preceding their numeric ASCII values with a backslash, for instance foo\15 is "foo" followed by a carriage return (octal numbers will be used in all the following examples).

While scanning, alphabetic case is ignored (a = A) unless you have SET INPUT CASE OBSERVE. If no search string is given, then the INPUT command will simply display all incoming characters on your screen until it times out or is interrupted.

If the INPUT command finds the specified string within the allotted amount of time, it terminates immediately without an error message, and the next command is executed. If the INPUT command fails to find the requested string, it will "fail." Failure is significant only if the command was issued from a TAKE command file, and INPUT TIMEOUT-ACTION is SET to QUIT. When a timeout occurs under these conditions, the command file is immediately terminated and control is returned to the invoking level, either the Kermit program prompt or a superior command file. If INPUT TIMEOUT-ACTION is SET to PROCEED, then the next command (if any) will be executed from the current command file.

The OUTPUT Command

Syntax: OUTPUT [*string*]

The given string is sent out the currently selected communication line. The string is in the same form as the INPUT string. Control or special characters may be included by prefacing their numeric ASCII values with backslash characters. Note that any terminating carriage return must be included explicitly, e.g., as \15. The string will also be echoed at your terminal.

The SCRIPT Command

Syntax: SCRIPT [*string*]

The SCRIPT command provides an escape clause to allow for system- or implementation-dependent script formats, such as the UNIX UUCP "expect-send" format. Normally, a Kermit program will not have a SCRIPT command if it has the INPUT and OUTPUT commands.

How to Use Login Scripts

Scripts can be used to automate the task of connecting and logging in. For instance, suppose you are using a DECSYSTEM-20 that is connected to a VAX UNIX system through a hardwired line on TTY line 13. To send a file to the VAX, you must connect to the VAX through the line, log in, run UNIX Kermit, escape back to the DEC-20, and issue the appropriate file transfer commands, then connect back to the VAX and log out. This may all be automated by means of the following set of commands stored in a DEC-20 file invoked by the Kermit TAKE command:

```
set line 13
output \15
input login:
out myuserid\15
in Password:
out mypassword\15
in 20 %
out kermit -r\15
send foo.bar
out \4
input
```

The first line points DEC-20 Kermit (Kermit-20) at the communication line. The next line sends a carriage return, which makes UNIX issue a login: prompt; the following INPUT command waits for this prompt to appear. When it does, Kermit-20 outputs *myuserid* followed by a carriage return. UNIX then prompts for a password; after the prompt appears, Kermit-20 supplies the password. Then Kermit-20 waits up to 20 seconds for the UNIX shell's % prompt. This allows time for various system messages to be displayed. When the shell prompt appears, Kermit-20 sends the command kermit -r, which tells UNIX Kermit to receive a file. Then a SEND command is given to Kermit-20. After the file is successfully transferred, Kermit-20 sends a logout command (\4, Control-D) to UNIX. The final INPUT command causes Kermit-20 to display any typeout (in this case the UNIX system's logout message) that occurs up to the default timeout interval.

The INPUT command is very important, because it ensures synchronization. One might expect to be able to simply send all the characters out the communication line at once, and let the remote host's typeahead and buffering facilities take care of the synchronization. In rare or simple cases, this might work, but it assumes that (a) the remote host allows typeahead, (b) the remote host's typeahead buffers are big enough to accommodate all the characters, *and* (c) the remote host never clears pending typeahead. These conditions rarely hold. For instance, UNIX clears its input buffer *after* issuing the Password: prompt; any typeahead will be lost. Interactive users as well as login script facilities must wait for the prompt before entering the password. This is the function of the INPUT command. On half-duplex systems, this function is critical. These systems cannot accept any input in advance of a prompt; there is no typeahead.

The Kermit script facility is not a programming language. There are no conditional execution of commands, no branching, no labels. Nevertheless, the SET INPUT command provides a degree of control. If the UNIX system were "down" in the sample script, Kermit-20 would still proceed merrily through the entire script, sending its output into the void and waiting the entire timeout interval on each INPUT command, and then attempt to send a file to a Kermit that wasn't there. It could take several minutes of timing out to terminate the script. This could be avoided by including the command

```
SET INPUT TIMEOUT-ACTION QUIT
```

at the top of the script. When the login: prompt failed to appear within the timeout interval, the rest of the script would be cancelled.

Nested command file capability combined with input timeout action selection can be used to provide a kind of "if-then-else" feature. Suppose you want to log in automatically to a system that *sometimes* asks you a question immediately after you log in. You don't want to always include the answer (say, "no"), because if you type the string "no" at normal system command level, it performs some undesirable function. You can handle the situation by writing a script that invokes another script. In this example, the system's prompt is % and the question's prompt ends in ?.

```
set input timeout quit
output \15
input login:
out myuserid\15
in 10 Password:
out mypassword\15
take question.cmd
in %
echo Logged in OK.
```

Here, after logging in successfully, the Kermit command file QUESTION.CMD is invoked from within the preceding command file. QUESTION.CMD looks like this:

```
input \77
output no\15
```

If the question mark appears (indicated here as \77 because a literal question mark would only produce a help message), Kermit-20 will answer "no." If not, a timeout will occur, and the *current* command file will be terminated without outputting the "no," returning control to the command file that invoked it.

The Kermit script facility allows complicated tasks to be performed routinely, since any Kermit commands can be included in a command file. For instance, suppose at your site all systems are reached through a port contention unit, which prompts you for a system and then connects you to it. That system may itself be another front end, which prompts you for yet another system. Each of these systems may have different characteristics as to duplex, parity, and so forth:

```
set parity none
set duplex full
set flow none
input Which system?
pause
output vm\15
input Select A or B
pause
output B\15
set duplex half
set parity mark
set handshake xon
output \15
input .\21
output login myuserid\15
input .\21
output mypassword
```

In this fragment, we talk full-duplex no parity to the port switcher, select the "vm" front end, then select the "B" system, then switch to mark parity, half-duplex, XON handshaking for system B. Then we log in to the half-duplex B system, which always issues a prompt of "." (dot) followed by an XON (^Q, ASCII 21 octal) when it is ready for input. Note the use of the PAUSE command, to give these often slow switching devices time to prepare themselves for input; the fact that they have issued a prompt is not always indication enough.

Perhaps the most common use for login scripts is the control of autodialers. Here's a simple script for dialing the number 765-4321 on a Hayes modem:

```
set input timeout quit
pause 1
output +++
pause 1
output AT\15
```

```
input OK
output ATD7654321\15
input CONNECT
connect
```

If the entire script succeeds, you will find yourself connected to the remote system. If any INPUT command fails, you'll find yourself back at local Kermit command level.

The Kermit script facility could be extended into a full-fledged programming language, complete with variables, labels, IF statements, loops, pattern matching, and so forth, but it hasn't happened yet.

Raw Download and Upload

Raw download is the term commonly used to describe the capture of a remote file on the local system without any kind of error detection or correction. This is how you obtain files from remote systems that do not have Kermit (or any other file transfer protocol that you also have), but this method entails the risk of loss or corruption of data.

Many Kermit programs provide raw downloading via the LOG SESSION command during CONNECT to a remote system (the session log is described on page 147). To use session logging to capture a file, do the following:

1. Run your local Kermit program.

2. Perform any required SET commands to condition Kermit for communication with the remote system. You may need SET PARITY, SET DUPLEX, SET FLOW, SET HANDSHAKE, etc., depending on the characteristics of the remote system and the communication medium.

3. CONNECT to the remote system and log in.

4. Set your terminal type on the remote system to as dumb a terminal as possible, and one that requires no padding, so that terminal control sequences and padding characters do not get mixed up in your file.

5. Condition your job on the remote system not to pause at the end of a screenful of text, and give whatever commands may be necessary to achieve a clean terminal listing—for instance, disable messages from the system or other users.

6. Type the appropriate command to have the desired file displayed at the terminal, *but without the terminating carriage return*. On most systems, the command would be TYPE; on UNIX it's "cat."

7. Escape back to Kermit on the local system and give the LOG SESSION command.

8. CONNECT back to the remote system and type a carriage return. The file will be displayed on your screen and recorded in the session log file.

9. Escape back to Kermit on the local system and give the CLOSE SESSION command.

You will probably find some editing necessary to remove extraneous prompts, messages, padding characters, or terminal escape sequences, or to fill in lost or garbled characters.

Raw upload means sending a file from the local system to a remote one, again without error detection or correction. Some Kermit programs provide a TRANSMIT command for this purpose.

The TRANSMIT Command

Syntax: TRANSMIT *filespec* [*prompt*]

The TRANSMIT command (which may be used in local mode only) sends the specified text file a line at a time, "raw" (as is, *without* using Kermit protocol), to the remote system, waiting for the specified prompt for each line. Only a single file may be sent with the TRANSMIT command; wildcards are not allowed in the filespec. The file should be a text file, not a binary file. Since protocol is not being used, no assurance can be given that the file will arrive at the destination correctly or completely.

The *prompt* is any string, for instance the prompt of a line editor in text insertion mode. The prompt string may include special characters by preceding their numeric ASCII values with a backslash, e.g., in octal, \12 for linefeed, \21 for XON (^Q). The syntax of the prompt string is the same as for the object string of the INPUT command.

If a prompt string is supplied, alphabetic case will be ignored in searching for it unless you SET INPUT CASE OBSERVE. If a prompt string is not supplied, then linefeed will be used by default unless you have performed a SET HANDSHAKE command, in which case the current handshake character will be used. If you really want to send the entire file without waiting for any prompts, specify a prompt of \0 (ASCII zero, NUL) (this is not advised).

The file will be sent using the current settings for duplex, parity, and flow control. There are no timeouts on input, as there are with the INPUT command. Most TRANS-MIT commands wait forever for the prompt to appear, and in that case a deadlock will occur if the prompt is garbled in transmission. If you observe that the transfer is stuck, there are three things you can do:

1. Type a carriage return to transmit the next line.

2. Type a Control-P to retransmit the previous line.

3. Type a Control-C to cancel the TRANSMIT command and get back to Kermit command level.

(Syntax may vary.)

TRANSMIT should be used as follows. CONNECT to the remote system, log in, and start up some kind of process on the remote system to store input from the terminal into a file. On a DEC-20 (that doesn't have Kermit), you could do

```
copy tty: foo.bar
```

or you could start a line editor like EDIT or Otto and put it into text insertion mode. On a UNIX system, you could

```
cat /dev/tty > foo.bar
```

or you could run "ed" and give it the "a" command. After you have made the remote system ready to collect text, escape back to the local Kermit and then issue the TRANSMIT command.

The TRANSMIT command will send the first line of the file immediately. Then it will wait for a prompt from the remote system before sending the next line. When performing a copy operation from the terminal to a file, the prompt will probably be a linefeed, \12, which is the default prompt. Most full-duplex systems expect you to type a line of text terminated by a carriage return. They echo the characters you type and then output a linefeed. Half-duplex systems, on the other hand, use some kind of line turnaround handshake character, like XON (Control-Q), to let you know when they are ready for the next line of input. Line editors like Wylbur or Otto may prompt you with a line number followed by a tab; in that case your prompt character would be \11. In any case, to assure synchronization, it is your responsibility to set up the target system to accept line-at-a-time textual input and to determine what the system's prompt will be when it is ready for the next line.

Each line is sent with a terminating carriage return, just as it would be if you were typing at the terminal. Linefeeds are not sent, since these are supplied by the receiving system if it needs them. The TRANSMIT command continues to send all the lines of the file in this manner until it reaches the end, or until you interrupt the operation by typing Control-C.

If you cannot make the TRANSMIT command work automatically, for instance because the remote system's prompt changes for each line, you may TRANSMIT manually by specifying a prompt string that will not appear and then typing a carriage return at your keyboard for each line you want to send.

If the TRANSMIT command completes successfully, then you must connect back to the remote system and type whatever command it needs in order to save or close the file there.

6

Common Problems and How to Fix Them

Connecting two computers can be a tricky business, and many things can go wrong. Before you can transfer files at all, you must first establish terminal communication— a feat in itself. But successful terminal connection does not necessarily mean that file transfer will also work. And even when file transfer appears to be working, the appearance can be deceptive.

If you are using a public X.25 network like Telenet or Datapac, be sure to read the discussion of public data networks starting on page 98. Table 4-4 shows the communication parameters that you can set on the PAD, and you probably *will* have to set some of these before file transfer can work. Sample settings for file transfer are shown in Table 4-5. You may also have to set certain Kermit parameters as well, including parity, packet length, timeout, and retry threshold.

Basic Connection Problems

If you have a version of Kermit on your microcomputer, but the CONNECT command doesn't work at all:

• Make sure all the required physical connections have been made and have not wiggled loose, and that all the devices involved are turned on.

• If you have more than one port on your micro, make sure you are using the right one (SET PORT, SET LINE).

• Make sure that all communication devices (ports, modems, etc.) are configured for the same baud rate.

• For a direct connection between two computers, you must use a null modem cable. Make sure the systems are configured correctly for the desired kind of communication (e.g., the remote system's terminal port is enabled for logins, the speed is set right). If all that seems OK, then your systems are probably refusing to communicate because some of the RS-232 modem signals (DTR, DSR, RTS, CTS, and RI) are not behaving appropriately. Try a different kind of null modem cable, or find a breakout box and start fiddling with the signals until the connection works, then fix up the cable accordingly. See the section in the data communication primer on null modem cables, page 102.

- If you are using a modem, make sure it's compatible with the one you have dialed (e.g., both are Bell-103, or Bell-212, or whatever), and that carrier is present (usually indicated by a light on the modem). If you still can't communicate, there may be a problem with the RS-232 signals between your port and your modem. First, make sure you are using a straight-through cable with pins 1–8, 20, and 22 connected. If not, get one and see if it fixes the problem. If not, then you can try setting configuration switches on the modem (e.g., for answer/originate mode, full/half-duplex, or whether the modem requires DTR from the PC, or whether RTS/CTS is to be used, etc.); see your modem manual. Failing that, you can supply the missing signals or disable the offending ones by fooling with the wires in your connector (for instance, if DTR is misbehaving on your PC, jumper DSR to DTR in the connector on the modem's end of the cable).

- If you are attempting to use an internal modem which takes the place of an RS-232 serial port, you may not be able to use Kermit unless (a) the modem perfectly mimics the characteristics and behavior of the serial port it replaces from the program's point of view, or (b) the program is written with explicit knowledge of the particular internal modem in question. In general, internal modems are not recommended for use with Kermit because most Kermit programs do not have the required explicit knowledge built in, and many of these modems do not mimic the regular serial port. And you can't fake the RS-232 signals as you can in a real De-connector.

- If you are using a "smart" modem that you normally use with a proprietary program, you should not expect Kermit to have the same built-in knowledge of the modem's functionality. In particular, you might have to type explicit setup and dialing commands to it after you give the Kermit CONNECT command. The modem might not echo these commands, so even if you're typing them correctly you may think "nothing is happening." Consult the manual that came with your modem.

If you've come this far, you should be seeing results on your screen when you CONNECT. But what results?

- Total Garbage on Screen. *Probable cause:* wrong baud rate. Adjust the baud rates of the appropriate devices. Use Kermit's SET BAUD (or SET SPEED) command if necessary, or else a system command or utility.

- Partial Garbage on Screen. *Probable causes:* noisy connection, parity set wrong, or your terminal type is set wrong on the remote system. If it's noise, try to make a new connection. If it's parity, use Kermit's SET PARITY command. If it's the terminal type, use the appropriate command on the remote system to let it know what kind of terminal your PC Kermit is emulating (if any).

- Missing Characters on Screen. *Probable causes:* unused or mismatched flow control or handshake (use Kermit's SET FLOW or SET HANDSHAKE to fix this); wrong parity— on some systems the port device driver will discard arriving characters that have "bad" parity (use SET PARITY to fix).

- No Echoing. You don't see the characters you type, only the computer's output. *Cause:* your PC is doing full-duplex communication and the remote system is doing half-duplex. *Cure:* SET DUPLEX HALF, SET ECHO LOCAL, or equivalent command to the local Kermit.

- Double Echoing. Every character you type comes out double. *Cause:* your PC is doing half-duplex communication and the remote system is doing full. *Cure:* SET DUPLEX FULL, SET ECHO REMOTE, or equivalent local Kermit command.

File Transfer Problems

Now terminal emulation works, but you can't transfer files. First, let's consider the case when not even the first packet makes it across.

- Missing Kermit. Are you sure you've started up the remote Kermit program and given it the desired command?

- Modem Signals. After escaping back from the remote system, communication stops. Perhaps your PC Kermit program turned off the DTR signal for some reason. Set your modem switches to ignore DTR, or install a jumper to make the modem think DTR is on.

- IBM Mainframes. If you're trying to communicate with an IBM mainframe through a full-screen terminal protocol converter, make sure it's the kind supported by Kermit. If not, try to find a line-mode TTY connection. If you're using a supported protocol converter or you have a line-mode connection, but file transfer still doesn't work, read on.

- Parity. If you do not inform the Kermit program that parity is being done, then Kermit's checksum or CRC calculations will be wrong, and packets will be rejected. *Cure:* SET PARITY to agree with what the remote system or the communication path uses or requires. May be necessary on both ends.

- Flow Control. If your connection is to a full-duplex system, both systems must use the same kind of flow control (XON/XOFF, ENQ/ACK, etc.). If there is not a flow-control option that both systems share then SET FLOW NONE, on both ends if necessary.

- Handshake. If your connection is to a half-duplex system, you'll almost certainly have to turn off any kind of full-duplex flow control, and enable the appropriate kind of line turnaround handshaking. Use SET FLOW NONE and SET HANDSHAKE XON (or whatever) for this. Note: IBM protocol converters are full-duplex front ends for half-duplex systems. The PC Kermit communicates with them in full-duplex, usually with XON/XOFF and no handshake.

- Packet Terminator. Most Kermit programs use carriage return to terminate their packets. A few systems might require other characters, like linefeed or ETX. If you are trying to receive files, then the other system's Send-Initiation packet will automatically inform your Kermit about this, but if you are sending files, then your initial packet might have the wrong terminator. Use the SET SEND END-OF-PACKET command to change the terminator on your initial outbound packet to what the other Kermit expects.

• Echoing. The remote system, its front end, or some communication box between here and there (maybe even your own modem) is echoing your packets back at you. Some Kermit programs are smart enough to ignore echoed packets, but for those that are not the workaround is to give local Kermit the SET SEND START-OF-PACKET command and the remote Kermit the SET RECEIVE START-OF-PACKET command to make outbound packets different from inbound ones, so those that bounce back are ignored. Alternatively, you can attempt to cope with the offending box. For instance, one such front end (used at a certain installation with Cray-1 computers) can be inhibited from echoing a line by preceding the line with a Control-Z character and ending it with a Control-W. Kermit's SET SEND/RECEIVE PADDING, PAD-CHARACTER, and END-OF-LINE commands are used to achieve the desired effect.

• ASCII/EBCDIC Translation. If you're trying to transfer files with an IBM mainframe, this could be the problem. In fact, it is almost always a problem when Kermit is being installed on an IBM mainframe for the first time. See the discussion on page 180.

If you've come this far, chances are you've got file transfer working, at least intermittently, or partially. A few packets are exchanged successfully and then things go sour. Or short files go, but long ones don't. If file transfer fails in random places, you may be suffering from:

• Line Noise. Just try again, possibly over a new connection. You can also try shortening your packets (SET SEND/RECEIVE PACKET-LENGTH) and increasing your retry threshold (SET RETRY).

• Message Interference. Issue whatever system commands are necessary to eliminate message or other interference.

• Interference from Other Users. If you're using a mainframe Kermit in local mode over an assigned terminal device, maybe some other user is using the same device at the same time. Some timesharing systems actually allow this.

• Buffer Overflow. Some systems have small input buffers but don't do flow control or handshake well enough to prevent overruns. It may be necessary to reduce the packet size (SET SEND/RECEIVE PACKET-LENGTH), or add a pause between packets (SET SEND/RECEIVE PAUSE).

• Delays. If you're connected to a timesharing system that is very busy, or that suddenly gets busy, or you're connected via a network that has intrinsic but variable delays, you should SET SEND/RECEIVE TIMEOUT and perhaps also SET RETRY to compensate.

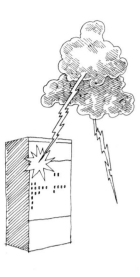

- Lack of Timeouts. Maybe neither of the Kermit programs is timing out; the first lost packet results in a deadlock. *Cure:* give the SET TIMER ON command to one of them. If that's not available, then monitor the transmission and whenever it seems to be stuck, type your program's interruption command for retransmitting the last packet (usually carriage return).

- Natural Disaster. The remote system crashed in the middle of the file transfer. The telephone connection dropped. A connector wiggled loose from its socket. A disk filled up. These things can happen. When disaster strikes, wait for it to go away, or attack the cause. Then try again.

If file transfer stops in a reproducible place, there could be several explanations:

- Translate Tables. Certain characters are mistranslated, causing the protocol to fail when they occur in the data, or in the packet sequence, length, or block check fields even if they aren't in the data. See page 180.

- Sacred Characters. A network, front end, PAD, or smart modem is opaque to some printable character or sequence that occurs in the data or one of the control fields (remember the modem that dialed Tasmania!). *Cure:* use the SET TRANSLATION command, if available, or find some communication channel that gets around the offending equipment.

- Parity. You may be trying to send an 8-bit binary file through a 7-bit channel, when the remote Kermit knows the channel is 7-bit, but your local Kermit does not. In this case, text files can be sent correctly, masking the problem. When a binary file is to be sent, the first few packets will be exchanged correctly, but the first packet that has an eighth bit on will fail. *Cure:* SET PARITY on your local Kermit.

- Disk Buffering. When downloading, your microcomputer might be accumulating data in a disk buffer in memory. If this buffer is sufficiently big and the disk is sufficiently slow, then the Kermit protocol might time out waiting for the buffer to be dumped. *Cure:* use some system command to reduce the size of the disk buffers, or use Kermit commands like SET RETRY or SET RECEIVE TIMEOUT (or SET SEND TIMEOUT on the other end) to increase retry threshold or the timeout interval.

In certain rare cases, Kermit programs have been known to consistently fail after transmitting some huge number of characters or packets. For instance, one Kermit program always crashed after transmitting its 65,535th packet (about 6 megabytes worth of data). The culprit here was a 16-bit word used to count the packets, purely for reporting purposes. But when it overflowed, havoc ensued.

If you suspect that character translation is causing a problem, try transmitting another file, preferably one containing only "bland" characters, like letters. If it stops at the same packet number as the first file, note the packet number (it should be between 0 and 63), then add 32 to it and look up the result in the decimal column of the ASCII table—that's probably the offending character (round up the usual suspects: ! [ ] ^ |).

The next common complaint is that Kermit transfers text files correctly, but not binary files:

- Does the documentation for your Kermit program say that it can transfer binary files? There are a few that can't.

- Did you issue the SET FILE TYPE BINARY (or equivalent) command at both ends?

- Maybe parity is interfering. Try using the SET PARITY command on one end or both. Maybe a box somewhere along the way is opaque to the high-order bit. Again, SET PARITY to something other than NONE (SPACE might be a good choice). Of course, SET PARITY produces the desired effect only if both Kermit programs include the eighth-bit prefixing option.

- If all else fails, preprocess (e.g., hexify) the file before sending, and postprocess it after receipt.

To verify that you can actually transfer binary files between a particular pair of systems, you can create a short file containing all 256 possible 8-bit bytes and send it back and forth, then use a file comparison utility to ensure that the result is correct.

Now we come to the annoying situation in which Kermit thinks it transferred the file correctly, but in reality it did not:

- A binary file is total garbage upon arrival. If it was supposed to be a program, let's hope it didn't do any damage when you tried to run it. *Probable cause:* you neglected to SET FILE TYPE BINARY on one or both sides. On record-oriented systems, you may also need to set special file attributes like block size, record format, and length, using SET FILE FORMAT or the equivalent. On systems with variable-length bytes, you might need to use SET FILE BYTE. Some systems, like UNIX, require that executable programs be stored with execute permission before you can run them (in UNIX, use "chmod +x"). *Another possible cause:* the file was stored incorrectly on the sending system in the first place.

- A text file is total or partial garbage upon arrival. *Probable cause:* you were previously transferring binary files, and then neglected to SET FILE TYPE TEXT again on one or both sides before transferring the text file.

- A text file arrives intact but has junk (perhaps one or more Control-Z's or NULs) at the end. *Probable cause:* the sending system does not record the end-of-file with precision and the Kermit program sent the entire last block. *Cure:* give the sending Kermit the SET EOF or equivalent command, if available, to inform it of the end-of-file convention to be used for the file in question. Failing that, use a text editor to trim the junk after arrival.

• A binary file arrives intact but has junk at the end. The cause is the same as above. But detecting that this has happened is not easy, because you don't normally look at binary files. The symptoms will vary widely, depending on what the file is used for, and could be severe. The cure is not obvious either. For instance, if the file is stored in the sending system that uses the Control-Z convention to mark the end of a file, you can't use that convention to determine the end of a binary file, because such files can easily contain Control-Z's as data. The best policy is not to store foreign binary files on systems that cannot record their length exactly.

Finally, we have files transferring correctly, but:

• An incoming file destroyed an existing file of the same name. *Cure:* SET FILE WARNING ON. If you always want this feature, put this command in your Kermit initialization file.

• Every packet is sent multiple times. This phenomenon is called resonating packets. *Probable cause:* you were using a Kermit server and had disconnected from it for a period of time, and several NAKs piled up in your system's input buffer. When you started your local Kermit program, it failed to clear the input buffer before reading its first packet, so each NAK caused a retransmission of the previous packet, an effect that can propagate throughout the entire transaction. *Possible cures:* (a) Use the SET SERVER TIMEOUT 0 command to disable the server's periodic command-wait NAKs; (b) Before using a server after a hiatus of more than a minute or two, CONNECT to it, let the NAKs type out on your screen, escape back, and then issue your commands; (c) Add code to your Kermit program to flush the input buffer.

• The transfer is very slow because of transmission delays. If the Kermit programs you are using support the sliding window protocol extension, try setting a window size higher than zero. Experiment until you hit the optimum window size. Or if the Kermit programs support the long packet extension, try that.

• The transfer is very slow because of echoed packets. This means your Kermit program has the intelligence to ignore reflected packets, but they still slow the transfer down. The only workaround is to attack the offending box, either physically or by sending it some magic sequence of characters.

• You connect back to the remote system and nothing happens. *Probable cause:* the remote Kermit printed its prompt or some other message while the PC Kermit was not actively handling port input, so the PC sent an XOFF (some PCs do this of their own accord). *Cure:* type an XON (usually Control-Q).

• You issue a command to a server that has been sitting idle for a long time and nothing happens, or many retries occur in rapid succession. *Probable cause:* the server's periodic NAKs might have filled your system port's input buffer, possibly causing an XOFF condition. *Cure:* issue a CONNECT command, type a Control-Q, escape back, and resume.

ASCII/EBCDIC Translation

Almost every IBM mainframe site that attempts to install Kermit runs into problems with its translation tables. ASCII/EBCDIC translation was discussed on page 61, and IBM mainframe communication was discussed on page 108. Let's see how all of this applies to Kermit.

Kermit packets are transmitted as ASCII characters, and the block check is based upon the numeric ASCII values of the characters in the packet. For an IBM mainframe Kermit to validate the block check of incoming packets and to construct a correct block check for outbound packets, it must use ASCII characters. But the system's access method for ASCII line-mode terminals translates incoming ASCII to EBCDIC, and assumes outbound characters are EBCDIC and so translates them to ASCII. This means that the Kermit program itself must either circumvent the access method or else apply the inverse translation internally.

Most IBM mainframe Kermits use the system's built-in access method, and so must keep their own internal translate tables. When an ASCII packet arrives, it is translated to EBCDIC by the system's access method, so the Kermit program must immediately translate it back to ASCII. The result must be identical to the packet originally transmitted. Similarly, after IBM mainframe Kermit constructs an ASCII packet, it translates it to EBCDIC and then sends it out the communication line, where the access method translates it back to ASCII. Again, the translation must match the original exactly. The process is shown in Figure 6-1.

IBM mainframe Kermits are distributed with internal ASCII/EBCDIC translation tables taken from the IBM System/370 Reference Summary [29], the same translation that is shown in Appendix D. If your system does not use this translation, then Kermit file transfer will not work without some adjustment of either the Kermit program, or your system, or both.

Here are the steps you must take in order to install Kermit successfully on an IBM mainframe:

1. Follow the installation instructions that come with the program. Once you have it in runable form, try it out—maybe it will work. If so, you're done.

2. Try to find a copy of your system's ASCII/EBCDIC translation table. If you can't find one, try to construct your own by typing every ASCII character into an IBM host-resident text editor, and then translating each character to hexadecimal, e.g., by dumping the resulting file.

3. Inspect your system's ASCII-to-EBCDIC translate table to see that no value occurs more than once (an easy way to do this is to sort it so that duplicates will be adjacent). If there are duplicates, then the system's table must be changed to eliminate them, preferably in conformance with the System/370 Reference Summary table. The only exception would be in the control characters, since Kermit normally uses no more than three of them (for start-of-packet, end-of-packet, and padding). As long as these (normally

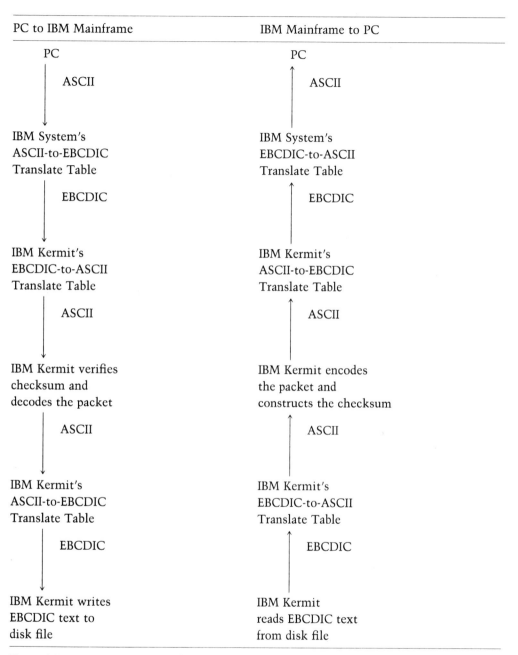

Figure 6-1. ASCII/EBCDIC Translation in Kermit

^A, carriage return, and null, respectively) are distinguished in the table, and different characters will not be selected for these functions, then the remaining control characters can be left alone.

4. If you have changed your system ASCII-to-EBCDIC table, then you must change its EBCDIC-to-ASCII table to agree with it.

5. Once your system's translation tables are purged of duplicates, they are invertible (from the ASCII viewpoint). You may now copy them into the Kermit program, if indeed they still differ from Kermit's tables.

6. Rebuild the Kermit program, if necessary, and try it out. If it still doesn't work, look a little harder at the tables.

A good way to test all this is to use Kermit to transfer a file containing all the ASCII characters to the mainframe and back, and back again, and then to compare the resulting files on both sides.

If All Else Fails

Kermit programs are, after all, creations of ordinary mortals. They may suffer the same imperfections as their creators; they may have (shudder, gasp) *bugs*—programming or logic errors. Perhaps more insidiously, they may have been written correctly, but under a set of assumptions whose validity has since changed. For example, the Kermit program that runs under Version 3.9 of your machine's operating system might (and if experience is any indicator, probably will) stop working when you install Version 4.0.

For that matter, operating systems themselves are imperfect, and exceedingly complex, creations. At times, a flaw will unexpectedly expose itself. This happened once at precisely 11:53:51 A.M. EDT, August 24, 1983, when all the DECSYSTEM-20 Kermits in the world stopped working because an internal format time overflowed into the sign bit, making it appear negative. The result was a Kermit program with rapid-fire timeouts, so fast that no packet could get past them. The cure in this case was to fix the operating system. But tracking down the problem was an education in itself.

If you've made all the checks suggested in this chapter and Kermit is still failing, the most likely explanation is a Kermit program bug, a system bug, or a system change. What can you do?

1. Try to reproduce the failure as simply as possible. For instance, find or create the shortest possible file whose transfer will cause the failure.

2. If the failure occurs during file transfer, use the Kermit LOG DEBUG and LOG PACKETS commands on both ends (if available) to create log files for the failing file transfer.

3. If the program crashes, record any information displayed by the system on your screen (error number, error message, program address, etc.), and use any available system-level commands to close the log files. Also, get a dump, if possible (UNIX creates a "core" file automatically; some other systems have "save" commands).

4. Describe the situation in writing, as succinctly as possible: the exact machines involved, including operating system and version; the Kermit programs involved, including version numbers; the sequence of commands and events that led to the problem; any error messages that were displayed. Indicate whether the problem is a new one, e.g., that started happening only since new hardware or operating system software was installed.

5. Send your description along with any data file and log files to your local Kermit maintainer. If you *are* the local Kermit maintainer, then send it to the author(s) of the Kermit program(s) involved, whose addresses are usually listed in the documentation or source code.

The truly stouthearted can delve into the Kermit source code themselves. Bug reports—especially when they come with fixes—are always appreciated.

7

Bootstrapping

Kermit programs are distributed mostly on magnetic tape or over computer networks, which means that when Kermit files first arrive at an organization, they are probably stuck on a mainframe disk in the organization's central computer center. How do you get Kermit from there onto your microcomputer?

Bootstrapping to the Local Micro

There are many approaches to this. If you already have some other communication program on your micro, you can probably use that. If not, most microcomputer Kermit programs come with some kind of "bootstrapping" mechanism—a short program you would type into your micro to download the Kermit program itself (usually some printable encoding, like hex, of the actual binary executable program), but with no error checking. Then there may be a second level—another program, which you get with the first program, which decodes the encoded Kermit program. All this can become quite tedious and frustrating when it doesn't work perfectly the first time (and it rarely does). It is far preferable to get the Kermit program on a diskette in the first place, and all Kermit contributors (and users too!) are urged to pass along copies to user groups or low-cost mail order distributors to spare others this tedium and frustration.

But there is also another way to download Kermit onto your micro initially— Kermit itself! What follows is a listing of a complete receive-only Kermit program, short enough for you to type on your microcomputer in a few minutes. It is written in Microsoft BASIC, which is available on a wide variety of micros. The logic should be clear enough to allow translation into other languages. It is not a model of structured or modular programming; the goal here is brevity, not beauty. You only have to use the program once.

When you run this program, it acts exactly like a "real" Kermit program that has been given the RECEIVE command: it waits for files to arrive from the remote Kermit, which must already have been given the SEND command. But how did you manage to use your PC to log in on the remote system and start the remote Kermit in the first place? Well, if you have Microsoft BASIC, your manual probably includes a short "dumb terminal" program in the communications section, or with the description of the OPEN COM statement, but it seems to be different for every system. For this reason (and to avoid legal entanglements) the terminal program is not reproduced here.

Back to our baby Kermit program. You probably shouldn't try to run it at speeds above 1200 baud. On the systems where it has been tested, it tends to get "Device I/O Errors" (overruns) at higher speeds. Nothing would be gained by higher speeds anyway, because the BASIC interpreter is so slow that 90 percent of the time is spent in inter-packet computation.

The program is as short and portable as possible. There is no command parser. There is no timeout facility; the other Kermit is expected to supply that. There's no manual intervention facility other than that provided by the system (e.g., typing CTRL-BREAK to stop the program). An 8-bit-wide data path is assumed, and nothing is done about parity or handshake. There is no repeat-count compression. On the positive side, the program is fairly robust, recovers from transmission errors as all good Kermits should, allows reception of multiple files, and even handles binary files correctly (as long as an 8-bit data path is available).

The program may be run in the BASIC environment, or it may be compiled and run standalone. A compiled version will run faster, but not everyone has a BASIC compiler. The interpreted version chugs along at an effective speed of about ten characters per second, so be prepared to find something to occupy yourself with if you expect to download any big files this way. During the file transfer, the program updates your screen by printing the name of each file that arrives, a dot (.) for every four packets, a percent symbol (%) for every retransmission, (OK) at the end of each file successfully transferred, and (Done) when all files have arrived successfully. If a fatal error occurs, a message will be printed. In any case, the program beeps when it's finished. Here's the program; an explanation follows.

A Receive-Only Kermit Program in Microsoft BASIC

```
100   RESET : RESET : RESET
110   ON ERROR GOTO 9000
120   DEFINT A-Z

1000  ' Initialize sequence number, retransmit buffer, and open comm line.
1010  N = 0 : SNDBUF$ = CHR$(1)+"# N3"+CHR$(13)
1020  OPEN "COM1:1200,N,8,,CS,DS" AS #1

2000  ' Get Send Initialization packet, exchange parameters.
2010  PRINT "Waiting..."
2020  GOSUB 5000
2030  IF TYP$ <> "S" THEN D$ = TYP$+" Packet in S State" : GOTO 9500
2040  IF LEN(PKTDAT$) > 4 THEN EOL=ASC(MID$(PKTDAT$,5,1))-32 ELSE EOL=13
2050  IF LEN(PKTDAT$) > 5 THEN CTL=ASC(MID$(PKTDAT$,6,1)) ELSE CTL=ASC("#")
2070  D$ = "H* @-#N1" : GOSUB 8020

3000  ' Get a File Header packet.  If a B packet comes, we're all done.
3010  GOSUB 5000
3020  IF TYP$ = "B" THEN GOSUB 8000 : GOTO 9900
3030  IF TYP$ <> "F" THEN D$ = TYP$+" Packet in F State" : GOTO 9500
```

```
3040 PRINT "Receiving "; MID$(PKTDAT$,1,L);
3050 OPEN MID$(PKTDAT$,1,L) FOR OUTPUT AS #2
3060 GOSUB 8000

4000 ' Get Data packets.  If a Z packet comes, the file is complete.
4010 GOSUB 5000
4020 IF TYP$ = "Z" THEN CLOSE #2 : GOSUB 8000 : PRINT "(OK)" : GOTO 3000
4030 IF TYP$ <> "D" THEN D$ = TYP$+" Packet in D State" : GOTO 9500
4040 PRINT #2, MID$(PKTDAT$,1,P);
4060 GOSUB 8000
4070 GOTO 4000

5000 ' Try to get a valid packet with the desired sequence number.
5010 GOSUB 7000
5020 FOR TRY = 1 TO 5
5030   IF SEQ = N AND TYP$ <> "Q" THEN RETURN
5040   PRINT #1, SNDBUF$;
5050   PRINT "%";
5060   GOSUB 7000
5070 NEXT TRY
5080 TYP$ = "T" : RETURN

6000 ' Send a packet with data D$ of length L, type TYP$, sequence #N.
6010 SNDBUF$ = CHR$(1)+CHR$(L+35)+CHR$(N+32)+TYP$+D$+" "+CHR$(EOL)
6020 CHKSUM = 0
6030 FOR I = 2 TO L+4
6040   CHKSUM = CHKSUM + ASC(MID$(SNDBUF$,I,1))
6050 NEXT I
6060 CHKSUM = (CHKSUM + ((CHKSUM AND 192) \ 64)) AND 63
6070 MID$(SNDBUF$,L+5) = CHR$(CHKSUM + 32)
6080 PRINT #1, SNDBUF$;
6100 RETURN

7000 ' Routine to Read and Decode a Packet.
7010 LINE INPUT #1, RCVBUF$
7020 I = INSTR(RCVBUF$,CHR$(1))
7030 IF I = 0 THEN TYP$ = "Q" : RETURN

7100 CHK   = ASC(MID$(RCVBUF$,I+1,1)) : L   = CHK - 35
7110 T     = ASC(MID$(RCVBUF$,I+2,1)) : SEQ = T - 32 : CHK = CHK + T
7120 TYP$  =     MID$(RCVBUF$,I+3,1)  : CHK = CHK + ASC(TYP$)
7130 P = 0 : FLAG = 0 : PKTDAT$ = STRING$(100,32)

7200 FOR J = I+4 TO I+3+L
7210   T = ASC(MID$(RCVBUF$,J,1))
7220   CHK = CHK + T
7240   IF TYP$ = "S" THEN 7300
7250     IF FLAG = 0 AND T = CTL THEN FLAG = 1 : GOTO 7400
7260       T7 = T AND 127
```

```
7270      IF FLAG THEN FLAG = 0 : IF T7 > 62 AND T7 < 96 THEN T = T XOR 64
7300    P = P + 1
7310    MID$(PKTDAT$,P,1) = CHR$(T)
7400  NEXT J
7420  CHK = (CHK + ((CHK AND 192) \ 64)) AND 63
7430  CHKSUM = ASC(MID$(RCVBUF$,J,1)) - 32
7450  IF CHKSUM <> CHK THEN TYP$ = "Q"
7460  RETURN

8000  ' Routine to send an ACK and increment the packet number...
8010  D$ = ""
8020  TYP$ = "Y" : L = LEN(D$) : GOSUB 6000
8030  N = (N + 1) AND 63
8040  IF (N AND 3) = 0 THEN PRINT ".";
8050  RETURN

9000  ' Error handler, nothing fancy...
9010  D$ = "Error " + STR$(ERR) + " at Line" + STR$(ERL)
9020  PRINT D$

9500  ' Error packet sender...
9520  L = LEN(D$) : TYP$ = "E" : GOSUB 6000

9900  ' Normal exit point
9910  CLOSE
9920  PRINT CHR$(7);"(Done)"
9999  END
```

The program is composed of the following sections:

• Lines 100–999

The RESET command clears things up—open files, port buffers, and so on. In borderline
cases, it seems to help. The ON ERROR command specifies invocation of the no-frills
error handler at line 9000 upon any kind of error—disk full, illegal file name, communication line I/O error, etc. All such errors are fatal. The error and program line numbers
are printed and are sent in an error packet to the sending Kermit. You can look up the
error number in your BASIC manual. DEFINT A-Z declares all numeric variables to be
integers, both for speed, and because integer arithmetic is required in the checksum and
sequence number calculations.

• Lines 1000–1999

Here the packet sequence number N is initialized, a "previous packet" is fabricated (a
NAK for packet zero), and the communication line is opened. The cryptic symbols in
the OPEN statement are explained in your BASIC manual, under OPEN COM. The
OPEN statement shown here specifies 1200 baud, no parity, 8 data bits per character,
and no waiting for or timing out on modem signals. You may need to alter some of
these parameters.

• Lines 2000–2999

Here we wait for the first packet from the remote Kermit, called the Send Initiation packet. This is the mechanism by which the two Kermits negotiate parameters with each other. When the desired packet arrives (the packet type must be S), two parameters are extracted from it—EOL, the end-of-line character the remote Kermit expects our packets to be terminated with, and the remote Kermit's own control-character prefix. Then we send back our own parameters in the ACK (acknowledgment, type Y). The H tells the other Kermit to send shorter-than-usual packets (40 characters). The * requests it to time out after 10 seconds. The – asks it to terminate its packets with a carriage return. The # is the control-character prefix we'll be using. No repeat count or eighth-bit prefixing is done. You can find the details in the next part of this book.

• Lines 3000–3999

Here's where we get the file header, containing the name of the file that's arriving, which is opened by the OPEN statement. If the file can't be opened, the program automatically takes the error exit at line 9000. We come back here after the file has arrived completely to see if any more files are coming. If so, there will be another F packet; otherwise we'll get a B (Break transmission) packet to indicate the transfer is done.

• Lines 4000–4999

The file data arrives in D packets. Each packet's worth of data is written to the file. Any error that occurs (e.g., disk filling up) automatically invokes the error exit. When the file has been completely transmitted, we get a Z (end-of-file) packet, at which point we close the file and go back to 3000 to see if another is on the way.

This is the main structure of the program. The remaining sections are procedures (subroutines) that take care of the details.

• Lines 5000–5999

This procedure tries five times to get a valid packet, that is, a packet with the correct sequence number and a correct checksum. If anything else arrives, the program simply ignores it and retransmits its own previous packet, presumably the ACK that was lost. This prevents the same data from being written to the file twice. In the case of packet zero, the "previous" packet is the NAK with which the transmit buffer was initialized.

• Lines 6000–6999

This procedure sends a packet, assembling it from the variables containing the data length, current sequence number, packet type, data, and terminator. It adds a Control-A, the normal Kermit start-of-packet marker, onto the front and inserts a checksum at the end, between the last data character and the terminator. Then it sends the packet.

• Lines 7000-7499

This procedure reads and decodes a packet. When a packet arrives, the procedure picks out the length, sequence, and type fields, and it computes the checksum based on the observed characters. It also takes care of Kermit's control-character prefix encoding (which is used to keep all the data in a Kermit packet printable; for instance, Control-X is represented as #X). Two minor wrinkles complicate matters: first, the control prefix is also used to prefix itself when it occurs as part of the data, and second, the Send-Initiate packet is not prefix-encoded, so it must not be decoded. Finally, the checksum that was calculated from the arriving data is compared with the one that was sent with it. If the checksums agree the packet is accepted; otherwise it is rejected.

- Lines 8000–8999

This routine acknowledges the current packet, increments the packet number, modulo 64, and prints a blip on the screen for every fourth packet. The special entry point at 8020 is used if there is something to put in the data field.

- Lines 9000–9499

This is error handler. We get here upon any BASIC or system error. The error number and program line are printed on the screen and are also sent to the other Kermit in an error packet, which terminates the file transfer cleanly. Then the program exits through the common exit point at line 9900.

- Lines 9500–9599

This routine sends an error packet, whose text is provided in the variable D$.

- Lines 9900–9999

Here the program terminates. The communication line is closed, along with any disk file that happens to be open (perhaps because an error occurred during transfer). A message is printed, including a beep to wake you up, and the program stops.

Addition of other features is left as an exercise for the ambitious reader. But don't get carried away; BASIC is not a good language for a "serious" Kermit program—whether you like its style or not, it's simply too slow.

Bootstrapping in the Other Direction

If you need to bootstrap Kermit to a remote system, you can try converting the program to some language found there. The only difference in operation is that a remote Kermit should not print screen messages during file transfer, because they can interfere with the packets. Just remove all the PRINT statements that aren't followed by #1 or #2.

I was able to translate the program to BASIC-Plus-2 as found on most DEC mini-computers, but not without some aggravation:

- The RESET statements had to be removed.

- Multiple statements had to be separated with "\" rather than ":".

- The syntax of the OPEN statements had to be changed, and LINE INPUT had to become INPUT LINE. The communication line (i.e., the console) was opened with

```
OPEN "TTY:" AS #1 \ X = NOECHO(1)
```

to prevent echoing of inbound packets.

- BASIC-Plus-2 has no DEFINT command, so every numeric variable and constant having to do with sequence numbers or checksums, or used in any arithmetic, needed to have a % tacked on, and regular division (/) was used because no integer division operator (\) was available.

- The outbound start-of-packet character had to be changed from Control-A (CHR$(1)) to Control-G (Beep, CHR$(7)), because BASIC-Plus-2 would not output a bare Control-A (or rather, it had no way of telling the operating system not to translate it to circumflex and letter A).

Then, to use the remote BASIC Kermit, the local Kermit had to be given these commands:

```
set parity even
set receive start 7
```

The BASIC program had no way of telling the operating system not to use its normal parity (even) on outbound characters, so binary files couldn't be transferred. Some BASICs (but not the one I used) support a MODE clause in the OPEN statement to put the terminal in "binary" mode. This would have let bare Control-A's and 8-bit data get through.

For Many, the End

It is my profound hope that the material presented so far, when used in conjunction with specific Kermit program documentation, can make you a self-sufficient creator and user of reliable data communication links. I've tried to include only what you need to know in each situation, which, sad to say, can sometimes amount to quite a heap. It's a complicated world, and I hope it gets simpler.

The rest of this book, except for the Glossary and Appendixes, is for programmers. There is an informal but complete presentation of the Kermit file transfer protocol, including programming examples and implementation suggestions. This is followed by a comparison of Kermit with some other file transfer protocols, some performance measurements, and a list of some of the lessons we've learned.

PART FOUR

Programmer Guide

8

How to Write a Kermit Program

Before you embark on a serious Kermit programming venture, please send a note to

Kermit Distribution
Columbia University Center for Computing Activities
612 West 115th Street
New York, NY 10025
USA

indicating what you propose to do—the machine, operating system, and programming language involved, how serious you are about it, your tentative schedule (if any), and how you can be reached. If you are the first to tackle this particular system, your name will be added to the list of potential Kermit contributors, and you will be given a prefix for your implementation (you can suggest one yourself if you like). If someone else is already working on the same thing, or if the Kermit you propose to write already exists, or if similar programs are good candidates for a base to work from, you'll be advised. This saves a lot of duplicated effort and sometimes results in productive cooperation.

Programming Language

Kermit programs have already been written in a variety of languages, including C, PASCAL, LISP, FORTRAN, PL/I, ALGOL, BLISS, and various assemblers. The easiest way to bring Kermit to a new system is to adapt one of the existing programs, perhaps adding features along the way.

The language to be used in writing a Kermit program is more than a matter of taste. The primary consideration is that the language provide the necessary function and speed; here are just a few criteria:

• The program should be able to run fast enough to keep up with the highest baud rate usable on your system. Even if you don't expect to be using it at more than 1200 baud, someone else may want to run at 9600. For this reason, interpreted BASIC is almost always a poor choice.

• In order to do terminal emulation, the language must permit (a) simultaneous input and output processes (if the underlying system supports them), (b) communication line or keyboard input event trapping, or (c) nondestructive sampling of keyboard and communication port input buffer or access to the communication port device status registers. Remote-only mainframe Kermit programs need not meet these requirements.

• In order to send and receive packets, the language must permit unformatted variable-length line-at-a-time or character-at-a-time input from the desired device (port or console). It must not be sensitive to commas or other field separators. On mainframes, the language must allow the terminal modes to be obtained, altered, and restored. During packet operations, the following functions that may be performed by the console driver must be disabled:

  • Echoing (on full-duplex systems)
  • Alphabetic case conversion
  • Interference with Control-A
  • Line wrap
  • Pause at end of screen
  • Line editing or similar functions tied to printable characters
  • Display of terminal messages

• In order to transfer binary files efficently, the language should allow 8-bit data characters, or have a way to tell the system to allow them, e.g., by disabling any parity processing normally done by the system.

Another consideration is portability. It is best to choose a language that people are likely to have a compiler for, either because it comes as a standard part of the system (as C does with UNIX, or an assembler does with most systems) or because it is a low-cost and popular option. It is better still if the language chosen runs on a wide variety of computers, with conversion between machines requiring very little work. The advantages of portability are obvious:

• The program can be adapted to an unlike system with relative ease.

• Users can track down and fix bugs themselves if the program is written in a language they can compile, and they can add new features. Assuming they send their changes back to you (or whoever takes over responsibility for the program when you're done with it), everyone benefits.

An additional wrinkle to portability concerns the legality of distributing source code written for a given compiler, or object code produced by that compiler, especially when the object code includes proprietary runtime libraries. Don't write the program in a language, or using utilities or libraries, when your license for these tools does not let you distribute the resulting source or object code without restriction.

Programming Style

Remember that your source program is its own best documentation, so please take pains to write it not only for the computer but also for the people who must read it.

Include lots of comments that reflect what the code is doing. If you change some code, remember to change the corresponding commentary too.

The form and organization of the program are also important:

- Try to isolate machine or operating system dependencies into well-defined modules that can be easily replaced for other machines or operating systems. When more than one system is to be supported, you must decide whether to have a separate system-dependent module for each system, or to use conditional compilation or assembly within a single system-dependent module. Conditional compilation has the advantage that redundant code need not be replicated in multiple files (which brings danger that these files will someday get out of sync) and the drawback that as the number of systems goes up, it becomes very hard to manage. Sometimes a combination works best.

- Try to isolate the "user interface" similarly, so it can be easily replaced by one of a different style (e.g., so that an interactive dialog program can be moved to a menu-oriented system).

- If you're including support for dialout modems, try to make it table-driven to allow easy addition of other types of modems.

- Try to avoid case sensitivity. If your compiler is case-sensitive (e.g., A and a are different identifiers), please don't use identifiers that are distinguished only by case. This makes it very hard to transport your program to another similar compiler that is not case-sensitive.

- Avoid long variable names, for the benefit of those who wish to transport your program to a more restrictive compiler.

- Keep lines of source text within 80 characters in length so they can fit on a regular-size CRT screen or printed page. Your program might have to be written on tapes or sent over communication links that mimic 80-column punched cards.

- Make sure to include a program version number that appears prominently in the source code, and that is displayed to the user at runtime. Increase the version number each time you issue a new release of the program. The version number allows those who support Kermit programs to help users with their problems and to report problems back to the author. The version number may have several parts, including a major version, a minor version, and an edit number, for example, 4C(057).

A few conventions should also be observed in organizing the program and naming the files:

- Please try to keep the number of files as small as possible. A balance must be struck between modularity and ease of distribution. On labeled magnetic tapes (a major medium for Kermit distribution), each file requires a label and a file mark. Many short files will take up a *lot* more space on a tape than the same data collected into fewer, longer files. If you prefer to work with a large number of source files, then for distribution purposes please collect them together into a single file, in which the boundaries are marked with some kind of textual marker that includes the actual filename of each file, and provide some procedure for picking this big file apart into its component pieces.

- The names of all the files belonging to a particular Kermit implementation must begin with the same two- or three-character prefix, to allow them to appear together in an alphabetical directory listing and to distinguish them from all the other Kermit programs in the Kermit distribution area. For instance, the MS-DOS Kermit files all have names starting with MS, the VAX/VMS with VMS, and so on. Please check with Columbia before making up a prefix, to make sure yours is unique.

- File names should not be longer than six characters in the name part and three characters in the extension or file-type part. This is because Kermit tapes are sent to many systems whose file systems have this restriction, where files whose names are not unique within the 6.3 paradigm will overwrite any other file that shares the same characters in these positions of its name.

The User Interface

What an awful phrase . . . With a program like Kermit, which runs on many different kinds of systems, the perennial question is whether all the versions ought to have the same "user interface" (like the one described in this book) so that all the Kermit programs can be talked about in the same way, or should mesh with the normal style of the system (menus and arrow keys, windows and mice) so that it will feel familiar to the user of a particular system. There's no good answer.

But there are a few things that can be said about what the program should do for the user, besides its basic function of transferring files:

- Provide help text for commands and fields. The user shouldn't have to thumb through thick manuals (or books!) to find out what the commands are or what the next field of a command is. The program should have built-in help on as many levels as possible, e.g., a general HELP command, specific HELP commands for each topic or Kermit command, ?-style help within commands, or pop-up or pull-down menus.

- Display what's going on during file transfer. The user should be able to monitor the progress of a file transfer by watching the screen of a local Kermit program to see how many packets, how many retransmissions, how many K of data, percent done, and current status (working, complete, interrupted, failed). The style of this display is discussed below, but the important thing is to keep the user informed.

• Signal when done. When a file transfer is finished, the program should make some noise or striking visual display to get the user's attention.

• Display meaningful error messages. When something goes wrong, a brief message should describe it clearly, like "Disk full" or "Carrier dropped" rather than, say, "I/O error."

• Keep logs. The user should be able to create logs of protocol transactions, so that long unattended transfers can be checked for success or failure. And there should be some way for the user to log debugging information (variables, states, packets) in order to track down problems or provide "software support" with meaningful information.

Displays can be as fancy as you like. Typically, a form is put up on the screen during file transfer, and fields are filled in by a jumping cursor. For instance, one popular Kermit's file transfer display looks like this:

```
          File Name: FOO.BAR
   KBytes Transferred: 17
  Percent Transferred: 58%
             Sending: In Progress

   Number of Packets: 193
   Number of Retries: 2
          Last Error: None
        Last Warning: None
```

with all the data on the right being updated continuously, and more or less at random. This is fine for most users, but it's not too helpful to blind people who are having screen output translated into speech or Braille by some special device. They can't see which quantity goes with what label, and Braille devices are too slow to keep up with rapid-fire screen output. In this case, a strictly sequential display is better:

```
Sending FOO.BAR.........%..%%.....Done
Sending FOO.BAZ.....^X Interrupted <BEEP>
Kermit-xx>
```

This will make a lot more sense when fed into a speaking machine. A dot stands for, say, four packets, a percent sign means a retransmission occurred. This format is also more useful to someone who returns to the screen after an absence. When the transfer is done, the beep gets the user's attention, and the new prompt is read. If the speaking machine is intelligent enough to know what to do with question marks, then the user could

```
SET PROMPT KERMIT-XX COMMAND?
```

to make the prompt sound like a question.

The opposite considerations come into play for the deaf. Some visual device like blinking, boldface, or inverse video, rather than a noise, should be used to get the user's attention at the end of a file transfer.

Some thought should also be given to making it easy for people with motor impairments to enter commands. Commands should not be long and complicated. It should be possible to shorten keywords to their minimum unique prefix, and even then special exceptions should be made for the most common commands (S for SEND, even though there is also a SET, R for RECEIVE, etc.). There should not be an overreliance on control characters, since some people can press only one key at a time.

When writing a Kermit program in a particular environment, try to think how that environment might be used to advantage by blind, deaf, or physically impaired people. For instance, while the window-and-mouse style is entirely inappropriate for the blind, it can be very handy for those with motor impairments, who will go out of their way to find systems that don't require a lot of typing. In this case, it makes sense for the Kermit program to use the mouse to its fullest advantage.

And don't forget that many people in the world don't speak English. Try to isolate the text messages embedded in the program in such a way that they can be easily translated to other languages.

A final word about the user interface on microcomputer Kermit programs. The trend today is toward windows. Major hardware and software manufacturers are promoting the idea of the "desktop" with multiple simultaneous applications running (or at least memory-resident), each in its own window on the screen. Some applications fit into this environment better than others, but like them or not, windows are on the way. Kermit programs, therefore, should be written defensively from the standpoint of windows, and should expect to coexist with other applications. What this might mean in a particular case, I can't say. Usually it means being careful about saving and restoring things like interrupts, not assuming you have the full width and length of the screen to play with, not bypassing operating system services and going straight to the hardware, and so on. Unfortunately, these requirements are often at odds with considerations of speed and efficiency.

Documentation

Each Kermit program should come with a handout that explains how to use it, what the commands are, and how the commands differ from the norm described in this book. The document should contain the following sections:

• Credits: Authors of the program and documentation, along with organization (if any) and address.

• Particulars about your Kermit program: programming language (and version if it makes a difference), Kermit program version number, and release date for the given version.

- Requirements: machine and operating system (and version if it makes a difference), any special memory or device requirements, limitations (will work on the serial port but not on the built-in modem, maximum baud rate, etc.).

- List of features, like the one shown in Table 8-1.

- Description of the file system: types of files (e.g., the distinction between text and binary), text file format and encoding, filename syntax, wildcard (file group) syntax, end-of-file detection and marking, and any peculiarities users should know about. Hints for pre- and postprocessing special kinds of files.

- How to invoke the program, what it's called, its prompt, the name and location of its initialization file (if any). How to interrupt the program, continue it, restart it, run it in the background. What measures (if any) must be taken before running Kermit.

- General but very brief description of what Kermit does and how to use it, for the benefit of those who have no other documentation.

- Command summary, including the syntax of each command and brief descriptions. More detailed descriptions of any commands or options peculiar to this version.

- Detailed descriptions of any peculiarities or special features like fancy terminal emulation.

- Installation instructions, including the recommended bootstrapping technique.

- A separate "beware" file, listing known bugs and limitations, how to report newly discovered bugs.

- A separate update history, in which the changes from one version to the next are recorded.

Frills

The major function of a Kermit program is to transfer files and other information using the Kermit protocol. Optional features of the protocol allow faster file transfer, remote file management, and so forth. A particular Kermit program can be expected to implement the basic Kermit protocol and any desired optional protocol features, and to provide a minimal terminal emulation function if it is to operate in local mode. Other features are nice to have in Kermit, or any other communication program:

- Fancy Terminal Emulation: A microcomputer Kermit can provide any desired degree of terminal emulation. It can even surpass the terminal being emulated by providing features like screen rollback, screen dump to disk or printer, saving lines that scroll off the top of the screen, key redefinition, graphics, and so forth. But only dumb terminal emulation is required, and then only for local Kermit operation.

Table 8-1. Sample Kermit Capabilities List

Local operation:	Yes
Remote operation:	Yes
Login scripts:	Yes
Transfer text files:	Yes
Transfer binary files:	Yes
Wildcard send:	Yes
File transfer interruption:	Yes
Filename collision avoidance:	Yes
Can time out:	Yes
Eighth-bit prefixing:	Yes
Repeat count prefixing:	Yes
Alternate block checks:	Yes
Terminal emulation:	VT102
Communication settings:	Parity, Duplex, Baud, Handshake, Flow
Transmit BREAK:	Yes
Support for dialout modems:	Hayes, Racal-Vadic
IBM mainframe communication:	Yes
Transaction logging:	Yes
Debug logging:	Yes
Session logging:	Yes
Raw file transmit:	Yes
Act as server:	Yes
Talk to server:	Yes
Advanced server functions:	Yes
Local file management:	Yes
Command/Init files:	Yes
Command macros:	Yes
File attributes packets:	No
Extended packets:	No
Sliding windows:	No

- Login Scripts: Given the intelligence that the Kermit program already has about all the communication parameters, it is not very hard to add a login script capability (provided it doesn't have to act like a full-fledged programming language).

- Raw Upload and Download: Also fairly easy to include, once you support communication parameters and can do a CONNECT command.

- Autodial Modem Control: Kermit programs should work on as wide a variety of systems as possible. Since modems and computers can occur in endless combinations, it is much harder to support each combination than to simply draw the line and ask users to control their modems manually. However, some Kermit programs include support for one or more autodial modems.

- Support for Internal Modems: These are the hardest devices to deal with because they usually must be controlled at the device level rather than with simple serial I/O. Each modem/system combination is different, probably requiring its own very specific, detailed control code. The only exception is when the internal modem perfectly mimics the system's normal serial port.

- Statistics about File Transfer: the error rate, the effective data rate, the amount of data transferred, the number of packets, the number of files, the encoding overhead, the packet overhead, the round-trip packet delay, and so on.

Testing

All the aspects of your program's protocol, file handling, and communications capabilities should be thoroughly tested. Any deficiencies or limitations that you uncover should be corrected, or else clearly noted in the documention. In addition to your own tests, you might want to subject your program to a variety of users, both naive and experienced. Their reactions might help you to make some aspects of the program's operation or documentation a little clearer. Here are some things to try:

Communications:

- Does it work with a modem? Without a modem?

- Does it work with parity? With no parity?

- Does it work on a full-duplex connection? With XON/XOFF? Without?

- Does it work on a half-duplex connection with handshake?

- Does it work with IBM mainframes?

Files: Put together a collection of files to form a kind of "validation suite." These might include:

- A file that fits exactly in a disk block

- A file that's one character shorter than a disk block

- A file that's one character longer than a disk block

- A file containing all the ASCII characters

- A file containing all possible 8-bit bytes

- A text file containing one long string of characters with no line terminators

- An executable program from the local system

- An executable program from a foreign (unlike) system

- A null (empty) file

- A nonsequential file (your program should refuse to send it)

- A file containing the Kermit prefix characters in all sorts of combinations

- A file containing random numbers of repetitions of printable, control, and 8-bit characters

- A very long file

- Whatever other kinds of files are pathological cases on your system or any other system you have access to

Protocol: Run through the validation suite against systems that:

- Are and are not IBM mainframes

- Do and don't do timeouts

- Do and don't do eighth-bit prefixing

- Do and don't do repeat count compression

- Do and don't do sliding windows

- Do and don't do type 2 and 3 block checks, requesting both 2 and 3.

And also:

- Run it in local and remote mode.

- Exercise the file interruption commands.

- Run it over Telenet or another public network.

- Run it against itself.

Once you've added all the features you're going to add, and fixed all the bugs you're going to fix, make sure the documentation reflects the true operation of the program. Now you're ready to unleash it upon the world.

Submission

Here are the steps for contributing your Kermit program:

1. Collect the source into a manageable number of files, all with prefixed names, as described previously.

2. If practical, and unless it's written in a portable language for many systems, include the binary executable program image, and also some printably encoded (e.g., hexified) version of the executable program image suitable for distribution on ANSI-labeled magnetic tape or transmission via electronic mail.

3. Don't include any proprietary or licensed material.

4. Include instructions for decoding the encoded program image. Better still, include a program to do it.

5. Write the necessary instructions for installation. For microcomputers, include a bootstrapping procedure, preferably a "miniature Kermit" like the one on page 186.

6. Submit it to one or more user groups on a native medium for your system, with the binary executable program included, along with documentation.

7. Make it available on any networks or dialup bulletin boards you may have access to.

8. Submit it to Kermit Distribution on a mutually agreeable medium, and list any networks, bulletin boards, or user groups you submitted it to, along with their addresses and/or phone numbers.

9

Protocol Specification

The next few chapters describe the Kermit protocol, mostly from the top down, with increasing attention to detail as we proceed. This chapter presents the basic protocol. Chapter 10 introduces some optional encoding and error-checking techniques. Chapter 11 discusses the client/server model. Chapter 12 describes advanced features for transmitting file attributes and for improving performance with extended-length packets or sliding windows. Finally, Chapter 13 presents some discussion and analysis of the protocol: implementation tricks, comparison with other protocols, performance measurements, and some of the lessons we've learned.

Kermit features are described in the order in which they were added to the protocol, more or less, so that this protocol description might be used not only as a guide to writing a new Kermit program, but also to adding newer features to older Kermit programs. It is assumed that you have a reading knowledge of the C programming language [19] and that you understand all the previous parts of this book.

A protocol is a set of rules governing the behavior of those who agree upon their importance. Here, for example, is the protocol recommended by Emily Post in 1922 [27] for a gentleman to manage his hat when encountering a lady on the street:

... he takes his hat off with his left hand, leaving his right free to shake hands, or he takes it off with his right and transfers it to his left. If he has a stick, he puts his stick in his left hand, takes off his hat with his right, transfers his hat also to his left hand, and gives her his right. If they walk ahead together, he at once puts his hat on; but while he is standing in the street talking to her, he should remain hatless.

The Kermit protocol bears a certain resemblance to this procedure. The file sender's behavior is governed by circumstances like the presence or absence of (more) files or data to send (as is the gentleman's by the presence or absence of a lady, or a stick), whereas the file receiver merely responds to the sender's actions. The lady is unconcerned with what the gentleman must do in order to extricate his right hand from his haberdashery; she only expects him to extend it. Similarly, the file receiver is indifferent to the efforts of the sender in locating, opening, and getting data from files; it only expects the files to arrive in the agreed-upon manner.

Basic File Transfer

Table 9-1 shows the basic Kermit packet types. Details of their function and format will emerge as we go along.

Table 9-1. Basic Kermit Packet Types

S	Send Initiation. I'm about to send files, and here are my parameters.
F	File Header, the name of the file which is about to come.
D	File Data.
Z	End of File.
B	Break Transmission, end of transaction.
Y	Acknowledgment.
N	Negative Acknowledgment.
E	Fatal Error.

The basic protocol takes place over a "transaction." Every transaction is independent of every other transaction. The transaction is driven by the file sender; the file receiver simply acknowledges each packet it gets. The packets are short—96 characters at most—and each party waits for a packet from the other before sending the next packet. Thus, Kermit is a "stop-and-wait" protocol. Each packet is checked for errors, and retransmission takes place whenever an error is detected. Data is encoded within packets for maximum transparency through communication equipment and host console terminal drivers.

The transaction begins when the file sender transmits a Send-Initiation packet to indicate that files are coming. This is followed by a File-Header packet, in which the sender tells the receiver the name of the file that is to come. Then come as many Data packets as are necessary to transfer the contents of the file, a Z packet at the end of the file (EOF), and finally a B packet to indicate that the transaction is finished. The File-Header/Data/EOF sequence can be repeated for each file to be sent within the transaction. A sample transaction was shown in Figure 2-3, back on page 17.

Let's restate all this in a more compact notation, in which each letter means a packet of the indicated type together with its acknowledgment, parentheses are used for grouping, and the character "*" means zero or more repetitions of the preceding quantity:

```
S (F D* Z)* B
```

If you ever studied formal languages, this notation will be familiar to you. It is used to write a class of grammars called "regular expressions" [1, 21]. A regular expression can be recognized by a "finite state automaton" (FSA), which is usually written in the form of a state diagram like the one in Figure 9-1. This FSA will recognize (or produce) all strings of the form "S (F D* Z)* B" including SB, SFZB, SFDZB, SFDDDDZB, SFDDDDDDZFZFDDZB, etc.—all the legal Kermit transactions.

The File Sender

How do we translate the state diagram into a program? First let's look at the file sender, the one that generates the SFDZB strings. We'll fudge the diagram a little and label the arrows according to what causes the automaton to choose one path over another, as in Figure 9-2.

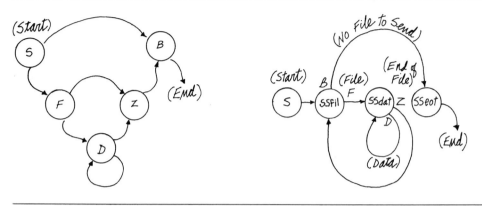

Figure 9-1. Kermit State Diagram   Figure 9-2. State Diagram for Sending Files

As you can see, the automaton is driven by the combination of its current state and some input, in this case, whether there is a file to send and whether there is data within the file. These are decisions that will be made by the program. Allowing the program to make these decisions while inside a state lets the diagram be rendered more simply. For instance, from Start state, we always enter `ssfil` state, but we don't send an F packet unless there is a file to send. Similarly, we always enter `ssdat` state from `ssfil` state, but send a D packet only if there is data. The emission of a packet is shown by writing the packet type, if any, on an arrow leaving a state.

A handy language for writing FSA programs is Lex, the UNIX lexical analyzer generator [22]. We use only a tiny subset of Lex, easily translatable (as you'll see) into ordinary "if" statements. Lex notation is used because it's compact and corresponds well to the state diagrams. Our Lex statements have this syntax:

[<*state1*[,*state2*[,...]]>]*input-character* { *action* }

The optional state field, enclosed in angle brackets, tells the state or states the program must be in to perform the indicated action. If no state is specified, then the action can be performed regardless of the current state. If more than one state is specifed, then the action can be performed in any of the listed states. Multiple states are separated by commas.

The input field is required. It consists of a single literal character, corresponding (in our case) to the packet type. When in the indicated state, if the arriving packet is of the specified type, the associated action will be performed. The character "." (dot) matches any packet type.

The state table is scanned from top to bottom for each input, and only the first statement that matches the current state and input is executed.

Here's a sample Lex statement (caution: see note, page 17):

```
<foo>X { xcount++; }
```

which is read, "if in state foo and input X arrives, perform the action xcount++;" (increment the x-counter). Another example:

```
<foo,bar>E { tmsg(ermsg); exit(); }
```

which translates to "if in state foo or state bar and the input is E, print an error message and exit." And one last example:

```
E { tmsg(ermsg); exit(); }
```

This is the same as the previous example, except that the indicated action will be taken in any state if E is input.

Here, using Lex notation, is how we might turn the state diagram in Figure 9-2 into a program:

```
%states ssfil ssdat sseot
%%
s { sinit(); BEGIN ssfil; }                     /* Send S */

<ssfil>Y { if (gnfile() > 0) { sfile(); BEGIN ssdat; }
           else { seot(); BEGIN sseot; }        /* Send F or B */

<ssdat>Y { if (sdata() == 0) { seof(); BEGIN ssfil; } }
                                                /* Send D or Z */

<sseot>Y { return; }                            /* Done */

  { error("Bad Packet Type"); }                 /* No ACK, error */
%%
```

Lex is a preprocessor for the C language; Lex notation is imbedded within a C program, enclosed between %% markers, and the actions specified in Lex statements are expressed in ordinary C. You should recognize most of the actions as C language "if-else" statements and function invocations. BEGIN is a Lex directive for changing the state; it is equivalent to

```
state =
```

"s" is a dummy packet type to start things off by invoking the sinit() function to transmit the Send-Initiation packet and then changing the state to ssfil (presumably the "user interface" has obtained the specification of the file or files to be sent and has set the initial input to s). At the end of the action portion of this (and each) Lex statement, the program waits for the next packet to arrive and then selects the next Lex statement based on the current state and the packet type. Since the file sender must always have an acknowledgment (packet type Y) for each packet it sends, this table looks rather uniform. Changing of states is governed in this case not so much by the arriving packet, but by what goes on in the actions: end-of-file, no more files, etc. Compare this with the state diagram for the file receiver shown in the next section in Figure 9-3.

In the ssfil state, the gnfile() (get next file) function is invoked to see if there is a file to send. If so, the sfile() function is called upon to open the file and to send a File-Header (F) packet, and then the state switches to ssdat. Otherwise the seot() function transmits a Break Transmission (B) packet and the state becomes sseot, whence the protocol exits.

In ssdat state, the sdata() function is called upon to send a packet's worth of data. If it succeeds, the state remains unchanged, so that the acknowledgment that arrives will simply cause the next data packet to be sent. If it fails, it is assumed that the end-of-file has been reached, and so the input file is closed, the seof() function is invoked to send an End-of-File (Z) packet, and the state changes back to ssfil to send another file or to end the transaction. Finally, if in any state a packet of any type other than Y arrives, an error procedure is invoked.

In practice, much can go awry even at this high level. For instance, any of the functions that transmit a packet, like sinit(), could fail for some reason, say, a communication line I/O error of some kind. The sfile() function could fail because the desired file could not be opened. The sdata() function could fail not only because it reached the end of the file but also because a file I/O error had occurred.

Also, there's one minor wrinkle that we didn't account for, and which is explained later. The acknowledgment of the Send-Initiation packet is special, and contains data that must be processed by the spar() function. A special state could be added to account for this, but instead we use a flag, filcnt, so that we can enter the relatively complicated ssfil state from both Start state and ssdat state. Here's the result of all this:

```
%states ssfil ssdat sseot
%%
s {                                 /* - Start State - */
    tinit();                        /* Initialize transaction. */
    if (sinit('S') < 0) { ERR("sinit"); }   /* Build, send Send-Init. */
    else {                          /* If successful, */
        filcnt = 0;                 /* initialize file counter, */
        BEGIN ssfil;                /* and switch to ssfil state. */
    }
}
<ssfil>Y {                          /* - Send File State - */
    if (filcnt++ == 0) spar(rdatap); /* Set parameters if 1st time. */
    cx = 0;                         /* Reset file interruption flag. */
    bctu = bctr;                    /* Switch to negotiated block check */
    if (gnfile() > 0) {             /* Is there a file to send? */
        if (sfile() < 0) { ERR("sfile"); }   /* Yes, open it, send F packet, */
        else BEGIN ssdat;           /* and if no error, switch state. */
```

```
      } else {                              /* No (more) files to send, */
        if (seot() < 0) { ERR("seot"); }    /* so send B packet, */
        else BEGIN sseot;                    /* and switch to sseot state. */
      }
}
<ssdat>Y {                                   /* - Send Data State - */
    if ((x = sdata()) == 0) {                /* Send data packet if data left. */
        if (seof((cx | cz) ? "D" : "") < 0) { /* If not, send Z packet */
            ERR("seof");
        }
        else BEGIN ssfil;                    /* and go back to ssfil state. */
    } else if (x < 0) { ERR("sdata"); } /* Handle file i/o errors. */
}
<sseot>Y { RESUME; }                         /* - Send B, done. - */
%%
```

ERR and RESUME are macros defined, for now, as follows:

```
#define ERR(x) error(x); RESUME
#define RESUME return
```

The error messages are deliberately terse to keep the listing neat. The real program would issue more informative messages, like "Can't open file," "Can't close file," and so on (preferably the reason would also be given, like "read access required," "disk is full," etc.). The tinit() function is used to initialize a transaction. It starts the packet number off at zero and clears any transaction-related variables or buffers.

The File Receiver

Figure 9-3 shows the automaton for recognizing "S (F D* Z)* B" strings, i.e., for receiving files.

In this case, the state transitions are governed by the type of packet that arrives. Not shown in the diagram is the transition to an error state if a packet arrives that is not valid in the current state; this happens in each state. Here's the Lex program:

```
%states srini srfil srdat
%%
v { tinit(); rinit(); BEGIN srini; }    /* - Receive - */

<srini>S { spar(rdatap); ackl(rpar()); bctu = bctr; BEGIN srfil; }

<srfil>B { ack(); RESUME; }

<srfil>F { if (rcvfil() < 0) { ERR("rcvfil"); } else { ack(); BEGIN srdat; } }

<srdat>D { if (decode() < 0) { ERR("decode"); } else ack(); }

<srdat>Z { if (closof() < 0) { ERR("closof"); } else { ack(); BEGIN srfil; } }
%%
```

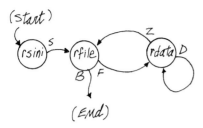

Figure 9-3. State Diagram for Receiving Files

The file receiver starts out by calling upon tinit() to do whatever is necessary to initialize a transaction, and rinit() to initialize a receive operation. Then it waits passively for an S packet from the file sender. When the S packet arrives, the parameters are set by spar() and the receiver's own parameters are set by rpar() and sent back to the sender in the acknowledgment by the ackl() function (which is for sending an acknowledgment that includes data), and then the state switches to srfil.

In srfil state, first we check for a B packet, which indicates no (more) files are coming and the transaction is complete. If an F packet comes, we call upon the rcvfil() function to attempt to create a new file of the given name. If it succeeds, it sends an acknowledgment and switches to srdat state.

Two inputs (packet types) are legal in srdat state: D and Z. The Z packet indicates that a file has been sent completely, in which case the file is closed and the state is switched back to srfil to see if any more files are coming. D packets contain data for the current file, encoded for transmission. The decode() function is used to decode the data and add it to the current file, and then the Data packet is acknowledged.

The B packet is the closing bracket of the transaction, and it serves as a "rear guard" on the files that preceded it. The B packet will not be sent until the preceding Z packet is acknowledged, and the Z packet is not acknowledged until the file is completely written to disk and closed.

When we combine the two Lex programs, we have a Kermit program that is capable of sending and receiving files. We only need to fill in the underlying functions and to supply a "user interface" to invoke this program.

Layers

We've now seen a Kermit transaction from both ends. At this point, it might be a good idea to say a few words about layered protocols. These are all the rage, and indeed they provide a useful model for discussing communication protocols in general. The most widely discussed layered protocol is the 7-layer ISO Open Systems Interconnection (OSI) Reference Model [17]; here is a very simplified summary of it:

1. The Physical Layer. The communication medium and the hardware that manages it, converting the computer's binary bits into signals appropriate to the medium, and vice versa.

2. The Data Link Layer. The hardware or software that breaks data up into block-checked frames, or packets, for transmission over the physical link, and detects errors upon receipt.

3. The Network Layer. Manages routing of packets through a multinode network.

4. The Transport Layer. Calls upon the network layer to ensure that packets are delivered and received with no errors and in proper sequence.

5. The Session Layer. Establishes a logical link between two processes, and calls upon the transport layer to provide the processes with reliable streams of data.

6. The Presentation Layer. Performs conversion between the format, encoding, and display conventions of different systems.

7. The Application Layer. Provides the user or programmer with transparent access to a remote system's resources.

Layers 1–3 are often implemented in special communication front ends, outside the host computer, which form a "communication subnet." Layering is reflected in the layout of a packet—the outermost fields belong to the lowest layers, the innermost fields to the highest. As an arriving packet moves up through the hierarchy, each layer peels off and processes its own fields, and passes the remainder up to the next layer. As outbound packets proceed downward through these layers, each adds its own fields to the beginning or end. Figure 9-4 shows the layers of the OSI model, and how they relate to Kermit (other interpretations are also possible [18]).

OSI	Kermit
Application layer	(None. Kermit does not provide a transparent interface.)
Presentation layer	Format and character set conversion for filenames and textual data.
Session layer	S (F D* Z)* B
Transport layer	Sequence assurance. ACK/NAK.
Network layer	(Null. Kermit is point-to-point.)
Datalink Layer	Data integrity: packet framing, block check, encode/decode, etc.
Physical layer	RS-232, parity, system-level flow control.

Figure 9-4. Kermit and the ISO OSI Reference Model

In a layered protocol, each layer communicates only with its adjacent layers locally, through well-defined, standardized interfaces, and with its peer layer on the other end through its inferior layers over the communication link. As one observer points out [26], if you picture the ISO model as a high-rise apartment building, you must climb down the stairs and then back up to visit a neighbor whose apartment is on your own floor. The idea behind layered protocols is that the module implementing any layer can be replaced by another module that works differently but presents itself to its neighboring and peer layers in the same way. For instance, a file transfer application can be replaced by a virtual terminal application, or a telecommunications datalink layer by Ethernet.

Kermit is *not* such a protocol. It is not designed to communicate with "Open Systems" that conform to the OSI model. Nevertheless, Kermit programs tend to be organized in layers, if only for the sake of clarity and elimination of redundant code. The part that we've been looking at so far corresponds roughly to the ISO session layer, in which a specific period of communication is initiated by the S-packet exchange and terminated by the B-packet exchange. Thus a Kermit transaction corresponds approximately to an OSI session. Dealings are on the packet level, but the assumption is that packets arrive in sequence and uncorrupted, with no loss or duplication. It is the responsibility of the transport layer to deliver packets in this way.

The Transport Layer

Kermit's tranport layer is invoked implicitly by its session layer when Lex calls upon the input( ) function to supply the next packet type. Let's digress a moment and show how Lex translates its statements into ordinary C, so that we can see where the input( ) function fits in.

The Lex %states (or %start) directive simply enters the given state names into Lex's symbol table, where Lex assigns numbers to them, like

```
#define ssini 1
#define ssfil 2
#define ssdat 3
```

Then, the section bracketed by %% markers is translated to something like this:

```
while (type = input()) {
    action = table[f(type,state)]
    switch(action) {
        case 1: { action } break;
        case 2: { action } break;
        etc.
    }
}
```

where *f*( ) is a function that produces an index into an action table containing an entry for every valid combination state and input; Lex creates this table from all the Lex statements that appear within the %%...%% brackets. The same result could be obtained without the use of Lex by doing something more cumbersome in straight C, like:

```
while (type = input()) {
    if (type == 'S' && state == rsini) { action }
    else if (type == 'B' && state == rsini) { action }
    else if (type == 'F' && state == rfile) { action }
    else if (etc...)
}
```

This may not look so bad, but it gets worse when multiple states go with one input, and there are many combinations to account for—Lex lets the computer do the accounting for you. The purpose here is not to explain or justify Lex but to illustrate that the input() function is invoked each time through the loop, and it returns a packet type.

How does the input() function manage to return uncorrupted packets in correct sequence? Let's take a look at a typical input function:

```
input() {
    int type, try;              /* Local variables */

    if (start != 0) {           /* Start state in effect? */
        type = start;           /* Yes, call it a packet type, */
        start = 0;              /* nullify the start state, */
        return(type);           /* and return the type. */
    }
    type = rpack();             /* No start state, read a packet. */

    for (try = 0; rsn != seq || strchr("TQN",type); try++) {
        if (try > limit) {      /* If too many tries, */
            error("Timed out"); /* give up. */
            return(0);
        }
        if (type == 'N' && rsn == (seq+1) & 63) {
                                /* NAK for next packet */
                return('Y');    /* is ACK for current. */
        } else {                /* Otherwise, */
            resend();           /* resend previous packet. */
        }
        type = rpack();         /* Try to read response. */
    }
    ttflui();                   /* Got a good one, clear buffer. */
    return(type);               /* Return its type. */
}
```

You're probably wondering how such a short function can do so much. The answer is that it really doesn't do much at all, just sequence assurance. It calls upon the datalink layer (the rpack() function) to do the dirty work; rpack() returns the packet type of the packet received, or else one of the dummy packet types T (timeout) or Q (corrupted packet). If the sequence number of the received packet (rsn) is not the desired one (seq), or if the packet type is N (negative acknowledgment), T, or Q, then the previous packet is retransmitted, and we try again to read the desired one, up to the retry threshold MAXTRY.

Actually, there's a little more to it. At the session layer, you saw invocations of functions like ack(), ackl(), sinit(), sfile(), sdata(), seof(), and seot(). These are the functions that transmit packets of the desired types. Each of these functions, in turn, calls upon a function nxtpkt() to increment the packet sequence number, modulo 64, and the datalink function spack(), which not only constructs and transmits the packet but also saves a copy of it so that it may be retransmitted by the resend() function if necessary.

The input() function shields the upper layers from having to worry about replicated or missing packets. It works for both sending and receiving files, and it ensures that functions like sfile(), rcvfil(), and sdata() are called only at appropriate times regardless of how many copies of a packet arrive. This prevents the same file from being opened multiple times, the same data from being written to the file more than once, and so forth.

In the file transfer schematic in Figure 2-3 on page 17, you may have noticed how the file receiver sent a NAK when packet 4 was corrupted in transmission. Such behavior is quite permissible, and it's how most Kermit programs handle the situation. But our input() function is above all that: it works for both file sender and file receiver, and it's fully unaware of the direction of the file transfer. Whenever the desired packet does not arrive intact, whether because of a timeout or corruption, or because a valid packet with the wrong number appeared, the input() function simply retransmits its last packet.

Let's enumerate the kinds of things that can go wrong. . .

1. A packet arrives corrupted. The datalink layer returns its type as Q, and we immediately retransmit our last packet. How does the other Kermit view this? It will notice that the same packet arrived again, so it will ignore it and retransmit its own last packet, which is just the one we want.

2. An expected packet does not arrive. The datalink layer times out and returns a dummy packet type of T. We treat this exactly the same as a corrupted packet.

3. A packet we send is corrupted or lost. Assuming the other side behaves as we do, it retransmits its previous packet. But we have already received it and are now expecting the next one. Since the packet that has just arrived has the wrong sequence number, we resend our previous packet. Assuming the other Kermit receives it correctly, we're back in sync.

This covers all the cases, at least when both Kermits follow the simple strategy of resending the previous packet whenever anything goes wrong. However, the protocol also allows a Kermit program to explicitly NAK a packet that arrives corrupted, or not at all. If a packet we send is corrupted or lost, a NAK with the same packet number will arrive, and the retransmission method will work as intended. But suppose an ACK was sent to us, which never arrived. The other Kermit will be waiting for the next packet. If it times out before we do, it may send a NAK for the expected packet. If we simply retransmit our previous packet (because we got a NAK), then we'll get the same NAK back again, and the process will repeat up to the retry limit, causing the transaction to fail. But if we observe that the other Kermit would not be sending a NAK for the next packet unless it had already received and ACK'd the current one, we can break the cycle. Here the rule is "A NAK for the next packet implies an ACK for the current packet."

The key to sequencing is, naturally, the packet sequence number. For each transaction, the file sender initializes the sequence number to zero before sending the first packet and advances it, modulo 64, before sending each subsequent packet. The file receiver begins a transaction by expecting packet number zero, and then it advances the packet number after acknowledging each packet. Here is the function for advancing the packet number:

```
nxtpkt() {                       /* nexpkt() */
    seq = (seq + 1) & 63;        /* Next packet number, mod 64 */
}
```

Before proceeding, let's look at two simple functions that are invoked from the Lex code. First, tinit() is invoked at the beginning of a transaction to set the sequence number to zero and clear the filename, receive packet, and send packet buffers:

```
tinit() {                        /* Transaction initialization */
    seq = 0;                     /* Start off with packet zero */
    *filnam = *sndpkt = *rcvpkt = '\0'; /* Clear string buffers */
}
```

The ERR() macro terminates a transaction abnormally when a fatal error occurs. It calls upon the error() function to issue the given error message (if any) either on the screen or in a packet, depending on whether the program is local or remote, and then terminates the transaction by returning from the protocol interpreter. A simple error() function might look like this:

```
error(s) char *s; {                   /* Fatal error */
    if (local) {                       /* If in local mode */
        tmsg("Fatal Error: ");         /* Type message on console */
        tmsg(s);
    } else {                           /* Otherwise */
        spack('E',seq,strlen(s),s);    /* Send in error packet. */
    }
    return;
}
```

The tmsg() function invokes the system-dependent procedure for typing a message on the console.

For sending the error packet, the error() function, like the other packet-sending functions about to be presented, calls upon the datalink-level spack() function. The arguments to spack() are the packet type, sequence number, length of the data field, and the contents of the data field. Here are the functions used by the file receiver to acknowledge, positively (ACK) or negatively (NAK), the packets it receives:

```
ack() {                              /* ack() */
    int x;                           /* Empty acknowledgment */
    x = spack('Y',seq,0,"");         /* Send the packet */
    nxtpkt();                        /* Increment packet number */
    return(x);
}

ackl(s) char *s; {                   /* ackl() */
    int x;                           /* Acknowledgment with data */
    x = spack('Y',seq,strlen(s),s);  /* Send the packet */
    nxtpkt();                        /* Increment packet number */
    return(x);
}

nak() {                              /* nak() */
    int x;                           /* Negative acknowledgment */
    x = spack('N',seq,0,"");         /* Never has data! */
    return(x);
}
```

Since the transport layer ensures that the ACKing functions will be invoked only once per packet, it is safe for them to include the nexpkt() invocation.

Here are the functions used by the file sender. The sinit() function starts the transaction by filling in the initialization string and sending it in an S packet:

```
    sinit(c) char c; {               /* sinit() */
    char *s;
    s = rpar();
    if (local == 0 && c == 'S' && server == 0) {
      tmsgl("Escape back to local system, give RECEIVE command...");
      sleep(delay);
    }
    return(spack(c,seq,strlen(s),s));
}
```

In remote mode, sinit() gives a helpful message and waits for the specified delay period before sending the first packet, to give the user time to escape back and prepare the local Kermit program for receiving. For now, you can assume that the character argument is always S and that the server flag is always zero.

The sfile() function opens the file and sends the File-Header packet. It assumes that the global string pointer filnam references the file's name. If the file is opened successfully, sfile() invokes the zltor() function to translate the filename to canonic form, and then `encstr()` to encode the result for transmission. The `encstr()` function returns the length of the result, and stores the encoded string itself in the global area called `data`.

```
sfile() {                                       /* sfile() */
    int x;
    char pktnam[50];
    if (zopeni(filnam) < 0) return(-1);         /* Try to open the file */
    zltor(filnam,pktnam);                       /* OK, convert name */
    x = encstr(pktnam);                         /* Encode the result */
    if (local) {                                /* If in local mode, */
        tmsg("Sending ");                       /* let user know we're */
        tmsg(filnam);                           /* sending this file */
        tmsg(" as ");                           /* under */
        tmsg(pktnam);                           /* this name. */
    }
    first = 1;                                  /* Flag beginning of file */
    maxsiz = spsiz - (bctr + 3);                /* Maximum data length */
    nxtpkt();                                   /* Increment packet number */
    return(spack((xpkt ? 'X' : 'F'),seq,x,data)); /* Send packet */
}
```

If filename translation is to be selectable, a flag set by the command parser can govern whether `zltor()` is called at this point. The statement that sets the variable `first` can be ignored for now. The one that sets `maxsiz` (the maximum length for the data field) does so based on the maximum packet size `spsiz` minus the combined lengths of the control fields; `bctr` is the block check field length, which is 1. You can assume the global flag `xpkt` (used in server mode, to be covered later) is zero, so the packet is finally sent with a packet type of F.

The `sdata()` function calls upon `getpkt()` to get the next packet's worth of data; the argument to `getpkt()` tells it how much it is allowed to get, and it returns how much it actually got, with the data again stored in the global `data` array.

```
sdata() {                                       /* sdata() */
    int x;
    if ((x = getpkt(maxsiz)) == 0)              /* If no data left to send, */
        return(0);                              /* return EOF indication. */
    nxtpkt();                                   /* Increment packet number */
    return(spack('D',seq,x,data));              /* Send the Data packet */
}
```

The `getpkt()` function in turn invokes the functions that decide whether to and how to convert local text format into canonic text format.

Here are the last two sending functions; `seof()` closes the input file and sends a Z packet; `seot()` simply sends a B packet.

```
seof(s) char *s; {                      /* seof() */
    if (zclosi() < 0)                   /* Try to close the file. */
        return(-1);                     /* On error, return failure. */
    else {                              /* Otherwise, */
        if (local) tmsgl("OK");         /* if local, reassure user, */
        nxtpkt();                       /* increment packet number */
        return(spack('Z',seq,strlen(s),s)); /* and send Z packet. */
    }
}

seot() {                                /* seot() */
    nxtpkt();                           /* Increment packet number */
    if (local) tmsgl("Done");           /* Say transaction is done */
    return(spack('B',seq,0,""));        /* Send the B packet */
}
```

Several auxiliary functions are used at this level for finding, opening, and closing files:

```
gnfile() {                              /* Get next file to send */
    if (nfils-- > 0) {                  /* from list. */
        strcpy(filnam,*cmlist++);       /* Depends on "user interface" */
        return(1);                      /* setting up the list. */
    } else return(0);
}

rcvfil() {                              /* Receive a file */
    char myname[50];
    decstr(filnam);                     /* Decode name */
    zrtol(filnam,myname,warn);          /* Convert to local form */
    if (zopeno(myname) < 0) return(-1); /* Open the file */
    else {                              /* OK, if local give message. */
        if (local && !xflag) {
            tmsg("Receiving "); tmsg(filnam); tmsg(" as "); tmsg(myname);
        }
        return(0);
    }
}

closof() {                              /* Close output file, but */
    if (xflag) return(0);               /* not if it's the screen */
    if (zcloso(cx|cz) < 0) return(-1);
    return(0);
}
```

The gnfile() function assumes that the list of files to be sent is already stored in an array, such as that set up by the UNIX shell, with nfils set to the number of files in the list. On other systems, gnfile() might have to do the work itself, stepping through the directory and matching each entry with a wildcard file specification, or calling upon the system to do so.

The Datalink Layer

Before we discuss the datalink layer, we need to know the packet layout. As you recall, a Kermit packet starts with a single control character and then the rest of the characters in the packet are in the ASCII printable range (32–126). This means that when we need to include a numeric quantity in the packet, like a sequence number, length, or checksum, it has to be encoded in printable ASCII characters. Here are the functions used for encoding and decoding:

- `tochar(x)` = $(x + 32)$

Transforms an integer x, which is assumed to lie in the range 0 to 94, into a printable ASCII character; 0 becomes SP, 1 becomes "!," 3 becomes "#," etc. The result is called "excess 32" notation.

- `unchar(x)` = $(x - 32)$

Transforms the character x, which is assumed to be in the printable range (ASCII 32–126, SP through tilde), into an integer in the range 0 to 94.

- `ctl(x)` = $(x$ ^ $64)$

Maps between control characters and their printable representations, preserving the high-order bit, by toggling bit six (i.e., the seventh bit from the "right"). If x is a control character, then

```
x = ctl(ctl(x))
```

that is, the same function is used to "controllify" and "uncontrollify." The argument is assumed to be a true control character (0–31, or 127), or the result of applying `ctl` to a true control character (63–95). The transformation is the mnemonic one: ^A becomes A and vice versa. "^" is the C language notation for the bitwise exclusive OR operation, whose result has each bit set to 1 when the corresponding bits in the operands are different, and to 0 when the corresponding operand bits are the same.

Each field in the basic Kermit packet, except the data field, is one character long, as shown in Figure 9-5.

Figure 9-5. Kermit Packet Format

The fields are:.

MARK A single control character that marks the beginning of the packet, Control-A (SOH, ASCII 1) by convention, but it may be redefined.

LEN The number of characters within the packet that follow this field, up to and including the check field, in excess-32 notation. In basic Kermit, this number ranges from 3 (#) when the data field is empty to 94 (~) when the data field contains the maximum of 91 characters.

SEQ   The packet sequence number, modulo 64, ranging from `tochar(0)` (SP) to `tochar(63)` (_). Sequence numbers wrap around to 0 after each group of 64 packets.

TYPE   The packet type, a single literal ASCII character from among those shown in Table 9-1, or others to be presented later. A complete list is given in Appendix C.

DATA   The contents of the packet, if any contents are required in the given type of packet, encoded or interpreted according to the packet type and encoding options in effect.

CHECK   A block check on the characters in the packet between, but not including, the mark and the block check itself. A single-character arithmetic checksum is the normal block check, and all Kermit programs must support it. Only six bits of the arithmetic sum are included, and only eight bits are required to accumulate and calculate it. So that all the bits of each data character contribute to this quantity, bits 6 and 7 of the final value are added to the quantity formed by bits 0–5. Thus if s is the arithmetic sum of the ASCII characters,

CHECK = `tochar((`s` + ((`s` & 192)/64)) & 63)`

where "&" is the bitwise AND operator. The block check is based on the values of all the characters in the packet, starting with LEN and ending with the final character in the DATA field (or if the DATA field is empty, the packet type). The high-order bit is not included if it is being used for parity, but it is included if it is being used for data.

Kermit protocol options, to be described later, allow variations on the length and block check fields. The packet fields correspond to protocol layers roughly as shown in Figure 9-6.

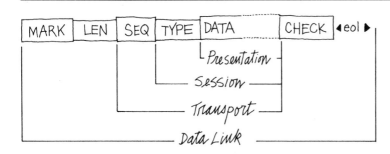

Figure 9-6. Packet Fields and Protocol Layers

Packet Terminator Any line terminator (shown as <eol> in the figure) required by the system may be appended to the packet. This is carriage return (ASCII 13) by default. Line terminators are not considered part of the packet and are not accounted for in the count or checksum. Terminators are not necessary to the protocol. However, most Kermit implementations require a terminator, either because they cannot do character-at-a-time input, or because they can't do it as efficiently as line-at-a-time.

The Parity Bit When communication line parity is in use (i.e., set to EVEN, ODD, MARK, or SPACE), the high-order bit of each character in the packet carries the selected parity, and the communication channel is said to be 7 bits wide. The parity bit is added to each character when the packet is sent, and stripped when the packet is received. It is *not* included in the sum s, which is the basis of the block check. When parity is not being done, the high-order bit of each character is available for data, and it *is* included in the block check calculation.

Encoding The data field of all packets described so far is encoded according to the options in effect, except for the data field of the S packet and its acknowledgment, since these packets are used to establish the encoding options in the first place. (The A and I packets, to be presented later, are not encoded either.)

Packet Formation and Decomposition The spack( ) function puts a packet together and sends it. It assumes all required encoding has already been done. The rpack( ) function receives a packet and picks it apart into its component fields. Here is a no-frills spack( ):

```
spack(type,n,len,d) char type, *d; int n, len; {
    int i = 0, j, k;
    sndpkt[i++] = smark;                     /* Packet mark */
    k = i;                                   /* Remember this place */
    sndpkt[i++] = tochar(len+3);             /* Length */
    sndpkt[i++] = tochar(n);                 /* Sequence number */
    sndpkt[i++] = type;                      /* Packet type */

    for (j = len; j > 0; j--) {              /* Data */
        sndpkt[i++] = *d++;
    }
    sndpkt[i] = '\0';                        /* Null-terminate for... */
    sndpkt[i++] = tochar(chk1(sndpkt+k));    /* ...checksum */
    sndpkt[i++] = seol;                      /* End of line */
    sndpkt[i++] = '\0';                      /* Null string-terminator */
    sndpkl = i;                              /* Remember length. */
    i = ttol(sndpkt,sndpkl);                 /* Send the packet. */
    if (local && !xflag) tchar('.');
    return(i);
```

Notice the printing of a dot on the console screen when in local mode. This keeps the user informed that packets are flowing (the use of xflag is explained later). The ttol() function is a system-dependent function that actually transmits the characters. The packet is constructed in the global area sndpkt, which is used later by the resend() function if retransmission is required:

```
resend() {                               /* resend() */
    int x;
    if (*sndpkt)
        x = ttol(sndpkt,sndpkl);         /* Send previous packet */
    else x = nak();                      /* or NAK if none */
    if (local && !xflag) tchar('%');     /* Let the user know. */
    return(x);
}
```

The resend() function prints a percent sign instead of a dot, to let the user know that there have been transmission problems. The nak() function is invoked if there is nothing in the resend buffer. This sends a negative acknowledgment for the desired packet, and as a by-product, fills in the resend buffer with the NAK packet in case another retransmission is needed.

The chkl() function computes the normal Kermit checksum based on the arithmetic sum of all the bytes in the packet, which in turn is calculated by the chksum() function according to the current parity setting. Note, by the way, that the arithmetic sum will fit into a 16-bit word. Even in the worst case (a 95-character packet composed of all 1-bits) the sum will be 95 x 255 = 24225, which fits into 15 bits (just barely).

```
chkl(packet) char *packet; {             /* Compute Kermit's */
    int s, t;                            /* 1-character block check. */
    s = chksum(packet);                  /* Get the arithmetic sum. */
    t = (((s & 192) >> 6) + s) & 63;     /* Fold it into 6 bits. */
    return(t);
}
chksum(p) char *p; {                     /* Compute the checksum */
    unsigned int m; long s;
    m = (parity) ? 0177 : 0377;          /* Mask for parity bit */
    for (s = 0; *p != '\0'; *p++)        /* For each character, */
        s += *p & m;                     /* accumulate the sum. */
    return(s & 07777);                   /* and then return it. */
}
```

Now let's look at a simple rpack() function. It returns the type of the packet that was read, or else dummy packet types T or Q. It calls upon the system-dependent ttinl() function to obtain a "line" of data (hopefully, a packet) from the communication medium; ttinl() presumably takes care of flow control, handshake, parity, timeouts, and so forth.

```
/*
 rpack reads a packet and returns the packet type, or else Q if the packet
was invalid, or T if a timeout occurred. Upon successful return, sets the
global variables:

    rsn    - the received sequence number
    rln    - length of the received data field
    rdatap - a pointer to the null-terminated contents of data field
*/
rpack() {
    int i, j, x, type, rlnpos;                 /* Local variables */
    char pbc[4];                               /* Packet block check */

    rsn = rln = -1;                            /* In case of failure. */

    *rcvpkt = '\0';                            /* Initialize receive buffer. */
    j = ttinl(rcvpkt,MAXRP,reol,parity); /* Try to get a "line". */
    if (j < 0) return('T');                    /* Timed out. */

    for (i = 0; rcvpkt[i] != rmark && (i < j); i++) /* Find mark */
        ;
    if (i == j) return('Q');                   /* If no mark, bad packet. */

    rlnpos = ++i;                              /* Got it, remember position. */
    rln = unchar(rcvpkt[i++]) - 3;             /* Data field length */
    rsn = unchar(rcvpkt[i++]);                 /* Sequence number */
    type = rcvpkt[i++];                        /* Packet type */
    rdatap = rcvpkt+i;                         /* The data itself */
    *pbc = rcvpkt[i+rln];                      /* Packet block check */
    rcvpkt[i+rln] = '\0';                      /* Null-terminate the data */
    if (unchar(*pbc) != chkl(rcvpkt+rlnpos)) /* Check checksum */
        return('Q');                           /* If bad, return Q */
    else return(type);                         /* Otherwise, packet type */
}
```

This completes the minimal datalink layer. The spack() and rpack() functions get
a bit more complicated when options and heuristics (tricks) are added.

The Physical Link Layer

The tt...() functions provide access to the physical communication link, or to the
operating system functions (device drivers) that control and service it. The content of
these functions is necessarily system-dependent, but their operation can be described
in a general way. As a matter of practice, these functions would be kept together in a
separate module with its own private global variables, allowing the functions to share
file descriptors, modes, and similar information. This system-dependent module should
be completely replaceable by an equivalent module for a different system. For the sake
of completeness, a listing of this module for UNIX is included in Appendix A.

Here are the system-dependent functions. Each returns 0 upon success and −1 on failure, unless otherwise indicated:

- `ttopen(name)`
Gains (presumably exclusive) access to, and opens, the named communication line, saving its current modes and settings for later restoration. Returns −1 if the line couldn't be accessed or opened. If the line was opened successfully, returns 0 if it is a remote line (i.e., the user's timesharing console), or 1 if local.

- `ttpkt(speed,flow,parity)`
Conditions the line for packet I/O. Turns off echoing, character translation, etc., and sets the speed to the one given (if it is a legal speed, greater than zero, and the line is not the controlling terminal). Enables the specified type of flow control (e.g., XON/XOFF, NONE). Establishes parity processing as indicated. Returns −1 if the line can't be conditioned as desired, otherwise clears the line's input buffer and returns 0.

- `ttres()`
Restores the original settings of the communication line.

- `ttclos()`
Closes and releases the communication line.

- `ttflui()`
Flushes the communication line input buffer, i.e., empties it, discarding its contents.

- `ttinl(dest,max,eol,timout)`
Gets a `line` from the communication medium, that is, a sequence of characters terminated by `eol`, or a string `max` characters long, whichever comes first, using the current settings of parity, flow, handshake, etc. If parity is being done, the parity bit is stripped from each incoming character. If handshake is being done, this function should be called with the handshake character as the `eol`. Returns the number of characters obtained, or −1 on error. If a time limit is specified, returns −1 if the limit expired before a line was read.

- `ttol(s,n)`
Outputs the string `s`, of length `n`, on the communication line, using the current settings for flow control and parity.

- `ttsspd(speed)`
Verifies that the given speed is legal. If so, it returns the system-dependent code for the given speed, otherwise −1.

There should also be several functions for console output: `tmsg()`, which simply types its string argument on the console; `tmsgl()`, which types the string followed by a line terminator; and `tchar()`, which displays a single character on the console.

The z... ( ) functions provide access to the local file system. These are kept together with the tt... ( ) functions, because they are also system-dependent. They insulate the program from specific knowledge of file format, file-name syntax, file descriptors, error codes, etc. Each returns 0 upon success, − 1 upon failure, unless otherwise indicated.

- zopeni(name)
Opens an existing local file of the given name for input.

- zopeno(name)
Creates a new file of the given name and opens it for output.

- zclosi()
Closes the input file opened by zopeni( ).

- zcloso(x)
Closes the output file opened by zopeno( ). If the parameter x is nonzero, the file is discarded; otherwise it is kept.

- zrtol(n1,n2,warn)
Translates the remote filename, n1, to a legal local one, n2. If the warn flag is nonzero, checks if a file by the resulting name already exists, and if so, constructs a unique new name in local format.

- zltor(n1,n2)
Translates the local filename, n1, to a remote (canonic) one, n2. Canonic form is a common intermediate representation for filenames, of the form *name.type*, containing only uppercase letters, digits, and at most a single dot, with at least one character before the dot. Any device or directory specifications are stripped, and funny characters are removed or replaced by letters or digits.

- zgetc(text)
Gets the next character from the input file. In text mode, performs any required translations from local format to canonic text format, e.g., record conversion, EBCDIC-to-ASCII translation, etc.

- zputc(c,text)
Outputs the character c to the output file. In text mode, performs any required conversions from canonic to local text file format.

The system-dependent module should also include definitions for intrinsically system-dependent variables, like the name of the controlling terminal, default local/remote status, default parity, and so on.

Encoding and Decoding of Data

Two distinct things can happen to data before it goes into the data field of a Kermit packet: (1) text files are translated into canonic form at the presentation layer, and (2) the data (canonic or not) is encoded for transmission at the datalink layer.

The Presentation Layer

An important goal of the Kermit protocol is that text files should remain useful after transfer between *any* pair of systems, no matter how different their text file formats. So that the Kermit program need not have detailed knowledge of the text file format of every conceivable system it could send text to, a common intermediate representation for text files is selected, which we call canonic form. Canonic form for text files is simply this: a stream of ASCII characters, one per 8-bit byte, with each line (record) terminated by a carriage return and a linefeed (CRLF). This format is chosen because it is economical and in common use. On many systems (such as MS-DOS), no conversion need be done at all. On others (such as IBM mainframes), both character set (EBCDIC/ASCII) and record format (block/stream) conversion are required.

Back in the sdata() function you may have noticed a function called getpkt(). This function reads a packet's worth of data and prepares it for transmission, using its own input and output functions. Its input function, gnchar(), gets the next character from the indicated source; the stream of characters returned by gnchar() is in canonic format. The output function, encode(), does the transmission-level encoding. The encode() function is called repeatedly until a packet's worth of data has been accumulated; upon each invocation, it deposits either a single character or a prefixed sequence into the packet data field. Here is a simple getpkt() function:

```
/*
 Fill a packet to the maximum.  Result goes in global data array,
 whose current length is indicated in global size.
*/
getpkt(maxlen) int maxlen; {
    int i, c;
    static char remain[6] = {'\0', '\0', '\0', '\0', '\0', '\0'};

/* Copy any leftovers that didn't fit in the last packet. */

    for (size = 0; (data[size] = remain[size]) != '\0'; size++) ;
    *remain = '\0';

/* Get, encode, and deposit the next character. */

    while ((c = gnchar()) > -1) {            /* Get next character. */
        osize = size;                        /* Remember current size. */
        encode(c);                           /* Encode the character. */

        if (size == maxlen) return(size); /* Just at end, done. */
```

```
        if (size > maxlen) {                  /* Past end, must save some. */
            for (i = 0; (remain[i] = data[osize+i]) != '\0'; i++) ;
            size = osize;                      /* Restore old size */
            data[size] = '\0';                 /* Restore old data */
            return(size);                      /* Return old size */
        }
    }                                          /* No more characters, done. */
    return(size);                              /* Return what we got. */
}
```

Here is the gnchar() function, which supplies getpkt() with the next character:

```
gnchar() {                                     /* Get Next Character */
    char c;
    if (isp) {                                 /* From string in memory, */
        return((c = *isp++) > 0 ? c : -1);
    } else return(zgetc(text));                /* or from a file. */
}
```

This function lets both file data and data in memory be treated the same way, so we can encode filenames or messages as well as file data. This shields getpkt() from having to know where the data is coming from.

Here's an example of the system-dependent function zgetc() that reads characters from a file and does the conversion to canonic form, in this case from UNIX text file format, in which lines are separated by a single "newline" character rather than CRLF. Other systems may need other conversions.

```
/*
 System-dependent function to return next character from file.
 If the text flag argument is nonzero, first convert to canonic
 form.
*/
zgetc(text) {                          /* Get next char from file */
#define MAXREC   100                   /* Size of record buffer */

    static char recbuf[MAXREC+1];      /* Record buffer */
    static char *rbp;                  /* Buffer pointer */
    static int i = 0;                  /* Buffer char counter */
    int c;                             /* Current character */

    if (i == 0) {                      /* If the buffer is empty, */
                                       /* read next line from file. */
        for (i=0; i < MAXREC - 1 && (c=getc(ifp)) != EOF && c != '\n'; i++)
            recbuf[i] = c;
        if (c == '\n') {               /* Got newline */
            if (text) {                /* If in text mode, */
                recbuf[i++] = '\r';    /* substitute CRLF. */
            }
            recbuf[i++] = c;           /* Put character in buffer */
        }
```

```
        recbuf[i] = '\0';          /* Done, terminate buffer. */
        if (i == 0) return(-1);    /* If empty, indicate EOF. */
        rbp = recbuf;              /* Remember position for next time. */
    }
    i--;                           /* Adjust the counter. */
    return(*rbp++ & 0377);         /* Return next character. */
}
```

zgetc() isolates the rest of the program from knowledge of the system's file format. Even though its purpose is to return the next character, its operation is record-oriented. When it runs out of characters, it gets the next record into its record buffer. This is to allow any required record format conversion to take place: stripping of trailing blanks, interpretation of record control words, etc. The "if (c == '\n') { ... }" section corresponds to the OSI presentation layer . In this example, record format conversion is done by translating UNIX "newline" characters (\n) to CRLFs. This is also where character set translation (like EBCDIC to ASCII) would take place, after the record is identified.

Datalink-Level Encoding

We've said repeatedly that only printable ASCII characters are allowed in packets, except that in 8-bit communication links the high-order bit may be used for data when transferring binary files. We take pains to encode control characters because, as you recall, mainframe console terminals as well as assorted communication boxes may be opaque to some of them. The required encoding is part of the packetizing process and is therefore a function of Kermit's datalink layer.

The basic encoding scheme is very simple. Any character whose low-order 7 bits fall into the control range (ASCII 0–31, and ASCII 127) is replaced by ctl() of itself and then prefixed by the control prefix character, which is normally "#." If the control prefix character itself occurs in the data, it is prefixed by itself, even if its high-order bit is on. The prefix character must be in the range ASCII 33–63 or 96–126 so that the ctl() function can work as intended. Table 9-2 shows some examples.

Table 9-2. Control Character Encoding

Character	Binary	Prefixed	Binary
A	01000001	A	01000001
A	11000001	A	11000001
Control–A	00000001	#A	01000001
Control–A	10000001	#A	11000001
Rubout	01111111	#?	00111111
Rubout	11111111	#?	10111111
#	00100110	##	00100110
#	10100110	##	10100110

In the Character and Prefixed columns, a character is shown in color to indicate that its high-order bit is on. The Binary columns show the binary ASCII value of the character (by itself, without the prefix) before and after encoding.

Here are simple encode() and decode() functions to produce the described effects. Every Kermit program is expected to have these. A prefixed sequence must not be broken across packets. If encode() emits a sequence that passes the packet boundary, getpkt() erases it and puts it aside for next time.

```
/*
 Encodes the character a into the global data array,
 and global size is updated.
 Global sctlq is the control prefix for sending data.
*/
encode(a) char a; {
    int a7;
    a7 = a & 127;                        /* Isolate low 7 bits */
    if (a7 < 32 || a7 == 127) {          /* If control character */
        data[size++] = sctlq;            /* insert control quote */
        a = ctl(a);                      /* and make printable. */
    } else if (a7 == sctlq) {            /* If data is control prefix, */
        data[size++] = sctlq;            /* also insert control quote */
    }
    data[size++] = a;                    /* Insert the character. */
    data[size] = '\0';                   /* Terminate string with NUL. */
}
```

Note that this function leaves the high-order bit of the character intact, allowing transfer of binary files through 8-bit-wide communication links. When the path is not 8 bits wide, binary files cannot be transferred without further measures, to be described later.

Here's the companion decoding function. It works on an entire data buffer rather than on a single character.

```
/*
 Decodes the data pointed to by the global pointer rdatap.
*/
decode() {
    char a, a7;

    while ((a = *rdatap++) != '\0') {/* For each character, a... */
        if (a == rctlq) {               /* Is it the control prefix? */
            a = *rdatap++;              /* Yes, get next character */
            a7 = a & 127;               /* and its low 7 bits. */
            if (a7 > 62 && a7 < 96)     /* Encoded control character? */
                a = ctl(a);            /* Yes, controllify. */
        }
        if (pnchar(a) < 0) return(-1); /* Output the character. */
    }
    return(0);                          /* Return successfully when done. */
}
```

The pnchar() function simply outputs the decoded character to the desired place, a string (osp = output string pointer), the screen (if xflag nonzero), or (in the normal case) a file:

```
pnchar(c) int c; {                    /* Put next character */
    if (xflag) {                      /* To screen if desired... */
        tchar(c);
        return(1);
    } else if (osp) {                 /* Or to string in memory... */
        *osp++ = c;
        return(1);
    } else return(zputc(c,text));     /* Otherwise to file. */
}
```

For file output, pnchar() calls upon the system-dependent function zputc(), which is the inverse of zgetc(). If in text mode, it assumes that its input is a stream of characters in canonic text format, and will do whatever is required to convert to local text format. Here's an example for UNIX:

```
zputc(c,text) int c, text; {          /* Put character in file. */
    unsigned int x;
    c &= 255;                         /* Undo any sign extension */
    if (text && c == '\r') {          /* If in text mode, */
        return(0);                    /* eliminate carriage returns */
    } else {                          /* Otherwise, */
        x = putc(c,ofp) & 255;        /* output the character. */
        if (c == 255) return(0);      /* Special for all ones. */
        return((x != c) ? -1 : 0);    /* Normal return code. */
    }
}
```

The zputc() function is where character set and record format conversion would take place if the local system differed from canonic format in these respects. The special case for 255 occurs in this example because the UNIX putc() function returns the same code after successfully outputting a byte of all 1's, as it does upon error.

Recall that the File-Header packet is sent with the filename encoded. Here are the functions that encode and decode strings in memory. They simply set up the string pointer and then invoke the same functions that are used with files (ignore the statement "first = 1;" for now).

```
encstr(s) char *s; {                  /* Fill a packet from the string. */
    first = 1;                         /* Start lookahead. */
    isp = s;                           /* Set input string pointer */
    getpkt(spsiz);                     /* Fill a packet */
    isp = NULL;                        /* Reset input string pointer */
    return(size);                      /* Return data field length */
}
```

```
decstr(s) char *s; {          /* Decode packet data into a string */
    osp = s;                  /* Set output string pointer   */
    decode();                 /* Decode the string */
    *osp = '\0';              /* Terminate string with NUL */
    osp = NULL;               /* Reset output string pointer */
}
```

The assumption behind Kermit's encoding scheme is that most files are transferred in text mode, and text files contain relatively few control characters. When this is true, the character stream is not significantly lengthened by quoting. For binary files, the expected prefixing overhead is 26.6 percent if all bit patterns are equally likely, since the characters that must be prefixed (the control characters, plus DEL, and "#" itself) comprise 26.6 percent of the 7-bit ASCII alphabet.

For text files (documents or program source), assuming an average line length of 40 with lines separated by CRLF (the only control characters normally found in the text file), we see about 5 percent overhead for prefixing of control characters. Assuming no line terminator for packets, no retransmissions or timeouts, and no time wasted for the line to turn around between packet and response, for average packet length p, using a single-character checksum, the Kermit protocol overhead consists of:

5 control field characters in the data packet
5 characters in the acknowledgment packet
+ 0.05p for control character quoting

This gives $10/p + 0.05$ overhead. If the packet length is 40, there is 30 percent overhead. If p is 96 (the maximum for unextended packets), the overhead is about 15 percent. These figures will vary with the average line length and the frequency of other control characters (like tabs and formfeeds) in the file. Encoding overhead is examined in more detail later.

Initial Connection Negotiation

Operations at Kermit's session layer commence with the exchange of parameters. This has turned out to be one of Kermit's most powerful features. It allows two Kermit programs to configure themselves to one another with respect to both communications and features. In particular, the indication of the presence or absence of a given feature allows the protocol to grow, yet remain "upwardly compatible" with old definitions. Because of this mechanism, the oldest, most primitive Kermit program can still communicate with the newest, most feature-laden version.

The Send-Initiation parameters are carried in the data field of the sender's S packet, and in the data field of the receiver's acknowledgment (Y) of the S packet. The basic protocol described so far requires only the negotiation of datalink options, shown in Figure 9-7, and even these have defaults.

Figure 9-7. Basic Kermit Initialization String

The fields are as follows ("I" and "you" are used to distinguish the two negotiating programs). Fields are encoded in printable excess-32 notation using the tochar() function, unless otherwise indicated.

• MAXL

The maximum length packet (i.e., the largest value of LEN) I want to receive, a number up to 94 (decimal). You respond with the maximum you want me to send. This allows systems to adjust to each other's buffer sizes or to the condition of the transmission medium. If not specified, 80 should be used.

• TIME

The number of seconds you should wait for a packet from me before timing out. You respond with the amount of time I should wait for packets from you. Negotiation of timeout allows the two sides to accommodate to different line speeds or other factors that could cause timing problems. Only one side needs to time out. If both sides time out, then the timeout intervals should not be close together. If not specified, 5 seconds should be used (if the system is capable of doing timeouts, and if its timer is enabled).

• NPAD

The number of padding characters I want you to precede each incoming packet with; you respond in kind. Padding might be used in half-duplex connections in lieu of handshake, or it might be used for inserting characters between packets in order to control communication equipment. If not specified, no padding will be done.

• PADC

The control character I need for padding, if any, transformed by ctl() (*not* tochar()) to make it printable. You respond in kind. Normally NUL (ASCII 0) for padding, but some systems use DEL (ASCII 127), and other control characters may be used for special purposes. This field is ignored if the value of NPAD is zero.

• EOL

The character I need to terminate an incoming packet, if any. You respond in kind. Most systems that require a line terminator for terminal input accept carriage return (CR) for this purpose, and if this parameter is not specified, CR should be used.

• QCTL

(Verbatim) The control prefix. The printable ASCII character I will use to quote control characters, normally and by default "#." You respond with the one you will use.

Here is a sample Kermit initialization string:

And here is what it means:

Field	Contents	Interpretation	Meaning
MAXL	~	(ASCII 126 - 32) = 96	Maximum packet length.
TIME	*	(ASCII 42 - 32) = 10	Seconds, timeout.
NPAD	SP	(Space, ASCII 32 - 32) = 0	No padding.
PADC	@	(ASCII 64 ^ 64) = 0	Pad character NUL.
EOL	–	(ASCII 45 - 32) = 13	End packets with CR.
QCTL	#	(Literal #)	Control prefix.

Additional fields, corresponding to optional protocol features, are added at the right. These are described in the next chapter. Old or basic Kermit programs do not expect to see such fields and should act as if they are not there. The default value for any field, indicated by blank, should result in the behavior that occurred before the new field was defined or added.

You might wonder why parity is not among the initiation parameters. The answer is simply that if the very first packet (the initialization packet itself) does not have the right parity, it will not pass through the datalink layer because the checksum will appear to be wrong. The use of parity prevents its negotiation. The same is true to some extent for EOL, but this can still be negotiated automatically when it is the sender that requires a nonstandard terminator.

Here is the spar() function, used for reading the information from an arriving initialization packet, and setting the corresponding parameters:

```
spar(s) char *s; {                      /* Set parameters */
    int x;

    s--;                                /* Line up with field numbers. */

/* Limit on size of outbound packets */
    x = (rln >= 1) ? unchar(s[1]) : 80;
    spsiz = (x < 10) ? 80 : x;

/* Timeout on inbound packets */
    x = (rln >= 2) ? unchar(s[2]) : 5;
    timint = (x < 0) ? 5 : x;

/* Outbound Padding */
    spadn = 0; spadc = '\0';
    if (rln >= 3) {
        spadn = unchar(s[3]);
        if (rln >= 4) spadc = ctl(s[4]); else spadc = 0;
    }
```

```
/* Outbound Packet Terminator */
    seol = (rln >= 5) ? unchar(s[5]) : '\r';
    if ((seol < 2) || (seol > 31)) seol = '\r';

/* Control prefix */
    x = (rln >= 6) ? s[6] : '#';
    rctlq = ((x > 32 && x < 63) || (x > 95 && x < 127)) ? x : '#';
}
```

Notice how spar() supplies defaults for missing fields. This makes it possible for a Kermit program to send an empty initialization string and still have the normal parameters set up. Here is the companion rpar() function:

```
/*  Fill the data array with my send-init parameters  */

char *
rpar() {
    data[1] = tochar(rpsiz);      /* Biggest packet I can receive */
    data[2] = tochar(rtimo);      /* When I want to be timed out */
    data[3] = tochar(rpadn);      /* How much padding I need (none) */
    data[4] = ctl(rpadc);         /* Padding character I want */
    data[5] = tochar(reol);       /* End-Of-Line character I want */
    data[6] = '#';                /* Control-Quote character I send */
    return(data+1);               /* Return a pointer to the string */
}
```

Figure 9-8 shows the packet exchange sample Kermit session, to give you an idea of what the packets actually look like.

The initialization exchange occurs in lines 1 and 2; the receiver requests short (40-character) packets and default timeout. The File-Header packet is sent in line 3, and acknowledged in line 4. Two data packets are sent and ACK'd in lines 5–8, but the data packet in line 9 is corrupted by noise, NAK'd in line 10, and retransmitted in line 11. The next two data packets are sent and ACK'd, but the ACK to the data packet in line 17 is lost. The sender times out and retransmits the same packet in line 18. Line 20 shows the final packet of the file. It's shorter than the others. The EOF packet is sent in line 22, and the break-transmission packet in line 24. The acknowledgment in line 25 completes the transaction.

The Missing Pieces

The code supplied so far is all you need for a basic Kermit program—one that can send and receive files. All you need, that is, except a main program to put it all together, and the definitions of the system-dependent primitive functions. The main program would include data definitions, the "user interface," some initialization, and the activation of the protocol functions. For the sake of completeness, the main program, a minimal

```
 1.  ^A, Sp+ @-#Yl~U
 2.  ^A% YH &
 3.  ^A+!FFRED.TXTD
 4.  ^A#!Y?
 5.  ^AD"DImagine you have written a book, K
 6.  ^A#"Y@
 7.  ^AD#Dand you want to submit the manuscW
 8.  ^A##YA
 9.  ^AD$Dript to y~~~|xxxppppM#Jpublisher, Fred, A
10.  ^A#$N7
11.  ^AD$Dript to your#M#Jpublisher, Fred, A
12.  ^A#$YB
13.  ^AD%Dwhose office is behind a high fen
14.  ^A#%YC
15.  ^AD&Dce, marked ''SUBMIT#M#JMANUSCRIPTO
16.  ^A#&YD
17.  ^AD'DS HERE,'' with an arrow pointing _
18.  ^AD'DS HERE,'' with an arrow pointing _
19.  ^A#'YE
20.  ^A2(Dto the top.#M#JA
21.  ^A#(YF
22.  ^A#)ZH
23.  ^A#)YG
24.  ^A#*Bl
25.  ^A#*YH
```

Figure 9-8. Sample Kermit Session

UNIX-style command parser, and a system-dependent module for UNIX are included in Appendix A. Whatever style of user interaction is employed by the command parser, its ultimate purpose is as follows:

- Set the global parameter variables, like `speed`, `parity`, `flow`, `rpsiz`, `rpadn`, `rpadc`, `turn`, `text`, `warn`, etc., based on its own defaults, or commands from the user.

- Set the variable `start` to "s" for send, "v" for receive.

- If sending, fill an array pointed to by `**cmlist` with pointers to names of files to send, with a null element at the end of the list.

- Point `cmarg` at any single string argument (such as a "generic command," discussed in Chapter 11.

After the commands are parsed, the main program calls upon the protocol function built by Lex from the protocol state tables, which you may combine into a single file, as follows:

- Include all the necessary C declarations at the top; make sure each such line starts with a space.

- Include a definition for Lex's `yywrap()` function.

- Include `%states` declarations for all states above the first `%%` marker.

- Put the send states and receive states together, between the `%%`...`%%` markers.

- After the closing bracket, include the line "`#undef input`" so that our own `input()` function will be used, rather than Lex's built-in one.

The result should look like this:

```
extern char *rdatap, *rpar();                          /* -*-C-*- */
extern int local, start, bctu, bctr;

int filcnt, x;

yywrap() { return(1); }

/* Declare Lex states. */

%states ssini ssfil ssdat sseot
%states srini srfil srdat
```

```
%%
include('uksend.l')
include('ukrcv.l')
E { if (local) error(rdatap); return; }
. { error("Unexpected Packet Type"); }
                              /* Handle unwanted packet types. */
%%
#undef input
```

The "include()" statements are replaced by the appropriate sections of Lex code, the first with the sending states and the second with the receiving states.

10

Optional Features

This chapter describes several optional datalink features, including a method for passing 8-bit binary data through a 7-bit communication link, a rudimentary form of data compression, and alternative block check methods. Also, a method is presented for gracefully interrupting a file transfer.

Eighth-Bit Prefixing

When the communication channel is only 7 bits wide because parity is being used, 8-bit binary files cannot be transferred by basic Kermit. However, a protocol option called eighth-bit prefixing allows 8-bit binary data to fit through, provided both Kermit programs agree to use it. Eighth-bit prefixing is simple in execution, but the preliminary negotiation is a bit complicated.

Assume we've agreed to do eighth-bit prefixing, and to use the ASCII ampersand character (&) as the prefix. Then data is encoded as before (the control prefix applied based on the low-order 7 bits of the character), but then if the eighth bit is on, the character receives another prefix, &, in front of the control prefix, if any. If this prefix character itself appears in the data, it too is prefixed by the control prefix. Table 10-1 shows some examples. As in Table 9-2, a character whose eighth bit is on is shown in color, and the value in the second Binary column corresponds with the final character in the Prefixed column. A "p" in that column means that the high-order bit is used for parity.

Table 10-1. Eighth-Bit Prefix Encoding

Character	Binary	Prefixed	Binary
A	01000001	A	p1000001
A	11000001	&A	p1000001
Control-A	00000001	#A	p1000001
Control-A	10000001	&#A	p1000001
Rubout	01111111	#?	p0111111
Rubout	11111111	&#?	p0111111
#	00100011	##	p0100011
#	10100011	&##	p0100011
&	00100110	#&	p0100110
&	10100110	&#&	p0100110

Eighth-bit prefixing introduces a 100 percent overhead for each character that has its eighth bit on, but no overhead for those that don't; for this reason, it is preferable to simple hex encoding, which entails 100 percent overhead for each character.

Negotiation of eighth-bit prefixing takes place in field 7, QBIN, of the initialization string, shown in Figure 10-1. Because of the extra overhead, this option is to be avoided when unnecessary. Moreover, it must be possible for the file receiver to request it, even after the sender has already transmitted its S packet, in case the receiver knows that the channel is 7 bits wide, but the sender doesn't. These issues complicate the negotiation.

Figure 10-1. Kermit Initialization String with Eighth-Bit Prefix

The values that QBIN may take are:

Y   Yes, I agree to do eighth-bit prefixing if you request it.

N   No, I refuse to do eighth-bit prefixing.

&   (or any valid prefix character distinct from the control prefix): I request that eighth-bit prefixing be done using this prefix.

Anything else, or field missing, is equivalent to N.

A valid prefix character is any character in the ranges ASCII 33–62 or 96–126, but there should never be a reason to use an eighth-bit prefix other than &. In the negotiation, either the file sender or the receiver may initiate eighth-bit prefixing. It will occur if one side specifies a prefix character and the other side provides a Y or the same prefix character. Table 10-2 lists some possible scenarios.

Table 10-2. Eighth-Bit Prefix Negotiations

Sender	Receiver	Prefixing?
Y	&	Yes
&	Y	Yes
&	&	Yes
Y	Y	No
&	N	No
N	&	No
&	%	No
Y	(blank)	No

In the table, "&" stands for any valid prefix character distinct from the control prefix, and "%" stands for some other valid prefix character. As you can see, there are many combinations that don't work (including YY. You've heard of double negatives? This is a double affirmative.) and only three that do. If eighth-bit prefixing is not selected, then its normal prefix "&" should not be prefixed when it appears in the data (but no harm will be done if it is).

Eighth-bit prefixing is normally tied to parity. Those Kermit programs which can do it at all will request it only when parity is other than NONE—i.e., ODD, EVEN, MARK, or SPACE. Otherwise, they will put a Y in QBIN field. Here is the code for the rpar() function:

```
switch (rqf) {                        /* 8th-bit prefix */
    case -1:
    case  1: if (parity) ebq = sq = '&'; break;
    case  0:
    case  2: break;
}
data[7] = sq;
```

This code is written so that it can be executed either before or after the companion code in spar(), in the next example. The rqf flag is initialized to −1 by tinit() before the transaction begins. If rpar() runs before spar() then eighth-bit prefixing is requested only if parity is being used. Otherwise spar() has set the value already, based on the contents of the QBIN field of the other Kermit's initialization string. Here is the part of spar() that handles eighth-bit prefix negotiation:

```
rq = (rln >= 7) ? s[7] : 0;           /* 8th-bit prefix */
if (rq == 'Y') rqf = 1;
else if ((rq > 32 && rq < 63) || (rq > 95 && rq < 127)) rqf = 2;
else rqf = 0;

switch (rqf) {
    case 0: ebqflg = 0; break;
    case 1: if (parity) { ebqflg = 1; ebq = '&'; } break;
    case 2: if (ebqflg = (ebq == sq || sq == 'Y')) ebq = rq;
}
```

Here, the variable rq is set to the other Kermit's QBIN field, or to zero if the QBIN field was omitted. Then the requested-quote-flag rqf is set to 1 if rq was a Y, to 2 if it was a valid prefix character, and otherwise to zero. Then, based on rqf, the flag that actually controls whether eighth-bit prefixing is done, ebqflg, is set to 0 if the other Kermit did not indicate a willingness to do this, to 1 if the other Kermit was willing and parity is in use, or if the other Kermit explicitly requested it, and the eight-bit prefix character is set accordingly. If you think about these two pieces of code enough, your head will start to spin. It might help to think of them as coroutines. The additions to `tinit()` are as follows:

```
ebqflg = 0;                     /* 8-bit quoting off */
sq = 'Y';                       /* Normal 8-bit quote bid */
rqf = -1;                       /* Flag other's bid not seen yet */
```

The additions to `encode()` and `decode()` to support eighth-bit prefixing are relatively straightforward, and are shown in the next section.

Run-Length Encoding

When the same byte appears four or more times in a row in the data, it may be replaced by a shorter prefixed sequence of the form

<prefix><length><byte>

where the prefix is another prefix character, distinct from the control and eighth-bit prefixes but chosen from the same range (ASCII 33–62 or 96–126), normally tilde (~), ASCII 126. The *<length>* is a single-character field encoded by `tochar()` exactly like the packet length and can represent values from 0 to 94. The *<byte>* is the data byte, possibly prefixed by control and eighth-bit prefixes.

Run-length encoding is the only data compression option supplied by Kermit. It is simple and cheap, requiring no extra passes through the data, no big buffers, and no complex algorithms. Other compression techniques can be used for pre- and post-processing the data (outside of Kermit) if desired. The major beneficiaries of run-length encoding are fixed-block files with trailing blanks, highly indented outlines or program source text, and binary files (which tend to contain lots of consecutive zero bytes).

The repeat prefix, like the other prefixes, must be prefixed by the control prefix when it appears in the data itself. The repeat sequence must always precede any other prefix character. The count field is entered literally, meaning that if it happens to coincide with a prefix character, it needs no further prefixing: # or & immediately following a ~ denote repeat counts, not control characters or 8-bit characters.

Table 10-3 shows some examples.

If a character appears more than 94 times in succession, it is "cut off" at 94, emitted with all appropriate prefixes, and "restarted." For example, 120 NUL characters (ASCII 0) would come out like this:

```
~~#@~:#@
```

Table 10-3. Repeat Prefix Examples

Character	With Repeat Prefix for 30 (= >) and with Eighth-Bit Prefix: On	Off
A	~>A	~>A
A	~>&A	~>A
Control-A	~>#A	~>#A
Control-A	~>&#A	~>#A
Rubout	~>#?	~>#?
Rubout	~>&#?	~>#?
#	~>##	~>##
#	~>&##	~>##
&	~>#&	~>&
&	~>&#&	~>&
~	~>#~	~>#~
~	~>&#~	~>#~

The repeat-count negotiation takes place in field 9, REPT, of the initialization string, shown in Figure 10-2. (Field 8 will be discussed in the next section.) The REPT field is set to "~" (or any other valid and distinct prefix character) by the sender, and the receiver indicates willingness to decode compressed data by responding with the identical character in the same field:

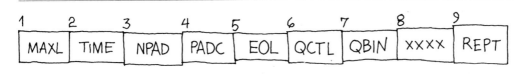

Figure 10-2. Kermit Initialization String with All Encoding Options

From tinit():
```
    rptflg = 0;                     /* No repeat counts by default */
```
From rpar():
```
    if (rptflg) data[9] = rptq; else data[9] = '~';
```
From spar():
```
    if (rln >= 9) {                 /* Repeat prefix */
        rptq = s[9];
        rptflg = ((rptq > 32 && rptq < 63) || (rptq > 95 && rptq < 127));
    } else rptflg = 0;
```

In rpar(), the repeat-flag rptflg will be set if spar() has already received a request for repeat-prefixing from the other Kermit. Otherwise, we enter our own bid to do it. In spar(), we set rptflg if the other Kermit's initialization string contains a valid prefix in the REPT field. If run-length encoding is not selected, then its normal prefix "~" should not be prefixed when it appears in the data (but no harm will be done if it is).

And now, here are expanded getpkt(), encode(), and decode() functions that handle all the encoding options. First, getpkt() has been changed to do one-character lookahead, so that encode() can accumulate the repeat count. Special action is required at the beginning of the file or string; this is controlled by the variable first. Its value starts as 1; after the first character has been obtained from the file, its value becomes zero. When the end-of-file is reached, it becomes −1.

```
/*
 Fill a packet to the maximum.  Result goes in global data, with
length indicated in global size.
*/
getpkt(maxlen) int maxlen; {
    int i, next;
    static int c;
    static char remain[6] = {'\0', '\0', '\0', '\0', '\0', '\0'};
    if (first == 1) {                   /* If first time thru...  */
        first = 0;                      /* remember not to do this next time, */
        *remain = '\0';                 /* discard any old leftovers, */
        c = gnchar();                   /* get first character of file,  */
        if (c < 0) {                    /* watching out for null file. */
            first = -1;
            return(size = 0);
        }
    } else if (first == -1) {    /* EOF from last time? */
        return(size = 0);
    }
    for (size = 0; (data[size] = remain[size]) != '\0'; size++) ;
    *remain = '\0';

    rpt = 0;                            /* Initialize repeat counter. */
    while (first > -1) {                /* Until end of file or string... */
        next = gnchar();                /* Look ahead one character. */
        if (next < 0) first = -1; /* If none, we're at EOF. */
        osize = size;                   /* Remember current size. */
        encode(c,next);                 /* Encode the character. */
        c = next;                       /* Old next char is now current. */

        if (size == maxlen) return(size); /* If just at end, done. */
```

```
        if (size > maxlen) {          /* Past end, must save some. */
            for (i = 0; (remain[i] = data[osize+i]) != '\0'; i++) ;
            size = osize;
            data[size] = '\0';
            return(size);              /* Return size. */
        }
    }
    return(size);                      /* EOF, return size. */
}
```

When you consider that a prefixed sequence may be up to five characters long (like
"~$&#A"), you can see why it's worth saving overflow for next time. Here is the new
encode() function, which handles run-length encoding and eighth-bit prefixing according to the negotiations:

```
/*
 Encode character a into global data array, update global size.
 Global maxsiz is the maximum length of the data field.
*/
encode(a,next) int a, next; {
    int a7, b8;
    if (rptflg) {                       /* Doing run-length encoding? */
        if (a == next) {                /* Yes, got a run? */
            if (++rpt < 94) {           /* Yes, count. */
                return;
            } else if (rpt == 94) {     /* If at maximum */
                data[size++] = rptq;    /* Emit prefix, */
                data[size++] = tochar(rpt); /* and count, */
                rpt = 0;                /* and reset counter. */
            }
        } else if (rpt == 1) {          /* Run broken, only two? */
            rpt = 0;                    /* Yes, do the character twice */
            encode(a,-1);               /* by calling self recursively. */
            if (size <= maxsiz) osize = size; /*Watch for boundary. */
            rpt = 0;                    /* Call self second time. */
            encode(a,-1);
            return;
        } else if (rpt > 1) {           /* Run broken, more than two? */
            data[size++] = rptq;        /* Yes, emit prefix and count */
            data[size++] = tochar(++rpt);
            rpt = 0;                    /* and reset counter. */
        }
    }
    a7 = a & 127;                       /* Get low 7 bits of character */
    b8 = a & 128;                       /* And "parity" bit */
    if (ebqflg && b8) {                 /* If doing 8th-bit prefixing */
        data[size++] = ebq;             /* and 8th bit on, insert prefix */
        a = a7;                         /* and clear the 8th bit. */
    }
```

```
    if (a7 < 32 || a7 == 127) {       /* If in control range */
        data[size++] = sctlq;         /* insert control prefix */
        a = ctl(a);                   /* and make character printable. */
    } else if (a7 == sctlq)           /* If data is control prefix, */
        data[size++] = sctlq;         /* prefix it. */
    else if (ebqflg && a7 == ebq)     /* If doing 8th-bit prefixing, */
        data[size++] = sctlq;         /* ditto for 8th-bit prefix. */
    else if (rptflg && a7 == rptq)    /* If doing run-length encoding, */
        data[size++] = sctlq;         /* ditto for repeat prefix. */

    data[size++] = a;                 /* Finally, emit the character. */
    data[size] = '\0';                /* Terminate string with null. */
}
```

The only tricky bit here is the way encode() avoids issuing a repeat count if the character is repeated only twice. In that case, the repeat sequence would usually be longer than the two literal characters. Finally, here is the new decoding procedure:

```
/*
 Decodes the data pointed to by the global pointer rdatap.
*/
decode() {
    int a, a7, b8;                      /* Local variables */

    while ((a = *rdatap++) != '\0') {   /* For each character, a, do... */
        rpt = 1;                        /* Initialize repeat count. */
        if (rptflg) {                   /* Repeat processing? */
            if (a == rptq) {            /* Yes, have repeat prefix? */
                rpt = unchar(*rdatap++); /* Yes, get count */
                a = *rdatap++;          /* and following character. */
            }
        }
        b8 = 0;                         /* Assume 8th bit not on. */
        if (ebqflg) {                   /* Doing 8th-bit prefixing? */
            if (a == ebq) {             /* Yes, have 8th-bit prefix? */
                b8 = 128;               /* Yes, remember bit 8 on */
                a = *rdatap++;          /* and get following character. */
            }
        }
        if (a == rctlq) {               /* Control quote? */
            a = *rdatap++;              /* Yes, get next character */
            a7 = a & 127;               /* and its low 7 bits */
            if (a7 > 62 && a7 < 96)     /* Encoded control character? */
                a = ctl(a);             /* Yes, controllify. */
        }
        a |= b8;                        /* OR in the 8th bit. */
        for (; rpt > 0; rpt--)
            if (pnchar(a) < 0) return(-1); /* Output character. */
    }
    return(0);                          /* Return successfully when done. */
}
```

Encoding Summary

- Prefix encoding for control characters is mandatory. The file sender indicates the prefix character it will use in the QCTL field of the initialization string. The prefix is normally #.

- Eighth-bit prefixing is optional and is negotiated between the sender and receiver via the QBIN field of the initialization string. This type of prefixing is to be avoided when unnecessary, since it adds overhead. The normal prefix is &. When the communication path allows transmission of 8 data bits, then the data character itself, after any required transformations (e.g., by ctl( )), should retain the original value of its high-order bit.

- Run-length encoding is optional. The file sender bids to use it in the REPT field of the initialization string; the receiver agrees or disagrees. When used, it improves performance. The normal repeat-count prefix is ~.

- When more than one type of prefixing is in effect, a single data character can be preceded by more than one prefix character, in this order (from left to right): (1) repeat count, (2) eighth-bit prefix, (3) control prefix. The control prefix # is most closely bound to the data character, then the eighth-bit prefix, then the repeat prefix and count. To illustrate, observe that &#A (a Control-A with its high bit on) is *not* equivalent to #&A (the literal character & followed by a letter A).

- Prefixed sequences must not be broken across packets. A prefixed sequence means a single character and all its prefixes, like ~%&#X, *not* a sequence like #M#J, which is *two* prefixed sequences.

- Control, eighth-bit, and repeat-count prefixes must be distinct.

- Prefix characters used for eighth-bit or repeat quoting must be quoted with the control prefix when they appear in the data when these types of quoting have been agreed upon. Otherwise they should not be quoted. The control prefix is applied based on the low-order 7 bits.

- Data fields of all packets must pass through the prefix-encoding mechanism, except for S, I, and A packets, and ACKs to those packets. (The I and A packets have not been presented yet.)

Encoding Performance

This section presents some statistics based on typical collections of files. Table 10-4 shows selected facts about 7-bit text files (about 14 megabytes of Kermit program source files and documentation). The characters are counted according to how Kermit would

Table 10-4. Text File Character Distribution

Files:	457
Total Characters:	14,241,014
Control Characters:	1,177,368
Runs:	272,190
Run Lengths:	3,057,027
Average Run Length:	11

Run Length Distribution:

4:	74,651	20:	2,704
5:	28,781	30:	699
6:	33,864	40:	610
7:	14,195	50:	566
8:	19,847	60:	128
9:	23,504	70:	415
10:	14,253	80:	113
11:	3,891	90:	1
12:	6,419	100:	1
13:	2,601	120:	1

encode them. Control characters are those whose low order 7 bits are in the control range. Runs are counted when the same character appears at least four times in succession.

Control characters, predominantly carriage returns and linefeeds, account for about 8.2 percent of all the characters in this large collection, and since a prefix character is added for each one, the encoding overhead they introduce is 8.2 percent. But there are also over a quarter of a million runs. Replacing the 3,057,027 characters involved by their run-length encoded equivalents (3 × 272,190 = 816,570) results in a net reduction of 2,240,457 characters, about twice as many characters as were added by control prefixing. The net encoding efficiency is therefore:

$$\frac{14,241,014}{14,241,014 + 1,177,368 - 2,240,457} = 108.07\%$$

It is also worth noting that the run-length distribution for text files is very well behaved: the shorter the run, the more runs there tend to be. The number of runs of length n drops off very rapidly as n increases.

Table 10-5 shows character distribution in binary files, in this case 135 files in the /bin and /usr/bin directories on a VAX UNIX system (about 2.8 megabytes of data). As you can see, binary files have a much higher proportion of control characters, about

Table 10-5. UNIX Binary File Character Distribution

Files:	135
Total Characters:	2,809,840
Control Characters:	1,356,728
Zero Bytes:	783,930
Eighth-Bit Characters:	834,457
Runs:	11,276
Run Lengths:	423,803
Average Run Length:	38

Run Length Distribution:

4:	2,811	20:	112	200:	0
5:	1,575	30:	4	250:	1
6:	3,064	40:	4	300:	1
7:	1,227	50:	1	341:	132
8:	148	60:	2	400:	0
9:	191	80:	0	450:	1
10:	235	100:	2	>500:	254

48 percent, against 8.2 percent for text files. Even more noteworthy is the fact that more than half the control characters are NULs (ASCII zero). This is no doubt a consequence of the fact that the files in question are executable programs, which tend to have their static data areas (variables, arrays) initialized to zeros. It is also worth observing that while run frequency tends to decay with length, the spread is not as great as for text files, and there are some interesting singularities: for some reason, there were a great many runs of length 341. Also, the 254 runs of lengths greater than 500 account for more characters than all the most frequent runs combined.

Let's take a look at the figures. The overhead introduced by control prefixing is

$$\frac{1,356,728}{2,809,840} = 48.28\%$$

and the efficiency is

$$\frac{2,809,840}{1,356,728 + 2,809,840} = 67.44\%$$

When run-length encoding comes into play, we replace 423,803 repeated characters by $3 \times 11,276 = 33,828$, for a net reduction of 389,975, yielding an efficiency of:

$$\frac{2,809,840}{1,356,728 + 2,809,840 - 389,975} = 74.4\%$$

If, however, the data must be transferred through a 7-bit communication path, a prefix character must be added for each character that has its eighth bit on, and in this sample there are 834,457 of these:

$$\frac{2,809,840}{1,356,728 + 2,809,840 - 389,975 + 834,457} = 60.9\%$$

This is why eighth-bit prefixing is to be avoided when it's not necessary, and why the rule of T. H. White's Antland—"Everything not forbidden is compulsory"—does not apply here.

For comparison, Table 10-6 shows the same data for 3.6 megabytes of MS-DOS binary files from the \BIN area. We see similar behavior here. The encoding efficiencies are remarkably similar to those for UNIX:

Efficiency with control prefixing:	67.47%
and run-length encoding:	76.38%
and eighth-bit prefixing:	62.35%

Table 10-6. MS-DOS Binary File Character Distribution

Files:	23
Total Characters:	363,449
Zero Bytes:	81,363
Control Characters:	175,260
Eighth-Bit Characters:	107,080
Runs:	747
Run Lengths:	62,880
Average Run Length:	84

Run Length Distribution:

4:	127	20:	6	200:	1
5:	100	30:	1	300:	1
6:	59	40:	1	400:	0
7:	38	50:	1	> 500:	19
8:	45	60:	3		
9:	30	80:	8		
10:	33	100:	2		

Sacred Characters

The Kermit protocol expects to be able to use the entire 95-character printable ASCII character set, plus at least one control character as a packet mark, plus perhaps two other control characters: one for packet termination, one for padding. Unfortunately, no method is provided for encoding any of these characters when they simply cannot make it through the communication channel intact. The control characters generally present no problem, since one can usually select two or three from the set of 33 that pass from one end to the other unmolested. Opacity to printable characters, on the other hand, can pose an insurmountable problem for Kermit. "Semiopacity," however, can sometimes be dealt with by doubling or otherwise quoting the offending character(s). For instance, a network terminal concentrator that uses "@" as an attention character might pass through a single @ if you send it two of them in a row.

To embody tricks like this in a Kermit program, you need to include a SET TRANS-LATION command in the "user interface," and code in the spack() function to apply the specified translations blindly, i.e., without affecting the block check or length field of the packet. Presumably, if such translations are to work, the packet will arrive at its ultimate destination with all the translations undone by the intervening opaque apparatus, so that the packet arrives in the right format.

Block Check Options

The Kermit 8-bit-folded-into-6-bit checksum has proven remarkably robust in practice, much more so than straightforward analysis would suggest. Arithmetic sums seem to be good at catching the bursty kinds of errors that typify telecommunication. Nevertheless, one might still claim that since the block check has only six significant bits, the chances are 1 in 64 that bad data will go undetected. The chances of undetected errors are greatest with binary files, since the high-order bit of all the characters in the packet is reflected only in a single bit of the checksum.

Kermit provides two optional block check types: a two-character 12-bit checksum, and a three-character 16-bit cyclic redundancy check (CRC). The 12-bit checksum is broken into two 6-bit quantities, and each is transformed by tochar() into a printable quantity, like this:

	1	2
...data	tochar(b6-b11)	tochar(b0-b5)

The CRC calculation treats the data as a string of bits with the low-order bit of the first character first and the high-order bit of the last character last. The 16-bit CRC is the remainder after dividing the data bit string by the CCITT polynomial

$$X^{16} + X^{12} + X^5 + 1$$

in which the value of X is 2, making the value of the polynomial equal to 1000100000100001_2. Software such as Kermit generally uses a byte-oriented method for calculating this quantity. The result is represented as three printable characters at the end of the Kermit packet, as follows:

	1	2	3
...data	tochar(b12–b15)	tochar(b6–b11)	tochar(b0–b5)

Kermit's CRC technique agrees with common hardware implementations like the VAX CRC instruction.

The probability that an error will not be caught by a correctly transmitted arithmetic checksum is the ratio of the number of possible errors that cancel each other out to the total number of possible errors, which works out to be something like $1/2^n$, where n is the number of bits in the checksum, assuming all errors are equally likely. This is 1/64 for the single-character checksum, and 1/4096 for the two-character checksum. But one must also consider the probability that an error will actually occur in a particular packet, i.e., the bit error rate for the line normalized to the packet length. For instance, if the probability that a 1-bit error will strike a packet is 1/1000, then the likelihood of an undetected error is the product of this number and 1/64, or 1/64,000. Similarly, the likelihood of an undetected double-bit error is $1/1000^2 \times 1/64$, or 1/64,000,000. The probability of undetected higher-order errors, according to this analysis, is negligible, so that the 1-bit case predominates.

In practice, not all kinds of errors are equally likely; bursts of 2–10 bits in length typically predominate on noisy telephone lines. These will usually cause framing errors, which should be caught by Kermit at the physical link level, causing immediate rejection of the packet. When a framing error is not detected, an error burst will almost certainly be caught by the checksum.

The 16-bit CRC has been explained and analyzed in great detail in the literature, and it is the preferred block check in network and hardware applications. It will detect all single- and double-bit errors, all messages with an odd number of bits in error, all error bursts shorter than 16 bits, and better than 99.99 percent of longer bursts [24]. These probabilities all assume, of course, that the block check is where it belongs.

The block check type is negotiated in field 8 (CHKT) of the initialization string, shown in Figure 10-3.

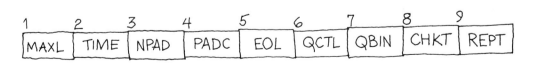

Figure 10-3. Kermit Initialization String with Block Check Option

The possible values are:

1. (Literal character "1") The normal one-character 6-bit checksum

2. Two-character 12-bit checksum

3. Three-character 16-bit cyclic redundancy check (CRC)

Anything else in this field, or the absence of this field, automatically selects block check type 1. Here is the code for negotiating the block check type:

From `tinit( )`:

```
    bctu = 1;                        /* Block check back to 1 */
```

From `rpar( )`:

```
    data[8] = bctr + '0';            /* Block Check Type */
```

and from `spar( )`:

```
    x = 1;                           /* Block check */
    if (rln >= 8) {
        x = s[8] - '0';
        if ((x < 1) || (x > 3)) x = 1;
    }
    bctr = x;
```

The variable `bctr` is the block check type requested, either by the user at command level, or by the other Kermit in an S packet. Again, the two pieces of code have to work in either order. (And another variable might be required to remember the block check type requested by the user in a SET command, if the program is to run interactively and perform multiple transactions). Note that the file sender controls the block check type; a way out of this dilemma is presented in Chapter 11.

A somewhat thornier dilemma also presents itself: since higher-order block checks are optional features, how does one negotiate with a Kermit program that does not support them? The answer is that the S packet and its acknowledgment must always be transmitted with type 1 block checks. The switch occurs only after the S packet is acknowledged. This accounts for the statement

```
bctu = bctr;
```

that you may have noticed in a couple of places back in the Lex code. The block check type used (`bctu`) switches to the block check type requested (`bctr`) after the S packet is acknowledged.

Here is a new `spack( )` function that includes the three block check options, plus the generation of padding (which was omitted in the first version):

```
spack(type,n,len,d) char type, *d; int n, len; {
    int i = 0, j, k;
    for (i = 0; i < spadn; i++) sndpkt[i] = spadc;
                                                /* Do requested padding */
    sndpkt[i++] = smark;                        /* Packet mark */
    k = i;                                      /* Remember this place */
    sndpkt[i++] = tochar(len+bctu+2);           /* Length */
    sndpkt[i++] = tochar(n);                    /* Sequence number */
    sndpkt[i++] = type;                         /* Packet type */

    for (j = len; j > 0; j--) {                 /* Data */
        sndpkt[i++] = *d++;
    }
    sndpkt[i] = '\0';                           /* Null-terminate */
    switch (bctu) {                             /* Block Check Type Used? */
        case 1:                                 /* Type 1 - 6 bit checksum */
            sndpkt[i++] = tochar(chk1(sndpkt+k));
            break;
        case 2:                                 /* Type 2 - 12 bit checksum*/
            j = chksum(sndpkt+k);
            sndpkt[i++] = tochar((j >> 6) & 077);
            sndpkt[i++] = tochar(j & 077);
            break;
        case 3:                                 /* Type 3 - 16 bit CRC-CCITT */
            j = chk3(sndpkt+k);
            sndpkt[i++] = tochar((j >> 12) & 017);
            sndpkt[i++] = tochar((j >> 6) & 077);
            sndpkt[i++] = tochar(j & 077);
            break;
    }
    sndpkt[i++] = seol;                         /* End of line */
    sndpkt[i++] = '\0';                         /* Null string-terminator */
    sndpkl = i;                                 /* Remember length. */

    i = ttol(sndpkt,sndpkl);                    /* Send the packet. */
    if (local && !xflag) tchar('.');
    return(i);
}
```

It is also worth mentioning that transmission-level character set translation should be performed in this function if necessary before the block check calculation, but only on the control fields. Any character set translation in the data should be done at presentation level.

Here is the corresponding rpack() function:

```
/*
rpack reads a packet and returns the packet type, or else Q if the
packet was invalid, or T if a timeout occurred.  Upon successful
return, sets the global variables:
```

```
        rsn    – the received sequence number
        rln    – length of the received data field
        rdatap – a pointer to null–terminated contents of the data field
*/
rpack() {
        int i, j, x, type, rlnpos;            /* Local variables */
        char pbc[4];                          /* Packet block check */

        rsn = rln = -1;                       /* In case of failure. */

        *rcvpkt = '\0';                       /* Initialize receive buffer. */
        j = ttinl(rcvpkt,MAXRP,reol,timint);  /* Try to get a "line". */

        if (j < 0) return('T');               /* Timed out. */

        for (i = 0; rcvpkt[i] != rmark && (i < j); i++) /* Find mark */
            ;
        if (i == j) return('Q');              /* If no mark, bad packet. */

        rlnpos = ++i;                         /* Got it, remember position. */
        rln = unchar(rcvpkt[i++]) - bctu - 2; /* Data field length */
        rsn = unchar(rcvpkt[i++]);            /* Sequence number */
        type = rcvpkt[i++];                   /* Packet type */
        rdatap = rcvpkt+i;                    /* The data itself */
        j = rln + i;                          /* Position of block check */
        if (j > MAXRP) return('Q');           /* Be defensive! */
        for (x = 0; x < bctu; x++)            /* Copy the block check */
            pbc[x] = rcvpkt[j+x];
        rcvpkt[j] = '\0';                     /* Null–terminate the data */

        switch (bctu) {                       /* Which block check type? */
            case 1:
                if (unchar(*pbc) != chk1(rcvpkt+rlnpos)) return('Q');
                break;
            case 2:
                x = unchar(*pbc) << 6 | unchar(pbc[1]);
                if (x != chksum(rcvpkt+rlnpos)) return('Q');
                break;
            case 3:
                x = unchar(*pbc) << 12 | unchar(pbc[1]) << 6 | unchar(pbc[2]);
                if (x != chk3(rcvpkt+rlnpos)) return('Q');
                break;
            default:
                error("Impossible block check type");
        }
        if (local && !xflag) tchar('.');
        return(type);                         /* Good packet, return type. */
}
```

By the way, notice how the program checks to make sure the length field does not point beyond the end of the buffer. In theory, this would never happen, but in fact it can occur any time a lot of extraneous characters precede the packet on the communication line (a terminal message, for instance), pushing the packet "to the right" in the buffer. Without this check, the statement "rcvpkt[j] = '\0';" could write into random memory, with potentially terrible results.

Finally, here is the function for calculating the CRC:

```
/*  C H K 3  ——  Compute a type-3 Kermit block check.  */
/*
Calculate the 16-bit CRC of a null-terminated string using a
byte-oriented tableless algorithm devised by Andy Lowry (Columbia
University). The magic number 010201 is derived from the
CRC-CCITT polynomial x^16+x^12+x^5+1.
*/
chk3(s) char *s; {
    unsigned int c, q;
    long crc = 0;

    while ((c = *s++) != '\0') {
        if (parity) c &= 0177;
        q = (crc ^ c) & 017;                /* Low-order nibble */
        crc = (crc >> 4) ^ (q * 010201);
        q = (crc ^ (c >> 4)) & 017;         /* High order nibble */
        crc = (crc >> 4) ^ (q * 010201);
    }
    return(crc);
}
```

Before we leave this topic, there's one last complication. With the code presented so far, what would happen if Kermit A sent an S packet requesting, say, type 3 block checks, and Kermit B acknowledged in agreement, but the acknowledgment was lost? Kermit A would time out and retransmit its S packet with a type 1 block check, but Kermit B would not be able to read it, because it would already have switched to type 3. But, as luck would have it, its old acknowledgment is still sitting in its retransmission buffer, so if it behaves according to the rules presented so far, the two Kermits will get back in phase. Unfortunately, not all Kermit programs can be counted on to retransmit the previous packet when they get a block check error. Some send a NAK for the desired packet instead, and the NAK in this case would contain a type 3 block check. Therefore, it may be necessary to do something to rpack() to account for this. The following tricks are not absolutely necessary. They merely avoid the the bouncing back and forth of incompatible packets up to the retry threshold.

If rpack() is allowed to examine the packet type (in flagrant violation of layering principles), it can (a) always look for a type 1 block check on an S packet, and/or (b) always deduce the block check type on a NAK (N) packet, because NAK packets never contain data (block check type = packet length − 2).

Graceful Interruption of File Transfer

It is often desirable to interrupt file transmission for some reason—an undesired file is being transmitted, the transmission or file parameters have been set incorrectly, etc. It is always possible to interrupt a file transfer by halting the local Kermit program or turning off the PC, but this leaves the remote Kermit program waiting for the next packet. Even if it can time out, the remote Kermit will go through its timeout-retry cycle up to the retry threshold, which could take some time. An optional feature of the Kermit protocol allows one Kermit to interrupt another gracefully and cleanly, provided both support this feature. If one does but the other doesn't, the interruption won't occur and the file transfer will continue.

To interrupt sending a file, send an EOF (Z) packet in place of the next data packet, including a D (for discard) in the data field. The recipient reacts normally to the Z packet but does not retain the file. This does not interfere with older Kermits on the receiving end. They will not inspect the data field and will close the file normally (but will also retain it). The mechanism can be triggered by typing an interrupt character at the console of the sending Kermit program. If a (wildcard) file group is being sent, it is possible to skip to the next file or to terminate the entire batch. The protocol is the same in either case, but the desired action could be selected by different interrupt characters, e.g., CTRL-X to skip the current file, CTRL-Z to skip the rest of the batch.

To interrupt receiving a file, put an X in the data field of an ACK for a data packet. To interrupt receiving an entire file group, use a Z. The user could trigger this mechanism by typing an interrupt character, say CTRL-X or CTRL-Z, respectively, at the receiving Kermit's console. A sender that was aware of this feature, upon finding one of these codes, would act as described, i.e., send a Z packet with a D code. A sender that did not implement this feature would simply ignore the codes and continue sending. In this case, and if the user wanted the whole batch to be cancelled (or if only one file were being sent), the receiving Kermit program, after determining that the sender had ignored the X or Z code, could send an Error (E) packet to stop the transfer.

The sender may also choose to send a Z packet containing the D code when it detects that the file it is sending cannot be sent correctly and completely. For instance, after sending some packets correctly, it gets an I/O error reading the file. Or it notices that the "eighth bit" of a file byte is set when the file is being sent as a text file and no provision has been made for transmitting the eighth bit.

The code for carrying out this protocol is very simple, but largely system-dependent. The system-dependent part monitors the keyboard of the local Kermit during file transfer for CTRL-X or CTRL-Z commands (or whatever keys or buttons these functions may be assigned to) and sets appropriate flags, say cx and cz, when they occur.

Then, when sending, in ssdat state (where you have an acknowledgment for the data packet), check the cx and cz flags. If either one is on, or if the data field of the Y packet contains an X or a Z, then set the corresponding flag and invoke seof() with an argument D (seof("D")). Then in gnfile() check the cz flag; if on, return as if there were no more files.

When receiving, in `srdat` state, check the flags. If `cx` is on, send an acknowledgment with an X in the data field (`ackl("X")`); if `cz` is on, then `ackl("Z")`. If you receive a Z packet with a D in the data field, discard the file rather than closing it normally.

Interruption protocol requires no negotiation. Its use will have no effect on Kermit programs that do not understand it. Even when both Kermits support file interruption, it can work only after initial connection negotiation has been completed and file transfer is in progress.

11

The Client/Server Model

The Kermit programs we've presented so far, even with all their options, still require a lot of tedious escaping back and forth as well as detailed knowledge of the command structure and file management functions of both systems. A Kermit server alleviates both these problems. Once started, it requires no further direct interaction with the user, and it provides a range of generic file management commands that shield the user from having to know the particulars of the system.

Server operation is optional. Not all Kermit programs can act as servers, and not all Kermit programs know how to behave as proper clients. When server or client operation is provided, only a certain subset is required; the rest is optional.

A Kermit server is completely passive. No interactions are initiated by the server. It receives all its commands in the form of packets from the "client" Kermit program. The commands accepted by a server are shown in Table 11-1.

Commands to servers are always sent with packet number 0 and block check type 1. The server's response always begins with packet 0 and block check type 1. The S and R commands are required, plus at least one G command (corresponding to either BYE or FINISH). The rest are optional.

The S, R, G, and C packets (with some exceptions) initiate transactions. The I packet is used for setting parameters prior to a transaction. Between transactions, the server waits for command packets to arrive, until it receives a generic command to finish (F) or logout (L).

An S packet sent to a server works exactly like an S packet sent to a regular Kermit that has been given the RECEIVE command, except that the server is still a server at the end of the transaction.

The R, G, and C command packets are interesting, because they are not normally acknowledged by the server. Rather, the server (usually) responds by initiating a transaction with an S packet, effectively changing the direction of the logical connection. That is, the side that was ACKing and NAKing is now sending "interesting" packets, and vice versa. There are several possible scenarios:

1. The R command elicits the S (F D* Z)* B response.

2. The G and C commands elicit the S (X D* Z)* B response.

3. The R, G, or C commands elicit a single acknowledgment (Y).

4. Any of the above elicit an error packet (E).

Table 11-1. Kermit Server Command Packet Types

S	Send-Initiation: I'm about to send files, and here are my parameters.
R	Receive-Initiation: Please send me the specified file(s).
I	Initialization: Here are my parameters.
G	Generic command (many possible: see Table 11-3).
C	Host command (arbitrary).

The final case results when a client sends a command to a server that the server does not support. The server responds with an error message like "Unsupported server command."

The G and C commands tell the server to do something and then to send you the results. If these results are very short, short enough to fit into one packet, they may be sent back in the data field of the acknowledgment. This is called the short-form response.

The long-form response looks exactly like a regular transaction, except the F (File-Header) packet is replaced by an X (Text-Header) packet. The X packet tells the receiver to display the following data on the screen instead of putting it in a file.

The I Packet

The I packet and its acknowledgment are exactly like the S packet and its acknowledgment. They contain initialization strings constructed by rpar( ), and upon arrival are processed by spar( ), and their data fields are not subject to encoding. The difference is that receipt of an I packet does not cause transition to a file-receiving state, i.e., it does not start a Kermit transaction. It is a complete interaction (session) in itself, and the packet number remains 0 afterward, and the block check type remains 1. Recall that most initialization parameters are determined by the sender. If there were no I packet, then it would be impossible for a client to specify that higher-order block checks be used if the server had not already been set up to do that. If the client uses an I packet to request type 2 or 3 block checks, then the server (if it is capable of doing them) will set the CHKT field in its next S packet accordingly, and the switch will be made after the S packet has been acknowledged, exactly as described before.

The matter is complicated, however, by the fact that the server, after having received and ACK'd an I packet, may skip sending the S packet in response to the next R, G, or C command and go on directly to the X or F packet. This will happen only (but not necessarily) when the I-packet negotiation has not specified a higher-order block check, in which case a second negotiation would be entirely redundant.

Affairs are further complicated by the fact that the server may not support the I packet at all, since it is optional. This means that the client program that sends an I packet must be prepared to receive and ignore any Error (E) packet it gets in response.

The Client

The client Kermit program must provide GET, SEND, and either BYE or FINISH commands at minimum, and optionally a selection of REMOTE commands (REMOTE DIRECTORY, REMOTE SPACE, REMOTE HOST, etc.), and it must translate them into server command packets. The SEND command needs no special attention. It works exactly as it does in a regular Kermit program. The GET and REMOTE commands require the following packets, with the data field containing the indicated material:

R   Remote file specification.

C   Command in the syntax of command processor of the server's host system.

G   String of the form

```
<code>[<L1><arg1>[<L2><arg2>[...]]]
```

in which <code> is a single letter denoting the generic command, followed by zero or more fields, each consisting of a single-character length field (encoded by tochar() in the customary manner) followed by a string of the specified length.

Table 11-2 shows the packet sequences that are generated and recognized by the client, taking into account the short- and long-form server responses as well as the optional nature (from both the client's and the server's point of view) of the I packet. A vertical bar (|) in a regular expression means "or." "(Y | E)" means "Y or E." In our case, the second half of the table can be ignored, because our client always precedes a server command with an I packet (the server, however, must take I-packetless operation into account).

The generic command string will be encoded in the normal way, so it may include control characters or any other data. If a length field turns out to correspond to an active prefix character, then it is prefixed at the datalink level. For example, to send a generic command with two fields, "ABC" and "ZZZZZZZZ," first each field would be prefixed by tochar() of its length, in this case tochar(3) and tochar(8), giving "#ABC(ZZZZZZZZ". But "#" is the normal control prefix character, so it must be pre-

Table 11-2. Kermit Client States

Client Generates	Client Recognizes
I (G | C)	(Y | E) Y | E | (S (X D* Z)* B) | ((X D* Z)* B)
I R	(Y | E) Y | E | (S (F D* Z)* B) | ((F D* Z)* B)
G | C	Y | E | (S (X D* Z)* B)
R	Y | E | (S (F D* Z)* B)

Table 11-3. Kermit Server Generic Commands

I	Login [<%user[%password[%account]]>]
C	CWD (change working directory) [<%directory[%password]>]
L	Logout (Bye)
F	Finish (Shut down the server, but don't logout).
D	Directory [<%filespec>]
U	Disk Usage Query [<%area>]
E	Erase (delete) <%filespec>
T	Type <%filespec>
R	Rename <%oldname%newname>
K	Copy <%source%destination>
W	Who's logged in? [<%user ID or network host[%options]>]
M	Send a short Message <%destination%text>
H	Help [<%topic>]
Q	Server Status Query
P	Program <%[program-filespec][%program-commands]>
J	Journal <%command[%argument]>
V	Variable <%command[%argument[%argument]]>

fixed itself, and the eight Z's can be condensed to three characters using a repeat prefix (if that has been negotiated), so the result after encoding might be "##ABC(~(Z" (assuming the repeat prefix is tilde). The recipient decodes this back into the original "#ABC(ZZZZZZZZ" before attempting to extract the two fields.

Since a generic command must fit into a single packet, the program sending the command should ensure that the command actually fits and should not include length fields that point beyond the end of the packet. Servers, however, should be defensive and not attempt to process any characters beyond the end of the data field, even if the argument length field would lead them to do so.

Table 11-3 shows the generic commands. The contents of the data field are enclosed in <> angle brackets, optional material in [ ] square brackets, and percent sign (%) represents the single-character length field. Of these commands, only F or L are required; the rest are optional. Almost any of these can have either short or long replies. For instance, the Generic Erase (GE) command may elicit a simple ACK or a stream of packets containing the names of all the files it erased (or didn't erase). Furthermore, any of these commands may elicit an Error (E) packet, for either of two reasons: (1) the requested service is not available (the server does not understand or support the command) or (2) the requested operation could not be performed (for instance, the specified file could not be found or could not be accessed in the specified way).

In either case, an appropriate error message should be furnished. The generic commands are now described in more detail:

I   (Login). For use when a Kermit server is kept perpetually running on a dedicated line. This lets a new user obtain an identity on the server's host system. If the data field is empty, the user's identity and file access rights are removed, and the server is left waiting for a new login command.

L   (Logout, Bye). This shuts down the server entirely, causing the server itself to log out its own job. This is for use when the server has been started up manually by the user, who then wishes to shut it down remotely. For a perpetual dedicated server, this command is equivalent to an empty login command.

F   (Finish). This is to allow the user to shut down the server, putting its terminal back into normal (as opposed to binary or raw) mode, and putting the server's job back at system command level, still logged in, so that the user can connect back to the job. For a perpetual dedicated server, this command behaves as the L (BYE) command.

C   (CWD). Change working directory. This sets the default directory or area for file transfer on the server's host. With no operands, this command sets the default area to be the user's own default area.

D   (Directory). Sends a directory listing to the user. The client program can display it on the terminal or store it in a file, as it chooses. The directory listing should contain file sizes and creation dates as well as filenames, if possible. A wildcard or other file-group designator may be specified to ask the server to list only those files that match. If no operand is given, all files in the current area should be shown.

U   (Disk Usage Query). The server responds with the amount of space used and the amount left free to use, in K bytes (or other units, which should be specified).

E   (Erase, Delete). Deletes the specified file or file group. The response may be an empty ACK, an ACK with data, or an entire transaction.

T   (Type). Sends the specified file or file group, indicating (by starting with an X packet rather than an F packet, or else by using the Type attribute) that the file is to be displayed on the screen rather than stored on disk.

R   (Rename). Changes the name of (or moves) the file or files as indicated. The string indicating the new name may contain other attributes, such as protection code, permitted in file specifications by the host.

K   (Copy). Produces a new copy of the file or file group, as indicated, leaving the source file(s) unmodified.

W   (Who's Logged In?) With no arguments, lists all the users who are logged in on the server's host system. If an argument is specified, provides more detailed information on the specified user or network host.

M   (Short Message). Sends the given short (single-packet) message to the indicated user's screen.

P   (Program). This command has two arguments, program name (filespec), and command(s) for the program. The first field is required, but may be left null (zero length). If it is null, the currently loaded program is "fed" the specified command. If not null, the specified program is loaded and started. If a program command is given it is fed to the program as an initial command (for instance, as a command line argument on systems that support that idea). In any case, the output of the program is sent back in packets as either a long or short reply, as previously described.

J   (Journal). This command controls server transaction logging. The data field contains one of the following:

+   Begin/resume logging transactions. If a filename is given, close any currently open transaction and then open the specified file as the new transaction log. If no name is given, but a log file was already open, resume logging to that file. If no filename was given and no log was open, the server should open a log with a default name, like TRANSACT.LOG. The filename should be returned in the ACK.

−   Stop logging transactions, but don't close the current transaction log file.

C   Stop logging and close the current log.

S   Send the transaction log as a file. If it was open, close it first.

Transaction logging is the recording of the progress of file transfers. It should contain entries showing the name of each file transferred, when the transfer began and ended, whether it was completed successfully, and if not, why.

V   (Set or Query a Variable). The command can be S or Q. The first argument is the variable name. The second argument, if any, is the value.

S   Set the specified variable to the specified value. If the value is null, then undefine the variable. If the variable is null, then do nothing. If the variable did not exist before, create it. The server should respond with an ACK if successful, and Error packet otherwise.

Q   Query the value of the named variable. If no variable is supplied, display the value of all active variables. The server responds with either a short or long reply, as described above. If a queried variable does not exist, a null value is returned.

Variables are named by character strings, and have character string values, which may be static or dynamic. For instance, a server might have built-in variables like "system name" or "version number" which never change, or others like "mail status" which, when queried, cause the server to check to see if the user has any new mail.

Because we've already developed almost all the tools we need, most of the code required for the client goes in the Lex portion of the program, where it calls upon these tools:

```
%states sipkt srgen
%%
...
r { tinit(); ssc = 0;    sinit('I'); BEGIN sipkt; } /* Get */
c { tinit(); ssc = 'C'; sinit('I'); BEGIN sipkt; } /* Host */
g { tinit(); ssc = 'G'; sinit('I'); BEGIN sipkt; } /* Generic */
<sipkt>Y {                          /* Got ACK for I packet */
    spar(rdatap);                   /* Set parameters from it */
    start = 'E';                    /* Force entry into next state */
}
<sipkt>E {                          /* Got E for I packet */
    if (ssc) {
        if (scmd(ssc,cmarg) < 0) { ERR("scmd"); }
        else BEGIN srgen;
    } else {
        if (scmd('R',cmarg) < 0) { ERR("scmd"); }
        else BEGIN srini;
    }
}
<srgen>Y { xflag = 1; decode(); RESUME; }

<srgen>S { spar(rdatap); ackl(rpar()); bctu = bctr; BEGIN srfil; }

<srgen,srfil>X { xflag = 1; ack(); BEGIN srdat; }
...
%%
```

We rely upon the "user interface" to set the start state to r, c, or g, and to set up any generic or host command string in the variable cmarg. The major complication here is that we have to remember the start state while we send the I packet, and then send the appropriate command afterward, even if the server responds to the I packet with an Error packet. Also, note the trick used to accomplish the equivalent of a "goto" from <sipkt>Y state to <sipkt>E state after setting the parameters. This saves having to replicate the whole section of code in each state.

In srgen state we must be prepared for an X, an S, or a Y packet, for the reasons explained. Notice that the action taken when receiving an S in srgen state is identical to that taken in srini state. Lex would allow these two lines to be combined under the heading

```
<srini,srgen>S { action }
```

The xflag is yet another global control for pnchar() (put next character). It tells the function to put the character not into a file, not into a string in memory, but onto the screen. It is cleared (by tinit()) at the beginning of each transaction:

```
xflag = 0;                    /* Output normally to file */
osp = NULL;                   /*  ... */
```

and it's used in the pnchar() function as was shown previously. Only one new function has been introduced. It merely encodes a preformatted (by the "user interface") generic command string and sends it:

```
scmd(t,s) char t, *s; {       /* Send a packet of the given type */
    encstr(s);                /* Encode the command string */
    spack(t,seq,size,data);
}
```

All things considered, it has been pretty easy to add client operation to our Kermit program. The state strings given in Table 11-2 have translated rather easily into Lex code. In fact, most of it was already there.

The Server

Table 11-4 shows the states recognized and generated by the Kermit server.

Table 11-4. Kermit Server States

Server Recognizes	Server Generates
I	Y
S (F D* Z)* B	Y*
R	Y | E | (S (F D* Z)* B)
G | C	Y | E | (S (X D* Z)* B)

It will respond to an I packet with an ACK (Y). If you send it a regular S transaction sequence, it will accept it. The interesting cases are the R, G, and C commands. Each of these can elicit a single ACK, possibly with data (a short-form response), an Error packet (indicating the requested service is not available or cannot be performed), or an entire transaction (long-form response). A long-form response consists of file data for the R command or screen data for the G and C commands.

To turn Kermit into a server, we need the following preliminaries:

• A server flag, nonzero if Kermit is acting as a server.

• An xpkt flag, initialized to zero in tinit(), which becomes nonzero if outbound data is to be preceded by an X packet rather than an F packet.

• Two new Lex states: %states sserv ssgen

• The RESUME macro redefined:

```
#define RESUME if (server) { SERVE; } else return
```

• One new macro:

```
#define SERVE tinit(); BEGIN sserv
```

Here is the Lex code for server operation. The "user interface" has set the start state to "x." Upon entering this state, the program turns on its server flag, so that when a transaction is complete, it will go back to server command wait rather than return. If the server gets an I packet, it sets parameters, ACKs, sets the packet sequence number back to zero, and remains in the same state. Otherwise, it attempts to process the GET (R), SEND (S), FINISH (G), or other REMOTE command. This example does only enough to show how server operation works. The REMOTE HOST (C) and the BYE (GL) commands are not shown here because they are necessarily system-dependent. Of the generic commands, only FINISH (GF) and TYPE (GT) are shown. The others require system-dependent methods to provide the requested service and direct the results to the outbound packet stream.

```
%states sserv ssgen
%%
...
x { server = 1; SERVE; }
<sserv>I {                                /* Got I packet */
    spar(rdatap); ackl(rpar());           /* Set parameters, respond */
    seq = 0;                              /* Set sequence number to 0 */
}
<sserv>R {                                /* GET command. */
    decstr(strbuf);                       /* Decode the filename. */
    nfils = 1;                            /* Indicate there's one file */
    *cmlist = strbuf;                     /* Point to name for gnfile() */
    if (sinit('S') < 0)                   /* Send S packet. */
        { ERR("sinit"); }
    else                                  /* If OK, switch to ssfil state. */
        { filcnt = 0; BEGIN ssfil; }
}
<sserv>S {                                /* Server gets S packet */
    spar(rdatap); ackl(rpar());           /* Set, send init parameters */
    bctu = bctr;                          /* Switch block check type */
    BEGIN srfil;                          /* Switch state */
}
<sserv>G {                                /* Generic command */
    decstr(strbuf);                       /* Decode it */
    start = *strbuf;                      /* New start state for input() */
    xpkt = 1;                             /* Use X instead of F packets */
    BEGIN ssgen;                          /* Switch to generic state */
}
```

```
<sserv>E { SERVE; }                         /* Ignore error packets */
<sserv>. {                                  /* Issue this message for others. */
    ERR("Unknown server command");
    SERVE;
}
<ssgen>F {                                  /* Generic FINISH command */
    ack(); server = 0; return;
}
<ssgen>T {                                  /* Generic TYPE command */
    decstr(strbuf);                         /* Decode it */
    nfils = 1;                              /* Indicate there's one file */
    *cmlist = strbuf+2;                     /* Point to name for gnfile() */
    if (sinit('S') < 0)                     /* Send S packet. */
        { ERR("sinit"); }
    else                                    /* If OK, switch to ssfil state. */
        { filcnt = 0; BEGIN ssfil; }
}
...
%%
```

The GET command handling does exactly what the command parser does when you give it a SEND command: it sets up a pointer, `**cmlist`, to a list of pointers to the names of the files to be sent, and it indicates the number of files, `nfils`, in the group. Only a single file can be handled by the GET command shown here. A "production version" would call upon system-dependent facilities to expand wildcard or other file group notation. The action taken when an S command is received is identical to that taken in `srini` or `srgen` state, so these could all be combined as

```
<srini,srgen,sserv>S { action }
```

The G command is handled by getting the first character from its data field and making that the start state. This tricks the `input()` function into returning a value the next time through, without reading a packet. In `ssgen` state, the program takes whatever action is associated with the generic command thus obtained.

One minor complication, not shown in the examples, is that the server must not exit from server command wait because it has had too many timeouts. The `input()` function needs to know when the server is in this state, so that it will never fail because the retry threshold is exceeded. Also, the timeout interval should be increased considerably from the normal one (usually 5 or 10 seconds) to 30–60 seconds. If the client program is capable of timing out, the server can completely dispense with timeouts.

12

Advanced Options

This chapter presents a method for transmitting and preserving file attributes and two protocol extensions designed to improve Kermit's efficiency.

The Capabilities Mask

The protocol options described in this chapter require additional fields in the initialization string. The first new field, field 10, the capabilities mask, is used to indicate the presence or absence of selected features. It is shown in Figure 12-1.

1	2	3	4	5	6	7	8	9	10
MAXL	TIME	NPAD	PADC	EOL	QCTL	QBIN	CHKT	REPT	CAPAS

Figure 12-1. Kermit Initialization String with Capabilities Mask

The CAPAS field is a bit string, in which each bit position corresponds to a capability of Kermit. A bit is set to 1 if the corresponding capability is present, and to 0 if it is not. If the CAPAS field is not present in the initialization string, then none of the capabilities may be used. Each character contains a 6-bit field (transformed by `tochar()`), whose low-order bit is set to 1 if another capability byte follows, and to 0 in the last capability byte. Thus the CAPAS field, unlike fields 1–9, is a variable length field. This is to allow additional capabilities to be added in the future. The capabilities defined so far are:

#1 *Reserved*
#2 *Reserved*
#3 Ability to accept "A" packets (file attributes)
#4 Sliding window protocol extension
#5 Long packet protocol extension

The capability mask as defined so far would look like this:

bit5	bit4	bit3	bit2	bit1	bit0
#1	#2	#3	#4	#5	0

If capabilities 1–5 were all "on," the value of the byte would be 76 (octal). When capability number 6 is added, the mask will look like this:

bit5	bit4	bit3	bit2	bit1	bit0		bit5	bit4	bit3	bit2	bit1	bit0
#1	#2	#3	#4	#5	1		#6	–	–	–	–	0

Initialization string fields that come after the capability mask are not in a fixed position. The spar( ) function must find the first CAPAS byte whose value after application of unchar( ) is even. For convenience, we'll refer to the positions of the fields following the mask as CAPAS + 1, CAPAS + 2, etc.

To handle the capabilities mask, global flag variables must be added for each defined capability, and spar( ) and rpar( ) need code to set those variables.

Declarations:

```
int capas = 10;        /* Final Position of inbound capas mask */
int atcapb = 8;        /* Attribute capability bit */
int atcapr = 0;        /* Attribute capability requested */
int atcapu = 0;        /* Attribute capability used */
int swcapb = 4;        /* Sliding window capability bit */
int swcapr = 0;        /* Sliding window capability requested */
int swcapu = 0;        /* Sliding window capability used */
int lpcapb = 2;        /* Long packet capability bit */
int lpcapr = 0;        /* Long packet capability requested */
int lpcapu = 0;        /* Long packet capability used */
```

From rpar( ):

```
data[10] = tochar(atcapr?atcapb:0 | lpcapr?lpcapb:0 | swcapr?swcapb:0);
```

From spar( ):

```
atcapu = lpcapu = swcapu = 0;
if (rln >= 10) {
    x = unchar(s[10]);
    atcapu = (x & atcapb) && atcapr;
    lpcapu = (x & lpcapb) && lbcapr;
    swcapu = (x & swcapb) && swcapr;
    for (capas = 10; (unchar(s[capas]) & 1) && (rln >= capas); capas++) ;
}
```

The rpar( ) function is very simply coded, because it knows it's sending only one capability byte. The variables atcapr, lpcapr, and swcapr have been set in program initialization, or by the "user interface." In spar( ), the capability flags are set according to whether what has been requested locally matches the other Kermit's capabilities, and the capas variable is set to act as a base from which subsequent fields are offset, even if extra capability bytes arrive whose meaning is unknown to us. When capabilities are defined that spill into additional bytes, the rpar( ) and spar( ) codes will become more complex.

Transmitting and Preserving File Attributes

The optional Attributes (A) packet provides a mechanism for the sender of a file to provide additional information about it. This packet can be sent if the file receiver has indicated its ability to process it by setting the attributes bit in the capability mask. If both sides set this bit in the Kermit capability mask, then the sender, after sending the filename in the F packet and receiving an acknowledgment, may (but does not have to) send zero or more A packets to provide file attribute information. In regular expression notation, a transaction with Attribute packets looks like this:

```
S ((F | X) A* D* Z)* B
```

Setting the attributes bit in the capability mask does *not* indicate support for any particular attributes, only that the receiver is prepared to accept the A packet.

The attributes are given in the data field of the A packet. The data field consists of zero or more subfields, which may occur in any order. Each subfield is of the following form:

```
ATTRIBUTE  LENGTH  DATA
```

where ATTRIBUTE is a single printable character from among those defined below, LENGTH is the number of data characters (0–94), transformed to a printable character by `tochar()`, and DATA is *length* characters worth of data, all printable characters. The A packet, like the I and S packets, is *not* encoded before transmission.

More than one A packet may be sent. The only requirement is that all the A packets for a file must immediately follow its File-Header (or X) packet, and precede the first Data packet.

There may be 93 different attributes, one for each of the 93 printable ASCII characters other than space. These are assigned in ASCII order.

! (ASCII 33)   Length. The data field gives the length of the file, as it is stored on the sender's system (before any conversions, e.g., to canonic form) in K (1024) bytes, as a printable decimal number, e.g., "!#109" for 109KB = 111616 bytes. This field allows the receiver to determine in advance (approximately) whether there is sufficient room for the file, to preallocate the space if necessary, to estimate how long the transfer will take, and to be able to report percent complete during the transfer.

" (ASCII 34)   Type. The data field can contain some indicator of the nature of the file. Operands are enclosed in { } braces, optional items in [] brackets.

A[{xx}]   ASCII text, logical records (lines) delimited by the (quoted) control character sequence {xx}, represented here by its printable counterpart (MJ = CRLF, J = LF, etc.). For instance, AMJ means that the appearance of #M#J (the normal prefixed CRLF sequence) in a file data packet indicates the end of a record, assuming the current control prefix is "#." If {xx} is omitted, MJ will be assumed.

B[{xx}] Binary. {xx} indicates in what manner the file is binary:

8   (Default) The file is a sequence of 8-bit bytes, which must be saved as is. The eighth bit may be sent "bare," or prefixed according to the negotiation about eighth-bit prefixing.

36 The file is a 36-bit format binary file, in which five 7-bit bytes are fitted into one 36-bit word, with the final bit of each word being represented as the high-order bit of every fifth character (perhaps prefixed). For use with DEC, Honeywell, Sperry, and other 36-bit word machines.

I[{x}]   Image. The file is being sent exactly as it is represented on the system of origin. For use between like systems. There are {x} usable bits per character, before prefixing. For instance, to send binary data from a system with 9-bit bytes, it might be convenient to send three 6-bit characters for every two 9-bit bytes. Default {x} is 8.

(ASCII 35) Creation date, expressed as "[yy]yymmdd[hh:mm[:ss]]," e.g., 860208 23:59. The time is optional. If given, it should be in 24-hour format, and the seconds may be omitted. A single space should separate the time from the date.

$ (ASCII 36) Creator identification, expressed as a character string of the given length.

% (ASCII 37) Account to charge the file to, character string.

& (ASCII 38) Area in which to store the file, character string.

' (ASCII 39) Password for above, character string.

((ASCII 40) Block Size. The file has, or is to be stored with, the given block size.

) (ASCII 41) Access:

N   New, the normal case—create a new file of the given name. If a file of the given name already exists, the receiver acts according to its FILE WARNING setting.

S   Supersede (overwrite) any file of the same name, regardless of the receiver's FILE WARNING setting.

W   Warn. Don't overwrite an existing file of the same name. Create the file with a new, unique name, regardless of the receiver's FILE WARNING setting.

A   Append to file of the given name. If no such file exists, create one.

* (ASCII 42)   Encoding. This attribute mechanism allows alternative transmission-level data encoding methods to be used. While it might appear that use of these methods might circumvent the "sacred character" problem, they do not. No matter how the data is encoded, any printable ASCII character may still show up in the LEN or CHECK packet fields.

A   ASCII, normal ASCII Kermit encoding with any negotiated prefixing.

E   EBCDIC (sent as if it were a binary file).

X   Encrypted.

H   Hexadecimal "nibble" (2-for-1) encoding.

3   3-for-2 encoding: three printable 6-bit bytes for every two 8-bit file bytes.

4   4-for-3 encoding: four printable 6-bit bytes for every three 8-bit file bytes.

Q{x}   Huffman encoding for compression, and transmitted in normal Kermit B format. The first x bytes of the file are the key.

+ (ASCII 43)   Disposition (operands are specified in the syntax of the receiver's host system):

M{user(s)}   Send the file as Mail to the specified user(s).

O{destination}   Send the file as a lOng terminal message to the specified destination (terminal, job, or user).

S[{options}]   Submit the file as a batch job, with any specified options.

P[{options}]   Print the file on a system printer, with any specified options, which may specify a particular printer, forms, etc.

T   Type the file on the screen (even if sent with an F packet).

L[{aaa}]   Load the file into memory at the given address, if any. The address is specified in decimal notation.

X[{aaa}]   Load the file into memory at the given address and eXecute it.

A   Archive the file. Save the file together with the attribute packets that preceded it, so that it can be sent back to the system of origin with all its attributes intact. A file stored in this way should be specially marked so that the Kermit program that sends it back will recognize the attribute information as distinct from the file data.

, (ASCII 44)   Protection code for the file, in the syntax of the receiver's host file system. With no operand, store according to the system's default protection for the destination area.

– (ASCII 45)   Protection code for the file with respect to the "public" or "world," expressed generically in a 6-bit quantity (made printable by `tochar( )`), in which the bits have the following meaning:

b0: Read Access

b1: Write Access

b2: Execute Access

b3: Append Access

b4: Delete Access

b5: Directory Listing Access

A 1 in the bit position means to allow the corresponding type of access; a 0 means to prohibit it. For example, the letter E in this field would allow read, execute, and directory listing access:

`unchar("E") = 69 − 32 = 37 = 100101`$_2$

(ASCII 46)   Machine and operating system of origin. This is useful in conjunction with the archive disposition attribute. It allows a file, once archived, to be transferred among different types of systems, retaining its archive status, until it finds its way to a machine with the right characteristics to de-archive it. The systems are denoted by codes. The first character is the major system designator, the second designates the specific model or operating system. A third character may be added to make further distinctions, like operating system version. The following systems do not form a complete collection. Many more can and probably will be added.

A   Apple microcomputers

1   Apple II, DOS
2   Apple III
3   Macintosh
4   Lisa

B Sperry (Univac) mainframes

 1 1100 series, EXEC, or OS-1100
 2 9080, VS9

C CDC mainframes

 1 Cyber series, NOS
 2 Cyber series, NOS-BE
 3 Cyber series, NOS-VE
 4 Cyber series, SCOPE

D Digital Equipment Corporation Systems

 1 DECsystem-10/20, TOPS-10
 2 DECsystem-10/20, TOPS-20
 3 DECsystem-10/20, TENEX
 4 DECsystem-10/20, ITS
 5 DECsystem-10/20, WAITS
 6 DECsystem-10/20, MAXC
 7 VAX-11, VMS
 8 PDP-11, RSX-11
 9 PDP-11, IAS
 A PDP-11, RSTS/E
 B PDP-11, RT-11
 C Professional-300, P/OS
 D Word Processor (WPS or DECmate), WPS
 E PDP-8, OS8, or RTS8

E Honeywell mainframes

 1 MULTICS systems
 2 DPS series, CP-6
 3 DPS series, GCOS
 4 DTSS

F Data General machines

 1 RDOS
 2 AOS
 3 AOS/VS

G PR1ME machines, PRIMOS

H Hewlett-Packard machines

 1 HP-1000, RTE
 2 HP-3000, MPE

I   IBM 370-series and compatible mainframes

1   VM/CMS
2   MVS/TSO
3   DOS/VSE
4   MUSIC
5   MVS/GUTS
6   MTS

J   Tandy microcomputers, TRSDOS

K   Atari computers

1   Home computers, DOS
2   ST series

L   Commodore micros

1   Pet
2   64
3   Amiga

M   Miscellaneous mainframes and minis with proprietary operating systems

1   Gould/SEL minis, MPX
2   Harris, VOS
3   Perkin-Elmer minis, OS/32
4   Prime, Primos
5   Tandem, Nonstop
6   Cray, CTSS
7   Burroughs (subtypes may be necessary here)
8   GEC 4000, OS4000
9   ICL machines
A   Norsk Data, Sintran III
B   Nixdorf machines

N   Miscellaneous micros and workstations:

1   Acorn BBC Micro
2   Alpha Micro
3   Apollo Aegis
4   Convergent, Burroughs, and similar systems with CTOS, BTOS
5   Corvus, CCOS
6   Cromemco, CDOS
7   Intel x86/3x0, iRMX-x86

8   Intel MDS, ISIS
9   Luxor ABC-800, ABCDOS
A   Perq
B   Motorola, Versados

O-T   *Reserved*

U   Portable operating or file systems

1   UNIX and derivatives
2   Software Tools
3   CP/M-80
4   CP/M-86
5   CP/M-68K
6   MP/M
7   Concurrent CP/M
8   MS-DOS
9   UCSD p-System
A   MUMPS
B   LISP
C   FORTH
D   OS-9

/ (ASCII 47)   Format of the data within the packets, before encoding.

A {xx}   Variable-length delimited records, terminated by the character sequence {xx}, where xx is a string of one or more control characters, represented here by their unprefixed printable equivalents, e.g., MJ for ^M^J (CRLF). This is the normal case.

D{x}   Variable-length undelimited records. Each logical record begins with an {x}-character ASCII decimal length field (similar to ANSI tape format D). For example, "D4" would indicate four-digit length fields, like 0132. As with ANSI length fields, the value includes the length of the length field itself, so that 0004 indicates a null record.

F{xxxx}   Fixed-length undelimited records. Each logical record is {xxxx} bytes long.

R{x}   For record-oriented transfers, to be used in combination with one of the formats given above. Each record begins (in the case of D format, after the length field) with an x-character-long position field indicating the byte position within the file at which this record is to be stored.

M{x}	For record-oriented transfers, to be used in combination with one of the formats given above. Maximum record length for a variable-length record.
0 (ASCII 48)	Special system-dependent parameters for storing the file on the system of origin, for specification of exotic attributes not covered explicitly by any of the Kermit attribute descriptors, or for expressing attributes conveniently in the system's own notation, like a list of DCB parameters in IBM Job Control Language, or a DEC FILES-11 control block.
1 (ASCII 49)	Exact byte count of the file as it is stored on the sender's system, before any conversions (e.g., to canonic form). Of limited usefulness when transferring text files between unlike systems.

2–@ (ASCII 50–64): *Reserved*

Other attributes can be imagined, and can be added later if needed. However, two important points should be noted:

- The receiver may have absolutely no way of honoring, or even recording, a given attribute. For instance, CP/M-80 has no slot for creation date or creator's ID in its FCB; UNIX has no concept of block size.

- The sender may have no way of determining the correct values of any of the attributes. This is particularly true when sending files of foreign origin.

The A-packet mechanism only provides a way to send certain information about a file to the receiver, with no provision or guarantee about what the receiver may do with it. This information may be obtained directly from the file's directory entry (FCB, FDB, . . .), or specified via user command.

The ACK to the A packet may in turn have information in its data field. However, no complicated negotiations about file attributes may take place, so the net result is that the receiver may either refuse the file or accept it. The receiver may reply to the A packet with any of the following codes in the data field of the ACK packet:

<null>	(Empty data field) I accept the file; go ahead and send it.
N[{xxx}]	I refuse the file as specified; don't send it. {xxx} is a string of zero or more of the attribute characters listed above, to specify what attributes I object to. For instance, "!" means it's too long, "&" means I don't have write access to the specified area. The sender should respond to this with a Z (end-of-file packet) containing the D (discard) code in the data field.
Y[{xxx}]	I agree to receive the file, but I cannot honor attributes {xxx}, so I will store the file the best way I can.
Y	(Degenerate case of Y{xxx}, equivalent to <null>, above)

How the receiver actually replies is an implementation decision. A NAK in response to the A packet means, of course, that the receiver did not receive the A packet correctly, not that it refuses to receive the file. An E response means that the A-packet capability must have been improperly negotiated.

To date, very few Kermit programs have implemented the Attribute packet option, and there has been little experience with it, especially between unlike systems. In addition to complications arising from the system-dependent aspects of determining and setting file attributes, the protocol itself requires the addition of several new states. For the sender, it's not very complicated. The flag atcapu is nonzero if attributes have been agreed upon in the negotiations. In ssfil state, the code that used to read

```
if (sfile() < 0) error("sfile"); else BEGIN ssdat;
```

becomes something like

```
if (sfile() < 0) error("sfile");
else if (atcapu) BEGIN ssatr; else BEGIN ssdat;
```

and then new states ssatr and ssatx are added:

```
<ssatr>Y {
    if ((x = sattr()) < 0) ERR("sattr");  /* Send attributes */
    else if (x > 0) BEGIN ssatx;          /* Switch to next state */
    else BEGIN { start = 'Y'; BEGIN ssdat; }
                                          /* Pass Y to ssdat state */
}
<ssatx>Y {
    if (rdattr(rdatap) < 0) {             /* get response */
        if (seof("D") < 0) ERR("seof");   /* If refused, send Z */
        else BEGIN seot;                  /* with Discard code */
    }
    if ((x = sattr()) < 0) ERR("sattr");  /* Else send next A */
    else if (x == 0) { start = 'Y'; BEGIN ssdat; } /* No more */
}
```

The sattr() function would have to be filled in to send the desired attributes (most commonly the file's size and date). It would return a positive value if it sent an attribute packet, a zero if it did not (e.g., there were no attributes left to send), or a negative number if there was a fatal error. After sending the first A packet, the sender switches to another state ssatx, in which the ACK packets are interpreted by the rdattr() function. This function would print any warning messages if in local mode, and if the receiver refused to accept the file, rdattr() would return a negative value.

Receiving a file is a bit more difficult, because an indeterminate number of attribute packets will arrive between the F (or X) packet and the first data packet (if any). The new file should not be opened until all the attributes are known, which happens when the first data packet arrives or (in the case of a null file) the Z packet.

```
<srfil>F { ack(); BEGIN sratt; }          /* Got F, go look for A's */
<srfil>X { ack(); xflag = 1; BEGIN sratt; }
                                           /* X, like F, but set X-flag */

<sratt>A {                                 /* Got A-packet */
    ackl(setatt());                        /* Set attributes */
}
<sratt>D {                                 /* Got first D packet */
    if (rcvfil() < 0) {                    /* Try to open file */
        ERR("rcvfil");                     /* Give up on error */
    } else {                               /* Otherwise */
        if (decode() < 0) {                /* Decode, write out file data */
            ERR("decode");
        } else { ack(); BEGIN srdat; }
                                           /* Switch to normal data state */

    }
}
<sratt>Z {                                 /* Got Z packet—null file */
    if (rcvfil() < 0) {                    /* Open the file */
        ERR("rcvfil");
    } else {
        if (*rdatap == 'D') cx = 1;        /* Check for discard code. */
        if (closof() < 0) {                /* Close the file. */
            ERR("closof");
        } else { ack(); BEGIN srfil; }
    }
}
```

When the F or X packet arrives, we switch to the new sratt state, in which we read and interpret A packets. In this state, we expect A, D, and Z packets. If an A packet arrives, the new setatt() function reads and interprets the attributes and sets up the responses for the data field of the acknowledgment. An unlimited number of A packets may arrive and be acknowledged in this manner. If setatt() determines that it does not want the file to arrive, it begins the ACK's data field with an N, and the sender presumably responds with a Z packet with the Discard code. When the first data packet arrives, we call rcvfil() to open the file and write out the first data packet, and switch to data-receiving state. The rcvfil() function, which actually opens the file, should be changed to take the attributes accumulated by setatt() into account. The receiver's Lex code takes no account of the atcapu flag. It will work whether attribute packets arrive or not. The file sender, of course, must not send attribute packets unless the file receiver has agreed to accept them.

Performance Options

This section describes two extensions to the Kermit file transfer protocol, long packets and sliding windows. Both address one of Kermit's weakest areas: performance. Both extensions are designed to allow extended Kermits to work transparently with older Kermit programs that are ignorant of the extensions, as has always been the rule for additions to the protocol.

As originally designed, Kermit is a "stop and wait" protocol. Each packet must be acknowledged before the next one is sent. A Kermit packet includes a single-byte length field expressed as a printable ASCII character, limiting the packet length to 94. The original design has been quite effective for several reasons:

1. Kermit programs are simple to write.

2. The restriction on packet length guaranteed that Kermit would work on practically every system, including the many whose terminal input buffers cannot tolerate long bursts of input.

3. The stop-and-wait strategy gives the operating system time to consolidate its input buffers.

As Kermit grows in popularity, it has found use in situations where its basic design results in poor performance. Two examples:

• Connections with built-in delays, like public networks or satellite links. Unlike direct or dialup connections, these connections do not have a dedicated channel. Response varies with the current load on the medium, and also with the "diameter" of the network. Delays can slow down the performance or stop it altogether if they exceed Kermit's timeout parameters.

• Direct, clean connections to systems with big input buffers. When the error rate is very low, throughput is unreasonably impeded by stop-and-wait for short packets.

At first glance, it would seem that a single solution could address both problems. First, note that any performance extension must require the receiver of a file to have big input buffers. Since many systems don't, any extensions must be negotiable. The question is whether to send one long packet or a bunch of short packets end-to-end (or both).

Assuming that each packet must be acknowledged, the advantage would seem to go to long packets, since fewer acknowledgments would be required per unit data. But when errors occur, the amount of data to be retransmitted is less with shorter packets, so continuous transmission of short packets could result in less retransmission overhead in a noisy environment. But since the acknowledgments must still arrive during this continuous transmission, a full-duplex communication channel is required. The mechanism that allows a certain number of acknowledgments to remain outstanding without blocking the sender is called a sliding window. It might still be possible to do packet windowing on half-duplex connections, but then the windows would lurch rather than slide, with a batch of packets sent, and a batch of ACKs and NAKs arriving in response after the line "turns around."

Longer packets are simpler to specify and program. Windowing is harder to specify and program, and for true full-duplex operation it also requires either multiprocessing (e.g., separate input and output processes) or else interrupt-driven buffered port I/O.

Currently during initial connection, two unextended Kermits tell each other the longest packet they are prepared to accept, up to the maximum of 94. Each computer bases this number on some knowledge about its input buffers. But there are also external factors that may be unknown to the computers. For instance, the connection may have been made through a public packet-switched network or a local area network whose interface devices might have smaller buffers than the computers themselves. These factors have rarely interfered with original ("classic"?) Kermit, because even its biggest packets are acceptable to most of these devices. When Kermit is extended to allow transmission of much longer bursts of continuous data, all bets are off. The burden will shift to the user to understand the communication environment enough to elect the best parameters and options. One should consider whether the benefits in performance are worth the cost in complexity for specification, programming, and "user education."

The sliding window and long packet extensions are compatible. It is theoretically possible to do both at once, but it doesn't make much sense. Long packets are for clean and/or half-duplex connections. Sliding windows are for potentially noisy and/or full-duplex connections.

Long Packets

The normal Kermit packet codes the packet length in a single-character field, restricting the overall length to 96 characters (including all the control fields). To allow transmission of longer packets, a mechanism is provided for extended headers that can express greater length values.

For long packets to be exchanged, the sender must set capability #5 in the CAPAS field of the initialization (S or I) packet, and also furnish the MAXLX1 and MAXLX2 (extended length 1 and 2) fields, as shown in Figure 12-2.

Figure 12-2. Kermit Initialization String with Long Packet Parameters

MAXLX1 and MAXLX2 are each a printable ASCII character in the range SP (space, ASCII 32) to "~" (tilde, ASCII 126), formed as follows:

```
MAXLX1 = tochar(m / 95)
MAXLX2 = tochar(m MOD 95)
```

where m is the intended maximum length, and integer division is used. The receiver responds with an ACK packet having the same bit also set in the CAPAS field, and with the MAXLX1 and MAXLX2 fields set to indicate the maximum length packet it will accept. The maximum length expressible by this construct is $95 \times 94 + 94$, or 9024.

Since the sender cannot know in advance whether the receiver is capable of extended headers, the initialization string MAXL field must also be set in the normal manner for compatibility. If the receiver responds favorably to an extended-length packet bid (that is, if its ACK has capability #5 set in the CAPAS field), then the combined value of its MAXLX1 and MAXLX2 fields is used. If capability #5 is set but MAXLX1 and MAXLX2 are missing, then the value of MAXL should be used instead. If the response to the long-packet bid is unfavorable (capability #5 is not set in the CAPAS field), then extended headers will not be used and the MAXL field will supply the maximum packet length.

Here is the negotiation code from a Kermit program that is capable of receiving 1000 characters at a time:

Declarations:
```
#define MAXSP 2000          /* Maximum length packet to send */
#define MAXRP 1000          /* Maximum length packet to receive */

    int rpsiz = MAXRP;      /* Packet size to ask for */
    char rcvpkt[MAXRP+200]; /* Receive packet buffer */
    char sndpkt[MAXSP+100]  /* Send packet buffer */
```
From rpar():
```
    data[1]  = tochar(94);    /* In case no long packets */
    data[12] = tochar(rpsiz / 95);  /* Set maximum packet length */
    data[13] = tochar(rpsiz % 95);
```
From spar():
```
    if (lpcapu) {                    /* Flag already set above */
        if (rln > capas+2) {
            x = unchar(s[capas+2]) * 95 + unchar(s[capas+3]);
            spsiz = x > MAXSP ? MAXSP : x;
        }
    }
```

Note the extra space allocated in the packet buffers. It is important that room be allowed for reception and construction of padding or other interpacket characters.

After the initialization string has been sent and acknowledged with agreement to allow extended headers, all packets up to and including the B or E packet that terminates

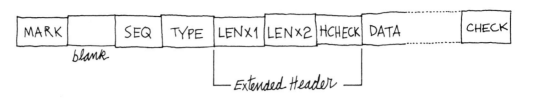

Figure 12-3. Kermit Extended-Length Packet

the transaction (and its acknowledgment) are allowed, but not required, to have extended headers. Extended and normal packets may be freely mixed by both Kermits.

The normal Kermit packet length field (LEN) specifies the number of bytes to follow, up to and including the block check. Since at least three bytes must follow (SEQ, TYPE, and CHECK), a value of 0, 1, or 2 is never encountered in the LEN field of a valid unextended Kermit packet. When extended packets have been negotiated, the LEN field is treated as follows for the duration of the transaction:

• If unchar(LEN) > 2, then the packet is a normal, unextended packet.

• If unchar(LEN) = 0, then the packet has a "Type 0" extended header.

• If unchar(LEN) = 1 or 2, the packet is invalid and should evoke an error.

"Lengths" of 1 and 2 are reserved for future use in type 1 and 2 extended headers, yet to be specified. The layout of a Type 0 extended packet is shown in Figure 12-3. The blank length field (SP = tochar(0)) indicates that the first three bytes of what is normally the data field is now an extended header of type 0, in which the number of bytes remaining in the packet, after the extended header, up to and including the block check, is

Extended length = (95 x unchar(LENX1)) + unchar(LENX2)

and HCHECK is a header checksum, formed exactly like a type-1 Kermit block check, but from the sum of the ASCII values of the LEN, SEQ, TYPE, LENX1, and LENX2 fields, as they appear in the packet:

s = LEN + SEQ + TYPE + LENX1 + LENX2
HCHECK = char((s + ((s & 192)/64)) & 63)

Since the value of the extended-length field must be known accurately in order to locate the end of the packet and the packet block check, it is vital that this information not be corrupted before it is used. The header checksum prevents this.

The extended header, like the normal header itself, is *not* prefix-encoded. This is because it is used at datalink level, before decoding takes place. Therefore, the entity responsible for encoding data must leave three spaces at the beginning of the data field, and the datalink function spack( ) fills in LENX1, LENX2, and HCHECK based on the data actually entered into the packet, after encoding. The packet receiving mechanism (rpack( )) behaves accordingly.

The packet block check is formed in the usual manner, based on all packet bytes beginning with LEN and ending with the last character in the data field. The block check may be type 1, 2, or 3, depending on what was negotiated, but longer packets are more likely to be corrupted than shorter ones and should therefore have higher-order block checks if possible. With long packets, the possibility exists that the arithmetic sum of the characters in a packet will exceed 2^{15}, and will overflow a 16-bit word, or become negative. The checksum function would have to be modified to guard against this, for instance, by always setting the high four bits of the sum to zero before adding in the next byte.

The only code required to handle long packets goes into the datalink functions spack( ) and rpack( ). If the length argument to spack( ) is greater than the maximum permissible for a regular packet (i.e., greater than 95 − bctu), then a long packet is constructed.

```
. . .
    sndpkt[i++] = smark;              /* Packet mark */
    k = i++;                          /* Remember this place */
    sndpkt[i++] = tochar(n);          /* Sequence number */
    sndpkt[i++] = type;               /* Packet type */
    j = len + bctu;                   /* True length */
    if (j > 95) {                     /* Long packet? */
        sndpkt[k] = tochar(0);        /* Set LEN to zero */
        sndpkt[i++] = tochar(j / 95); /* High part of length */
        sndpkt[i++] = tochar(j % 95); /* Low part of length */
        sndpkt[i] = '\0';             /* Header checksum */
        sndpkt[i++] = tochar(chkl(sndpkt+k));
    } else sndpkt[k] = tochar(j+2)    /* Regular packet length */

    for (j = len; j > 0; j--) {       /* Data */
        sndpkt[i++] = *d++;
    }
    sndpkt[i] = '\0';                 /* Null-terminate */
. . .
```

The companion code for rpack( ) would be something like this:

```
. . .
    if ((j = unchar(rcvpkt[i++])) == 0) {     /* Long packet? */
        j = rlnpos+5;                         /* Yes, check header */
        if (j > MAXRP) return('Q');           /* Be defensive */
        x = rcvpkt[j];
        rcvpkt[j] = '\0';
        if (unchar(x) != chkl(rcvpkt+rlnpos)) return('Q');
        rcvpkt[j] = x;
        rln = unchar(rcvpkt[j-2]) * 95 + unchar(rcvpkt[j-1]) - bctu;
        j = 3;
```

```
    } else {
        rln = j - bctu - 2;              /* Regular packet */
        j = 0;                           /* No extended header */
    }
    rsn = unchar(rcvpkt[i++]);           /* Sequence number */
    type = rcvpkt[i++];                  /* Packet type */
    i += j;                              /* Account for extended header */
    rdatap = rcvpkt+i;                   /* The data itself */
    j = rln + i;                         /* Position of block check */
...
```

Extra Long Packets

Hold the presses! The type 1 extended header has just been specified! (No kidding, this "final" addition to the protocol was made just before press time, and is being inserted into the book at this point not only to make the material public, but also to illustrate yet again how Kermit lends itself to extension.)

Recent technological advances have brought high-speed, error-correcting asynchronous dialup modems into the marketplace, and it won't be long until they are affordable by ordinary mortals. The first question some people ask when they learn of these devices is whether their error-correcting capability has made Kermit obsolete. The answer is an emphatic *no*, for at least two reasons. First, although error-free transmission may be guaranteed from modem to modem, it cannot be assured between modem and computer. Second, even when the connection between computer and modem is clean, problems of file delimitation, file representation, and computer-to-computer synchronization are not solved by these modems.

When new communication technologies provide high-speed, potentially error-free paths, then file transfer performance is unreasonably hampered by Kermit's short packets and its stop-and-wait operation. But (you ask) won't the long packet extension solve this problem? Perhaps, for some modems. But others, already on the market, will not perform at their peak unless they handle data in bursts even longer than the 9024-byte maximum provided by this extension. One such modem, operating in half duplex, wants data in chunks of at least 16K–20K, and others may need even more.

Successful transmission of very long packets, especially at high speeds, requires effective end-to-end full-duplex flow control. When modems or other intermediate devices are involved, each device along the chain must be able to control the flow of data from the devices "upstream." For instance, if the receiving computer cannot keep up with arriving data, it must be able to stop the modem, and when the modem's buffers approach fullness, it must stop the other modem, which in turn must be able to stop the sending computer, all without loss of a single byte of data.

But given a virtually error-free path with reliable end-to-end flow control, Kermit's maximum packet length can be further increased by employing a second kind of extended header, which is just like the long-packet (LP) header, except with a 3-byte, rather than 2-byte, extended length field. The presence of a 3-byte length field is signalled when the LEN field of the packet indicates (after decoding) a length of one. The DATA field of such a packet begins with an extended header in which the first three bytes are the 3-digit base-95 length, and the 4th byte is the header checksum. This allows for lengths up to 857,374 (95 cubed minus 1).

To ensure that this extension is compatible with Kermit programs that are unaware of it, we must include it in the negotiations. Rather than extend the capability mask into a second byte, we take over one of the reserved bits, and assign capability #2 (bit 4 of the first capability byte, corresponding to a value of 16) for extra long packets (ELP). The rest of the initialization string stays the same, but the interpretation of the MAXLX1 and MAXLX2 fields, which appear at CAPAS+2 and CAPAS+3, respectively, is different. If the ELP capability bit is set (regardless of the setting of the LP bit), then the 2-digit base-95 quantity given by MAXLX1 and MAXLX2 should be multiplied by 95 to obtain the intended length. In other words, MAXL1 is the "9025's place" (rather than the 95's place), and MAXLX2 is the 95's place (rather than the 1's place). For instance, if the maximum length is to be 30,000, the encoding could be "#>" (3 × 9025 + 30 × 95 = 29,925) or "#?" (30,020).

As with regular long packets, the file receiver tells the sender the maximum length packet to send. But now there are more possibilities, since either Kermit program may support one or the other or both (or neither) long packet extension. If the receiver does not support LP or ELP, the sender will send only normal packets (NP). If a Kermit program supports ELP, then it should also support LP, so that it can fall back to LP rather than to NP when the receiver supports LP but not ELP.

The interesting case arises when the sender supports only LP, but the receiver supports both LP and ELP. If the receiver puts the ELP maximum length in MAXLX1 and MAXLX2, then the sender (which is unaware of the ELP extension) will interpret these numbers as the LP maximum length, 95 times smaller than what the receiver intended. But since the sender goes first in the negotiation, the receiver sees that the sender does not have ELP capability, and in this case it can specify a suitably large LP maximum length (like 9024) in its own initialization string, rather than an ELP maximum length that the sender would misinterpret. Without this trick, fallback would occur to a much smaller size.

A few final words of caution are necessary. First, the longer the packet, the more rigorous the required error-checking technique; it would be unwise to transmit packets of thousands of characters guarded by anything less than a 16-bit CRC. Second, extra long packets are untried as of this writing; even if the technique works, performance might be disappointing if the implementation follows the straightforward path suggested in all the foregoing code. When packets are very long, the transmission line can sit idle for extended periods while packets are being assembled and disassembled. Although idleness is unavoidable while the receiver is checking and processing the packet before ACKing it, the sender can make use of this time to begin assembling its next packet, so that additional idle time after the ACK is received is avoided. This trick requires an additional packet transmission buffer, which, for very long packets, might be hard to find. Finally, users must know the required conditions for successful use of long packets, and must request extended packet sizes explicitly; too many things can go wrong if long packets are used by default.

Sliding Window Protocol Extension

So far, we've seen Kermit's flow control accomplished at two separate levels. At the physical link level, the system's terminal drivers take care of it with full-duplex XON/XOFF, half-duplex handshake, or similar method. At the transport level, the Kermit program itself stops and waits for an acknowledgment for each packet before sending the next one. This operation does not incur an untoward penalty over standard direct-dial land-based phone lines, but public data networks or satellite links can introduce delays of up to several seconds per round trip. As a result, the sending system can spend much more time waiting for replies than actually sending data.

A well-known technique for boosting performance under these circumstances is called the sliding window. Support for sliding windows has been grafted onto the Kermit protocol with a minimum of disruption. No new packet types are added, and most phases of Kermit's operation remain unchanged. Still (and partly for this reason), the specification is complicated, and so too is the implementation.

This discussion is adapted from the sliding window design specification and related documents from The Source (see the Acknowledgments).

Introduction The sliding window extension allows the file sender to transmit data continuously, and the receiver to transmit acknowledgments continuously, by introducing a new transport-level flow-control technique in which multiple packets may be sent before acknowledgment is required. The number of ACKs that may be outstanding is called the window size. As the file sender forms and sends packets from the file data, the packets are kept in a list so that they may be retransmitted, and the active window is said to "slide" over the list. Whenever the earliest packet in the sender's list is ACK'd, the window advances a notch, as in Figure 12-4. The file receiver keeps a similar list, allowing packets to be received out of sequence, with the holes filled in by retransmission.

Conceptually, the window slides over a list of packets that represents the file from beginning to end. In practice, the window is stationary and the list, which contains only as many packets as will fit in the window, is "rotated" within it. The suggested standard window size is about 8 packets, and the maximum is 31 packets, to prevent ambiguous (modulo 64) sequence numbers within a window.

The file sender continuously transmits data packets until its window is full. If ACKs arrive in sequence before the window fills up, the window will be rotated before it is full, and transmission will be continuous. Otherwise, complications arise, which the windowing extension handles on a case-by-case basis.

To ease the impact on existing Kermit programs, windowing is in effect only while data packets are being transmitted. It begins with the first data (D) packet, stops with the next Z packet (to avoid having more than one file open at once), and resumes with the first D packet of the next file, if any.

Sliding Window Specification There are five stages to a Kermit transaction, each corresponding to one of the letters in the expression "S (F D* Z)* B." Three of these

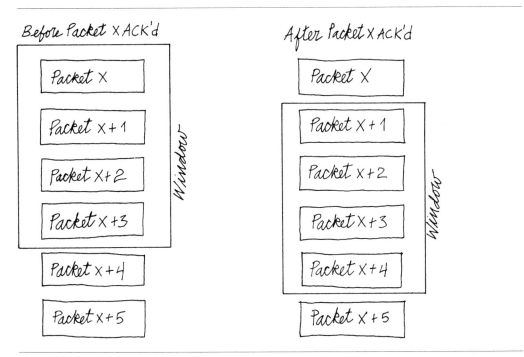

Figure 12-4. A Sliding Window

stages (1, 3, and 4, which handle S, D, and Z packets) must be changed in order to accomplish sliding windows.

1. Propose and accept windowing. The file sender requests windowing in the initialization string of the Send Initiation (S) packet. The file receiver accepts or refuses windowing in its reply (Y).

2. Send and accept File-Header packet. The file sender transmits the File-Header (F) packet and waits for the file receiver to acknowledge it prior to transmitting any data. If there are no files to send, the file sender proceeds to stage 5.

3. Transfer data. The file sender transmits Data (D) packets one after the other until the window is closed. The receiving side ACKs good data, storing it on disk as required, and NAKs bad data. When the sender receives an ACK, its window may be rotated and the next packet sent. If the sender receives a NAK, the indicated data packet is retransmitted.

4. Send and accept EOF packet. The sender will eventually reach the end of the file. At that point, it waits until all outstanding data packets have been acknowledged and then sends an EOF (Z) packet. When the receiver gets the Z packet it stores the rest of the data on disk, closes the file, and acknowledges. The protocol then returns to stage 2, sending and acknowledging any further File Header (F) packets.

5. End of transmission. Once the EOF packet has been sent and acknowledged and there are no more files to send, the sender transmits the End-of-Transmission (B) packet to terminate the transaction. Once the receiver ACKs this packet, the transaction is over and the logical connection closed.

Stage 1, Propose and Accept Windowing

Sliding windows are negotiated in the CAPAS field and CAPAS+1 field, as shown in Figure 12-5. Capability #4 specifies the ability to do windowing. In the first field after CAPAS, designated WINDO, the sender specifies the window size it wishes to use, that is, the maximum number of outstanding packets, and the receiver replies with its own window size. The window size actually used is the minimum of the two. If the receiver replies with capability #4 off, or with a window size of zero, then windowing will not be done.

Figure 12-5. Kermit Initialization String with Sliding Window Parameters

Stage 3, Transfer Data

The sequence of events required for the transmission of data packets and confirmation of receipt is the main job of the windowing extension. There are four main parts to the job:

1. The sender's processing of the data packets.

2. The receiver's handling of incoming packets.

3. The sender's handling of confirmations.

4. The error handling on both sides.

The following discussion details the specific actions required for each of these functions. Refer to the state table on page 296 for the specific action taken on a received-message basis for the full protocol.

The file sender forms and transmits data packets in the normal manner, one after another, until its window is full. Each outbound packet is saved in a Send Table. A Send Table entry consists of the data packet itself (which makes it possible to resend any NAK'd packet from the window), a flag which keeps track of whether the packet has been ACK'd (the ACK'd bit), and a retry counter.

While all this is going on, the sender must also handle confirmations. The method used depends on the implementation. There may be separate packet input and output processes communicating via semaphores or shared memory, or a low-level interrupt-driven buffered packet input function, whose status is checked by the sender before each transmission. In any case, whenever a confirmation arrives, the sender updates the Send Table status flags and counters appropriately, and rotates the window if possible. Transmission stops if the window fills up.

The receiver keeps its own table of incoming data packets. This allows packets to arrive out of order and still be written to disk correctly. A Receive Table entry consists of the data packet itself, a bit which keeps track of whether a good version of the packet has been received (the ACK'd bit), and a retry counter for the NAKs sent to request retransmissions of the packet. The table is large enough to hold all the packets for the protocol window.

To simplify the following discussion, we define several variables:

WSIZE   The negotiated window size

HIGH   The "highest," "latest" table entry (chronologically)

LOW   The lowest, earliest table entry

SEQ   The current, expected sequence number

PSN   The sequence number of the packet that has just arrived

The different possibilities for a received packet are:

1. $PSN = SEQ = HIGH + 1$, the usual case. The packet is ACK'd, and the Receive Table is checked for space. If it is full, the oldest entry is written to disk (assuming its ACK'd bit is set; otherwise a fatal error has occurred) to make room for the new packet, which is then stored in the Receive Table, with its ACK'd bit set.

2. $PSN \neq SEQ$, a new packet, but not the next sequential one. If the packet received has a sequence number in the range $HIGH + 2$ to $HIGH + WSIZE$, it is a new packet but one or more intervening packets have been lost. The upper limit here represents the highest packet the sender could send within its window. Note that the requirement to test for this case is what limits the maximum window size to half the range of possible sequence numbers, namely 31.

We respond by ACKing the new packet, and NAKing all intervening missing packets from $HIGH + 1$ to $PSN - 1$. Then the Receive Table is checked. It may have to be rotated to accommodate the new packet, as in case 1, but this time, several table entries may have to be written to disk. As before, if any of these do not have the ACK'd bit set, a fatal error is triggered. Finally, the packet is stored in the table with its ACK'd bit set.

3. $LOW \leq PSN \leq HIGH$, an old, presumably missing, packet, retransmitted. The packet is ACK'd, then placed in the table, setting the ACK'd bit.

4. $PSN < LOW$ or $PSN > HIGH$, an unexpected, undesired data packet. Such a packet is simply ignored.

5. If any packet is received with a bad checksum, we must decide whether to generate a NAK, and with what sequence number. The best action may depend on the configu-

ration and channel error rate. For now, we adopt the following heuristic: If there are unACK'd entries in our Receive Table, we send a NAK for the oldest one. Otherwise we ignore the packet. In the most common case, when things have been going smoothly and one packet gets garbled, the bad packet will be NAK'd after a subsequent good one is received.

A packet could also be written to disk when it is a good packet and it is the earliest entry in the Receive Table. This approach has the disadvantage that you don't know at this point that the sender has received your ACK, so you have to be prepared to handle the same packet later on if the sender never gets the ACK, times out, and sends the same packet again. Thus, you have to be prepared to deal with packets previous to the current window. You will have to ACK such a packet if it has been received properly before.

By writing the oldest packet to disk when the Receive Table becomes full, you know that the sender has received your ACK (otherwise the sender could not have rotated the window to the WSIZE + 1 position to send the current packet). This makes it very easy to stay synchronized with the sender. The disadvantage of this approach is that when you receive the End-of-File packet, you have to take the time to write all the remaining packets in the Receive Table to disk.

The concept that an ACK would also ACK all previous packets seems attractive at first, since it would appear to reduce overhead. However, it introduces a major complication when errors occur. Once you have an error, you have to send a NAK, and then stop and wait for a retransmission of the NAK'd packet before you can send out any more ACKs. If you sent out an ACK for a later packet, it would imply that you had received the NAK'd packet. Not until you safely get the retransmission can you go ahead. This would prevent the continuous transmission, even during error recovery, that the method described allows (as long as the window does not become blocked).

The sender's receipt of confirmations controls the rotation of the Send Table and normally returns the sender to a sending state. The sender's action depends on the packet checksum, the type of confirmation (ACK or NAK), and whether the confirmation is within the high and low boundaries of the Send Table.

- If the checksum is bad, the packet is ignored.

- When the sender receives an ACK, the sequence number is examined. If the sequence number is outside of the current table boundaries, the ACK is also ignored. If the sequence number is inside of the current table boundaries, the ACK'd bit for that packet is marked. If the entry is at the low boundary, the table is rotated, and the low boundary is changed to the next sequential entry for which the ACK'd bit is not set, freeing space in the table for further transmissions.

- When a NAK arrives inside the table boundaries, the sender checks whether its retry counter has exceeded the threshold. If so, a fatal error has occurred. Otherwise, the retry counter is incremented and the packet is retransmitted. A NAK outside of the table boundaries causes the sender to transmit the earliest unACK'd packet, or if all have been ACK'd, the next packet (in which case, SEQ is incremented first). The retry counter is tested and incremented as above.

Three kinds of errors must be taken care of: sender timeout, receiver timeout, and invalid packets. If the sender's timeout condition is triggered, then it will retransmit its oldest unACK'd packet, the first one in the Send Table. If the receiver's timeout condition is triggered, then it will send a NAK for the "most desired packet." This is defined as either the oldest unACK'd packet, or if none are unACK'd, then the next packet to be received (HIGH + 1). The packet retry count is not incremented by this NAK. Instead we depend on the timeout retry count. For either the sender or receiver, the timeout retry count is incremented each time a timeout occurs. Each side resets the retry count to zero whenever it receives a packet. If the timeout retry limit is exceeded, then a fatal error has occurred.

In addition, as with unextended Kermit, any invalid packet types received by either side will cause a fatal error.

Stage 4, Send and Accept End-of-File Packet

There are several ways to end the file transfer:

1. Sender reaches end-of-file.

2. User interruption of sender.

3. User interruption of receiver.

4. Fatal error.

When the sender reaches the end of file, it must wait until all data packets have been acknowledged before sending the EOF (Z) packet. To do this it sets an EOF flag. Then if an ACK causes the Send Table to be emptied and if the EOF flag is on, the Z packet can be sent and the next file started or (if no more files) the transaction completed. When the receiver gets the Z packet, it writes the contents of the Receive Table to the file (suitably decoded) and closes the file. If any entries do not have the ACK'd bit set, or if errors occur in writing the file, the receiver signals a fatal error. If the operation is successful, the receiver sends an ACK. It then sets its sequence number to the Z packet's sequence number and goes back to receive-file state.

Whenever the sending program checks for input from the data communication line, it should also check for user input. If that indicates that the file transfer should be stopped, or if an ACK is received with an X or a Z in its data field, the sender should go directly to the Send-EOF state and send a Z packet with the Discard indication, a Z(D) packet for short. It will not have to wait for outstanding packets to be ACK'd. When the receiver gets the Z(D) packet, it discards the file, sets its sequence number to the Z packet's sequence number, and goes to receive-file state.

If the receiver detects a user keyboard interruption, it places an X or a Z in the data field of its next ACK, according to whether the current file or the entire batch is to be interrupted, respectively. When the sender gets such an ACK, it goes to send-EOF state and sends a Z(D) packet with sequence number PSN + 1 (PSN is the sequence number of the ACK with the interruption request). When the receiver gets the Z(D) packet, it discards the file, sets its sequence number to the Z packet's sequence number, and goes to receive-file state.

Low-Level Protocol Requirements To be used to fullest advantage, the windowing extension requires a full-duplex channel to allow messages to be sent and received simultaneously. Half-duplex operation is possible, but cumbersome. The sender blasts the packets out until its window fills up. Then it stops sending, and this gives the receiver a chance to send some ACKs. However, some special arrangement may be necessary to turn the line around, like sending the handshake character or EOL only after the last packet in a group.

The ability to buffer several received messages at the physical link level before processing them at the Kermit datalink level is desirable, because the higher layers may take a while to process one input, and meanwhile several others may arrive. System-level XON/XOFF or other full-duplex flow control may be used to prevent overruns, but it should work bidirectionally, to prevent XOFF deadlocks.

Kermit Windowing Protocol State Table

Table 12-1 shows the inputs expected, the actions performed, and the succeeding states for sending and receiving data with windowing. If both sides agree on windowing in the parameter exchange, then instead of entering the old send-data or receive-data states, they enter the new send-data-windowing or receive-data-windowing states and take it from there. The code to implement windowing is a bit too complex to show in this book, and key parts of it are system-dependent. Most of the code you have seen already has to be redone, and then used with a window size of one for communication with non-windowing Kermit programs. The sliding window option is finding its way into some of the major Kermit implementations, so if you're interested you can consult the source code as it becomes available.

Some Analysis

As you increase the baud rate of a connection, the transmission speed of the data increases, but you do not change the delay caused by the communication path. As a result, the delay becomes more and more significant as the transmission rate rises.

Assume, for example, that your communication path introduces a delay of 1 second each way for packets, for a total delay of 2 seconds round trip. Assume also that your packets have 900 bits in them, so it takes you 3 seconds to send a packet at 300 baud (this is roughly equivalent to a typical Kermit packet).

Without windowing, here is what happens:

If you transmitted data for 3 seconds (sending 900 bits) at 300 baud, then waited 2 seconds for each acknowledgment, your throughput would be roughly 180 baud. (Total time for each transmission = 5 seconds. 900/5 = 180).

Table 12-1. Kermit Sliding Window State Table

SEND_DATA_WINDOWING (SDW)

Rec'd Msg	Action	Next State
No input/Window closed	(1) Wait for input	SDW
No input/Window open	(2) Read file, encode packet, Place in table, mark unACK'd, Send packet	SDW
ACK/X or Z	(3) set interrupt indicator (X/Z)	Send_Eof
ACK/outside table	-ignore-	SDW
ACK/inside table	(4) mark packet ACK'd, if low rotate table, if file eof & table empty then goto Send_Eof	SDW or Send_Eof
NAK/outside table	-ignore-	SDW
NAK/inside table	(5) test retry limit, re-send DATA packet	SDW
Bad checksum	-ignore-	SDW
Timeout	(6) re-send oldest unACK'd packet	SDW
User interrupt	(7) set interrupt indicator (X/Z)	Send_Eof
Other	(8) send Error packet	Quit

RCV_DATA_WINDOWING (RDW)

Rec'd Msg	Action	Next State
DATA/new	(1) send ACK if table full: file & rotate store new packet in table	RDW
DATA/old	(2) send ACK, store in table	RDW
DATA/unexpected	-ignore-	RDW
Z/discard	(3) discard file	Rcv_File
Z/	(4) write table to file & close if OK send ACK, else Error	Rcv_File or Quit
Bad checksum	(5) send NAK for oldest unACK'd packet	RDW
Timeout	(6) send NAK for most desired packet	RDW
User Interrupt	(7) Set interrupt indicator X or Z	RDW
Other	(8) send Error packet	Quit

However, if you went to 2400 baud, you would transmit data for 3/8 second, then wait 2 seconds for an acknowledgment. (Total time for each transmission = 2 and 3/8 seconds). The throughput would increase only to about 378 baud. (900 / 2.375 = 378).

The delay becomes the limiting factor. In this case, with this packet size, the delay sets an outside limit of 450 baud (900/2 second delay = 450), no matter how fast the modem speed.

With windowing, the throughput should be close to the actual transmission speed. It should be possible to send data nearly continuously. The exact speed will depend on the window size, length of transmission delays, and error rate.

It is possible to see the desired relationship between packet size and windowing for various baud rates and communications delays. For the common case of an error corrected by one retransmission of the corrupted packet, the minimum window size needed for continuous throughput (the window never gets blocked) can be calculated by:

$$\text{WSIZE} > 1 + \frac{4 \times \text{delay} \times \text{baud rate}}{\text{packet size} \times 10}$$

where the denominator is the number of bits in the packet. Windowing always helps, as long as the window size is greater than 1.

In the preceding relation, the "4" derives from the fact that a corrupted packet has 4 transit times involved:

• Original (bad checksum) packet

• NAK for the packet

• Retransmission of packet

• ACK for retransmission.

All of this must happen before the window becomes blocked.

The "delay" is the effective maximum one-way communications path delay, which includes any CPU delays. Strictly speaking, the "packet size" should have the length of the ACK packets added to it. As an example, if you assume a 2-second (one-way) delay at 1200 baud, with a packet size of 94, the minimum window size for continuous throughput would be:

$$\text{WSIZE} > \frac{4 \times 2 \times 1200}{94 \times 10} = 10.2$$

Under these circumstances, a window size of at least 11 should be chosen, if possible.

13

Discussion and Analysis

In this, our final chapter, we tie up some loose ends. Some tricks are mentioned that you can use to make your Kermit program work better; Kermit is compared with the Christensen protocol; and some lessons are drawn.

Kermit Implementation Tricks

Special tricks can often be used to improve Kermit's operation, but usually at the expense of portability, layering, or some other worthy principle. Some of these tricks are now discussed. They are all outside the protocol in that they are unilateral actions one Kermit program can take without the knowledge or consent of the other.

Problems Starting a Transaction

It often happens that the initial packet simply does not get through because the sender and receiver's parity are mismatched, or the receiver needs a different packet terminator than the one supplied by the sender.

The sender can take care of the end-of-line problem by terminating its first packet (usually S or I) with a variety of common terminators—carriage return, linefeed, XOFF, etc. When the S or I packet gets through, the receiver's response will indicate (in the EOL field) what terminator it really needs, and the sender will know which one to use from then on.

The parity problem can be overcome by the receiver under certain conditions. Most Kermit programs do not send parity unless instructed to do so, and they don't expect to see it on arriving packets. Now, the initial packet of a transaction, no matter whether it's an I, S, G, or C packet, will never contain 8-bit data. Therefore, if the receiver detects that any eighth bits are on, it can tell that parity is being used. In fact, it can even tell *which* parity is in use, as long as it can find two characters in the packet that would have opposite "sense." For instance, a normal S packet begins with a Control-A (ASCII 1, with an odd number of 1-bits) in the MARK field and includes an S (ASCII 83, with an even number of bits) in the TYPE field:

MARK	TYPE	Parity
00000001	01010011	None (or Space)
00000001	11010011	Odd
10000001	01010011	Even
10000001	11010011	Mark

This trick (in this case) is almost foolproof. The only ambiguity is between SPACE parity and NONE, but SPACE parity is hardly ever used. If you don't have an S packet, look through whatever packet you have for a character with an even number of 1-bits in the low-order 7 positions and use it instead.

Usually, it's enough just to know that parity is being used. If the receiver detects that any eighth bits are on in a control packet (any packet of type other than D), it can act as it would had the user given a SET PARITY ODD (or whatever) command, namely, set the parity variable nonzero, so that the parity bit will be stripped from all incoming packets before the block check calculation.

Problems Terminating a Transaction

Just as it's sometimes hard to say hello, it can also be hard to say goodbye. It can happen that transactions get stuck at the very end, usually when the RECEIVE/escape-back/SEND model is in use. The file receiver, upon receiving a B (Break, End-of-Transaction) packet, acknowledges it and then exits. But what happens if the file sender does not receive the ACK? It retransmits the B packet, of course. But the other Kermit has stopped reading packets. So the sender times out, retransmits, and so on, up to its retry threshold, and then finally exits. The process may take quite some time, and will certainly mystify, or at least frustrate, the poor user.

The B packet serves a very useful purpose. As was mentioned before, it acts as a kind of rear guard on the transaction, to ensure that the (last) file that was sent was received and closed properly. The file sender does not send the B packet until it has received an acknowledgment for its previous Z packet, and therefore it knows that the file it has just sent was indeed received and closed. So if it fails to get an ACK for the B packet, no harm will have been done. It can exit after one or two timeouts, by setting its retry threshold to 1 or 2.

This situation comes up in real life more often than you might expect. It happens not only when the ACK is corrupted or lost in transit, but also as a by-product of the file receiver closing or resetting the terminal after sending the final ACK, with the close or reset taking effect before the packet is all the way out of the system. It can happen not only after a file transfer but also to any "final" ACK, such as the ones that come from the server in response to BYE or FINISH command. To reduce the likelihood that the door will be slammed before the final packet is all the way out, a Kermit program should sleep for a second or so before resetting and closing the communication device.

Server Command Wait Timeouts

A Kermit server should not assume that the other Kermit will provide timeouts. Since a Kermit server, unless otherwise occupied, is always waiting for a command, it will time out when the command does not arrive, and when it times out, it sends a NAK for packet zero (the familiar "# N3"). Since the normal timeout interval is something like 5 seconds, and the retry threshold is a small integer, a server would not remain a server for long unless certain steps were taken. First, the retry threshold should become infinite, so that the server does not exit without being explicitly instructed to do so. Second, the timeout interval during command wait should be increased, so that NAKs do not pile up and eventually clog the client system's input buffer, which is what will happen if the client system is not actively doing input from the communication line.

Resonating Packets

The periodic NAKs from a server, even when they are stretched out at 30 or 60 second intervals, will pile up in the client system's input buffer until overruns occur, or the client system successfully silences the server with an XOFF or similar flow control. In either case, however, some number of NAKs has built up in the client system's buffer. In the latter case, there are still more of them trapped in the server system's output buffer.

This is just one of many situations that can give rise to the phenomenon of "resonating packets." When the user of the client system decides to make use of the server after some hiatus, the client Kermit program is directed to send a command or initialization packet to the server, which it does; let's say it's an S packet. The response will be the first NAK from the input buffer, which may have been sitting there for hours. But the client Kermit program doesn't know that, so it behaves according to protocol and retransmits its most recent packet. Then it reads the response. Another NAK. So it retransmits again. And so on.

Eventually, if it has not exceeded the retry threshold, the client comes across the response to the first packet it sent, in this case an ACK for the S packet. At last! It sets its parameters from it, and then sends the F packet. And then reads the response. Guess what . . . another ACK for the S packet. So it sends another F packet. And so on, throughout the entire transaction. In the worst case, every packet will be sent and acknowledged *n* times, where *n* is the retry threshold.

No real harm is done. The protocol prevents redundant data from being written to disk, so the files are still transferred intact. But it is clearly desirable that the operation not take three, four, or more times longer than it needs to. How can we stop packets from resonating?

The first, and most common, technique is to clear the input buffer at certain critical times. This is the job of the system-dependent `ttflui()` function. The buffer should be cleared by a client before sending a command to a server, and it should be cleared in the `input()` function after the desired packet has been successfully read, *unless* windowing is being done. Unfortunately, not all systems provide a clear-buffer function. Of those that don't, however, some provide a "tell me how many characters are waiting in the input buffer" function, which allows you to read and discard them without risk of blocking on input.

A second, and perhaps more effective, method is to ignore redundant ACKs. Windowing Kermit does this anyway; it only retransmits a particular packet when it gets a NAK for it. Windowless Kermit, however, can take special measures in its `input()`

function. If the packet type is Y and the sequence number is the previous one, then it simply waits for the next packet. If it doesn't arrive, then one side or the other will time out and retransmit.

Echoing Packets

Certain communications equipment insists on echoing characters back at devices it believes are terminals, but which may well be PCs sending Kermit packets. A simple check can be performed in the input() function, similar to the one just mentioned: if the type of the packet received is the same as the one just sent, ignore it and wait for the next packet. Or, if we're willing to abuse our layers, we can do this more efficiently and reliably within rpack(): if the packet type is the same as the one just sent, don't bother processing the rest of it, just jump back and read in the next one.

The user also has some recourse here, if both Kermit programs provide a SET SEND/ RECEIVE START-OF-PACKET command. If the packet marker is different in the two directions, then the echoed outbound packets will not be in valid format for inbound packets, and will therefore be ignored as interpacket garbage.

Adjusting Packet Size

It has been said several times that the longer a packet, the greater the probability that it will be corrupted, and the longer the time required to retransmit it. But the shorter the packet, the greater the per-packet overhead. Assuming we have a wide range over which to vary the length, as we do with the long packet extension, it would be a good idea to have the program automatically adjust the length based on the error rate. The noisier the line, the shorter the packet, and the cleaner, the longer. This is entirely an implementation decision, transparent to the protocol, as long as the maximum negotiated length is not exceeded. In fact, a technique like this could be essential for the protocol to work at all when two systems have negotiated a packet size that exceeds the capacity of some intervening apparatus.

The error rate should be kept weighted so that the most recent behavior counts most heavily, to allow rapid response to changing conditions. In the extreme example, only the most recent packet would count. The packet size could be reduced (say, halved) for each successive failure, and increased (e.g., doubled) after each success, up to the maximum. The halving should stop too, at some reasonable cutoff, to avoid Zeno's paradox.

Adjusting Retry Threshold

The retry threshold is intended to catch the case in which the other Kermit has stopped cooperating—died, hung, crashed, disappeared. We patiently give it x chances to send its next packet, and then give up. However, when the connection is very noisy, it's always possible that the other Kermit is still there, valiantly trying to send the packet.

There's no good reason to abandon ship when it might not sink. The two cases can be distinguished at transport level. The input() function gets a pseudotype of Q when a packet arrived with a bad checksum, and a T if it didn't arrive at all. A clever Kermit would assign less wieght to a Q than to a T. But this is tricky. First of all, T should have substantial weight at the outset, to catch the case where parameters are mismatched. For instance, if the parity gremlin is at work, the checksum will almost always be wrong, which means that we don't want the first packet retried infinitely (unless we adjust our idea of what the parity is with each retry). Second, there may be some other kind of consistent failure, like an ASCII/EBCDIC mistranslation of some unusual character like "{," which will eventually show up in a length field or block check.

Adjusting Timeout

Transmission errors are only one external factor that can affect the protocol. Another is transmission delay, caused by a heavily loaded shared resource like a timesharing computer, or a packet switched network. When delay is constant (e.g., because each packet must bounce off a satellite), then static adjustments can be made—the timeout interval can be increased to account for the delay. But when the delay varies, it is desirable for the timeout interval to vary accordingly. Otherwise, throughput will suffer if it is set too high, and unnecessary retransmissions will occur if it is set too low.

A mainframe Kermit program can exert some control if it is able to ascertain the system load average. It can weight the per-packet timeout interval accordingly. But when the delays have external causes, more complicated measures might be required, like a weighted average of the perceived round-trip packet delay.

Text versus Binary Files

One of the major headaches with Kermit stems from its special handling of text files. While this is a highly desirable service, it produces complications and confusion among users who also want to transfer binary files. If they forget to give the proper SET commands—usually on both ends—the results will be useless. Even when they understand the difference, they are still thwarted because they can't transfer a mixture of text and binary files in a single transaction, and there's usually no convenient way to switch modes when using a server (the REMOTE SET command is not widely implemented).

It would be far better if Kermit programs could recognize files as text or binary based on their attributes or contents. In fact, some Kermit programs can do this. But sending a file in the correct mode does no good if it is not received in the same mode. The Attributes packet mechanism provides a way out of this dilemma, but like REMOTE SET it is rarely found in real Kermit programs. Until its use becomes widespread, and to some extent also thereafter, some tricks could be employed:

• In the absence of any other identifying attributes, the file sender could do a quick scan of the file before sending it to determine whether any telltale signs of binary files were present: bytes with the eighth bit set, a preponderance of control characters, etc. *Quick* is the key word here; the operation should not cause the receiver to time out.

• The file receiver could keep a substantial buffer in memory for file data. After the first bufferful had been accumulated, it could scan for the telltale signs, change modes if necessary, and then do any required reformatting before writing the data out to disk.

These tricks are probably not worth doing unless there is a strong probability that they will work. Consistency is more comforting to the user than caprice; certainly, it's easier to explain.

Kermit versus Other Protocols

Kermit is but one of many "asynchronous" protocols. Many such protocols are of a proprietary nature, and there's no point comparing Kermit with them more than we have already—that is, on an economic, organizational basis. Two others are worth a brief inspection, so that when their names are bandied about you'll have some feeling for what's behind them.

ASCII, or XON/XOFF

Many communication programs are said to support "ASCII" or "XON/XOFF" protocol. By now, you should be able to guess what this means. What you get is flow control that works so long as the system on the other end pays attention to it, but that includes no error detection or correction, and no way of distinguishing between file and screen data. In other words, it works just like the Kermit session log for downloading files, and like Kermit's TRANSMIT command for uploading.

The Christensen Protocol

The Christensen protocol, invented by Ward Christensen in 1977, was intended to provide reliable file transfer between CP/M microcomputers over communication lines. His original file transfer program was called MODEM. It has since been enhanced in various ways, and the resulting variants have names like MODEM2, MODEM7, XMODEM, and YMODEM. If one believes the makers of the many communication programs that claim to support it, XMODEM is the most popular of these.

To summarize MODEM operation very briefly, it is equivalent to the "D* Z" portion of Kermit protocol. A MODEM packet starts with a mark, ASCII Control-A, like Kermit's (but the mark character can also appear elsewhere in the packet). Then it has a packet number, the data, and a block check. The data field is exactly 128 characters long, corresponding to a CP/M disk block. The data is sent exactly as it appears on disk, with no conversions. Both data and control fields are 8-bit bytes, unencoded. The file sender transmits as many packets as there are disk blocks in the source file and then sends a single EOT (ASCII Control-D) character to indicate the end of the file. The file receiver responds to each packet, and to the EOT, with an ACK character (*not* packet), ASCII Control-F, or NAK, ASCII Control-U. The packet number (or more properly the "block" number) appears twice in succession, with the second copy being the 1's complement of the first, so that when they are combined, the result should be zero. This serves as a kind of header checksum. There is only one type of packet, equivalent to the Kermit Data packet. Basic MODEM protocol provides no file headers. The file transfer begins when the receiver sends a NAK.

Over the years, additions were made to this protocol in much the same vein as those made to Kermit:

- "Batch mode," which allows a group of files to be sent in a single operation.

- 16-bit CRCs instead of 8-bit checksums, selected when the receiver sends C instead of NAK. This feature was added after MODEM2, and may or may not be present in any particular MODEM7 or XMODEM program.

- Remote single-file operation, interruptible by sending CAN (ASCII Control-X). This is the distinguishing characteristic of XMODEM, which is the basis for many Remote CP/M systems. Roughly equivalent to remote Kermit, except that XMODEM does not necessarily provide batch mode.

- 1K packets, indicated by starting a packet with STX (Control-B) instead of SOH, first implemented in YMODEM.

Kermit was first developed in 1981 in total ignorance of the Christensen protocol (which we'll call MODEM for short). The purpose of Kermit was to provide error-free file transfer among a diverse set of computers with various characteristics through a perverse set of communication media, whereas MODEM was intended only for CP/M-to-CP/M transfers over transparent, 8-bit-wide, relatively clean channels. Still, the two are remarkably similar in both their original design and in their evolution.

Datalink Level

Both protocols call for back-and-forth ACK/NAK ("stop-and-wait") packet transfer over asynchronous telecommunication lines. However, MODEM sends fixed-length 132-byte packets of 8-bit bytes whereas Kermit sends variable-length packets up to 96 characters in length with either 7- or 8-bit data bytes. (Extensions to both Kermit and MODEM allow for longer packets.) The MODEM packet control fields use all 8 bits, but Kermit control fields use only 7. There are several consequences of all this:

- MODEM can't work at all over a 7-bit channel, even for text files, because the checksum and block-number fields will be wrong. This means that MODEM can't be used over public packet-switched networks like Telenet (except in the rare cases when the host puts the user's PAD into 8-bit transparency mode), or with hosts (like IBM mainframes) that require use of character parity. Kermit can send both text and binary files over either 7-bit channels or 8-bit channels, but the data gets longer if you have to squeeze it through a narrower hole.

- Certain computing or communication equipment cannot accept 132 characters at a time. Their input buffers aren't that big. Kermit can adapt to this situation; MODEM cannot. On the other hand, when the buffers are big enough, standard MODEM packets are a bit longer than standard Kermit packets, and therefore incur less overhead.

- Communication devices or mainframe hosts often cannot accept ASCII control characters transparently at the console terminal. MODEM provides no mechanism for encoding otherwise taboo characters. Kermit allows 8-bit and control characters to be encoded for safe transmission. Neither MODEM nor Kermit encodes 7-bit printable characters.

- MODEM cannot transmit through equipment that does XON/XOFF or any other in-band flow control, because its packets can contain XOFF or any other characters. The packet number of block 19 is a Control-S.

MODEM is more sensitive to transmission errors than Kermit because MODEM's packetizing is done only in one direction. The receiver's confirmations are single characters, and when these are corrupted into something else that is significant to a MODEM program (for instance, an ACK becomes a CAN, or a spurious EOT arrives at the file receiver), the protocol stops working. On the other hand, MODEM's default checksum of eight bits is more robust (in one direction only) than Kermit's default six-bit checksum.

Transport Layer

Even though MODEM packets have sequence numbers that span a greater range (1–127) than Kermit's (0–63), MODEM cannot be extended to support sliding windows because the file receiver's confirmations do not contain the block number. In view of this fact, there is no reason for MODEM packets to use more than one bit for sequencing—a packet is either "this one" or "the last one."

Kermit packet numbers proceed in sequence, modulo 64. MODEM packet numbers skip over zero. YMODEM uses packet zero as a file header.

Session Layer

A session between MODEM programs begins when the file receiver transmits a single character to indicate its readiness, originally the NAK character. This mechanism has since become the vehicle for selection of options, like CRC. It is not error-checked. Since it consists of only one character, it is also not very flexible. There is no guaranteed compatibility on a per-feature basis between variant MODEM programs, such as that provided by Kermit's error-checked, extensible Send-Initiation exchange at the beginning of a Kermit session.

In the MODEM world, there are two different batch-mode techniques: (a) MODEM7 uses a character-by-character handshaking of the 8.3 CP/M-format filename and a checksum (which goes on indefinitely until the checksums match), and (b) YMODEM uses a regular block transfer with the filename in an otherwise ignored block zero. The MODEM program on the receiving end may understand one or both of these conventions, or neither of them. Kermit has a standard, error-checked method of marking the beginning of a file, and transmitting its name. Batch mode is an intrinsic part of the Kermit protocol. YMODEM, unlike Kermit, includes the file date, time, and size along with the filename in block zero.

MODEM's end-of-file indicator (a single EOT character) is not error-checked. MODEM receiver programs may be coded to verify that an EOT is real by NAKing the first EOT to make the sender repeat it, but this technique is not widespread. Also, there is variation in how a file begins, depending on whether batch mode is in use or not, and which kind of batch mode. There is no session-level mechanism for the two programs to settle this. Kermit, on the other hand, encloses files between error-checked File-Header and End-of-File packets that work the same in all Kermit programs.

The basic single-file MODEM session is terminated by EOT, and the MODEM7 batch session is finished when two EOTs arrive in succession. The YMODEM batch session is complete when the sender transmits a block number zero containing no filename. Kermit encloses a session within the S and B packets, so that the Kermit protocol need not distinguish between single-file and multifile sessions.

Presentation Layer

The MODEM protocol says a file should be sent as CP/M disk blocks, exactly as is. Kermit treats text and binary files differently, converting text files to a common intermediate representation. Some MODEM implementations take it upon themselves to do something like this, but there is no requirement that they do so.

Non-CP/M systems, which do not necessarily allocate files in units of 128 bytes or follow the CTRL-Z end-of-file convention, will tend to have junk at the end of a file received from MODEM unless they take special precautions to strip it away. When sending, non-CP/M MODEM programs have to pad out the last packet when the file doesn't end on a 128-byte boundary. There is always uncertainty about the effects this padding will have on any particular system. Kermit has no problem sending a short final packet; Kermit packets have length fields that make padding unnecessary.

Implementation

Much greater attention has been given in MODEM programs to modems themselves, and MODEM programs are typically able to control dialout modems from various manufacturers and to run in "remote mode" when dialed up from the "back port" of a micro (some Kermits also have this ability, but it is not their hallmark). Public-domain CP/M implementations of MODEM come with "overlays" to support a vast array of microcomputers and modems.

Performance

Table 13-1 compares XMODEM, windowless Kermit, and Kermit-with-windows. The tests were done at The Source Telecomputing using a 2400 baud (240 cps) dialup connection to a Telenet PAD at 11:00 A.M. on a weekday. The Kermit programs did not use data compression. The connection was eight bits wide (unlike most Telenet connections), and Kermit did not use eighth-bit prefixing.

These figures show that XMODEM's 132-character unencoded packets, and its single-character responses, result in greater throughput than Kermit's encoded, somewhat shorter packets, and block-checked responses, under the same conditions. The relative performance of the two protocols would remain about the same on a direct, point-to-point connection, but the efficiency (bytes/sec/240) would be higher. When data compression comes into play, Kermit begins to look better, particularly for binary files (recall the statistics in Tables 10-5 and 10-6 on page 250). However, both protocols fare poorly in the Telenet environment, when each packet takes a second or more to arrive at its destination. The continuous transmission provided by Kermit with windows overcomes these delays, resulting in a dramatic improvement in speed.

It's Too Late Now

Kermit was never designed to be the ultimate protocol. It was intended only for transferring files. The design is fairly flexible in terms of datalink options and so it has spread to a remarkably wide variety of systems, large and small. And it has proved itself adaptable to other applications that resemble file transfer: the generic commands (REMOTE DIRECTORY, REMOTE TYPE, REMOTE WHO, etc.) are all based on the built-in file transfer mechanism.

But Kermit is not suited for applications that are intrinsically interactive or message-oriented, because the flow of data is one-way throughout a transaction. The datalink

Table 13-1. Kermit versus XMODEM over Telenet

	Min:Sec	Bytes/Sec	Efficiency
File 1: 22042 bytes (binary)			
Kermit (no windows)	9:36	38	16%
XMODEM	5:46	63	26%
Kermit (windows)	2:39	139	58%
File 2: 20000 bytes (text)			
Kermit (no windows)	6:17	53	22%
XMODEM	4:40	71	29%
Kermit (windows)	1:37	206	86%

function is all there, but there is no separation of session control from the application itself. An error in the application is fatal to the whole session. Using the tools presented in this book, you might be able to invent new applications, using the session brackets as a skeleton, and calling upon the transport layer for a reliable, sequential stream of packets. But each such application would have to be its "own protocol."

The Kermit protocol would have been much more readily adaptable to new applications had it allowed for another layer to be included above the session layer, namely an application layer. Kermit's "application layer," file transfer, is imbedded in the session layer. A more layered protocol would have defined just a few selected packet types at the session layer, concerned only with opening, closing, and renegotiating sessions. This would have allowed selection, activation, suspension, and termination of a variety of applications.

Such a protocol would allow options like block check type to be renegotiated on the fly at the session level, without the application's knowledge. Sliding windows could be used throughout the session, not just between F and Z packets. Large file transfers could be checkpointed and restarted. And so on . . . But it's too late now.

If we forget about the big picture, there are still a few minor areas where we'd do things differently if we could start again:

• We should have used Control-G for the packet marker, rather than Control-A. Control-G is the single control character that almost every operating system leaves alone.

• The packets should have had a header checksum, like the extended packet does.

• We should have used a CRC block check from the beginning. Or, if we had to provide a variety of block checks, the packet design should have allowed some way of specifying within each packet what kind of block check it had, to allow dynamic switching of block check types for adapting to changing line conditions.

• The character set might have been narrowed down a bit more, perhaps to the 64 least innocuous characters. Several of the exotic ASCII characters have proven quite troublesome in complicated communications environments, and in ASCII/EBCDIC translation. On the other hand, it's much easier to decode (and debug) Kermit packets when most of the data appears in plain text.

• The characters used in the block check should not have included space; although we've never encountered an instance of it, it is not inconceivable that some computers strip trailing spaces from terminal input.

• An automatic parity-detection scheme, like Hayes modems use on the "AT" sequence, should have been incorporated.

• The F packet should have had the file length in it, and possibly also the creation date. This would have eliminated 80 percent of the demand for attribute packets, which are not very clearly organized.

Kermit is what it is—a file transfer protocol, with a strong datalink function allowing it to adapt to the wide variety of asynchronous communication styles of the diverse collection of microcomputers, PCs, workstations, minicomputers, mainframes, and supercomputers that fill the world. The protocol is robust, simple enough that a minimal program can be written on two pages, yet extensible enough to produce a general-purpose file server with a full range of file management and related functions. The simplicity and flexibility of the basic Kermit design have contributed to its popularity, allowing the protocol to be adapted to hundreds of different systems within the space of a few years. The spirit of sharing and cooperation that animates those who create Kermit programs has been, and will continue to be, a major factor in its success. Because there will always be a need for user-initiated file transfer between otherwise unconnected or incompatible computers, there will always be a need for Kermit, or something like it. I hope that this book goes a little way toward taking the mystery out of data communications and putting reliable file transfer into the realm of the possible for everyone who needs to do it.

Appendixes

Appendix A

Remaining Pieces of the Kermit Program

This appendix lists the additional pieces you'll need to create a Kermit program, beyond those already listed in Chapters 9, 10, and 11. Though it may be possible to produce a working program by copying the code from this book, the recommended method is to obtain machine-readable source code from Columbia or elsewhere (see page 8) and work from that. Not only will this save you a lot of typing, but it will give you more up-to-date material to work from. While every effort has been made to ensure that the code presented in this book works as advertised, there can be no guarantees. The program has been built and tested under Berkeley UNIX.

Symbol Definitions and Variable Declarations

The following section defines and initializes symbols, macros, and global variables for "book-Kermit."

```
/* Definitions */

#define MAXSP 1000          /* Maximum send packet size  */
#define MAXRP 2000          /* Maximum receive packet size  */

#define CTTNAM  "/dev/tty"  /* Default controlling terminal name (Unix) */
#define MAXTRY  5           /* Max times to try reading a packet */
#define SP      32          /* ASCII space character */

/* Macros */

#define tochar(ch)  ((ch) + SP )            /* Number to character */
#define unchar(ch)  ((ch) - SP )            /* Character to number */
#define ctl(ch)     ((ch) ^ 64 )            /* Controllify/Uncontrollify */

/* General purpose reusable string buffer */

    char strbuf[500];

/* Declarations for Send-Init Parameters */

int spsiz = 90,             /* Biggest packet size we can send */
    rpsiz = 90,             /* Biggest we want to receive */
    timint = 5,             /* Timeout interval I use */
    rtimo = 7,              /* Timeout I want you to use */
    rpadn = 0,              /* How much padding to send */
```

```
        spadn = 0,                      /* How much padding to ask for */
        bctr = 1,                       /* Block check type requested */
        bctu = 1,                       /* Block check type used */
        ebq = '&',                      /* 8th-bit prefix */
        ebqflg = 0,                     /* 8th-bit quoting flag */
        rqf = -1,                       /* Flag used in 8bq negotiation */
        rq = 0,                         /* Received 8bq bid */
        sq = 'Y',                       /* Sent 8bq bid */
        rpt = 0,                        /* Repeat count */
        rptq = '~',                     /* Repeat prefix */
        rptflg = 0,                     /* Repeat processing flag */
        capas = 0;                      /* Capabilities */
    char spadc = 0,                     /* Padding character to send */
        rpadc = 0,                      /* Padding character to ask for */
        seol = '\r',                    /* End-of-Line character to send */
        reol = '\r',                    /* End-of-Line character to look for */
        rctlq = '#',                    /* Control prefix in incoming data */
        sctlq = '#';                    /* Outbound control character prefix */

/* Packet-related variables */

    int seq = 0,                        /* Current packet number */
        size,                           /* Current size of output pkt data */
        osize,                          /* Previous output packet data size */
        maxsiz,                         /* Max size for building data field */
        rln,                            /* Received packet length */
        rsn,                            /* Received packet sequence number */
        limit = MAXTRY,                 /* Packet retry threshold */
        sndpkl;                         /* Length of packet being sent */
    char sndpkt[MAXSP+100],             /* Entire packet being sent */
        rcvpkt[MAXRP+200],              /* Packet most recently received */
        *rdatap,                        /* Pointer to data field of rcvpkt */
        data[MAXRP+1],                  /* Packet data buffer */
        *isp = NULL,                    /* Input string pointer */
        *osp = NULL,                    /* Output string pointer */
        smark = '\1',                   /* Outbound packet-start character */
        rmark = '\1';                   /* Incoming packet-start character */

/* File-related variables */

    char filnam[50];                    /* Name of current file. */

    int nfils,                          /* Number of files in file group */
        cx = 0, cz = 0,                 /* Ctrl-X and Z flags */
        xflag = 0,                      /* Flag for input goes to screen */
        xpkt = 0;                       /* Flag to send X packet */

/* Communication line variables */

    char ttname[50];                    /* Name of communication line. */
    char *cmerrp;                       /* Error message pointer. */
```

```
int parity,                        /* Parity specified, 0,'e','o',etc */
    flow,                          /* Flow control, 1 = xon/xoff */
    speed = -1,                    /* Line speed */
    turn = 0,                      /* Line turnaround handshake flag */
    turnch = '\17',                /* Line turnaround character */
    duplex = 0,                    /* Duplex, 0 = full */
    escape = 034,                  /* Escape character for connect */
    delay = 5;                     /* Initial delay before sending */
/* Flags */
int
    text  = 1,                     /* Flag for binary file */
    local = 0,                     /* Flag for external tty vs stdout */
    server = 0,                    /* Flag for being a server */
    first = 0,                     /* Flag for first input from file */
    keep = 0;                      /* Keep incomplete files */
/* Variables passed from command parser to protocol module */
char start  = 0;                   /* Starting state for automaton */
extern char **cmlist;              /* Pointer to file list in argv */
/* Miscellaneous */
char **xargv;                      /* Global copies of argv */
int  xargc;                        /* and argc (Unix) */
char *dftty = CTTNAM;              /* Default controlling terminal name */
int dfloc = 0;                     /* Default location, 0=remote */
int dfprty = 0;                    /* Default parity, 0=none */
int dfflow = 1;                    /* Default flow control, 1=xon/xoff */
char *rpar();                      /* Forward declaration of rpar() */
```

The Main Program

Our main program is a typical UNIX main program. It calls upon the "user interface function," cmdlin(), to parse the command line. Then, if any protocol action has been selected, it opens the communication line, puts it in packet mode, and calls the Lex-generated yylex() protocol module to execute the desired protocol. Also, options are provided for engaging in terminal emulation before or after the protocol operation, or both.

```
main(argc,argv) int argc; char **argv; { /* Main Program */
    int x;
    char *strcpy();
    xargc = argc;                  /* Make global copies of argc */
    xargv = argv;                  /* ...and argv. */
    start = 0;                     /* No default start state. */
```

```
    seq = 0;                        /* Packet sequence number. */
    strcpy(ttname,dftty);           /* Set up default tty name. */
    local = dfloc;                  /* And whether it's local or remote. */
    parity = dfprty;                /* Set initial parity, */
    flow = dfflow;                  /* and flow control. */

    if (argc > 1) {                 /* Command line arguments? */
        start = cmdlin();           /* Yes, parse. */
        if (start == 0 && cflg == 0 && cnflg == 0) {
            fprintf(stderr,"no start state");
            return;
        } else {                    /* Have action, try to open line */
            if ((local = ttopen(ttname)) < 0) {
                fprintf(stderr,"Can't open line\n");
                return(-1);
            }                       /* Open OK, put it in packet mode */
            x = (local) ? speed : -1;
            if (ttpkt(x,flow,parity) < 0) {
                printf("Can't condition line\n");
                return(-1);
            }                       /* OK, do requested actions. */
            if (cflg) conect();     /* Connect before */
            if (start) yylex();     /* Protocol */
            if (cnflg) conect();    /* Connect after */
            doexit(0);              /* Done, exit. */
        }
    } else usage();                 /* No action command, give help */
}

doexit(x) int x; {                  /* Exit */
    ttres();                        /* Reset the communication line */
    ttclos();                       /* Close it */
    exit(x);                        /* Done */
}
```

The Command Parser

What follows is a rudimentary UNIX-style command parser. A real command parser in the recommended Kermit style would be too long and complicated to print in a book. This one accepts the following command-line options:

−x		*server*
−f		*finish*
−r		*receive*
−s	fn	*send*
−g	fn	*get*
−t	fn	*remote type*

−c	*connect before*
−n	*connect after*
−l dev	*line*
−b	*baud rate*
−i	*image binary*
−p x	*parity, x = o,e,m,s,n*
−1,2,3	*block check type*
−h	*help (this message)*

Also included is the setgen() function for building a generic command string. The commands are parsed according to the normal UNIX conventions regarding argument bundling, etc.; it is beyond the scope of this book to explain in greater detail. (Refer to "A Proposed Command Syntax Standard for UNIX Systems" by Kathy Hemenway and Helene Armitage in *UNIX/WORLD*, Vol. 1, No. 3, 1984.)

```
/*  C M D L I N  --  Get arguments from command line  */
/*
 Simple Unix-style command line parser, conforming with 'A Proposed
 Command Syntax Standard for Unix Systems', Hemenway & Armitage, Unix/
 World, Vol. 1, No.3, 1984.
*/

#include <stdio.h>

/* Externals */

extern int nfils, parity, speed, debug;
extern int text, warn, local, server, bctr, xargc;
extern char ttname[], *cmerrp, *cmarg, **xargv;

char *setgen();                     /* Makes generic commands */
char **cmlist;                      /* Pointer to file list in argv */

/* Variables and symbols local to this module */

char cmbuf[100];                    /* Buffer for building generic cmds */

int n,                              /* General purpose int */
    cflg,                           /* Command-line connect cmd given */
    cnflg,                          /* Connect after */
    action;                         /* Action selected on command line */

cmdlin() {
    char x;                         /* Local general-purpose int */
    cmarg = "";                     /* Initialize globals */
    action = cflg = 0;
    cmlist = xargv;                 /* Make this point to something */
```

```
    while (--xargc > 0) {              /* Go through command line words */
        xargv++;
        if (**xargv == '-') {          /* Got an option (begins with dash) */
            x = *(*xargv+1);           /* Get the option letter */
            x = doarg(x);              /* Go handle the option */
            if (x < 0) exit(0);
        } else {                       /* No dash where expected */
            usage();                   /* Give usage message */
            exit(1);
        }
    }
    return(action);                    /* Then do any requested protocol */
}

/*  D O A R G  --  Do a command-line argument.  */

doarg(x) char x; {
    int z; char *xp;

    xp = *xargv+1;                     /* Pointer for bundled args */
    while (x) {
        switch (x) {

case 'x':                              /* Server */
    if (action) fatal("conflicting actions");
    action = 'x';
    break;

case 'f':                              /* Generic Finish */
    if (action) fatal("conflicting actions");
    action = 'g';
    cmarg = setgen('F',"","","");
    break;

case 'r':                              /* Receive */
    if (action) fatal("conflicting actions");
    action = 'v';
    break;

case 's':                              /* Send */
    if (action) fatal("conflicting actions");
    if (*(xp+1)) fatal("invalid argument bundling after -s");
    nfils = 0;                         /* Initialize file counter, flag */
    cmlist = xargv+1;                  /* Remember this pointer */
    while (--xargc > 0) {              /* Traverse the list */
        *xargv++;
        nfils++;
    }
    xargc++, *xargv--;                 /* Adjust argv/argc */
    if (nfils < 1) fatal("missing filename for -s");
    action = 's';
    break;
```

```
      case 'g':                                 /* get */
          if (action) fatal("conflicting actions");
          if (*(xp+1)) fatal("invalid argument bundling after -g");
          *xargv++, xargc--;
          if ((xargc == 0) || (**xargv == '-'))
              fatal("missing filename for -g");
          cmarg = *xargv;
          action = 'r';
          break;

      case 't':                                 /* remote type */
          if (action) fatal("conflicting actions");
          if (*(xp+1)) fatal("invalid argument bundling after -t");
          *xargv++, xargc--;
          if ((xargc == 0) || (**xargv == '-'))
              fatal("missing filename for -t");
          cmarg = setgen('T',*xargv,"","");
          action = 'g';
          break;

      case 'c':                           /* Connect before */
          cflg = 1;
          break;

      case 'n':                           /* Connect after */
          cnflg = 1;
          break;

      case 'h':                           /* Help */
          usage();
          return(-1);

      case 'l':                           /* Set line */
          if (*(xp+1)) fatal("invalid argument bundling after -l");
          *xargv++, xargc--;
          if ((xargc < 1) || (**xargv == '-'))
              fatal("communication line device name missing");
          strcpy(ttname,*xargv);
          break;

      case 'b':                           /* Set baud */
          if (*(xp+1)) fatal("invalid argument bundling");
          *xargv++, xargc--;
          if ((xargc < 1) || (**xargv == '-'))
              fatal("missing baud");
          z = atoi(*xargv);                     /* Convert to number */
          if (ttsspd(z) > -1) speed = z;        /* Check it */
              else fatal("Unsupported baud rate");
          break;

      case 'i':                           /* Treat files as binary */
          text = 0;
          break;
```

```
case 'p':                                    /* Set parity */
    if (*(xp+1)) fatal("invalid argument bundling");
    *xargv++, xargc--;
    if ((xargc < 1) || (**xargv == '-'))
        fatal("missing parity");
    switch(x = **xargv) {
        case 'e':                                /* Even */
        case 'o':                                /* Odd */
        case 'm':                                /* Mark */
        case 's': parity = x; break;             /* Space */
        case 'n': parity = 0; break;             /* None */
        default:  fatal("invalid parity");
    }
    break;
case '1':                                    /* Block Check type 1,2,3 */
case '2':
case '3':
    bctr = x - '0';
    break;
default:                                     /* Anything else */
        fatal("invalid argument, type 'kermit -h' for help");
    }

    x = *++xp;                               /* See if options are bundled */
    }
    return(0);
}

/* Make length-encoded copy of string  */

char *
bldlen(str,dest) char *str, *dest; {
    int len;
    len = strlen(str);
    *dest = len + 32;
    strcpy(dest+1,str);
    return(dest+len+1);
}

/* Construct a generic command, up to 3 fields  */

char *
setgen(type,arg1,arg2,arg3) char type, *arg1, *arg2, *arg3; {
    char *upstr, *cp;
    cp = cmbuf;
    *cp++ = type;
    *cp = '\0';
    if (*arg1 != '\0') {
        upstr = bldlen(arg1,cp);
        if (*arg2 != '\0') {
            upstr = bldlen(arg2,upstr);
            if (*arg3 != '\0') bldlen(arg3,upstr);
        }
```

```
        }
        return(cmbuf);
}

fatal(msg) char *msg; {                    /* Fatal error message */
        fprintf(stderr,"\r\nFatal: %s\n",msg);
        exit(1);                           /* Exit indicating failure */
}

usage() {
        fprintf(stderr,"kermit -xfrsgtcnlbipl23h\n\n");
        fprintf(stderr,"-x      server\n");
        fprintf(stderr,"-f      finish\n");
        fprintf(stderr,"-r      receive\n");
        fprintf(stderr,"-s fn   send\n");
        fprintf(stderr,"-g fn   get\n");
        fprintf(stderr,"-t fn   remote type\n");
        fprintf(stderr,"-c      connect before\n");
        fprintf(stderr,"-n      connect after\n");
        fprintf(stderr,"-l dev  line\n");
        fprintf(stderr,"-b      baud rate\n");
        fprintf(stderr,"-i      image binary\n");
        fprintf(stderr,"-p      parity, o,e,m,s,n\n");
        fprintf(stderr,"-1,2,3  block check type\n");
        fprintf(stderr,"-h      help (this message)\n\n");
}
```

Kermit System-Dependent Functions for UNIX

Finally, here is the collection of system-dependent functions for UNIX (the Berkeley version, and probably also Bell Version 7) including a conect( ) function that implements a rudimentary CONNECT command.

```
/* Book-Kermit System Dependent Module for V7 and Berkeley UNIX */
/*
 Terminal emulation:
   conect

 Console Output:
   tmsg  - Type a message
   tmsgl - Type a line
   tchar - Type a character

 Communication Line:
   ttopen - Open
   ttpkt  - Put in packet mode
   ttres  - Restore normal mode
   ttclos - Close
```

```
    ttinl  - Input a line
    ttol   - Output a line
    ttflui - Flush input buffer
    ttsspd - Verify speed
 File:
   zopeni - Open input file
   zopeno - Open output file
   zclosi - Close input file
   zcloso - Close output file
   zrtol  - Remote-to-Local filename conversion
   zltor  - Local-to-Remote filename conversion
   zgetc  - Get character from input file
   zputc  - Put character into output file
Local private functions:
   dopar  - Add parity to character
*/
#include <stdio.h>                        /* Standard input/output */
#include <sgtty.h>                        /* TTY modes */
#include <ctype.h>                        /* Character types */
#include <signal.h>                       /* Interrupts */
#include <setjmp.h>                       /* Longjumps */

/* Private global variables */

int
  xp = 0,                                 /* Parity in use */
  xlocal = -1,                            /* Local/Remote flag */
  ttyfd = -1,                             /* Comm line file descriptor */
  raw = 0;                                /* Comm line rawmode flag */

static struct sgttyb                      /* Terminal mode data structure */
  ttold, ttraw;                           /* Old (normal), and raw */

static jmp_buf jbuf;                       /* Longjump buffer for timeouts */

FILE *ifp, *ofp;                          /* Input and output file pointers */

/* Console Functions */

tchar(c) char c; {                        /* tchar() */
    putc(c,stderr);                       /* Type character on screen */
}

tmsg(s) char *s; {                        /* tmsg() */
    fprintf(stderr,"%s",s);               /* Type message on screen. */
}

tmsgl(s) char *s; {                       /* tmsgl() */
    if (raw)
        fprintf(stderr,"%s\r\n",s);       /* Type message with CRLF */
    else fprintf(stderr,"%s\n",s);
}
```

```
/* Private Functions */
char
dopar(ch) char ch; {                              /* dopar() */
    int a, b;
    if (!xp) return(ch); else ch &= 0177;
    switch (xp) {
        case 'm':  return(ch | 128);              /* Mark */
        case 's':  return(ch & 127);              /* Space */
        case 'o':                                 /* Odd (fall thru) */
        case 'e':                                 /* Even */
            a = (ch & 15) ^ ((ch >> 4) & 15);
            a = (a & 3) ^ ((a >> 2) & 3);
            a = (a & 1) ^ ((a >> 1) & 1);
            if (xp == 'o') a = 1 - a;             /* Switch sense for odd */
            return(ch | (a << 7));
        default:   return(ch);
    }
}

/* Communication Line Functions */

ttopen(ttname) char *ttname; {          /* Open the communication line */
    if (ttyfd > -1) return(0);          /* Do nothing if already open */
    ttyfd = open(ttname,2);             /* Try to open it */
    if (ttyfd < 0) return(-1);          /* Return -1 upon failure */

    xlocal = (strcmp(ttname,"/dev/tty") == 0) ? 0 : 1;
                                        /* See if local */

    gtty(ttyfd,&ttold);                 /* Get modes. */
    gtty(ttyfd,&ttraw);

    return(xlocal);                     /* Return local/remote status */
}

/* Put comm line in packet mode */
ttpkt(speed,flow,p) int speed, flow, p; {
    int x;

    xp = p;                             /* Make local copy of parity */
    ttraw.sg_flags |= RAW;              /* Raw (binary) mode */
    if (flow) ttraw.sg_flags |= TANDEM;       /* XON/XOFF if requested */
    ttraw.sg_flags &= ~(ECHO|CRMOD);    /* No echo, etc */

    if (xlocal > 0 && speed > 0) {      /* If local, and speed requested */
        x = ttsspd(speed);              /* Check requested speed. */
        if (x > -1) ttraw.sg_ispeed = ttraw.sg_ospeed = x;
                                        /* Valid, use it */
    }
    if (stty(ttyfd,&ttraw) < 0) return(-1); /* Set modes */
    raw = 1;                            /* Flag we're now in raw mode */
    ttflui();                           /* Flush comm line input buffer */
    return(0);
}
```

```
ttclos() {                               /* Close comm line */
    if (ttyfd < 0) return(0);            /* Ignore if not open */
    close(ttyfd);                        /* Close it */
    ttyfd = -1;                          /* Flag no longer open */
    return(0);
}

ttres() {                                /* ttres() - reset */
    int x;
    sleep(1);                            /* Let output finish */
    if ((x = stty(ttyfd,&ttold)) == 0) raw = 0; /* Reset old modes */
    return(x);
}

ttflui() {                               /* ttflui() - flush input buffer */
    long n;
    if (ttyfd < 0) return(-1);           /* Ignore if line not open */
    n = 1;                               /* Specify read queue */
    return(ioctl(ttyfd,TIOCFLUSH,&n) < 0);  /* Flush */
}

timerh() {                               /* Timeout handler */
    longjmp(jbuf,1);
}

/*
 ttinl() - Input a line from the communication line

 Call with:
    dest - where to put it
    max  - maximum length
    eol  - line terminator
    timo - timeout (seconds)
 Returns length obtained, or -1 if error or timeout
*/
ttinl(dest,max,eol,timo) int max, timo; char eol, *dest; {
    int x = 0, ccn = 0; char c;          /* Local variables */
    if (ttyfd < 0) return(-1);           /* Error if not open */

    *dest = '\0';                        /* Clear destination buffer */
    signal(SIGALRM,timerh);              /* Enable timer interrupt */
    alarm(timo);                         /* Set it. */
    if (setjmp(jbuf)) {                  /* Timer went off? */
        x = -1;                          /* Yes, set this return code. */
    } else {                             /* Otherwise... */
        for (x = 0; x < max; x++) {      /* Get up to max characters */
            if (read(ttyfd,&c,1) < 0) {/* Read one character */
                x = -1;                  /* make it the return code */
                break;
            } else if ((dest[x] = xp ? c & 127 : c) == eol) {
                break;                   /* Got eol, done. */
```

```
            } else if (c == 3) {        /* Got ^C, count it. */
                if (++ccn > 1) {        /* If more than 1, let them out */
                    fprintf(stderr,"^C...");
                    ttres(); ttclos();
                    fprintf(stderr,"\n");
                    exit(1);
                }
            } else ccn = 0;             /* Reset ^C Counter */
        }
        dest[x] = '\0';                 /* Null-terminate whatever we got */
    }
    alarm(0);                           /* Turn off the alarm */
    signal(SIGALRM,SIG_DFL);            /* and associated interrupt */
    return(x);                          /* Return length, or failure. */
}

ttol(s,n) int n; char *s; {     /* Output a line of length n */
    int i; char *sl = s;
    if (ttyfd < 0) return(-1);    /* Error if line not open */
    if (xp)                       /* Add parity if requested */
        for (i = 0; i < n; i++) *sl = dopar(*sl);
    return(write(ttyfd,s,n));
}


ttsspd(speed) {                 /* Check speed, return internal code */
    int s, spdok;

    if (speed < 0) return(-1);
        spdok = 1;              /* Assume arg ok */
        switch (speed) {
            case 0:    s = B0;    break;
            case 110:  s = B110;  break;
            case 150:  s = B150;  break;
            case 300:  s = B300;  break;
            case 600:  s = B600;  break;
            case 1200: s = B1200; break;
            case 1800: s = B1800; break;
            case 2400: s = B2400; break;
            case 4800: s = B4800; break;
            case 9600: s = B9600; break;
            case 19200: s = EXTA; break;
            default:
                spdok = 0;
                break;
        }
        if (spdok) return(s); else return(-1);
}
```

```
/* File Functions */
zopeni(name) char *name; {          /* Open existing file for input */
    ifp = fopen(name,"r");
    if (ifp == NULL) return(-1); else return(0);
}

zopeno(name) char *name; {          /* Open new file for output */
    ofp = fopen(name,"w");
    if (ofp == NULL) return(-1); else return(0);
}

zltor(nl,n2) char *nl, *n2; {       /* Name from local to remote format */
    for ( ; *nl != '\0'; nl++,n2++) {
        *n2 = (islower(*nl)) ? toupper(*nl) : *nl;
    }
    *n2 = '\0';
}

/* Name from remote to local */
zrtol(nl,n2,warn) char *nl, *n2; int warn; {
    for ( ; *nl != '\0'; nl++,n2++) {
        *n2 = (isupper(*nl)) ? tolower(*nl) : *nl;
    }
    *n2 = '\0';
}

zclosi() {                          /* Close input file */
    if (fclose(ifp) == EOF) return(-1); else return(0);
}

zcloso() {                          /* Close output file */
    if (fclose(ofp) == EOF) return(-1); else return(0);
}

zgetc(text) {                       /* Get next char from file */
#define MAXREC  100
    static char recbuf[MAXREC+1]; /* Record buffer */
    static char *rbp;             /* Buffer pointer */
    static int i = 0;             /* Buffer char counter */
    int c;                        /* Current character */

    if (i == 0) {
        for (i = 0;
             i < MAXREC - 1 && (c = getc(ifp)) != EOF && c != '\n';
             i++)
            recbuf[i] = c;
        if (c == '\n') {            /* Got newline */
            if (text) {             /* If in text mode, */
                recbuf[i++] = '\r'; /* substitute CRLF */
            }
            recbuf[i++] = c;
        }
```

```
        recbuf[i] = '\0';
        if (i == 0) return(-1);      /* eof */
        rbp = recbuf;
    }
    i--;
    return(*rbp++ & 0377);
}

zputc(c,text) int c, text; {        /* Put character in file. */
    unsigned int x;
    c &= 255;                        /* Undo any sign extension */
    if (text && c == '\r') {         /* If in text mode, */
        return(0);                   /* eliminate carriage returns */
    } else {                         /* Otherwise, */
        x = putc(c,ofp) & 255;       /* output the character. */
        if (c == 255) return(0);     /* Special handling for all 1's. */
        return((x != c) ? -1 : 0);   /* Normal return code. */
    }
}
/* A very primitive CONNECT command */

conect() {
    char esc = '\034';               /* Escape character is ^\ */
    int pid, cf;                     /* Fork id, connected flag */
    char bel = '\07', c;             /* Beep, current character */
    static struct sgttyb             /* Terminal mode data structures */
        conold, conraw;              /*   for console */

    gtty(0,&conold); gtty(0,&conraw);  /* Put console in raw mode */
    conraw.sg_flags |= (RAW|TANDEM);
    conraw.sg_flags &= ~(ECHO|CRMOD);
    stty(0,&conraw);

    pid = fork();                    /* Create a fork input fork */
    if (pid) {                       /* This is keyboard input fork */
        cf = 1;                      /* Connected-flag */

        fprintf(stderr,"Connecting, CTRL-%cC to return...\r\n",(esc ^ 64));

        while (cf) {                 /* While connected, */
            read(0,&c,1);            /* Get a character from keyboard */
            c &= 127;                /* Strip parity */
            if (c == esc) {          /* Check for escape character */
                read(0,&c,1);        /* Got esc char, get next */
                c &= 127;
                if (c == esc) write(ttyfd,&c,1);  /* Double esc, send one */
                else if (c == 'c') {              /* C for Close */
                    cf = 0;                       /* Flag not connected */
                    write(0,"\r\n...",5);         /* Give some indication */
                } else write(0,&bel,1);           /* Not valid esc arg, beep */
            } else write(ttyfd,&c,1);             /* Not esc char, put on screen */
```

```
        }
        kill(pid,9); wait(0);      /* Close, kill keyboard fork */
        stty(0,&conold);           /* Restore console */
        fprintf(stderr,"Back at local system\n");
        return;
    } else {                       /* Port input fork */
        sleep(1);                  /* Wait a sec, then... */
        while (1) {                /* Forever (until killed), */
            read(ttyfd,&c,1);      /* read a character from port, */
            c &= 127;              /* strip parity, */
            write(1,&c,1);         /* and put it on the screen. */
        }
    }
}
```

Appendix B

Kermit Command Summary

No Kermit program will have all these commands, some Kermit programs may use different syntax, and some Kermit programs may include system-dependent commands not listed here. The only commands required for a minimal remote Kermit program are SEND and RECEIVE. A minimal local Kermit program also needs a CONNECT command. Interactive Kermit programs also need an EXIT or QUIT command. A minimal Kermit server requires a SERVER command (unless it goes into server mode automatically). To use a server, a local Kermit needs at least a GET command plus a BYE or FINISH command. Consult the documentation of your particular Kermit program for details about its commands.

The major Kermit commands are listed alphabetically, with the REMOTE commands and SET options listed at the end.

Top-Level Commands

BYE
Shut down and log out a remote server. [p. 140]

CLEAR
Clear communication input and output buffers. [p. 164]

CLOSE {DEBUG, PACKETS, SESSION, TRANSACTIONS}
Close the specified log file. [p. 148]

COMMENT [*string*]
Enter a comment in a TAKE file. [p. 145]

CONNECT [*line*]
Emulate a terminal on the specified communication line. [p. 122]

COPY *filespec1 filespec2*
Copy local file to local file. [p. 143]

CWD [*directory*]
Change working directory. [p. 143]

DEFINE *macroname* [*phrase*, [*phrase*, [...]]]
Construct a command macro. [p. 162]

DELETE *filespec*
Delete the specified local file(s). [p. 143]

DIAL *number*
Call a remote system using an autodial modem. [p. 125]

DIRECTORY [*filespec*]
List names of files on the local disk. [p. 143]

ECHO [*string*]
Display the given text on the screen. [p. 145]

EXIT
Terminate execution of the Kermit program. [p. 144]

FINISH
Shut down but don't log out remote server. [p. 140]

GET *filespec*
Request server to send specified file(s). [p. 138]

HANGUP
Hang up a phone (modem) connection. [p. 126]

HELP
Display information about Kermit commands. [p. 144]

HOST *command*
Execute the command on the local host. [p. 143]

INPUT [*interval*] [*string*]
Wait for the specified string from the communication line. [p. 165]

[LOCAL] *command*
Execute command on local system. [p. 142]

LOG {DEBUG, PACKETS, SESSION, TRANSACTIONS} [*filespec*]
Activate the given log file. [p. 146]

OUTPUT [*string*]
Send the string out the communication line. [p. 165]

PAUSE [*number*]
Suspend execution for specified number of seconds. [p. 165]

PRINT *filespec* [*options*]
Print the local file on a local printer. [p. 143]

PROGRAM *command*
Feed the command to the currently RUN program. [p. 143]

PUSH
Activate a system command interpreter that can be returned from. [p. 144]

QUIT
Terminate execution of the Kermit program. [p. 146]

RECEIVE [*filespec*]
Wait for a file to arrive from the other Kermit. [p. 137]

REMOTE *command*
Send the command to be executed by remote server, listed on page 334. [p. 140]

RENAME *filespec1* *filespec2*
Rename the local file. [p. 143]

RUN [*filespec* [*arguments*]]
Activate the specified program; return to Kermit when done. [p. 143]

SEND *filespec1* [*filespec2*]
Send the specified file or files to the other Kermit. [p. 135]

SCRIPT *string*
Execute a system-dependent script. [p. 166]

SERVER
Enter server mode. [p. 139]

SET *parameter* [*parameter*] [*value*]
Establish or modify a communication, protocol, or other parameter; listed on page 331.
[p. 148]

SHOW [*parameter*]
Display values of SET parameters. [p. 163]

SPACE [*directory*]
Display information about used or available disk space. [p. 143]

STATISTICS
Display information about most recent file transfer. [p. 146]

SUBMIT *filespec* [*options*]
Submit the file for background processing on the local system. [p. 143]

TAKE *filespec*
Execute Kermit commands from the given file. [p. 145]

TRANSMIT *filespec*
Send the specified file "raw," with no error checking. [p. 170]

TYPE *filespec*
Display the contents of the specified file(s) on the screen. [p. 144]

WHO [*user*]
List the named user, or all users who are logged in. [p. 144]

SET Commands

SET BAUD *number*
Communication line speed (baud rate). [p. 148]

SET BLOCK-CHECK {1,2,3}
Level of error checking. [p. 148]

SET DEBUG [*value*]
Enable/disable, or select level or type of, debugging. [p. 149]

SET DEFAULT *device*
Change disks (on micro). [p. 150]

SET DELAY *number*
How long to wait before sending first packet. [p. 150]

SET DESTINATION *device*
Alternative device for arriving files. [p. 150]

SET DISPLAY {ON, OFF, ...}
Control file transfer display. [p. 150]

SET DUPLEX {FULL, HALF}
Access to communication channel. [p. 150]

SET ECHO {LOCAL, REMOTE}
Which system does the echoing during CONNECT. [p. 151]

SET EOF *option*
End of file detection or marking method. [p. 151]

SET ESCAPE *character*
Escape character during CONNECT. [p. 151]

SET FILE {BYTE, DISPLAY, FORMAT, NAMES, TYPE, WARNING,...} *value*
File related parameters. [p. 151]

SET FLOW-CONTROL { NONE, ENQ/ACK, ETX/ACK, XON/XOFF, ...}
Enable/disable, or select type of, full-duplex flow control. [p. 153]

SET HANDSHAKE *option*
Enable/disable, or select type of, half-duplex handshake. [p. 153]

SET IBM [*option*]
Establish parameters to communicate with IBM mainframes. [p. 153]

SET INCOMPLETE {KEEP, DISCARD}
What to do with files that arrive incompletely. [p. 154]

SET INPUT *parameter value*
Timeout and pattern matching parameters for INPUT command. [p. 154]

SET KEY {SCAN *number*, Fn} *value*
Change key bindings or define a keystroke macro. [p. 154]

SET LINE [*terminal-designator*]
Communication line on a mainframe, changes local/remote status. [p. 155]

SET MODEM {NONE, *modem-type*}
Type of modem to be used with DIAL command. [p. 155]

SET PARITY {EVEN, ODD, MARK, SPACE, NONE}
Communication line parity. [p. 156]

SET PORT [*port-designator*]
Alternate communication port on a microcomputer. [p. 156]

SET PROMPT *string*
Change Kermit program's interactive command prompt. [p. 157]

SET RECEIVE *parameter value*
Protocol parameters to ask the other Kermit to use, see page 334. [p. 157]

SET RETRY [{INITIAL, PACKETS}] *number*
How many times to try transmitting a packet before giving up. [p. 158]

SET SEND *parameter value*
Protocol parameters to use when communicating with the other Kermit, see page 334. [p. 158]

SET SERVER *parameter value*
Server-related parameters, like TIMEOUT. [p. 159]

SET SPEED *number*
Communication line speed (baud rate). [p. 160]

SET TAKE {ECHO, ERROR} *option*
Command file processing options. [p. 160]

SET TERMINAL {NONE, *type*}
Terminal to be emulated. [p. 160]

SET TIMER {ON, OFF}
Enable/disable the local timer. [p. 160]

SET TRANSLATION *string1 string2*
Character translation during transmission. [p. 161]

SET WINDOW [*number*]
Unacknowledged packet window size. [p. 161]

SET SEND/RECEIVE **Commands** [pp. 157–158]

SET {SEND, RECEIVE} END-OF-PACKET *character*
Control character to use as packet terminator. Also, END-OF-LINE or EOL.

SET {SEND, RECEIVE} PACKET-LENGTH *number*
Maximum packet length, 10–94 (or 10–9000 with extension).

SET {SEND, RECEIVE} PAD-CHARACTER *character*
Character to use for pre-packet padding.

SET {SEND, RECEIVE} PADDING *number*
How many copies of pad character.

SET {SEND, RECEIVE} PAUSE *number*
How many seconds to pause between packets.

SET {SEND, RECEIVE} START-OF-PACKET *character*
Control character to mark start of packet.

SET {SEND, RECEIVE} TIMEOUT *number*
How many seconds to wait for a packet.

REMOTE **Commands** [pp. 140–142]

REMOTE CLOSE {DEBUG, PACKETS, SESSION, TRANSACTIONS}
Deactivate remote logging of the specified function.

REMOTE COPY *filespec1* *filespec2*
Copy remote file to remote file.

REMOTE CWD [*directory*]
Change working directory on remote system.

REMOTE DELETE *filespec*
Delete specified remote file(s).

REMOTE DIRECTORY [*filespec*]
List specified remote file(s).

REMOTE HELP
List available functions.

REMOTE HOST *command*
Ask the remote host system command processor to execute a command.

REMOTE KERMIT *command*
Ask the remote Kermit to execute the given command.

REMOTE LOG {DEBUG, PACKETS, SESSION, TRANSACTIONS}
Activate remote logging.

REMOTE PRINT *filespec* [*options*]
Print the remote file on a remote printer.

REMOTE PROGRAM [*command*]
Send command to most recently RUN remote program.

REMOTE RENAME *filespec1 filespec2*
Rename the remote file.

REMOTE RUN *program-name* [*command-line*]
Run the remote program on the remote system.

REMOTE SET *options*
Ask server to execute specifed SET command.

REMOTE SHOW [*option*]
Ask server to display specified SET options.

REMOTE SPACE [*directory*]
Ask about disk usage on the remote system.

REMOTE SUBMIT *filespec* [*options*]
Submit remote file for background execution.

REMOTE TYPE *filespec*
Display the remote file(s) on the screen.

REMOTE WHO [*user*]
List user, or who's logged in to the remote system.

Appendix C

Kermit Packet Summary

Basic Kermit Packet Layout

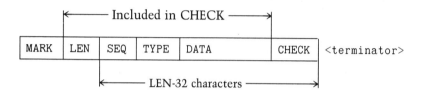

| MARK | LEN | SEQ | TYPE | DATA | CHECK | <terminator> |

Included in CHECK

LEN-32 characters

MARK   A real control character, usually CTRL-A.
LEN   One character, length of remainder of packet + 32, max 95
SEQ   One character, packet sequence number + 32, modulo 64
TYPE   One character, an uppercase letter
CHECK   One, two, or three characters, as negotiated.

<terminator>   Any control character required for reading the packet.

Kermit Extended Packet Layout

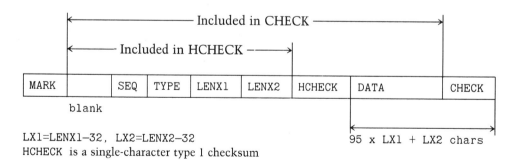

| MARK | | SEQ | TYPE | LENX1 | LENX2 | HCHECK | DATA | CHECK |

Included in CHECK

Included in HCHECK

blank

95 x LX1 + LX2 chars

LX1=LENX1–32, LX2=LENX2–32
HCHECK is a single-character type 1 checksum

Initialization String

1	2	3	4	5	6	7	8	9	10
MAXL	TIME	NPAD	PADC	EOL	QCTL	QBIN	CHKT	REPT	

10		CAPAS+1	CAPAS+2	CAPAS+3	
CAPAS	...	WINDO	MAXLX1	MAXLX1	

MAXL   Maximum length (0–94) +32
TIME   Timeout, seconds (0–94) +32
NPAD   Number of pad characters (0–94) +32
EOL   Packet terminator (0–63) +32
QCTL   Control prefix, literal
QBIN   Eighth bit prefix, literal
CHKT   Block check type {1,2,3}, literal
REPT   Repeat count prefix, literal
CAPAS   Extendable capabilities mask, ends when value–32 is even
WINDO   Window size (0–31) +32
MAXLX1   High part of extended packet maximum length (int(max/95)+32)
MAXLX2   Low part of extended packet maximum length (mod(max,95)+32)

Capabilities:
#1, #2   Reserved
    #3   Attribute packets
    #4   Sliding windows
    #5   Long packets

Packet Types

Y   Acknowledgment (ACK). Data according to what kind of packet is being acknowledged.

N   Negative Acknowledgment (NAK). Data field always empty.

S   Send Initiation. Data field contains unencoded initialization string. Tells receiver to expect files. ACK to this packet also contains unencoded initialization string.

I   Initialize. Data field contains unencoded initialization string. Sent to server to set parameters prior to a command. ACK to this packet also contains unencoded initialization string.

F   File Header. Indicates file data about to arrive for named file. Data field contains encoded file name. ACK to this packet may contain encoded name receiver will store file under.

X   Text Header. Indicates screen data about to arrive. Data field contains encoded heading for display.

A   File Attributes. Data field contains unencoded attributes. ACK may contain unencoded corresponding agreement or refusal, per attribute.

D   Data Packet. Data field contains encoded file or screen data. ACK may contain X to interrupt sending this file, Z to interrupt entire transaction.

Z   End of File. Data field may contain D for Discard.

B   Break Transmission.

E   Error. Data field contains encoded error message.

R   Receive Initiate. Data field contains encoded file name.

C   Host Command. Data field contains encoded command for host's command processor.

K   Kermit Command. Data field contains encoded command for Kermit command processor.

T   Timeout pseudopacket, for internal use.

Q   Block check error pseudopacket, for internal use.

G   Generic Kermit Command. Data field contains a single character subcommand, followed by zero or more length-encoded operands, encoded after formation:

    I   Login [<%user[%password[%account]]>]

    C   CWD, Change Working Directory [<%directory[%password]>]

    L   Logout, Bye

    F   Finish (Shut down the server, but don't logout)

    D   Directory [<%filespec>]

    U   Disk Usage Query [<%area>]

    E   Erase (delete) <%filespec>

    T   Type <%filespec>

    R   Rename <%oldname%newname>

    K   Copy <%source%destination>

    W   Who's logged in? [<%user ID or network host[%options]>]

M   Send a short Message <%destination%text>

H   Help [<%topic>]

Q   Server Status Query

P   Program <%[program-filespec][%program-commands]>

J   Journal <%command[%argument]>

V   Variable <%command[%argument[%argument]]>

Appendix D

The ASCII Character Set

ASCII Code (ANSI X3.4-1977)

There are 128 characters in the American National Standard Code for Information Interchange (ASCII), each assigned a numeric code. The characters are listed in numeric order; the columns are labeled as follows:

Bit	Even parity bit for ASCII character
ASCII Dec	Decimal (base 10) representation
ASCII Oct	Octal (base 8) representation
ASCII Hex	Hexadecimal (base 16) representation
EBCDIC Hex	EBCDIC hexadecimal equivalent for Kermit translate tables
Char	Name or graphical representation of character
Remark	Description of character

The first group consists of nonprintable control characters:

Bit	ASCII			EBCDIC		
	Dec	Oct	Hex	Hex	Char	Remarks
0	000	000	00	00	NUL	^@, Null, Idle
1	001	001	01	01	SOH	^A, Start of heading
1	002	002	02	02	STX	^B, Start of text
0	003	003	03	03	ETX	^C, End of text
1	004	004	04	37	EOT	^D, End of transmission
0	005	005	05	2D	ENQ	^E, Enquiry
0	006	006	06	2E	ACK	^F, Acknowledge
1	007	007	07	2F	BEL	^G, Bell, beep, or fleep
1	008	010	08	16	BS	^H, Backspace
0	009	011	09	05	HT	^I, Horizontal tab
0	010	012	0A	25	LF	^J, Line feed
1	011	013	0B	0B	VT	^K, Vertical tab
0	012	014	0C	0C	FF	^L, Form feed (top of page)
1	013	015	0D	0D	CR	^M, Carriage return
1	014	016	0E	0E	SO	^N, Shift out
0	015	017	0F	0F	SI	^O, Shift in
1	016	020	10	10	DLE	^P, Data link escape
0	017	021	11	11	DC1	^Q, Device control 1, XON
0	018	022	12	12	DC2	^R, Device control 2
1	019	023	13	13	DC3	^S, Device control 3, XOFF
0	020	024	14	3C	DC4	^T, Device control 4
1	021	025	15	3D	NAK	^U, Negative acknowledge
1	022	026	16	32	SYN	^V, Synchronous idle
0	023	027	17	26	ETB	^W, End of transmission block
0	024	030	18	18	CAN	^X, Cancel
1	025	031	19	19	EM	^Y, End of medium
1	026	032	1A	3F	SUB	^Z, Substitute
0	027	033	1B	27	ESC	^[, Escape, prefix, altmode
1	028	034	1C	1C	FS	^\, File separator
0	029	035	1D	1D	GS	^], Group separator
0	030	036	1E	1E	RS	^^, Record separator
1	031	037	1F	1F	US	^_, Unit separator

Note: The last four characters (28–31) are usually associated with the control version of backslash, right square bracket, circumflex (uparrow), and underscore, respectively, but some terminals do not associate them with these keys.

The following characters are printable:
First, some punctuation characters.

| Bit | ASCII | | | EBCDIC | | Remarks |
	Dec	Oct	Hex	Hex	Char	
1	032	040	20	40	SP	Space, blank
0	033	041	21	5A	!	Exclamation mark
0	034	042	22	7F	"	Doublequote
1	035	043	23	7B	#	Number sign, pound sign
0	036	044	24	5B	$	Dollar sign
1	037	045	25	6C	%	Percent sign
1	038	046	26	50	&	Ampersand
0	039	047	27	7D	´	Apostrophe, accent acute
0	040	050	28	4D	(	Left parenthesis
1	041	051	29	5D	)	Right parenthesis
1	042	052	2A	5C	*	Asterisk, star
0	043	053	2B	4E	+	Plus sign
1	044	054	2C	6B	,	Comma
0	045	055	2D	60	–	Dash, hyphen, minus sign
0	046	056	2E	4B	.	Period, dot
1	047	057	2F	61	/	Slash

Numeric characters:

| Bit | ASCII | | | EBCDIC | | Remarks |
	Dec	Oct	Hex	Hex	Char	
0	048	060	30	F0	0	Zero
1	049	061	31	F1	1	One
1	050	062	32	F2	2	Two
0	051	063	33	F3	3	Three
1	052	064	34	F4	4	Four
0	053	065	35	F5	5	Five
0	054	066	36	F6	6	Six
1	055	067	37	F7	7	Seven
1	056	070	38	F8	8	Eight
0	057	071	39	F9	9	Nine

More punctuation characters:

Bit	ASCII Dec	ASCII Oct	ASCII Hex	EBCDIC Hex	EBCDIC Char	Remarks
0	058	072	3A	7A	:	Colon
1	059	073	3B	5E	;	Semicolon
0	060	074	3C	4C	<	Left angle bracket
1	061	075	3D	7E	=	Equal sign
1	062	076	3E	6E	>	Right angle bracket
0	063	077	3F	6F	?	Question mark
1	064	100	40	7C	@	"At" sign

Uppercase alphabetic characters (letters):

Bit	ASCII Dec	ASCII Oct	ASCII Hex	EBCDIC Hex	EBCDIC Char
0	065	101	41	C1	A
0	066	102	42	C2	B
1	067	103	43	C3	C
0	068	104	44	C4	D
1	069	105	45	C5	E
1	070	106	46	C6	F
0	071	107	47	C7	G
0	072	110	48	C8	H
1	073	111	49	C9	I
1	074	112	4A	D1	J
0	075	113	4B	D2	K
1	076	114	4C	D3	L
0	077	115	4D	D4	M
0	078	116	4E	D5	N
1	079	117	4F	D6	O
0	080	120	50	D7	P
1	081	121	51	D8	Q
1	082	122	52	D9	R
0	083	123	53	E2	S
1	084	124	54	E3	T
0	085	125	55	E4	U
0	086	126	56	E5	V
1	087	127	57	E6	W
1	088	130	58	E7	X
0	089	131	59	E8	Y
0	090	132	5A	E9	Z

More punctuation characters:

Bit	ASCII Dec	ASCII Oct	ASCII Hex	EBCDIC Hex	Char	Remarks
1	091	133	5B	AD	[	Left square bracket
0	092	134	5C	E0	\	Backslash
1	093	135	5D	BD	]	Right square bracket
1	094	136	5E	5F	^	Circumflex, up arrow
0	095	137	5F	6D	_	Underscore, left arrow
0	096	140	60	79	`	Accent grave

Lowercase alphabetic characters (letters):

Bit	ASCII Dec	ASCII Oct	ASCII Hex	EBCDIC Hex	Char
1	097	141	61	81	a
1	098	142	62	82	b
0	099	143	63	83	c
1	100	144	64	84	d
0	101	145	65	85	e
0	102	146	66	86	f
1	103	147	67	87	g
1	104	150	68	88	h
0	105	151	69	89	i
0	106	152	6A	91	j
1	107	153	6B	92	k
0	108	154	6C	93	l
1	109	155	6D	94	m
1	110	156	6E	95	n
0	111	157	6F	96	o
1	112	160	70	97	p
0	113	161	71	98	q
0	114	162	72	99	r
1	115	163	73	A2	s
0	116	164	74	A3	t
1	117	165	75	A4	u
1	118	166	76	A5	v
0	119	167	77	A6	w
0	120	170	78	A7	x
1	121	171	79	A8	y
1	122	172	7A	A9	z

More punctuation characters:

Bit	ASCII			EBCDIC		Remarks
	Dec	Oct	Hex	Hex	Char	
0	123	173	7B	C0	{	Left brace (curly bracket)
1	124	174	7C	4F	|	Vertical bar
0	125	175	7D	D0	}	Right brace (curly bracket)
0	126	176	7E	A1	~	Tilde

Finally, one more nonprintable character:

0	127	177	7F	07	DEL	Delete, rubout

Appendix E

Binary, Octal, and Hexadecimal Numbers

Powers of two figure prominently in the computing lexicon, just as powers of ten dominate our perception of numbers in everyday life. Just as the decimal number 3749 means

$$(3 \times 10^3) + (7 \times 10^2) + (4 \times 10^1) + 9$$

the binary number 100101 means

$$(1 \times 2^5) + (0 \times 2^4) + (0 \times 2^3) + (1 \times 2^2) + (0 \times 2^1) + 1$$

The notation 2^n means "multiply two by itself n times." This is called raising two to the nth power. 2^n is pronounced "two to the n" or "two to the nth power." The second power is called the square, the third power is called the cube; 2^2 is two squared, 2^3 is two cubed. The binary number shown above (100101) is

$$32 + 0 + 0 + 4 + 0 + 1 = 37$$

Some powers of two are listed in Table E-1, and Table E-2 shows how some popular numbers appear in binary and other notations.

If you can raise two to the nth power, you should also be able to deduce which power two must be raised to in order to produce a given number. This is called "taking the logarithm (or log), base 2":

If $x = 2^n$, then $n = \log_2(x)$

and

$$n = \log_2(2^n)$$

(The subscript 2 means base 2.) If n is a power of two, then you can represent n different quantities in $\log_2(n)$ bits. For instance, you need two bits to represent four different things, because there are four different combinations of two bits: 00, 01, 10, and 11. Note that these binary numbers correspond to 0, 1, 2, and 3 in decimal notation. It is normal for computers to start counting from zero, rather than from 1, and to stop at $n - 1$, rather than at n. Note also that 2^n is written in binary notation as a one with n zeros after it, e.g.,

$2^7 = 10000000_2$

just as 10^n is written as 1 with n zeros after it in decimal notation (e.g., $10^3 = 1000$).

Binary arithmetic is easy. For addition, you just have to remember the following rules:

$$
\begin{array}{cccc}
0 & 0 & 1 & 1 \\
+0 & +1 & +0 & +1 \\
\hline
0 & 1 & 1 & 10
\end{array}
$$

Whenever you add two 1's together, you have to carry a 1:

$$
\begin{array}{cc}
101011 & 11111 \\
+011110 & +1 \\
\hline
1001001 & 100000
\end{array}
$$

Binary numbers also have certain properties that allow arithmetic operations to be realized very easily in hardware. For instance, subtraction can be done by inverting all the bits in the subtrahend and adding 1 to it, and then adding the result to the minuend:

$$
\begin{array}{ll}
101101 \leftarrow \text{minuend} & 101101 \\
-010101 \leftarrow \text{subtrahend} & +101011 \leftarrow \text{2's complement} \\
\hline
011000 & 011000
\end{array}
$$

The carry out of the last position is discarded. The name for this trick is two's complement arithmetic. It allows simple inverting and incrementing circuits to be substituted for potentially much more complicated subtracting logic. Another property of binary numbers allows multiplication and division to be done by shifting to the left and right, respectively. Note how the patterns are preserved:

$$
\begin{array}{c}
101101 \\
\times 100 \\
\hline
10110100
\end{array}
\qquad
\frac{110110}{10} = 11011
$$

The technique gets a little more complicated when there are additional 1's in the multiplier or divisor.

Some powers of two have special significance in computing circles:

$2^7 = 128$, which is the number of characters in the ASCII alphabet. This is why ASCII is called a 7-bit code. Its characters have numeric values 0 through 127, i.e., 0 through $2^7 - 1$.

$2^8 = 256$, the number of characters in the 8-bit EBCDIC alphabet, and 8 is the most common number of bits in a byte.

$2^{10} = 1,024$. Because 1,024 is close to 1,000, this quantity is often abbreviated K (for kilo) and combined with the abbreviation for byte (B) or word (W) to form expressions like 10KW (10,000 words, really 10,240 words), or 256KB (256 × 1,024 = 262,144 bytes).

$2^{20} = (2^{10} \times 2^{10}) = 1,048,576$. Since this number is close to 1,000,000, it is often abbreviated M (for mega, or million) and similarly combined with the abbreviations for byte or word.

$2^{30} = 1,073,741,824$, about a billion, abbreviated G (for giga).

Notice that I didn't say K, M, and G could be combined with the abbreviation b for bit. They can, but then they usually stand for the actual decimal numbers 1,000, 1,000,000, and 1,000,000,000, respectively. For instance, 9.6Kbps is really 9600 bits per second, not 9830.4.

Octal and Hexadecimal Notation

Decimal numbers are not handy for discussing bit patterns, because 10 is not a power of 2. It takes $\log_2(10) = 3.322$ bits (approximately) to represent ten different things—in this case, the decimal digits 0 through 9. But you can't have fractions of bits. To illustrate, the decimal number 27 is written in binary notation as 11011. Which binary digits correspond to which decimal digits? As you can see from Figure E-1, some of the bits clearly "belong" to the decimal 10's place and others in the 1's place. But notice how the bit in the 8's place must be "split" between the two decimal places.

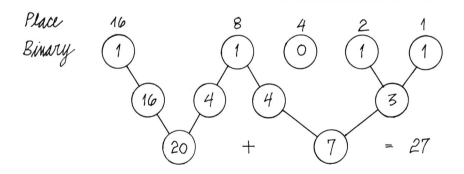

Figure E-1. Assignment of Bits to a Decimal Number

Two other notations are much more appropriate, because they are based upon powers of two, namely 8 $(= 2^3)$ and 16 $(= 2^4)$. Base 8 notation is called octal notation, and it uses only the digits 0 through 7. Each digit represents exactly three bits:

Binary:	000	001	010	011	100	101	110	111
Octal:	0	1	2	3	4	5	6	7

The octal number 10 is decimal 8; the octal number 123 is:

$$(1 \times 8^2) + (2 \times 8^1) + 3 = 64 + 16 + 3 = 83$$

It's easy to work with octal numbers. You can add, subtract, and multiply them just like decimal numbers except that you have to remember that 0 comes after 7 again instead of after 9, so that carries and borrows happen earlier:

$$
\begin{array}{rrrrr}
3 & 4 & 23 & 167 & 42 \\
+4 & +4 & -17 & +1625 & \times 20 \\
\hline
7 & 10 & 4 & 2014 & 1040 \\
\end{array}
$$

Hexadecimal, or base 16, numbers are a bit harder to work with. They use the digits 0 through 9 in the same way as the decimal system, but then the additional digits A through F represent the numbers 10 through 15. For example, the hexadecimal number 1D8A is

$$(1 \times 16^3) + (13 \times 16^2) + (8 \times 16^1) + 10 = 4096 + 3328 + 128 + 10 = 7562$$

The advantage of hexadecimal notation is that two "hex" digits (sometimes called nibbles) correspond exactly with one 8-bit byte. Notice how the hex and binary digits line up, this time with groups of four bits rather than three:

Hex:	1	D	8	A
Binary:	0001	1101	1000	1010

Table E-1. Powers of Two, Eight, Ten, and Sixteen

Power	Base 2	Base 8	Base 10	Base 16
0	1	1	1	1
1	2	8	10	16
2	4	64	100	256
3	8	512	1000	4096
4	16	4096	10000	65536
5	32	32768	100000	1048576
6	64	262144	1000000	16777216
7	128	2097152	10000000	268435456
8	256	16777216	100000000	4294967296
9	512	134217728	1000000000	68719476736
10	1024	1073741824	10000000000	1099511627776
11	2048	8589934594	100000000000	17592186044416
12	4096	549755813888	1000000000000	281474976710656
13	8192	4398046511104	10000000000000	4503599627370496
14	16384	35184372088832	100000000000000	72057594037927936
15	32768	281474976710656	1000000000000000	1152921504606846976
16	65536	2251799813685248	10000000000000000	18446744073709551616

Table E-2. The Numbers 0–32 in Various Bases

Decimal	Binary	Octal	Hex	Decimal	Binary	Octal	Hex
0	0	0	0	16	10000	20	10
1	1	1	1	17	10001	21	11
2	10	2	2	18	10010	22	12
3	11	3	3	19	10011	23	13
4	100	4	4	20	10100	24	14
5	101	5	5	21	10101	25	15
6	110	6	6	22	10110	26	16
7	111	7	7	23	10111	27	17
8	1000	10	8	24	11000	30	18
9	1001	11	9	25	11001	31	19
10	1010	12	A	26	11010	32	1A
11	1011	13	B	27	11011	33	1B
12	1100	14	C	28	11100	34	1C
13	1101	15	D	29	11101	35	1D
14	1110	16	E	30	11110	36	1E
15	1111	17	F	31	11111	37	1F
				32	100000	40	20

Glossary

This glossary provides brief definitions for the important technical terms used in this book, in letter-by-letter alphabetical order. For further detail, consult the Index.

ACK (a) ASCII character number 6, Control-F. (b) An acknowledgment packet (Kermit packet type Y).

Acoustic Coupler A device for transmitting sounds between the telephone handset and a modem. Falling into disuse since the advent of modular (RJ-type) phone jacks.

Address A location in memory, on a disk, or in a network, expressed as a number ranging from 0 to the number of the highest location. A location in memory may be a byte or a word; a location on disk is a block. Memory addresses are sequential, disk or network addresses usually are field-encoded.

Amplifier An electronic device that boosts the strength of an analog signal in the direction of transmission.

Analog Representing information by continuously varying waveforms rather than discrete values. *See also* Digital.

ANSI The American National Standards Institute, a nonprofit, nongovernmental organization supported by more than 1000 trade organizations, professional societies, and companies, which serves as the USA's representative to the International Organization for Standardization (ISO). ANSI issues standards for everything from screw threads to magnetic tape formats. ANSI standards relevant to asynchronous data communication include the ASCII specification [5], the character structure and parity standard [4], and the bit-sequencing standard [3].

Answer One of two modes a modem can be in. In answer mode the modem awaits a call on its answering frequency. *See also* Originate.

ASCII American Standard Code for Information Interchange [5], a 128-character code used almost universally by computers for representing and transmitting character data, in which each character corresponds to a number between 0 and 127. The ASCII alphabet is listed in Appendix D. Eight- or nine-bit codes of which the first 128 characters correspond to ASCII are called Extended ASCII; the additional characters are used to provide graphic characters for non-roman alphabets, special screen effects, etc.

Asynchronous Character- or byte-oriented data transmission in which no out-of-band coordination takes place between the sender and the receiver, where character boundaries must be deduced from the structure of the data itself. Delimitation is accomplished by start and stop bits.

Autoanswer A kind of modem that automatically answers a telephone call without manual intervention.

Autodial A kind of modem that simulates a telephone's dialing mechanism, rotary or touch-tone, in order to place a call, usually under computer control.

Bandwidth Formally, the frequency range assigned to a communication channel. Informally, any measure of how much information can pass through a communication channel per unit time.

Baud The number of discrete signalling events that occur on a transmission line in a second. For binary digital transmission, a baud is the same as a bit per second. Some modems, however, can transmit more bits per second than their baud rate, because they use multilevel signalling.

Bell-103 The standard modulation/demodulation technique for transmitting data at 110 or 300 bits per second over phone lines in both directions simultaneously in North America.

Bell-212 One of several modulation/demodulation techniques for transmitting data at 1200 bits per second over phone lines in both directions simultaneously in North America.

BERT Bit Error Rate Tester, a device for determining the noise level on a data transmission line.

Binary Referring to the number two. Binary notation is a way of writing numbers using only the digits 0 and 1. Binary computers are made out of switches that have only two states, on and off. Binary digital transmission is done with only two voltage levels.

Binary File A file that consists of seemingly random sequences of 0 and 1 bits, usually containing instructions or numbers in the computer's own hardware format and making sense only to the computer. Since the contents of binary files usually depend on some particular hardware, they should not be converted or translated in any way during transfer to another system.

Bipolar Representing binary data by two voltages of equal magnitude but opposite polarity, like $+12V$ and $-12V$.

Bit A binary digit, 0 or 1, irrespective of the form in which it is represented, abbreviated b.

Block A certain fixed number of data bytes in a row. The minimum addressable amount of data on a disk, or a message packet on a transmission medium.

Block Check A quantity formed from all the data in a block, for instance, by adding up all the bytes (a checksum) or combining them in some other way (like CRC), and then included with the block itself, so that the recipient of the block can determine whether it was corrupted in transit. Kermit supports three types of block checks, a one-character checksum (6 bits), a two-character checksum (12 bits), and a three-character CRC (16 bits).

bps Bits per second. Often, but not always, equivalent to Baud.

BREAK A space condition (binary zero, $+12V$ or so) on a communication line lasting about 0.275 second. Also, a "long BREAK" lasting about 1.5 seconds. A BREAK causes the UART to flag a framing error. The long BREAK is sometimes used to cause modems to hang up the phone.

Breakout Box A device to monitor RS-232 signals, inserted between a port and a cable. Lights show the signals, and switches or jumper cables allow easy alteration of the connections.

Buffer A place to put arriving data until the intended recipient can get around to reading it, or a place to queue outbound data until the transmitter gets around to sending it.

Bus A data connection along which data signals travel in parallel, with all attached devices receiving all transmissions, and with a method provided for arbitrating contention. Usually used to connect the internal components of a computer, but also the basis for "bus topology" communication networks, like Ethernet.

Byte A unit of storage intended to hold a character, usually 8 bits long, abbreviated B. Computer memory and disk capacity is often measured in thousands (K) or millions (M) of bytes, e.g., 256KB.

C The programming language [19] used predominantly on UNIX systems, and in this book.

Carrier A continuous signal capable of being modulated (in either amplitude or frequency) by another signal representing binary data. Used between modems through a telephone connection. The presence of carrier tells one modem that the other modem is in data transmission mode. The loss of carrier indicates the data connection is broken.

CCITT Comité Consultatif International Télégraphique et Téléphonique, a committee of the International Telecommunications Union (ITU), which in turn is an agency of the United Nations. The CCITT issues standards, called Recommendations, in the area of data communication. The X series of Recommendations (X.25, X.29, etc.) deals with digital networking, and the V series (V.21, V.22*bis*, V.26*ter*, etc.) addresses data transmission over the telephone network.

Cellular Radio A technique for transmitting data via radio broadcast, often involving a mobile station, which is serviced by different transmitters as it changes location.

Channel The communication path between a receiver and a transmitter. A full-duplex channel is actually two paths, either two separate wires, or one wire carrying signals at two frequencies.

Character A discrete unit of information, a byte corresponding to a member of a given character set, like ASCII or EBCDIC.

Checksum A block check based on the arithmetic sum of all the bytes in a block.

Circuit An electrical path providing communication between two points.

Circuit Board A flat rectangular board containing electronic circuits, usually implementing some component of a computer or communication device, designed to be plugged into a "slot," with signals passing through contacts on its edge.

Clock A device in a computer or communication device that controls its frequency, speed, etc. Also called an oscillator or a crystal.

Cluster Controller In the IBM world, a device, designated 3272 or 3274, that allows multiple 3270 Series terminals to communicate with the IBM mainframe over a single coaxial cable.

Coaxial Cable A transmission medium consisting of a central wire surrounded by an insulator and a wire mesh. Usually used in data communications for networking or synchronous communication, as opposed to twisted pair, the primary medium for asynchronous RS-232 communication.

Code In data communications, the numeric or internal representation for a character, e.g., in ASCII or EBCDIC. In programming, another word for program, as in "source code" (the program text as typed by the author), "object code" (the machine-language output of the compiler).

Communication Port A device allowing a computer or terminal to engage in data communication, usually manifested as an external connector for a cable to connect the device to a modem, a computer, or a terminal.

Concentrator A box to connect multiple terminal devices to a computer or a network through one wire, for example, a multiplexer, a terminal server.

Connector A plug, of either male or female gender, providing contacts for one or more wires within a cable, mating with a similar plug of opposite gender to provide the desired electrical circuits. The connectors used most commonly in asynchronous data communication are D-connectors (so called because they are shaped like the letter D) with either 25 pins (DB-25) or 9 pins (D-9). The DB-25 is often called an RS-232 or EIA connector, even though the EIA RS-232 standard does not discuss connector configuration at all. The D-9 connector layout is specified by EIA Standard RS-449 [12]

Console The primary input/output device with which a person controls a personal computer or a timesharing session on a shared computer.

Contention Multiple users competing for access to some shared resource, such as a transmission medium, or the read/write head of a shared disk.

Control Character An ASCII chararacter in the range 0 through 31, or ASCII character 127, contrasted with the printable, or graphic, characters in the range 32 through 126 (see Appendix D). Produced on an ASCII terminal by holding down the CTRL key and typing the desired character. Computer consoles and communication devices tend to be opaque to some of the control characters, but transparent to the printable set.

Conversational A style of communication between a person and a computer or device, characterized by a series of commands (or questions) and responses, in which each participant waits for the other's response before continuing. Also called interactive.

CP/M Control Program for Microcomputers. The first popular microcomputer operating system. From Digital Research, Inc.

CPU Central Processing Unit, the part of the computer that executes instructions, together with its memory, distinct from external devices (peripherals).

CR Abbreviation for Carriage Return (ASCII 13, Control-M).

CRC Cyclic Redundancy Check, a block check technique in which a block of data is viewed as a linear string of bits, to be divided by a certain binary number (there are several different ones in use), with the remainder used as the block check.

CRLF Abbreviation for Carriage Return, Linefeed, the sequence of ASCII characters (numbers 13 and 10) used on many systems to delimit lines in a text file, and used by Kermit in its canonic representation for text files.

CRT Cathode Ray Tube, the screen of a video terminal or personal computer. Also, a video display terminal (VDT).

CTS Clear to Send, the RS-232 signal that indicates readiness to accept data.

Cursor The blob on your CRT screen that indicates the current position.

Data Information as it is stored in, or transmitted by, a computer or terminal. Plural of Latin *datum* but in common use as an English collective (singular) noun.

Data Set (1) A file. (2) A modem. Sometimes spelled dataset.

DB Designation for a 25-pin RS-232 connector. D refers to the shape (it's shaped like a D), and B denotes the shell size. With the "d" in lowercase (dB) it's an abbreviation for decibels, a unit used in data communication to measure the signal-to-noise ratio of a communication channel.

DCE Data Communications Equipment. Any device that conforms to the description of a DCE in the RS-232 standard, for instance, a modem, multiplexer, terminal server, etc. DCEs are used to connect DTEs.

D-Connector See Connector.

Deadlock A condition in which a pair of supposedly cooperating processes or devices are blocked from operating because each is waiting for the other to complete some action.

Decrement Subtract 1 from.

Dedicated Line A communication line that connects two devices with relative permanence, for instance, a direct line from a terminal to a computer, or a leased telephone circuit. The opposite of a switched or dialup line.

Default The value that is used for some parameter when no other value is explicitly provided.

Delay The amount of extra time spent waiting for an expected response. For instance, the amount of time it takes for a packet to be acknowledged. Also, in Kermit programs, the amount of time to wait before sending the first packet, to give the user time to set things up on the other end.

Demodulation Restoring a modulated signal back to its original digital form. *See also* Modulation.

Device Driver A software component of a computer's operating system that controls or services an input/output device, such as a UART or a disk controller, in real time, providing a simple, buffered, time-independent "interface" to the application programmer.

Dialup A data connection established via telephone call, usually involving modems.

Digital Representation of data by discrete, rather than continuous, voltages or states. Opposite of analog.

Directory A file on a disk that contains a list of other files, with pointers to their physical locations on the disk, and possibly other information about them, such as size, creation date, protection.

Disk A rotating magnetic storage medium for digital information, similar to a phonograph record, but possibly having more than one platter mounted on a central spindle. Disks are generally classified as "hard" (usually permanent, with high capacity) and "floppy" (single platter, flexible, removable, moderate capacity). Floppy disks are also called diskettes.

DOS Disk Operating System. An operating system that uses a magnetic disk as its principal medium of permanent storage.

DTE Data Terminal Equipment. In the lexicon of data communication, a computer or a terminal; a device that is situated at one end of a connection, as opposed to an intermediate device like a modem.

Duplex A measure of the degree to which a channel permits two-way traffic. Half-duplex means traffic can go either way, but only one way at a time; full-duplex means traffic can go both ways at the same time. Echoplex means full-duplex with remote echoing.

EBCDIC Extended Binary Coded Decimal Interchange Code. The character code used on IBM mainframes. Not covered by any formal standards, but described definitively in the IBM System/370 Reference Summary [29] and discussed at length in [23].

Echo The process by which a character typed at a terminal, or a device emulating a terminal, is sent to the screen. Local echo means the terminal itself copies the character to the screen. This is usually associated with half-duplex communication. Remote echo means the system to which the character is transmitted sends it back to be displayed, possibly modified.

EIA The Electronic Industries Association. An organization of U.S. electronics manufacturers. Issues standards in the area of data transmission, such as the RS-232, RS-422, and RS-449 standards. Some EIA standards are adopted by ANSI.

ESC ASCII character 27, Control-[.

Escape Character A character used to get the attention of an otherwise transparent device or program (like Kermit in CONNECT mode). Not to be confused with ASCII ESC. Its particular value depends on the program or device; it could be ESC or anything else, usually a control character.

Escape Sequence A sequence of characters opaque to an otherwise transparent device or program, which causes it to enter conversational mode, or to take some other action. For instance Kermit, during CONNECT, will accept a variety of escape sequences as commands.

Even *See* Parity.

External Modem A modem that is not mounted internally in a PC. Usually portable, requiring its own power source, or drawing DC power from the phone.

FDM Frequency Division Multiplexing.

FDX Full-Duplex.

Fiber Optic A transmission medium for light waves rather than electrical current, typically a clear glass or plastic strand, capable of carrying laser-generated signals at very high speeds over relatively long distances.

File A named collection of data stored on a disk. A file group is a collection of files that can be referred to using a single file specification.

Flag A variable that can have two possible values, often implemented as a single bit, used to control the behavior of a program, or to indicate the success or failure of an operation.

Flow Control The process by which the flow of data in a particular direction is regulated so that the arrival of data is coordinated with the capacity of the receiver to process it.

FORTRAN One of the first "high-level" programming languages, intended mainly for numerical applications.

Framing The method used to delimit characters in asynchronous serial communications. Each character is preceded by a start bit (space) and followed by a stop bit (mark), with a continuous marking condition indicating no transmission.

Frequency The number of times a complete waveform repeats itself, crest-to-crest, per second, also called cycles per second, or Hertz (Hz). For instance, the sound wave from an "A" tuning fork has a frequency of 440 Hz.

Frequency Division Multiplexing A technique for establishing multiple channels on a single communication medium by assigning each to a different carrier frequency.

Frequency Modulation (FM) A way of transmitting information by varying the frequency of the carrier wave according to the data, while holding the amplitude constant. Contrast with Amplitude Modulation (AM) which varies the amplitude, leaving the frequency constant.

Frequency Shift Keying (FSK) An FM technique used for binary digital data, in which 0 is represented by one frequency and 1 by another.

Front End A communication processor for a host computer, which operates independently from it but is closely tied to it. The front end relieves the host from the burden of detailed control of multiple devices, and usually has direct access to the host's memory.

FSA Finite State Automaton. An abstract device that can generate or recognize Regular Expressions.

Full-Duplex A channel that permits simultaneous two-way data traffic between two devices, either by dedicating one wire to each direction or by some multiplexing technique.

G Abbreviation for giga, meaning either 1 billion, or else $2^{30} = 1,073,741,824$.

Gender The "sex" of a connector, male or female. Female connectors have holes; male connectors have corresponding pins. Connectors of opposite gender mate.

Gender Mender A double-ended connector whose purpose is to change the gender of another connector.

Ground An electrical connection to earth, used for safety (to prevent electrical shock), or for reference (to measure other voltages against).

Half-Duplex A channel that permits data transmission in both directions, but in only one direction at a time.

Handshake A method for granting permission to transmit, usually on a half-duplex channel, either in-band (XON) or out-of-band (RTS/CTS).

Hardwired Referring to a communication link that is installed with some degree of permanence and is not switched. Also said of a function that is incorporated inflexibly in the design of a piece of hardware or software. *See also* Point-to-Point.

HDX Half-Duplex.

Hertz Cycles per second, a measure of frequency. Abbreviated Hz.

Hex Slang for hexadecimal.

Hexadecimal Numeric notation in base 16, using the digits 0–9 and A–F to represent the numbers 0–15, with each hexadecimal digit corresponding to four bits.

Increment Add 1 to.

Input/Output The process of getting data into and out of a computer, whether from a peripheral device like a disk or tape, or via a communication line to a terminal or another computer. Called I/O for short.

Interactive *See* Conversational.

Interface Computer jargon for something that allows two otherwise incompatible components to work together by satisfying their respective physical and logical requirements and making any necessary conversions of format, timing, voltage, etc. A connector is a kind of interface; so is a UART. The aspect of a software program that interacts with a person is sometimes called the "user interface." Also, the console is said to be the user's interface to the system.

Interrupt In computing, an event that occurs at an unpredictable time, which a program might take special action to service, after which it returns to what it was doing before. Most device drivers and communication programs are "interrupt driven," allowing them to respond rapidly (in "real time") to arriving data, even if they're in the middle of doing something else, like transmitting.

I/O Input/Output.

ISO The International Organization for Standardization, a voluntary international group of national standards organizations, including ANSI, that issues standards in all areas, including computers and information processing, and whose technical committee also maintains liaison with CCITT.

Job In a timesharing system, a user session of indefinite duration, commencing with login and ending with logout (or system shutdown), possibly involving the invocation of one or more programs, in series or in parallel. A job is associated with a particular user and a particular controlling terminal or console. Also, batch job, print job.

Jumper A short wire used to establish a circuit, typically inside a connector or on a circuit board.

K Abbreviation for kilo, meaning 1000, or else $2^{10} = 1024$.

LAN Local Area Network.

Leased Line A permanent, dedicated communication line rented from the telephone or other company, usually used in conjunction with multiplexers or synchronous modems at speeds in the 4800–19200 baud range.

LED Light Emitting Diode. A small, low-power light bulb, used on modems, breakout boxes, and other communication equipment to convey the state of selected signals.

Line (1) A physical communication path, such as a telephone cable; (2) a computer's interface to or designation for such a path; (3) a sequence of characters in a text file intended to print on one line of a page or screen.

Line Card A circuit board for controlling a communication line, possibly with a UART.

Line Driver A device to boost RS-232 signals on a dedicated line, to allow communication over a longer distance than could otherwise take place.

Line Turnaround The amount of time it takes to switch the directionality of a half-duplex connection, or the mechanism used for doing so, such as XON handshake, RTS/CTS RS-232 signals, etc.

Link Another word for connection. Also, in program development, to collect object modules together into a single program, reconciling their references to each other.

Local Nearby, close to. When two systems or devices are connected, the local system is the "closer" one. When two Kermit programs are connected, the local Kermit is the one the user interacts with most directly (the one that has the CONNECT command).

Local Area Network A data communication network allowing computing devices in a building or on a campus to communicate at higher speeds than are possible with telecommunications.

Local Echo Immediate display on the local screen, by a local agent, of characters sent to a remote computer. Associated with half-duplex communication.

Long Haul Long distance, applied to connections, modems, or networks. Opposite of short haul. Also, wide area (opposite of local area).

Loopback A diagnostic method for determining the point where a connection stops working correctly by reflecting received data automatically back to the sender.

LSB Least Signicant Bit, e.g., of a word, byte, or character. Also called the low-order bit.

M Abbreviation for mega, meaning either one million, or else $2^{20} = 1,048,576$.

Mainframe Commonly used to mean a big computer, as distinct from a minicomputer or a microcomputer. In this book, it means any multiuser computer in which a user's console is also the user's only communication channel with the computer.

Mark (1) The voltage level used to express a binary 1 on a communication line. (2) A kind of character parity in which the parity bit of all characters is set to 1. (3) The single ASCII character that marks the beginning of a Kermit packet, usually SOH (Control-A).

Medium That through which data is transmitted—copper wire, coaxial cable, optical fiber, empty space, etc.—or which it is stored upon—magnetic disk, diskette, tape, etc.

Memory The internal, volatile, high-speed, solid state storage of a computer, as distinguished from external, permanent, lower-speed, rotating mechanical memories (e.g., disks, tapes) used for bulk storage.

Message A unit of information, usually consisting of multiple bytes or characters, cast into some specified format for transmission.

Microcode The instructions used by a computer's manufacturer to construct the computer's instruction set. Usually alterable by the manufacturer but not by the customer. Also called "firmware."

Microcomputer In this book, a single-user computer whose console is distinct from its communication line.

Microsecond One millionth of a second, abbreviated μsec.

Microwave A portion of the frequency spectrum used for line-of-sight data transmission through the open air, involving earth stations, satellites, or both.

Millisecond One thousandth of a second, abbreviated msec.

Modem Modulator/Demodulator, a device that converts between serial digital data as output from a UART and analog waveforms suitable for transmission on a telephone line.

Modem Eliminator *See* Null Modem.

Modulation In data communication, impressing data upon a steady carrier wave by changing its amplitude, frequency, or phase.

Modulo A maximum number to be used in counting, at which counting begins over again at zero. For instance, modulo-four counting proceeds like this: 0, 1, 2, 3, 0, 1, 2, 3, 0, . . . Any number *modulo n* is the remainder left upon dividing that number by *n*. For instance, the Kermit packet number is the true sequential number of the packet, modulo 64.

MSB Most Significant Bit, e.g., of a word, byte, or character. Also called the high-order bit.

MS-DOS Microsoft's Disk Operating System for microcomputers based on the Intel 8086 family of CPU chips. Called PC-DOS on the IBM PC family.

Multiplexer A device allowing multiple devices to share a single communication medium, using any of several techniques, including frequency division, time division, or some statistical method. Used in pairs, one at each end; the transmitter multiplexes, the receiver demultiplexes.

Mux Slang for multiplexer.

NAK (1) ASCII character 25, Control-U. (2) A Negative Acknowledgment packet (Kermit packet type N).

Network A permanent arrangement allowing two or more computers or devices to communicate with each other conveniently and reliably at high speeds, over dedicated media, typically requiring special hardware and operating-system-level software.

Nibble A four-bit quantity, half a byte expressible in one hexadecimal digit.

Node A device or computer on a network.

Noise Corruption of data during transmission.

NUL ASCII character number 0, as distinct from the number zero or the ASCII character digit "0" (ASCII 48).

Null Modem A pair of connectors, possibly with a length of cable between them, allowing two DTEs (computers or terminals) to be directly connected without intervening DCEs (modems or multiplexers), supplying the required RS-232 signals by means of cross-connections and jumpers. An asynchronous null modem consists only of wires and connectors; a synchronous null modem also provides a clock signal.

Octal Base 8 numeric notation, a convenient representation for binary numbers, in which each octal digit, 0–7, corresponds to three binary digits (bits).

Odd *See* Parity.

Off (1) Not in effect (said of an option). (2) Zero (said of a bit).

Off Line Not in data communication mode, said of a printer, a terminal, a network node, etc.

On (1) In effect (said of an option). (2) One (said of a bit).

On Line (1) Working, connected, able to communicate. (2) Stored on a disk.

Opaque A program or device whose normal function is to transmit characters, but which "swallows," modifies, or takes special action upon encountering certain character sequences, rather allowing them to pass through, is said to be opaque to those characters or sequences. Opposite of transparent.

Operating System The software program that controls a computer at the most basic level, consisting of a collection of device drivers, a scheduler, memory manager, etc. Operating system functions, particularly device drivers, operate in real time, as distinguished from user programs, which are scheduled and managed by the operating system, and which must call upon the operating system to perform critical functions like device input/output.

Operator (1) A person operating a computer console. Also, a user. (2) A symbol indicating an operation to be performed, e.g., " + ."

Optical Fiber See Fiber Optic.

OS Operating System.

OSI The Open System Interconnection reference model of the ISO, a commonly used basis for network design.

Out of Band Referring to a signal, typically for control purposes, sent outside of the data stream, or else imbedded within the data but in some form that is not legal or expected for data.

Overhead Extra work, or consumption of some resource, that must occur in order to achieve a particular objective. For instance, the start and stop bits in asynchronous data transmission, the bytes wasted at the end of the final disk block of a file, the control fields of a Kermit packet.

Overrun The overwriting of data in a buffer with new data before the old data has been retrieved for use, e.g., in a UART's holding register.

Packet A message consisting of fields whose locations and interpretation are agreed upon by the sending and receiving entities, to be transmitted (and possibly switched) as a whole, and typically containing sequencing, error checking, and other control information as well as data.

Packet Switching A technique, typically used in computer networks, to allow multiple users and hosts to share the same set of transmission media by breaking their data up into discrete packets, which may be intermixed and routed arbitrarily and still arrive at their various destinations in sequence and intact.

PAD Packet Assembler/Disassembler, a device connecting one or more terminals or computers to a packet-switched network, providing conversion from the unguarded asynchronous communication that occurs between itself and the terminal to packet-switched communication between itself and the host selected by the user.

Padding (1) A method for allowing a receiving device to keep up with sustained transmission, by including extra characters at critical points to tie up the transmission line while the device is busy servicing the data received so far. For instance, certain kinds of printers need padding after a carriage return character to give them time to move the printing head back to the left margin. Used in lieu of full-duplex flow control. (2) A Kermit communication parameter specifying how many of a specified pad character to transmit before the beginning of each Kermit packet.

Parallel All at once. In data communication, the transmission of all the bits in a byte (or word) together, each on its own wire, usually done only over very short distances. *See also* Serial.

Parameter A symbolic value, standing for, or to be replaced by, a real value.

Parity An error detection method in which one bit is set aside to indicate some property of the remaining bits in a byte or word. Usually, it is the number, modulo 2, of 1 bits in the quantity. Odd parity means the parity bit is set to make the overall number of 1 bits odd, Even makes the overall number of 1 bits even. Mark parity means the parity bit is always set to 1; space parity means it's always set to zero. No parity means the bit that would otherwise be used for parity may be used for data.

Pascal A high-level programming language noted for its approach to program structure.

PBX Private Branch Exchange, a telephone system serving the internal needs of an organization and providing connection to the external phone system. May be used for transmission data as well as voice within the organization. May be digital or analog.

PC Personal Computer. *See also* Microcomputer.

PDN Public Data Network.

Peripheral An input/output device connected to a computer. Usually said of a disk drive, tape drive, or printer.

Phase Shift Keying (PSK) A modulation technique in which the phase of the carrier wave is altered according to the data to be transmitted, typically used in 1200 and 2400 bps modems.

Plug A male connector.

Point-to-Point Said of a transmission path that is direct, with no intermediate routing nodes involved, but possibly including transparent switches. For instance, a dialup phone connection is point-to-point, but a packet-switched network connection is not. *See also* Hardwired.

Polarity The property of having two opposing poles, positive and negative. Said, for instance, of voltage or magnets.

Port *See* Communication Port.

Port Contention Unit A device allowing multiple terminals to be connected to multiple computers, in which terminal ports contend for computer ports. Typically the port contention unit engages in a dialog with the user, asking which computer the user wishes to connect to. The connection thus established may or may not be wholly transparent. Some units are opaque to certain character sequences, others to BREAK, and others are controlled by modem signals like DTR. Also called port selector, port switcher.

Protocol In data communication, a set of rules and formats for exchanging messages, generally incorporating methods of sequencing, timing, and error detection and correction.

Public Data Network A network, usually packet-switched, providing access to the public on a subscription basis to potentially widely scattered and diverse services.

QAM Quadrature Amplitude Modulation, another modulation technique used by 2400 bps dialup modems.

Queue A list in which the first element entered is the first removed. Also called a First-In-First-Out (FIFO) list.

Real Time Said of an environment in which events must be serviced promptly as they occur, rather than queued for later service.

Receptacle A female connector.

Regular Expression Notation used in this book for compact description of a sequence of packets. A letter stands for a packet type, parentheses are used for grouping, an asterisk means 0 or more repetitions of the preceding quantity, and a vertical bar signifies alternation. Example: Y | E | (S (F D* Z)* B) means a Y packet or an E packet or else an S packet followed by an F packet followed by zero or more D packets, then a Z packet (with the F-D-Z sequence occurring zero or more times), followed by a B packet.

Remote Said of the more distant, or less directly accessed, of two connected devices. A remote Kermit is the one running on the host that the local Kermit has connected to.

Repeater An amplifier for digital signals.

Response Time A measure of the interval between a stimulus and its response, for instance, how long it takes a character to echo on a full-duplex channel.

Retry A second or subsequent attempt of the same operation, e.g., transmission of a packet.

RJ Designation for connectors of the sort used in modular telephone jacks. The 6-position, 4-wire RJ11 is the most common model in voice and data communication.

ROM Read-Only Memory. High speed internal memory containing permanently recorded information.

RS-232-C An EIA standard that gives the electrical and functional specification for serial binary digital data transmission [9], the most commonly used interface between terminals (or computers) and modems (or multiplexers).

RS-422 An EIA standard for serial transmission over longer distances and at higher speeds than RS-232-C, employing balanced pairs of receive and transmit signals [10].

RTS Request to Send, one of the RS-232-C signals, typically used by a terminal or computer to ask permission of a modem to transmit data to it.

Satellite In data communication, an object circling the earth in a relatively permanent, often geostationary orbit (always above the same spot), relaying data between earth stations (possibly through other satellites) usually via microwave, typically introducing delays in response time because of the great distances and contention involved.

Serial In series, sequential, one after another. The dominant mode of transmission of binary data over distances greater than a few feet. *See also* Parallel.

Server A program, or intelligent device, that provides specified services to users, or "clients," in response to requests, usually over a communication line or network.

Session The period during which a user engages in dialog with a computer; the duration of a job. Also, a layer in the ISO OSI model.

Signal (1) An electrical, optical, radio, or other wave capable of carrying data from one point to another. (2) An interrupt.

Simplex Permitting data to travel in only one direction.

Smart Said, sometimes ironically, of a device that has some built-in functionality ("intelligence") not usually found in such a device, e.g., a smart terminal, a smart modem.

SOH Start-of-Header, ASCII character number 1, Control-A. Normally used to indicate the start of a Kermit packet.

Space (1) A binary 0 as represented on a transmission medium. (2) A blank, ASCII character 32. (3) A kind of parity in which the parity bit is always 0.

Start Bit In asynchronous serial transmission, the space (0-bit) that indicates that a character is starting to arrive, after one or more bit times of mark (1-bit) condition.

Statistical Multiplexer A multiplexer that allocates bandwidth dynamically based upon the expected or observed behavior of the multiplexed devices.

Stop Bit In asynchronous serial transmission, the mark (1-bit) that terminates a character. It lasts for at least one bit time, and thereafter until the next character starts to arrive.

Straight-Through Said of a cable in which the wires connect corresponding pins, with no crossovers or jumpers. An RS-232 cable that connects a modem to a terminal or computer is usually straight-through. *See also* Null Modem.

Switched Line A communication line subject to switching, typically a dialed telephone connection.

Synchronous A method of data communication in which characters (or arbitrary bit streams) may be transmitted without framing information (start and stop bits) to achieve greater throughput than possible with asynchronous communication, by using out-of-band timing signals, but also requiring occasional resynchronization by means of in-band "sync characters."

System (1) A way of doing things. (2) A computer.

T1 A long-haul medium capable of transmitting 1.544Mbps, typically multiplexed into 56Kbps or 64Kbps channels, originally used as telephone trunk lines, now seeing increasing use for data transmission.

TCAM IBM mainframe Telecommunications Access Method, a device driver for asynchronous terminals.

Telecommunication Asynchronous serial data communication, possibly (but not necessarily) involving dialup telephone connections and modems.

Telenet A public packet-switched network service.

Terminal A device allowing a person to interact with a computer, with the person typing characters on a keyboard to send them to the computer, and with the computer's responses appearing on a screen or paper. Sometimes includes the ability to interpret special character sequences to accomplish screen formatting, but in general differing from a computer by not having local permanent memory or general-purpose programmability. Most terminals are ASCII, asynchronous, and character-oriented, but there are also other kinds, for example, the IBM EBCDIC block mode 3270 series.

Terminal Emulation Behaving like a terminal. Said of software that runs on PCs or other computers, which sends the user's typein out the serial port, and sends the port input to the screen. Sometimes includes the ability to interpret the same special sequences that a specific real terminal would obey. The Kermit CONNECT command performs terminal emulation.

Terminal Server A network device allowing ordinary terminals with no networking capabilities of their own to participate in a network, provided hosts share a common protocol with the terminal server. The terminal server is probably not wholly transparent, requiring some means to regulate the flow of data and to interact directly with the user.

Text Computer data intended for a person to read, or typed by a person, consisting of only printable characters and those control characters necessary for format control (carriage return, linefeed, tab, etc.). Text files can be transferred between unlike systems and still remain useful. *See also* Binary File.

3270 A series of IBM synchronous, EBCDIC, block-mode, half-duplex terminals, the preferred (by IBM) type for use with IBM System/370 mainframes.

Throughput A measure of how much data passes through a particular point per unit time.

Timeout The process by which a program wakes up after waiting for some expected event (like input from a device) longer than a predetermined amount of time.

Transaction In Kermit jargon, the exchange of packets commencing with an S (Send-Initiation) packet and concluding with a B (Break-Transmission) or E (Error) packet, usually involving the transfer of one or more files.

Translation Table A list of the numeric representations of characters in a given character set. The position in the list is the numeric value of a character in the set being translated from; the number located at that position is the value to be translated to. Also called translate table.

Transparent Allowing data to pass through unmodified. Opposite of Opaque.

TTY Originally, Teletypewriter. Currently, any asynchronous ASCII terminal or computer that emulates one.

Turnaround (1) Response time. (2) Line turnaround.

Twisted Pair Pairs of insulated copper wire, 20-28 AWG, twisted around each other in helix fashion within an outer sleeve. Used for telecommunication.

Tymnet A public packet-switched network service offered by Tymnet, Inc.

Typeahead The ability to send characters to a computer or device before it has requested them, possible only on full-duplex connections.

UART Universal Asynchronous Receiver/Transmitter, the device that converts between parallel character data as stored in a computer's memory and asynchronous serial binary data as transmitted on a telecommunication line.

Unattended Referring to an operation that can proceed automatically, without human intervention.

Unguarded Said of data transmission in which no method of error detection and correction is employed.

UNIX A popular operating system developed at AT&T Bell Laboratories, noted for its portability.

User What we call a person who is using a computer.

User Interface The hardware and software with which a person communicates with a computer.

User Program A program that runs outside of the operating system's environment, whose scheduling is controlled by the operating system, and which must call upon the operating system to perform time-critical or privileged services.

V.22 An ISO Recommendation for 2400 bps modem operation.

V.26 Another ISO Recommendation for 2400 bps modem operation.

VA-3400 The original 1200 bps modem transmission technique, developed by Vadic (now Racal-Vadic).

Virtual Behaving as if it were a real (1) terminal, (2) circuit, (3) disk, (4) machine . . .

Virtual Terminal A common intermediate representation for a terminal and its control sequences and functions. Not the same as terminal emulation.

Voice Grade Said of a telephone connection, either dialed or leased, intended for carrying voice rather than digital traffic; usually noisier than a digital or specially conditioned line.

VTAM IBM mainframe Virtual Telecommunications Access Method; a device driver for asynchronous terminals and for network virtual terminals.

Wildcard A notation for referring to a group of files with a single filename, by including pattern-matching characters (like "*").

Word A unit of storage in a computer's memory, usually the one used for numbers and addresses, directly addressable by the computer.

Workstation A single-user computer, equivalent to a PC or microcomputer in that the console is separate from the communication line, but usually composed of more expensive components, intended for more ambitious uses.

XON/XOFF The most common in-band full-duplex flow-control method, in which the receiver sends an XOFF character when its input buffer is close to filling up, and an XON when it has made room for more data to arrive.

References

1. Aho, A. V., J. E. Hopcroft, and J. D. Ullman. *Computer Science and Information Processing: The Design and Analysis of Computer Algorithms*. Addison-Wesley, Reading, MA, 1974.

2. *ANSI X3.1-1976. Synchronous Signaling Rates for Data Transmission*. American National Standards Institute, 1430 Broadway, New York, NY 10018, 1976.

3. *ANSI X3.15-1976. Bit Sequencing of ASCII in Serial-By-Bit Data Transmission*. 1976.

4. *ANSI 3.16-1976. Character Structure and Character Parity Sense for Serial-By-Bit Data Communication in ASCII*. 1976.

5. *ANSI X3.4-1977. Code for Information Interchange*. 1977.

6. da Cruz, F. *Kermit Protocol Manual*. Columbia University Center for Computing Activities, New York, 1986.

7. da Cruz, F., ed. *Kermit User Guide*. Columbia University Center for Computing Activities, New York, 1986.

8. da Cruz, F., and B. Catchings. "Kermit: A File Transfer Protocol for Universities." *BYTE 9* (June, July 1984).

9. *EIA Standard RS-232-C, Interface Between Data Terminal Equipment and Data Communication Equipment Employing Serial Binary Data Interchange*. Electronic Industries Association, 2001 Eye Street N.W., Washington DC 20006, 1969.

10. *EIA Standard RS-422, Electrical Characteristics of Balanced Voltage Digital Interface Circuits*. 1975.

11. *EIA Standard RS-269-B, Synchronous Signalling Rates for Data Transmission*. 1976.

12. *EIA Standard RS-449, General Purpose 37-Position and 9-Position Interface for Data Terminal Equipment and Data Circuit-Terminating Equipment Employing Serial Binary Data Interchange*. 1977.

13. Hamming, R. W. "Error Detecting and Error Correcting Codes." *Bell System Technical Journal* 29 (April 1950): 147–160.

14. *Hayes Smartmodem 1200 User's Guide*. Hayes Microcomputer Products, Inc., 1985.

15. *ISO/DIS 2110: Data Communication—25-pin DTE/DCE Interface Connector and Pin Assignments*. International Organization for Standardization, 1972.

16. *ISO/DIS 4902: Data Communication—7-pin and 9-pin DTE/DCE Interface Connector and Pin Assignments*. 1972.

17. *ISO/TC97/SC16: Reference Model of Open Systems Interconnection.* 1972.

18. Jesty, P. H. *Computer Science Texts: Networking with Microcomputers.* Blackwell Scientific Publications, Oxford, 1985.

19. Kernighan, B. W., and D. M. Ritchie. *Prentice-Hall Software Series: The C Programming Language.* Prentice-Hall, Englewood Cliffs, NJ, 1978.

20. Knuth, D. E. *T$_E$X and METAFONT.* Digital Press and the American Mathematical Society, Bedford, MA, 1979.

21. Kohavi, Z. *Computer Science Series: Switching and Finite Automata Theory.* McGraw-Hill, New York, 1970.

22. Lesk, M. E. *Lex—A Lexical Analyzer Generator.* Computer Science Technical Report 39, Bell Laboratories, October 1975.

23. Mackenzie, C. E. *Coded-Character Sets: History and Development.* Addison-Wesley, Reading, MA, 1980.

24. Martin, J. *Teleprocessing Network Organization.* Prentice-Hall, Englewood Cliffs, NJ, 1970.

25. McNamara, J. E. *Technical Aspects of Data Communication.* Digital Press, Bedford, MA, 1982.

26. Padlipsky, M. A. *The Elements of Networking Style.* Prentice-Hall, Englewood Cliffs, NJ, 1985.

27. Post, E. *Etiquette in Society, in Business, in Politics, and at Home.* Harper & Row, New York, 1922.

28. Stallman, R. M. "EMACS, The Extensible, Customizable, Self-Documenting Display Editor." In *Proceedings of the ACM SIGPLAN SIGOA Symposium on Text Manipulation.* June 1981, 147–156.

29. *System/370 Reference Summary,* 6th ed., GX20–1850–5. IBM, 1984.

30. *V.5, Standardization of Data-Signalling Rates for Synchronous Data Transmission in the General Switched Telephone Network.* CCITT, Geneva, 1976.

31. *X.3, Packet Assembly/Disassembly Facility (PAD) in a Public Data Network.* CCITT, Geneva, 1977.

32. *X.25, Interface Between Data Terminal Equipment (DTE) and Data Circuit-Terminating Equipment (DTE) for Terminals Operating in the Packet Mode on Public Data Networks.* CCITT, Geneva, 1976, 1977.

33. *X.28, DTE/DCE Interface for a Start-Stop Mode Data Terminal Equipment Accessing the Packet Assembly/Disassembly Facility (PAD) in a Public Data Network Situated in the Same Country.* CCITT, Geneva, 1977.

34. *X.29, Procedures for the Exchange of Control Information and User Data Between a Packet Mode DTE and a Packet Assembly/Disassembly Facility (PAD).* CCITT, Geneva, 1977.

Trademarks

The following companies hold the following trademarks, or market the following products, mentioned in this book:

American Mathematical Society, Providence, RI: T_EX.

Apollo Computer, Inc., Chelmsford, MA: Apollo, Aegis.

Apple Computer, Cupertino, CA: Apple II, Apple III, Macintosh, Lisa.

Atari, Inc., Sunnyvale, CA: Atari 800, Atari 520 ST.

AT&T Information Systems, Morristown, NJ: Bell, Bell-103, Bell-202, Bell-212, UNIX, System III, System V, Touch-Tone.

Borland International, Scotts Valley, CA: Turbo Pascal.

British Broadcasting Corporation, London, UK: BBC, Acorn BBC Micro.

Burroughs Corporation, Detroit, MI: B6800, B7900.

Cisi Telematique, France: Cisipac.

Cray Research, Inc., Mendota Heights, MN: Cray-1, Cray-XMP.

Commodore International Ltd., West Chester, PA: Commodore 64, Pet, Amiga.

Control Data Corporation, Minneapolis, MN: CDC, Cyber, NOS, NOS-BE, NOS-VE, SCOPE.

Convergent Technologies, Santa Clara, CA: Convergent, CTOS.

Corvus Systems, Inc., San Jose, CA: Concept CDOS.

Cromemco, Inc., Mountain View, CA: CDOS.

Data General Corp., Westboro, MA: RDOS, AOS. AOS/VS.

Digital Communications Associates, Inc., Norcross, GA: DCA, IRMA.

Digital Equipment Corporation, Maynard, MA: The Digital logo, DEC, DECsystem-10, DECSYSTEM-20, TOPS-10, TOPS-20, PDP-11, VAX, VMS, VT52, VT100, Rainbow, Professional-300, Pro/RT, P/OS, RSX-11, RT-11, RSTS/E, IAS, OS8, RTS8, WPS.

Digital Research, Monterey, CA: CP/M-80, CP/M-86.

General Telephone and Electric, Stanford, CT: GTE, Telenet.

Gould Inc., Rolling Meadows, IL: MPX/32.

Harris Computer, Melbourne, FA: VOS.

Hayes Microcomputer Products, Inc., Norcross, GA: Hayes Smartmodem 1200.

Heath Company, Benton Harbor, MI: Heathkit, H-19, H-89.

Henson Associates, Inc., NY: Kermit.

Hewlett-Packard Co., Palo Alto, CA: RTE, MPE, SPL, HP-150, HP-1000, HP-3000.

Honeywell Information Systems, Waltham, MA: MULTICS, DPS, GCOS, CP6.

ICL, London, UK,: ICL.

Intel Corp., Santa Clara, CA: Intel 8080, 8086, 8088, 80286; iRMX-86, ISIS.

International Business Machines Corp., Armonk, NY: IBM, Series/1, VM/CMS, MVS/TSO, PC-DOS, DOS/VSE, 3270, 3271, 3272, 3273, 3274, 3276, 3277, 3278, 3279, 3705, 3725, Yale ASCII Communications System, System/360, System/370, System/34, System 36, System/38, Displaywriter, IBM PC, IBM PC/XT, IBM PC/AT, IBM PCjr, IBM RT PC, 370/148, 370/168, 3031, 3033, 4341, 4361, 3081, 3083, OS/360, OS/VS1, CICS, TCAM, VTAM, 7171, 4994.

Lisp Machine Inc., Los Angeles, CA: LMI, ZETALISP-PLUS.

Microsoft Corporation, Bellevue, WA: MS-DOS, Xenix, MASM.

Microware Systems Corp., Des Moines, IA, and Motorola Inc., Phoenix, AZ: OS-9.

Microware Systems Corp., Des Moines, IA: OS-9/68000.

Motorola, Inc., Phoenix, AZ: 6502, 6809, 68000, Versados, VME.

Perkin-Elmer, Oceanport, NJ: Perkin-Elmer, 3200, OS/32.

PERQ Systems Corp, Pittsburgh, PA: PERQ.

Prime Computer, Natick, MA: PRIMOS.

Racal-Vadic, Milpitas, CA: VA3400.

Regents of the University of California: BSD, UCSD PASCAL, UCSD p-System.

Sperry Corp, Blue Bell, PA: Sperry 1100, OS 1100, EXEC, 9080, VS9.

Sun Microsystems, Inc., Mountain View, CA: Sun Microsystems, Sun Workstation.

Symbolics, Inc., Cambridge, MA: Symbolics 3600.

Systems Engineering Laboratories, Fort Lauderdale, FL: SEL.

Tandem Computers Inc, Cupertino, CA: Nonstop, Guardian.

Tandy Corporation, Fort Worth, TX: Radio Shack, TRS80, TRSDOS, Color Computer.

Telecom Canada, Ottawa, Ontario: Datapac.

Teletype Corporation, Skokie, IL: Teletype.

The Source Telecomputing Corporation, McLean, VA: The Source.

Tymnet, Inc., San Jose, CA: Tymnet, X.PC.

US Telecom, Lenexa, KS: UNINET.

VentureCom, Inc., Cambridge, MA: VENIX.

Xerox Corporation, Stanford, CT: Diablo, Ethernet.

Yale University Computer Center, New Haven, CT: Yale ASCII Terminal Communication System, YTERM.

Zenith Data Systems, Glenview, IL: Z89, Z19, Z100.

Zilog, Campbell, CA: Z80.

Index (Also See Glossary)

Ordering Information

To order this book and related titles, fill in and mail this form or call the toll-free telephone number below. Orders under $50 must be prepaid by check or charge card; postage and handling are free on prepaid orders. There is a 10 percent discount on orders of two or more copies.

Digital Press/Order Processing
Digital Equipment Corporation
12A Esquire Road
Billerica, MA 01862

QTY.	TITLE	ORDER NO.	PRICE*	TOTAL
	da Cruz, *Kermit*	EY-6705E-DP	$25.00	
	McNamara, *Local Area Networks*	EY-00051-DP	$28.00	
	McNamara, *Technical Aspects of Data Communication*	EY-AX018-DP	$35.00	

Total	
Discount	
Add state sales tax	
Total remitted	

METHOD OF PAYMENT

_____ Check included (Make checks payable to Digital Equipment Corporation)

_____ Purchase order (Please attach)

_____ MasterCard/Visa

Charge Card Acc't No. _____

Expiration Date _____

Authorized Signature _____

Name _____ Phone _____

Address _____

City _____ State _____ Zip _____

TOLL-FREE ORDER NUMBER
To order books by MasterCard or VISA, call 1-800-343-8321. In Massachusetts, call 1-800-462-8006. Phone lines are open from 8:00 A.M. to 4:00 P.M., Eastern time.

*Price and terms quoted are U.S. only and are subject to change without notice. For prices outside the U.S., contact the nearest office of Educational Services, Digital Equipment Corporation.